Fiscal Institutions
and Fiscal Performance

A National Bureau
of Economic Research
Conference Report

Fiscal Institutions and Fiscal Performance

Edited by James M. Poterba and
Jürgen von Hagen

The University of Chicago Press

Chicago and London

WITHDRAWN
ITHACA COLLEGE LIBRARY

JAMES M. POTERBA is the Mitsui Professor of Economics at the Massachusetts Institute of Technology and director of the Public Economics Research Program at the National Bureau of Economic Research. JÜRGEN VON HAGEN is professor of economics at the University of Bonn, a director of the Zentrum für Europäische Integrationsforschung (Center for European Integration Studies) of the University of Bonn, and a fellow of the Centre for Economic Policy Research, London.

HJ
2005
.F567
1999

ADG-3335

The University of Chicago Press, Chicago 60637
The University of Chicago Press, Ltd., London
© 1999 by the National Bureau of Economic Research
All rights reserved. Published 1999

08 07 06 05 04 03 02 01 00 99   1 2 3 4 5
ISBN: 0-226-67623-4 (cloth)

Library of Congress Cataloging-in-Publication Data

Fiscal institutions and fiscal performance / edited by James M. Poterba
and Jürgen von Hagen.
     p.   cm.—(A National Bureau of Economic Research conference report)
    Includes bibliographical references and index.
    ISBN 0-226-67623-4 (alk. paper)
    1. Budget deficits—Congresses. 2. Fiscal policy—Congresses.
    3. Deficit financing—Congresses. I. Poterba, James M. II. Hagen, Jürgen von. III. Series: Conference report (National Bureau of Economic Research)
    HJ2005.F567   1999
    336.3—dc21   98-31598
                                               CIP
                                               Rev.

♾ The paper used in this publication meets the minimum requirements of the American National Standard for Information Sciences—Permanence of Paper for Printed Library Materials, ANSI Z39.48-1992.

National Bureau of Economic Research

Officers

John H. Biggs, *chairman*
Carl F. Christ, *vice-chairman*
Martin Feldstein, *president and chief executive officer*
Gerald A. Polansky, *treasurer*

Sam Parker, *director of finance*
Susan Colligan, *corporate secretary*
Kelly Horak, *assistant corporate secretary*
Gerardine Johnson, *assistant corporate secretary*

Directors at Large

Peter C. Aldrich
Elizabeth E. Bailey
John H. Biggs
Andrew Brimmer
Carl F. Christ
Don R. Conlan
Kathleen B. Cooper
George C. Eads

Martin Feldstein
Stephen Friedman
George Hatsopoulos
Karen N. Horn
Lawrence R. Klein
John Lipsky
Leo Melamed
Merton H. Miller

Michael H. Moskow
Robert T. Parry
Peter G. Peterson
Richard N. Rosett
Bert Seidman
Kathleen P. Utgoff
Marina v. N. Whitman
John O. Wilson

Directors by University Appointment

George Akerlof, *California, Berkeley*
Jagdish Bhagwati, *Columbia*
William C. Brainard, *Yale*
Glen G. Cain, *Wisconsin*
Franklin Fisher, *Massachusetts Institute of Technology*
Saul H. Hymans, *Michigan*
Marjorie B. McElroy, *Duke*

Joel Mokyr, *Northwestern*
Andrew Postlewaite, *Pennsylvania*
Nathan Rosenberg, *Stanford*
Harold T. Shapiro, *Princeton*
Craig Swan, *Minnesota*
David B. Yoffie, *Harvard*
Arnold Zellner, *Chicago*

Directors by Appointment of Other Organizations

Marcel Boyer, *Canadian Economics Association*
Mark Drabenstott, *American Agricultural Economics Association*
William C. Dunkelberg, *National Association of Business Economists*
Gail D. Fosler, *The Conference Board*
A. Ronald Gallant, *American Statistical Association*
Robert S. Hamada, *American Finance Association*

Rudolph A. Oswald, *American Federation of Labor and Congress of Industrial Organizations*
Gerald A. Polansky, *American Institute of Certified Public Accountants*
John J. Siegfried, *American Economic Association*
Josh S. Weston, *Committee for Economic Development*
Gavin Wright, *Economic History Association*

Directors Emeriti

Moses Abramovitz
George T. Conklin, Jr.
Jean A. Crockett

Thomas D. Flynn
Franklin A. Lindsay
Paul W. McCracken

Geoffrey H. Moore
James J. O'Leary
Eli Shapiro

Since this volume is a record of conference proceedings, it has been exempted from the rules governing critical review of manuscripts by the Board of Directors of the National Bureau (resolution adopted 8 June 1948, as revised 21 November 1949 and 20 April 1968).

Contents

Acknowledgments

This volume contains the papers presented at a conference cosponsored by the National Bureau of Economic Research and the Zentrum für Europäische Integrationsforschung (ZEI) in Bonn in June 1997. We are grateful for financial support from both institutions.

The NBER Conference Department, under the direction of Kirsten Foss Davis, together with its counterpart at ZEI under Heike Schnappertz, provided outstanding support organizing the conference. Deborah Kiernan, Elizabeth Gertsch, and especially Helena Fitz-Patrick, all of the NBER Publications Department, guided the volume through the editorial and publication process. We thank them for all their assistance.

The National Bureau of Economic Research was founded in 1920. It is a private, nonprofit, nonpartisan research organization dedicated to promoting a greater understanding of how the economy works. The NBER is committed to promoting unbiased economic research among public policymakers, business professionals, and the academic community. Although NBER research brings critical information to many important policy debates, the NBER remains impartial and makes no policy recommendations.

The Zentrum für Europäische Integrationsforschung was established in 1995 as an applied research institute at the University of Bonn. ZEI is a unique institution in Germany's university scene. It endeavors to bridge the gap between academia and public policy and business, and to contribute constructively to the solution of the political, institutional, and economic challenges of European integration and Europe's long-term development. The research of ZEI's economic group emphasizes policy-oriented and empirical work, as well as political economy and macroeconomics.

Introduction

James M. Poterba and Jürgen von Hagen

The rise and persistence of sustained budget deficits in many developed and developing nations during the last three decades is a subject of great concern and interest to both policymakers and researchers. The persistence of these deficits makes them incompatible with optimal fiscal strategies such as tax smoothing, and the observation that deficits rose simultaneously in many nations defies explanations focusing on particular economic developments in individual countries. Recent attempts to explain why governments run large and persistent deficits have, therefore, focused on political and institutional factors and their effect on fiscal outcomes. Turning to such factors, and by implication to differences in national political and institutional developments, may also be a promising avenue to explain why fiscal policies in countries exposed to similar economic shocks performed in remarkably different ways during the 1970s and 1980s. While precise evaluation of the economic effects of budget deficits is a difficult exercise, leading figures in many nations have called for deficit reduction, and there have been numerous policy debates concerning the design of fiscal institutions that will restrict budget deficits and limit the growth of national debt. Several nations—New Zealand, Denmark, Sweden, and Ireland, to name just a few—adopted institutional changes in the 1980s and 1990s hoping that this would enable them to achieve greater fiscal discipline.

The Maastricht Treaty's provisions for European Monetary Union (EMU) have also drawn increased attention to the relationship between fiscal rules and

James M. Poterba is the Mitsui Professor of Economics at the Massachusetts Institute of Technology and director of the Public Economics Research Program at the National Bureau of Economic Research. Jürgen von Hagen is professor of economics at the University of Bonn, a director of the Zentrum für Europäische Integrationsforschung (Center for European Integration Studies) of the University of Bonn, and a fellow of the Centre for Economic Policy Research, London.

The authors are grateful to the National Bureau of Economic Research, the University of Bonn's Zentrum für Europäische Integrationsforschung, and the National Science Foundation (Poterba) for research support.

fiscal policy outcomes. To avoid situations in which deficit spending by a member nation could necessitate a "bailout" by the European Central Bank, the treaty requires that EMU member nations avoid "excessive deficits," that is, deficits exceeding 3 percent of GDP. The Stability and Growth Pact signed in Amsterdam in June 1997 strengthened the Maastricht Treaty's original provision by adding a quasi-automatic review process and financial fines imposed on countries having excessive deficits. How such antideficit provisions will affect the fiscal performance of the EMU member countries, however, remains an open question. While it is easy to write such rules into a treaty, it is much more difficult to enforce them and to evaluate their net effect on fiscal policy. Member nations might respond, as the designers of the rules intended, by carefully avoiding large deficits and by reacting promptly to negative fiscal shocks by raising revenues and reducing outlays. But member nations might also respond by shifting expenditures to off-budget accounts or engaging in other types of "creative accounting" that would enable them to comply with the letter, but not the spirit, of the antideficit provisions.

The effect of budget institutions, including such deficit rules, on fiscal policy outcomes has been an active subject of theoretical and empirical research in the last decade. There is now a substantial literature that attempts to model the interaction between fiscal rules and fiscal outcomes, and that provides empirical evidence on the importance of these links. Stimulated in part by political processes such as European monetary unification and calls for a balanced-budget amendment in the United States, researchers have studied cross-country differences in fiscal institutions, the rare episodes of budgetary reform in individual nations, and the budgeting and financing rules of the U.S. states. These studies are designed to obtain new insight on the relationship between fiscal rules and fiscal policy outcomes. Research in this area involves a constant interplay between political-economic modeling, case study and institutional analysis, and statistical investigation.

In the inaugural research meeting of the University of Bonn's Zentrum für Europäische Integrationsforschung (ZEI), a group of researchers met in June 1997 at a conference cosponsored by ZEI and the National Bureau of Economic Research (NBER) to present their latest work on budget rules and fiscal policy. The program included thirteen papers addressing a range of questions relating to the economic effects of fiscal institutions. The papers presented covered three distinct areas of research: new theoretical models of what explains the rise and persistence of budget deficits; new empirical evidence on the relationship between fiscal rules and fiscal policy outcomes, such as deficits and the response of fiscal policy to aggregate economic shocks; and case studies of the effects of budget rules on the behavior of policymakers and other actors involved in the fiscal policy process.

This volume presents the research findings that were reported at the conference. The remainder of this introduction distills several broad lessons that emerged from the presentations and discussion at the conference, and then presents a brief summary of each of the research papers that follow below.

Common Themes

The research in this volume suggests several important conclusions about fiscal institutions and fiscal policy. First, there is an emerging consensus that persistent budget deficits can be modeled as the result of a rational choice by self-interested political actors. Deficits arise because the government's general tax fund is a "common property resource" from which projects of public policy are being financed, much like the aggregate stock of a resource in resource economics. This induces a "common-pool problem" in which competing political groups vie for government expenditures that are financed using broad-based tax instruments. As in models of geographically concentrated pork barrel spending, the costs of higher deficits are broadly dispersed, while the benefits of higher deficits, primarily higher spending on particular projects, transfer programs, or lower tax rates on particular types of income, are concentrated. This results in higher deficits than political actors who internalized the costs of spending and deficits would choose. This last aspect means that budgeting decisions under an unmitigated common-pool problem are inefficient in the sense that all actors involved would choose lower levels of spending and deficits if they took the full costs into account.

One critical implication of common-pool models is that fiscal rules that lead participants in the budgeting process to internalize the costs of budget deficits will lead to smaller budget deficits. The more fragmented the budget process is, that is, the less individual actors take into account the externality created by the general tax fund, the larger is the bias toward higher spending and larger deficits. *Fragmentation* can arise when there are many actors involved in the budget process, and when the decision-making processes in which these decision makers interact diffuses power. *Centralization* of the budget process involves institutional provisions conducive to internalizing the externality. This can be achieved by limiting the number of actors in the budget-making process, by centralizing budgeting authority in the hands of a fiscal entrepreneur, or by implementing decision-making rules, such as cooperative bargaining processes, among the relevant actors. The prediction that centralization leads to smaller deficits is one of those considered in several empirical papers in this volume.

Transparency is a key dimension of *centralization,* and one along which budget systems vary. It appears to be correlated with budget outcomes. A transparent budget process is one that provides clear information on all aspects of government fiscal policy. Budgets that include numerous special accounts and that fail to consolidate all fiscal activity into a single "bottom line" measure are not transparent. Budgets that are easily available to the public and to participants in the policymaking process, and that do present consolidated information, are transparent. Higher levels of transparency are associated with lower budget deficits.

A second common theme that emerges from the empirical work is broad agreement that fiscal institutions have important effects on fiscal policy outcomes. The empirical evidence supporting this proposition arises from empirical studies of OECD nations, states within the United States, provinces in Argentina, cantons in Switzerland, and cross-national evidence for Latin America. The empirical evidence suggesting that institutions matter is stronger than the evidence on the mechanisms by which these institutions matter.

Third, institutional environments of national fiscal policy are complex and, therefore, difficult to model and to characterize empirically. Empirical researchers have developed a number of different ways of characterizing budget rules, political institutions, and other factors that may affect fiscal policy. One branch of the recent research develops numerical indexes summarizing key aspects of the relevant institutions. Such indexes can be used in regression analysis, but hardly do full justice to the complex reality of budgets. Furthermore, they involve questionable assumptions of substitutability between individual institutional rules. Case studies, in contrast, make room for more detailed description, but defy statistical analysis. An important insight from the conference is, therefore, that different methodological approaches lead to similar conclusions regarding the role of fiscal institutions. In the end, different methodologies should, therefore, be regarded as complements rather than substitutes.

Fourth, while the evidence from both approaches strongly suggests that fiscal institutions are important determinants of fiscal outcomes, a recurrent theme of the discussion is that the institutions must themselves be regarded as endogenous. The questions when, and why, governments adopt institutional reforms remain important challenges for future research in the political economy of fiscal policy.

In the next section, we summarize the papers presented at the conference in three broad groups, corresponding to their different methods of inquiry.

The Relevance of Fiscal Institutions: Overview and Theory

The first chapter in the volume is a broad survey of theoretical as well as empirical work on budget policy. Alberto Alesina and Roberto Perotti's chapter, "Budget Deficits and Budget Institutions," presents a valuable overview on the existing state of research on the determinants of fiscal policy. The chapter outlines the existing theoretical models of budget determination, which draw on game theory, formal political science, macroeconomics, and public finance to develop an understanding of the factors that might affect budget outcomes. The authors emphasize models in which deficits arise because some of the actors in the fiscal policy process do not bear the full costs of raising revenue, even though they can receive the full benefits of additional expenditures. The chapter also surveys existing empirical work and thereby provides a motivation for the various data analyses presented in the second part of this volume. The authors argue that the available literature suggests that budget procedures and budget institutions, both procedural rules and balanced-budget laws, influence budget outcomes. The chapter concludes with a discussion of several unresolved issues, including the trade-offs between fiscal restraint and other factors that may be associated with tight budget rules, and the potential endogeneity of fiscal institutions.

The second chapter is Andrés Velasco's study, "A Model of Endogenous Fiscal Deficits and Delayed Fiscal Reforms." Velasco develops a dynamic, political-economic model of fiscal policy in which government resources are a "common property" out of which interest groups can finance expenditures on their preferred items. This setup has striking macroeconomic implications. First, fiscal deficits and debt accumulation occur even when there are no reasons for intertemporal smoothing of tax and expenditure burdens. This finding stands in contrast to much of the positive theory of intertemporal fiscal policy, which holds that governments run deficits when their current expenditure needs are high relative to their long-run needs, or their current tax capacity is low relative to long-run capacity. Second, the chapter shows that deficits resulting from this "common pool" problem can be eliminated through a fiscal reform, but such a reform may only take place after a delay during which government debt is built up.

The last chapter in this section, by Adriana Arreaza, Bent Sørensen, and Oved Yosha, considers the degree to which governments use fiscal policy to smooth private-sector consumption in the face of macroeconomic shocks. This chapter is directly relevant to debates about monetary union, because one of the important issues any time nations or states cede some authority to a centralized governing body is the degree to which this body will be able to carry out redistribution across member states. The chapter, "Consumption Smoothing through Fiscal Policy in OECD and EU Countries," compares the current consumption-smoothing patterns in the OECD and in the European Union (EU). The results suggest that EU countries rely more strongly than other OECD countries on government transfers, rather than government consumption, to smooth cyclical shocks. Furthermore, the evidence suggests that governments with persistently high deficits are less able to smooth consumption than governments with low average deficits. Finally, the authors show that countries with relatively strong elements of centralization in their budget processes achieve a higher degree of consumption smoothing through fiscal policy than countries with relatively fragmented budget processes. The implication is that fiscal institutions that reduce the government's deficit bias also strengthen its ability to run large deficits in responding to adverse economic shocks. This finding implies that the nature of budget rules can have an important impact on the government's power to carry out efficient fiscal stabilization.

Empirical Evidence on the Effects and the Choice of Fiscal Institutions

The results surveyed and presented in the first three chapters provide an important warrant for empirical analysis of the factors that determine budget outcomes. The majority of chapters in this volume present new empirical evidence, based on statistical analysis of cross-sectional or panel data, on the effect of budget rules or political variables on fiscal policy outcomes. Each of these chapters suggests that there is an important correlation between a set of budget rules or procedures and fiscal outcomes at the national or subnational level. Several of these studies develop new databases on fiscal institutions and fiscal policy outcomes in particular regions or nations. Taken together these studies represent substantial evidence supporting the importance of fiscal rules in determining tax and expenditure levels.

The first chapter in this spirit is by Yianos Kontopoulos and Roberto Perotti; it is titled "Government Fragmentation and Fiscal Policy Outcomes: Evidence from OECD Countries." This chapter explores the effects of political factors, procedural factors (such as the budget process), and ideology in shaping the fiscal outcomes for OECD countries throughout the 1960–95 period. The chapter begins with a theoretical model of how fragmentation affects the budget process. The empirical analysis suggests that fragmentation, particularly when measured by the number of participants in the deliberations that ultimately determine the budget, has an important effect on fiscal policy outcomes. It also indicates that ideology, as measured by the position of the ruling party on a liberal/conservative spectrum, is a substantively important determinant of fiscal policy.

Ernesto Stein, Ernesto Talvi, and Alejandro Grisanti also find support for the role of fiscal institutions in their chapter, "Institutional Arrangements and Fiscal Performance: The Latin American Experience." This chapter explores the links between electoral systems, budget institutions, and fiscal performance in Latin America. It considers four measures of fiscal performance: the level of government expenditures, the size of the deficit, the size of the public debt, and the response of fiscal policy to business cycle fluctuations. It finds evidence that electoral systems characterized by a high degree of proportionality (i.e., proportional representation) tend to have larger governments, larger deficits, and a more procyclical response to the business cycle, unless they are constrained by institutional rules producing greater centralization of the budget process. It also finds that more transparent and centralized budgetary procedures lead to lower deficits and debt. Furthermore, strengthening budget procedures for the central government can weaken the effect of proportional representation on fiscal policy outcomes.

The next chapter presents further analysis of fiscal institutions and fiscal policies in Latin America. Mark P. Jones, Pablo Sanguinetti, and Mariano Tommasi, in "Politics, Institutions, and Public-Sector Spending in the Argentine

Provinces," exploit the substantial cross-sectional variation in the fiscal rules within Argentina to develop and test models of political-economic interactions. They study the behavior of provincial public finances since Argentina's return to democracy in 1983. Their empirical model is based on the "common pool" theory of deficit determination, and the empirical results suggest that the tax-sharing mechanism, *coparticipacion fiscal,* by which the national government devolves taxes to the provinces, is an important determinant of provincial fiscal behavior. Budget procedures and other institutions are also crucial for fiscal performance. Party affiliation of the provincial governors in relation to most of the national executive is a key factor in ameliorating or exacerbating the incentive for provinces to "free ride" on the common pool. The latter finding is particularly intriguing, since it suggests that political factors may interact with fiscal rules in determining policy outcomes.

The next two studies also exploit variation in fiscal rules at the subnational level to provide evidence on the economic consequences of different rules. Lars P. Feld and Gebhard Kirchgässner, in their chapter "Public Debt and Budgetary Procedures: Top Down or Bottom Up? Some Evidence from Swiss Municipalities," study the effects of referendum approval of budget deficits. Referendum approval is a form of direct democracy: it essentially subjects the level of deficit spending or government borrowing to a popular vote. Their study analyzes a cross section of the 131 largest Swiss municipalities and develops a new database on fiscal institutions and fiscal outcomes in these municipalities. The data suggest that there is a great deal of heterogeneity in the budgeting rules used in different municipalities, so the Swiss experience provides a valuable setting in which to test alternative models of fiscal policy choice. The authors explore the link between institutional structure and fiscal outcomes and find that municipalities with direct-democracy provisions for the approval of new debt issues exhibit lower levels of debt per capita than those municipalities without such provisions.

The final chapter on subnational fiscal policy, by James M. Poterba and Kim Rueben, is entitled "State Fiscal Institutions and the U.S. Municipal Bond Market." The fiscal policy experiences of the U.S. states, which are autonomous but are linked through participation in a currency union (the United States), may provide useful lessons on the potential effects of European monetary union. This chapter presents new evidence on the effect of state fiscal institutions, particularly balanced-budget rules and restrictions on state debt issuance, on the yields on state general obligation bonds. The authors find that states with tighter antideficit rules, and states with more restrictive provisions on the authority of state governments to issue debt, face lower borrowing costs. The interest rate differential between a state with a very strict antideficit constitution, and one with a lax constitution, is between 10 and 15 basis points. States with binding revenue limitation measures tend to face higher borrowing rates by approximately the same amount. These results provide evidence that bond market participants consider fiscal institutions in assessing the risk characteristics of tax-exempt bonds, and further support the view that fiscal institutions have real effects on fiscal outcomes.

The last chapter in this section focuses on the experience of countries in the OECD or the European Union. Mark Hallerberg and Jürgen von Hagen explore the interplay between electoral systems, proportional representation versus plurality, and institutional arrangements to achieve a higher degree of centralization of the budget process. Their paper, "Electoral Institutions, Cabinet Negotiations, and Budget Deficits in the European Union," argues that electoral systems restrict the type of budgetary institutions at the government's disposal. In states with plurality systems, where one-party governments are the norm, centralization can be achieved effectively by delegating strong agenda-setting powers to the finance minister, who thus becomes the fiscal entrepreneur. The authors also show that in states with systems of proportional representation and where multiparty coalitions are the common form of government, the proper institutional solution to the "common pool" problem is a commitment to fiscal targets negotiated among the coalition partners. These institutional choices are determined by the different enforcement mechanisms implied by single and multiparty governments.

The empirical section of this chapter shows that, among the EU states, electoral systems help predict the choice of institution to achieve greater fiscal discipline. The implication is that one should not expect fiscal targets such as those imposed by the Maastricht Treaty to promote fiscal consolidation in states where single-party governments are the rule. The chapter also shows that the two mechanisms, delegation of decision-making powers to a strong finance minister and commitment to fiscal targets, contributed to reducing deficits in the EU states during the period 1980–94.

Case Studies of Budgetary Institutions

Analyzing data on the correlation between budget rules and budget outcomes, as the foregoing chapters do, provides a valuable source of evidence on the determinants of fiscal policy, but it may neglect important institutional features of the budget process. The last four chapters in the volume consider the evolution and effects of budget rules in one nation, or a small set of nations. While these chapters present quantitative evidence on budgeting procedures, they can also be viewed as case studies of particular budgeting rules.

The first is J. Edgardo Campos and Sanjay Pradhan's report, "Budgetary Institutions and the Levels of Expenditure Outcomes in Australia and New Zealand." This chapter extends previous research suggesting that key budgetary institutions are important in controlling aggregate spending. It looks beyond the issue of fiscal discipline and argues that aggregate fiscal discipline is necessarily linked to the issues of allocative and technical efficiency. Hence, in identifying the impact of budgetary institutions, the paper suggests taking a broader and more systemic perspective. Based on the reform experiences of New Zealand and Australia, it argues that these linkages embody transactions costs that could lead one country to adopt one set of institutions, and another a different (though overlapping) set. Specifically, it shows that New Zealand sought to control aggregate spending by focusing on improving technical efficiency, while Australia sought to do so by introducing mechanisms to facilitate strategic prioritization and to enhance allocative efficiency. These are aspects of the micro budget process that have important effects on the aggregate level of spending.

The second chapter, by Jakob de Haan, Wim Moessen, and Bjørn Volkerink, examines changes in the budget process in a small set of nations in the European Union. The chapter, "Budgetary Procedures—Aspects and Changes: New Evidence for Some European Countries," combines cross-sectional statistical analysis of a large data set on fiscal rules and fiscal policy, with a more specialized investigation of budgeting in several nations. This chapter addresses two problems that arise in the empirical literature on the link between procedures that lead to the formulation, approval, and implementation of the budget, and fiscal policy outcomes. First, budget institutions have many dimensions, and it is not clear which budget procedures have the greatest effect on policy outcomes. The chapter considers this issue using data from nations in the European Union. The results suggest that the position of the finance minister in the budget process and the presence or absence of binding constraints appear most important in determining the level of budget deficits. This supports the findings in earlier papers of the importance of centralization in budget procedures.

The second part of the chapter considers the evolution of budget rules in several nations that have adopted some procedural changes during the last fifteen years. In one case, Sweden, changes in the budgetary process were precipitated by an acute financial crisis. In several other nations that exhibit reported changes in the budget process during the last decade, it is more difficult to identify the motivation for reform, or to evaluate its impact on fiscal policy.

The third chapter in this section is Thomas J. Courchene's study, "Subnational Budgetary and Stabilization Policies in Canada and Australia." It focuses on the relationship between institutional structures and subnational fiscal and budgetary processes in two nations that were part of the British Empire, but which evolved quite different budget rules. The chapter explains the institutional arrangements that have led the Australian government to be more centralized and egalitarian than its Canadian counterpart and that have made the Canadian provinces more fiscally autonomous than the Australian states. One episode that receives particular attention is the expansion of borrowing by the Canadian province of Ontario in the late 1980s, and the effect of this borrowing on the aggregate government sector in Canada.

Courchene's analysis also focuses on the implications of government structure for the magnitude and structure of intergovernmental grants, for the degree of subnational fiscal stabilization policy, for subnational borrowing autonomy, and for the extent of economic and budgetary coordination between the national and subnational governments. It also considers the recent shift toward "hard budget constraints" in the Canadian provinces and presents some evidence, along the lines of Poterba and Rueben's evidence for the United States, suggesting that the credit ratings of Australian states and Canadian provinces is affected by their fiscal position.

The final chapter, by Maurice Wright, focuses on budgeting outcomes in Japan. In "Coping with Fiscal Stress: Illusion and Reality in Central Government Budgeting in Japan, 1975–1997," Wright describes how the Japanese government has coped with conditions of almost continuous fiscal stress, including budget deficits, accumulated debt, and increasing costs of debt servicing, during the last two and one-half decades. He concludes that policy choices were largely unsuccessful in achieving their stated fiscal objectives, which were to substantially reduce government deficits. An illusion of discipline and control was created through manipulation of the budgetary system and the exploitation of the rules of the game on the part of budget makers. In reality, the central government was either unable or unwilling to control the growth of government spending over this period. Wright's analysis is a cautionary note to those who suppose that merely enacting a deficit reduction target will lead to deficit reduction.

The Main Lessons

The research findings summarized in this volume represent an important addition to our knowledge of how fiscal policy is affected by budgeting institutions. A first, important insight is that the common-pool approach to the analysis of public spending and deficits is promising and powerful in explaining the emergence of large and persistent deficits. As the common-pool approach focuses on a problem of coordination failure among the decision makers involved in public budgeting, the implication is that large deficits may be avoided by strategic design of the budget process, that is, by institutions that distribute authority and facilitate agreement on the efficient outcome. Procedural design thus emerges as an important alternative to rules restricting the outcome of the budget process, such as balanced-budget laws.

Second, effective institutional design of the budget process to reduce the spending and deficit bias of governments promotes a comprehensive view of the costs and benefits of public policies. If *centralization* of the budget process relies on delegating power to an individual decision maker, the key is that this individual be driven less by particularistic spending interests than the spending ministers. If centralization relies on common agreements on fiscal targets, the key is that these targets be agreed upon early in the budget process, that the agreement is negotiated by all parties involved, and that the agreement is backed up by strong enough punishments for violation to make it binding throughout the budget process. Effective institutional design also includes elements assuring the enforcement of efficient agreements, such as limits on parliamentary amendments and a strong monitoring position of the treasury in budget implementation to prevent policymakers from reneging on the initial agreement.

The empirical work in several chapters emphasizes the richness of budget institutions by developing comprehensive characterizations of the entire budget process rather than by focusing on the existence or absence of individual rules. The implication is that reform of the budget process must consider the interaction of all stages of the process.

Third, the empirical work presented in this volume shows that fiscal institutions matter not only for the average deficit, but also for other aspects of fiscal performance. These include the government's capacity for consumption smoothing, its ability to conduct macroeconomic stabilization policies, its inclination to engage in political business cycles, and the cost of public debt. An important finding is that *centralization* of the budget process does not worsen the performance of budgetary policies in these other regards.

Finally, the work presented in this volume suggests an intimate connection between the design of the budget process and other dimensions of a country's constitution such as the position of the executive relative to the legislature, the strength of elements of direct democracy, and the type of electoral law. Budgetary institutions that work in one constitutional context may fail to work in others, because they do not provide the proper incentives and constraints to promote and enforce agreement on efficient levels of spending and deficits. The implication is that reform of the budget process cannot rely on a "one model fits all" approach but must consider a country's broader constitutional framework and tradition.

Future Directions

The presentations and discussion at the ZEI-NBER meeting raise a number of unresolved issues that stand as challenges for future research. The single most important issue for further work concerns the endogeneity of budget rules, and the factors that lead policymakers to reform budget processes. Virtually all of the empirical papers in this volume acknowledge the potential econometric problems that are posed by the fact that budget rules are not randomly assigned to nations or subnational jurisdictions, but rather are the product of deliberate choice by voters or their elected representatives. This makes it difficult to evaluate observed correlations between budget rules and budget outcomes: perhaps the observed relationships are simply due to a correlation between a third factor, voter preferences, and the these observed manifestations of voter preferences. Further work is clearly needed to explain where budget rules come from, and what factors lead to changes in these rules over time. Several papers argue that there are costs to changing budget rules, but there has been little analysis to date of what these costs are, and what makes some political actors willing to bear them, while others are not.

A second issue that bears further investigation is the interaction between political factors and budgeting institutions in determining fiscal outcomes. As noted above, some of the empirical papers in this volume and in other papers suggest that the effectiveness of budget institutions in reducing the deficit bias depends on the general political setting of the country considered. Providing further evidence on this issue will require careful empirical work, because budget rules and political variables are often highly correlated.

Finally, the research in this volume underscores the need for further theoretical and empirical research that sheds light on the *description* of budget institutions. Many of the empirical studies in this volume and the broader literature use indicator variables, "dummy variables," for the presence or absence of particular attributes of the budget process in particular nations or states. Others rely on indexes of budget stringency that are created by adding together sets of indicator variables, or by coding various aspects of budget policy on arbitrary scales. Such additive indexes assume a strong form of substitution between different components of the budget process, and there is little evidence to support the assumptions underlying such aggregation.

Existing empirical work clearly suggests that various aspects of budget institutions matter, but the next generation of research should attempt to fine-tune these findings with a more detailed investigation of budget rules. Moving ahead in this research program will require both theoretical development, to suggest the key features of the budget process that warrant measurement, and new efforts to codify and measure budget institutions. The proposition that budget rules are simply a veil, which a median voter or set of political actors can pierce in setting fiscal policy, is not credible in light of the evidence developed here and elsewhere. But the precise mechanism through which budget processes affect fiscal outcomes remains to be documented, modeled, and tested.

All of the methodologies featured in this book—theoretical model-building, empirical analysis, and case study research—can contribute to our further understanding of the economic effects of fiscal policy institutions. The fiscal pressures associated with the aging populations in many developed nations are likely to draw more, not less, attention to the factors that determine budget outcomes, and to make this a very promising area for research in the years and decades to come.

1   Budget Deficits and Budget Institutions

Alberto Alesina and Roberto Perotti

1.1   Introduction

In the last thirty years several OECD economies have accumulated large public debts. In fact, table 1.1 shows a very large variance in debt/GNP ratios in OECD countries, much larger today than twenty years ago. Several countries exhibit debt/GNP ratios close to or even greater than 100 percent, while others have ratios of about 30 percent. The increase in public debts has been accompanied by a marked transformation in the composition of government outlays. While twenty years ago purchases of goods and services were predominant in government budgets, in the last twenty years transfer programs have grown much more rapidly than government purchases of goods and services. Transfers are notoriously more difficult to cut; therefore this evolution of the composition of expenditures makes fiscal adjustments in the face of high debts particularly difficult.

In a previous paper (Alesina and Perotti 1995b) we asked two questions: (1) Why did certain countries accumulate large public debts while others did not? and (2) Why did these large debts appear in the last twenty years but not before?

In that paper we argued that economic variables alone cannot provide satisfactory answers to these questions, and we considered several politico-institutional explanations. In particular, we emphasized the role of electoral systems, party structure, government fragmentation, and political polarization. For instance, we agreed with those authors[1] who have argued that coalition

Alberto Alesina is professor of economics and government at Harvard University and a research associate of the National Bureau of Economic Research and of the Centre for Economic Policy Research, London. Roberto Perotti is professor of economics at Columbia University and a research associate of the Centre for Economic Policy Research, London.

1. See Roubini and Sachs 1989a, b; Grilli, Masciandaro, and Tabellini 1991; Alesina and Perotti 1995a; Perotti and Kontopoulos (chap. 4 in this volume); and Hallerberg and von Hagen (chap. 9

governments, typical of countries with proportional electoral systems, tend to delay fiscal adjustments, so that public debts accumulate more rapidly in these countries.

In this paper we focus more specifically on "budgetary institutions," defined as all the rules and regulations according to which budgets are prepared, approved, and carried out.

Our goal is to understand whether the budget procedures have significant macroeconomic effects on the size and composition of the budget and on the budget balance.[2] Specifically, we pose two related questions: (*a*) To what extent do budget institutions explain fiscal policy outcomes, and particularly, the budget balance? Can budget institutions explain why certain high-debt countries have more difficulties in adjusting than others? (*b*) What are the most effective budget procedures to insure "fiscal responsibility"? We conclude that fiscal institutions are important determinants of fiscal outcomes. In Poterba's (1996) words, "although the evidence is not conclusive, the preponderance of studies suggest that institutions are not simply veils . . . but are important constraints."[3]

This paper is organized as follows. Section 1.2 describes and summarizes our basic argument and provides an overview of the paper. This section briefly touches upon several issues that are then addressed in more detail in the following sections. Section 1.3 reviews the theoretical literature, and section 1.4 discusses the issues and problems left unsolved. Section 1.5 tackles a difficult but important issue, namely the transparency of the budget. Section 1.6 reviews the empirical literature that can shed light on our two questions.

1.2   Budgetary Institutions: An Overview

This section describes our basic argument and provides an overview of the entire paper.

1.2.1   Are Institutions Endogenous?

Budgetary institutions are all the rules and regulations according to which budgets are drafted, approved, and implemented. Since these institutions vary across countries, and, to a lesser extent, over time, they can be used as an explanation of cross-country differences in fiscal policy.

An obvious objection to this research strategy is that institutions are themselves endogenous. In particular, institutions may be changed as a result of unsatisfactory fiscal performance, and the choice of different institutions may

---

in this volume) for empirical work and Spolaore 1993 and Velasco (chap. 2 in this volume) for theoretical work.

2. For a more comprehensive discussion of legal, organizational, and economic aspects of budget procedures, see Wildasky 1986 and, in particular, Premchand 1983.

3. Poterba 1996 provides an excellent assessment of the literature on fiscal institutions that nicely complements the present one.

be a function of other socio-political-historical variables that may influence both the institutional choice and the fiscal outcome. If this is the case, institutions cannot be used as explanatory variables in regressions where fiscal outcomes are on the left-hand side of the equation, which is the procedure adopted in much of the empirical literature reviewed below.

Clearly, to some extent institutions are indeed endogenous, particularly to past fiscal outcomes. However, to the extent that institutions are reasonably difficult to change, and therefore are changed relatively infrequently, they can be considered predetermined, at least in the short-to-medium run. In other words, since it is costly and complex to change institutions, the existing ones have to be very unsatisfactory before it is worth changing them; as a result, there is a strong "status quo" bias in institutional reforms. Therefore, at least up to a point, one can use institutional features as explanatory variables. Nevertheless we believe that systematic research that tries to explain institutional building is overdue and is an excellent area of future work.

One can distinguish between two types of institutions: laws that prescribe numerical targets on the budget, and procedural rules.

1.2.2   Balanced-Budget Laws

The most typical example of a "numerical target" is a balanced-budget law. Two theoretical arguments suggest that a balanced-budget law would not be optimal. The first one is related to stabilization policies. Standard Keynesian anticyclical policies prescribe tax cuts, expenditure increases, and deficits in recessions and tax increases, expenditure cuts, and surplus in economic booms. Note, however, that the feasibility and opportunity of this kind of fine-tuning of fiscal policies have been questioned, starting with the famous argument on "long and variable lags" by Milton Friedman.[4]

A second theoretical argument that runs against the idea of balanced-budget laws is the tax-smoothing theory of budget deficits (Barro 1979; Lucas and Stokey 1983). According to this theory, budget deficits and surpluses should be used to "smooth" the distortionary cost of taxation, so that deficits should be permitted when spending is exceptionally and temporarily high, for instance during wars, natural calamities, and emergencies, or when revenues are temporarily low, for instance during recessions. Thus, a law that prescribes a balanced budget in every year would excessively constrain the use of budget deficits and surpluses as the "buffer" needed to implement the optimal tax policy.

Theoretically, one could think of a "contingent" budget balance law, with escape clauses to permit a certain amount of tax smoothing. However, a well-understood argument in the debate on rules versus discretion suggests that rules have to be simple.[5] Complicated rules can be circumvented and present

---

4. Even though Friedman was concerned about monetary policy, his argument applies also to fiscal policy.

5. See, for instance, Tanzi 1993.

monitoring problems, so that in the end they become almost useless. They may even be counterproductive if they create incentives to resort to "creative budgeting" and highly distorted policies chosen simply to circumvent the rules.

On the other hand, several arguments suggest that actual policies are not dictated by principles of optimal taxation, but are the result of various politically induced deficit bias (see the survey in Alesina and Perotti 1995b). In this case, a balanced-budget law may be a second-best solution. One would have to trade off the distortions of the balanced-budget law on the optimal tax policies, against the reduction of politically induced distortions on actual policies.

This paper argues that balanced-budget laws at the national level are neither necessary nor sufficient to insure fiscal discipline. We argue that *appropriate* procedures may not require numerical targets, so that one may maintain flexibility on the budget balance front (needed to implement tax-smoothing policies or stabilization policies) without giving up fiscal discipline. To evaluate this claim, we now turn to an overview of procedural issues.

1.2.3 Procedural Rules

One can identify three phases in the budget process: (1) the formulation of a budget proposal within the executive; (2) the presentation and approval of the budget in the legislature; and (3) the implementation of the budget by the bureaucracy.

This paper focuses mostly on the first two aspects, although we will briefly touch upon the third one as well. An exhaustive treatment of the role and organization of a bureaucracy goes beyond the scope of this paper.[6]

Two issues are crucial in our view: the voting procedures leading to the formulation and approval of the budget, and the degree of transparency of the budget. Voting procedures are clearly important because they establish who has an influence on the final budget outcome, and when. The transparency is equally important since "creative accounting" can circumvent even the most stringent voting procedures. In fact, the two issues are strictly connected: voting procedures have an impact on the final outcome if the latter can be monitored because it is transparent. We begin with voting procedures.

We focus upon a key trade-off between two types of institutions. One type, which we label, for lack of a better word, *hierarchical,* has the property that it limits the democratic accountability of the budget process. The second type, which for lack of a better word we call *collegial,* has the opposite features. Hierarchical institutions are those that, for instance, attribute strong prerogatives to the prime minister (or the finance or Treasury minister) to overrule spending ministers within intragovernmental negotiations on the formulation of the budget. Hierarchical institutions also limit in a variety of ways the capacity of the legislature to amend the budget proposed by the government. Colle-

---

6. See Premchand 1983 on this point.

gial institutions emphasize the democratic rule in every stage, like the prerogatives of spending ministers within the government, the prerogatives of the legislature vis-à-vis the government, and the rights of the minority opposition in the legislature.

We argue that there is a trade-off between these two types of institutions: hierarchical institutions are more likely to enforce fiscal restraint, avoid large and persistent deficits, and implement fiscal adjustments more promptly. On the other hand, they are less respectful of the rights of the minority, and more likely to generate budgets heavily tilted in favor of the interests of the majority. Collegial institutions have the opposite features.

This trade-off can have important positive and normative implications. From a positive standpoint we will argue, using the available evidence, that indeed, hierarchical institutions promote fiscal restraints. From a normative point of view we discuss what considerations should lead to a choice over this trade-off and how to "optimize" over it. Generally speaking, institutional choices close to the extremes of this institutional trade-off are unlikely to be optimal. Also, this institutional choice depends upon the "initial conditions." For example, a country with a high debt/GDP ratio that is contemplating an institutional reform should look more favorably toward hierarchical institutions than, ceteris paribus, a country with a low debt/GDP ratio. The theoretical arguments underlying this trade-off are discussed in sections 1.3 and 1.4.

The second important set of issues concerns the transparency of the budget and the nature of those institutions that are supposed to "control" the budget process. Modern budgets of OECD countries are extremely complicated, sometimes unnecessarily so. One has to wonder whether the degree of complexity of a budget is unavoidable, or whether it is a way of creating opportunities for "creative budgeting." Typically, governments "hide" liabilities, by either shifting them to future budgets, or using funds that are "outside the budget." A related common practice is that of adopting overoptimistic projections of macroeconomic variables, so that revenues are overestimated and spending needs are underestimated. Then, at the end of the fiscal year, "bad luck" is held responsible for the "unexpected" additional deficit.

One can think of two ways of dealing with the problem of transparency. One is to set certain standards to be followed. The other is to have independent agencies that provide a "check" on the accuracy of the budget. We will conclude in favor of the second solution, in section 1.5, which specifically addresses the issue of transparency.

1.3   Institutions, Procedures, and the Budget: Theory

1.3.1   General Issues

Without any restrictions on procedures, without any "structure" and rules, Arrow's impossibility theorem (1951) implies that a legislature would never produce a budget but only legislative "chaos." Influential work by Shepsle (1979a,b) shows that the restrictions ("structure") imposed by procedural rules generally solve Arrow's problem and lead to predictable legislative outcomes.

A vast literature in formal political science has studied how different voting procedures in legislatures lead to different outcomes, and a good portion of this research focuses on the budget. Typically this literature is inspired by American institutions and focuses almost exclusively on the legislature, namely on the American Congress. However, if viewed *cum grano salis,* this line of research can shed light on institutions of other countries.

Much of this research is based, directly or indirectly, upon a view of the budget as the result of conflicting interests of representatives with geographically based constituencies. In particular, it addresses two problems: the determination of the size of the budget and the allocation of projects among different districts.

Weingast, Shepsle, and Johnsen (1981) provide one of the clearest discussions of these issues by arguing that representatives with geographically based constituencies ask for spending programs that benefit their district and are financed nationwide. Thus, representatives systematically do not internalize the "true" costs of financing such projects. The idea is that the voters of the ith district receive benefits for a certain public project in their district, but have to pay $1/N$ of the total costs of this project, if N is the number of districts and if taxes are equally distributed among districts. A geographically elected representative does not fully internalize the effects of spending in his district on the tax burden of the country. The aggregate effect of rational representatives facing these incentives is an excessive demand of public goods with geographically targeted benefits and diffuse financing costs.

While Weingast, Shepsle, and Johnsen do not address directly the question of how all of these demands for pork barrel projects lead to an aggregate budget, the critical feature of a voting equilibrium that leads to an oversupply of pork barrel projects is "reciprocity." Namely, a representative of the ith district votes in favor of a project for district j, expecting the same favor in return from the representative of district in the next vote.

The literature on procedures has addressed three related questions: what procedural rules mitigate or aggravate the problem of oversupply of pork barrel projects? What procedural rules make the choice of projects, given a certain total budget, more or less efficient? How do different procedural rules influence the final allocation of net benefits among districts? Two issues are particularly interesting for our purposes: (*a*) the sequence of voting on the budget, and (*b*) the type of admissible amendments on the proposed budget.

1.3.2   Timing of Voting on the Budget

One of the most important features of the Budget Act of 1974 in the United States, which substantially reformed budget procedures, was to change the sequence of congressional votes on the budget. Until then, Congress would vote on a series of appropriation bills, and the overall size of the budget was determined residually. After the Budget Act, Congress is required to vote at the beginning of the process on the overall size of the budget. The motivation of this reform was to enforce an ex ante discipline on the legislature, so as to fix an agreed-upon overall size of the budget, rather than letting it be determined by the accumulation of bills. The emergence of large budget deficits in the eighties raises some questions concerning the success of this reform.[7]

Motivated by this puzzle, Ferejohn and Krehbiel (1987) study theoretically the determination of the size of the budget under the two alternative voting procedures. They assume that the budget can be allocated to two projects and different legislators have different preferences for the relative benefits of these two projects. These authors reach a rather provocative conclusion: It is not always the case that the size of the budget is smaller when the legislatures vote first on the size and then on the composition, relative to the case in which the overall budget size is determined as a residual. While the size of the budget is in general *not* independent of the order of votes, the relative size of the budget with different orders of votes depends on the distribution of legislatures' preferences for budget composition. The same issue has been revisited recently by Hallerberg and von Hagen (1997).

The critical intuition of these results is that rational legislators should be forward looking: for example, when voting on the first item of the budget, they will calculate how their first vote will affect the final outcome both in terms of size and of composition. Conversely, when voting on the size first, rational legislators can compute how a certain size will then lead to a certain composition in the following vote. These results are obtained with the assumption of perfect information—each legislator knows the distribution of preferences of the legislatures. Thus, at the moment of the first vote, the legislators can compute the final voting equilibrium. While this assumption is clearly not realistic, it is not obvious in which direction the results would change if one allowed for imperfect information.

An unfortunate feature of these results is that they cannot really illuminate the question of which of the two procedures one should choose to limit the spending bias of legislatures. In fact, it is hard to derive a simple link between certain observable characteristics of the distribution of legislatures' preferences and the policy outcomes under the two different procedures. Thus, one should read these papers as a very useful warning against oversimplifying the effect of certain procedures on final outcomes.

1.3.3   Amendment Rules

In an influential series of papers, Baron (1989, 1991) and Baron and Ferejohn (1989) study the question of how legislatures reach agreement on how to

---

7. Naturally, one may argue that fiscal discipline in the United States would have been even more relaxed without the Budget Act, but this is a difficult point to prove empirically.

choose pork barrel projects. Specifically, they study both how the legislature chooses the allocation of benefits of a certain budget among legislators representing different districts and how the legislature chooses among different budgets, more or less efficiently.

This line of research emphasizes a distinction between *closed rules* and *open rules* in amendments. A closed rule is one in which a proposal made by a member of the legislature has to be voted immediately up or down. If it is approved, the "game is over"; if it is rejected, a new member of the legislature can make another proposal, which again is voted up or down. An open rule is one in which the proposal made by the member selected is subject to amendments on the floor.

In actual legislatures the agenda setter in the budget process is the government. Thus, closed rules attribute more power to the government and less to the floor of the legislature. The result is that closed rules are more hierarchical. The implication is that with closed rules budgets are approved rapidly and typically reflect more closely the preference of the government. On the other hand, the preferences of various minority groups in the legislatures are taken into account less, precisely because the procedures are less collegial.

In practice, closed rules are those that make it impossible for the legislature to amend the size of the deficit; that is, if the legislature wants to increase spending, it also has to increase taxes. Even more stringent procedures make it impossible for the legislature to increase not only the deficit, but even total spending. In this case the legislature can only change the allocation of spending and revenues, but not their total.

The discussion about the possible amendments of the legislature highlights very clearly several aspects of the trade-off between hierarchical and collegial procedures. With a closed rule you achieve quick approval of a proposal, at the cost of implementing "unfair" budgets. Budgets are unfair in the sense that they are tilted in favor of those who make the first proposal, and always distribute benefits to the smallest possible majority.

Two implications on the choice of rules follow. First, a closed rule is preferable if avoiding delays is an important consideration. This is likely to be the case in high-debt countries and/or in periods of macroeconomic instability, when the rapid adoption of fiscal adjustments is critical. On the other hand, in countries and time periods of low debt and fiscal stability, considerations of allocative efficiency and fairness may be predominant, leading to the adoption of an open rule.

1.3.4   An Analogy with Electoral Laws

Before closing this section it is useful to highlight an analogy between the trade-off between collegial and hierarchical institutions and the trade-off between proportional and majoritarian electoral systems. Proportional electoral systems tend to produce multiparty systems with large coalition governments.

Majoritarian systems tend to produce biparty systems (or some approximation of them) and single-party governments. Coalition governments are the analogue of collegial procedures: they generate delays in policymaking but avoid extreme partisanship. In fact, coalition governments require approval of several parties to govern, and the veto power of each coalition member can delay the legislative process. Majoritarian systems have the opposite features, since they imply that, when in office, a party is unconstrained. Alesina and Drazen (1991) and Spolaore (1993) provide formalization of these ideas. Grilli, Masciandaro, and Tabellini (1991), Roubini and Sachs (1989a,b), Alesina and Perotti (1995a), Perotti and Kontopoulos (chap. 4 in this volume) and Hallerberg and von Hagen (chap. 9 in this volume) discuss empirical evidence on fiscal deadlocks and delayed fiscal adjustments in coalition governments in OECD countries. A related discussion refers to "divided government" in the United States, which occurs when the party of the president does not hold a majority in Congress. This situation can be a source of policy delays but also of policy moderation, as argued theoretically and empirically by Alesina and Rosenthal (1995).

In summary, the choice of an electoral law implies an institutional trade-off that is very similar to the one that we have highlighted for budget procedures.

1.4 Discussion

The formal literature discussed above has made important progress in analyzing legislatures in general and the U.S. Congress in particular. For those, like us, who are interested in the effects of procedures on budget deficits in a comparative perspective, this literature leaves several questions open.

1. First, this literature addresses specifically the size and the geographical composition of the budget, while it is silent on the budget balance. One needs a dynamic model in order to analyze deficits, while the models reviewed so far are static. The technical difficulty lies in the fact that in a dynamic model each legislative vote determines the state of the world (in particular the level of public debt) inherited by the following legislature, or the following vote by the same legislature. Thus, rational legislators should vote today taking into account the effects of their decision on future voting equilibria, with different levels of debt. This problem is hard to solve, except in very simple models where the complexity of procedural rules and of the composition of the legislature is vastly simplified.[8]

Chari and Cole (1993) make some progress in this direction, by considering together the insights of Weingast, Shepsle, and Johnsen (1981), reviewed above, and the point made by Alesina and Tabellini (1990). The latter suggest that public debt can be used "strategically" by today's policymaker to influence

8. For example, see Alesina and Tabellini 1990, Persson and Svensson 1989, and Tabellini and Alesina 1990.

the choice of tomorrow's policymaker if the two policymakers (today's and tomorrow's) have different spending priorities. Chari and Cole consider a legislature with the kind of bias emphasized by Weingast, Shepsle, and Johnsen and show how this legislature will choose to issue debt to spend as much as possible in the first period. The reason for the high-spending/high-debt policy is a combination of the "district bias" argument and the "strategic debt" argument.

Velasco (chap. 2 in this volume) uses a model based on the "tragedy of the commons" framework and studies a noncooperative game between multiple spending authorities drawing on a common amount of tax revenues. All of these spending authorities attempt to free ride on common public resources (tax revenues) to spend on the desired program.

In summary, one has to choose between models that are relatively rich in institutional details but are static and dynamic models that are poor in institutional realism. For the empirical and policy-oriented researcher this is a serious problem, since results on the size of spending do not necessarily translate into results on the size of deficits. In fact, one can point to examples of countries (e.g., France) with a large government sector, but a low level of public debt.

2. The second limitation of this literature lies in its emphasis on pork barrel projects, that is, on public projects with geographically concentrated benefits. While this emphasis was empirically grounded two decades ago, it has been less and less so in recent years. As argued above, the share of OECD budgets devoted to projects that can be considered pork barrel and geographically based is shrinking relative to transfer programs and entitlement, which are broadly based. Clearly, some transfer programs have a geographical base—for instance, Florida has a high concentration of pensioners; disability pensions have been used in Italy as an indirect transfer from the north to the south.[9] However, the emphasis placed by this formal literature on pork barrel projects is disproportionate relative to the current relevance of these projects in the budget. In fact, Alesina and Perotti (1995a) argue that the recent experience of fiscal adjustments in OECD countries shows that successful and long-lasting fiscal consolidations cannot avoid cuts in entitlement, broad-based transfer programs, and government wages and employment. Formal models of legislative votes on pork barrel projects cannot be directly applied to questions of spending allocation to transfer programs, social security, and entitlement in general.

3. A third problem is the almost exclusive emphasis of this literature on the legislature, with reasonably little attention to the executive.[10] One can argue that this emphasis is justified for the case of the United States, but, in our view, it is beyond doubt that one needs to focus more on the formulation of budget within the government in parliamentary democracies. Particularly in situations where the role of the legislature is limited in how it can amend the budget

---

9. See Emerson 1988 for data on this point.
10. An exception is Velasco (chap. 2 in this volume).

proposed by the executive, intragovernment negotiations can be very important for the final outcome.

Some of the literature on committees, procedural rules, order of voting, closed versus open rules, can be applied mutatis mutandis to the decision process within the government. For example, our previous discussion on the order of voting (on the overall size first and the composition later) could be well applied to voting within a cabinet of ministers.

However, several additional issues arise when we consider the budget formation within the executive in parliamentary democracies. For instance, one crucial factor is the relative position, de jure or de facto, of the spending ministers versus the Treasury minister and/or the prime minister. Specifically, the issue is whether the person who is ultimately responsible for presenting the budget to the legislature (typically the Treasury minister) has a higher standing in the intragovernment budget negotiations relative to the spending ministers. In some cases, more than one person is responsible for the preparation of the budget. In what follows, we indicate with *Treasury minister* the person(s) responsible for the overall budget. More hierarchical procedures grant to the Treasury minister higher standing relative to spending ministers, while more collegial procedures are more egalitarian, within the government. The constituencies of spending ministers are groups and industries who benefit from certain spending programs, while, at least in theory, the constituency of the Treasury minister is the "average" taxpayer. Thus the spending ministers do not internalize the aggregate costs of certain spending programs, while the Treasury has an incentive to internalize.

One can think of an analogy with the case of the United States. Spending ministers are like congressmen, whose constituencies favor specific spending programs. The president in the United States and the Treasury minister in parliamentary democracies, should be more sensitive to the broad-based interests of the average taxpayer. Chari, Jones, and Marimon (1997) provide an interesting formalization of this idea for the case of the United States. They argue that the American voters often prefer to elect a "big spender" (i.e., a Democrat) in their legislative district, but a "fiscal conservative" (i.e., a Republican) as president. By doing so, these voters maximize their chances of bringing spending to their districts while keeping the overall size of the budget, thus the level of taxes, low.[11] The analogy with parliamentary governments is that the voters should favor "generous" spending ministers and a conservative Treasury minister.

The incentives for "spending ministers" to increase the size of the budget are even stronger if we consider their role as heads of a bureaucracy. We know from the work by Niskanen (1971) and of the "public choice school" (see

---

11. A devil's advocate may note that Democratic presidents are sometimes elected and that the Republican administrations in the eighties were far from "fiscally conservative" in a traditional sense. The November 1994 midterm election produced a configuration of divided government that is opposite from the one predicted by Chari, Jones, and Mariman 1997.

Mueller 1978 for a review) that bureaucracies strive to maximize their budget allocation. In fact the status, salary, and influence of bureaucrats is often positively correlated with the size of the budget that they manage.[12]

In summary, any procedural arrangement that increases the relative power of the Treasury minister is likely to increase fiscal discipline.

4. A fourth set of issues that assumes somewhat different features in the American context and in parliamentary democracies is the relationship between executive and legislature in the budget process. Typically, both in the United States and in parliamentary democracies, legislators are viewed as big spenders, trying to undermine the attempt of governments to be more fiscally responsible. Thus, as argued above, procedures that limit the type of amendments that the legislature can propose should lead to fiscal restraint, at the cost of less collegiality. An important procedural aspect concerns the consequences of a rejection of the budget proposed by the executive. The consequences could be very "serious," implying de jure or de facto the resignation of the government and even new elections. On the opposite extreme, the consequences can be very "mild," simply requiring a new budget proposal from the executive.

Von Hagen (1992) argues that the more "serious" for the government are the consequences of a parliamentary defeat on the budget, "the more it is in government's interest to propose a budget that can be expected to find a solid majority in parliament" (von Hagen 1992, 35). On the other hand, the legislature and, in particular, the parties supporting the government may refrain from defeating a budget proposal for fear of creating an institutional crisis. Which of the two arguments prevails may depend on the circumstances. Generally, if the government can choose "what is at stake" in any given vote on the budget, it achieves a strategic advantage, turning a vote for or against the budget into a vote for or against the government. This choice may be helpful to "bring to order" parliamentary debates where members of the parties in government threaten to vote with the opposition on the budget. For instance, Huber (1992) discusses these types of procedures (the *guillotine* and the *package vote*) for the case of France. He argues that these procedures are used quite frequently in the Fifth Republic and were introduced as a response to the cabinet fragility of the Fourth Republic. He suggests that the use of these procedures significantly helped the executive to pass the desired legislation, and these procedures were often used within the budget approval process.

5. In section 1.3.3, we discussed the relative merits of closed and open rules, but several additional issues are left open. In particular, the open-rule regime can be of very different types. For instance, amendments can be permissible only if they do not increase the size of the deficit, or if they do not increase the size of spending. For instance, one can think of a closed rule on the size of the

---

12. Fiorina and Noll (1978) discuss the interaction of bureaucrats interested in increasing the size of the budget and legislators interested in increasing the size of pork barrel programs for their districts.

budget, and an open rule on its composition. This would strengthen the position of the executive when needed to implement fiscal adjustments, but preserve collegiality on purely allocative issues. Theoretical work on these points is not yet available.

1.5 Transparency of the Budget

The budgets of modern economies are very complex, sometimes unnecessarily so. This complexity, partly unavoidable, partly artificially created, helps in various practices that "hide" the real balance (current and future) of costs and benefits for the taxpayers. Politicians have incentives to hide taxes, overemphasize the benefits of spending, and hide government liabilities (the equivalent of future taxes). Politicians have little incentive to produce simple, clear, and transparent budgets.

At least two theoretical arguments support this claim. The first, the theory of "fiscal illusion," is illustrated particularly clearly by Buchanan and Wagner (1977). According to this view, the voters typically overestimate the benefits of public spending and underestimate the costs of taxation, current and future. Lack of transparency of the budget can increase the voters' confusion and reduce politicians' incentives to be fiscally responsible. Elsewhere (Alesina and Perotti 1995b) we have raised some doubts about the role of fiscal illusion as the main explanation of large and persistent deficits, such as those of countries with debt/GDP ratios of 100 percent or more. However, lack of transparency and voters' confusion can certainly interfere negatively with effective budget control, particularly when substantial fiscal adjustments are needed.

The second argument does not rely on voters' irrationality and confusion. Several papers, although in different contexts (e.g., Cukierman and Meltzer 1986; Alesina and Cukierman 1990), highlight the benefit for policymakers of a certain amount of ambiguity even when they face a rational electorate. The idea is that by creating confusion and, in particular, by making it less clear how policies translate into outcomes, policymakers can retain a strategic advantage versus rational, but not fully informed, voters. This advantage would disappear with "transparent" procedures; therefore, the policymakers would often choose to adopt ambiguous procedures. In particular, at least up to a point, the less the electorate knows and understands about the budget process, the more the politicians can act strategically and use fiscal deficits and overspending to achieve opportunistic goals.

Rogoff and Sibert (1988) and Rogoff (1990) make a similar point in the context of political business cycle models. They show that if the voters cannot easily observe the composition of the budget (on the spending or on the financing side), then policymakers can follow loose fiscal policies before elections and increase their chances of reappointment.

The literature reviewed in this section makes interesting points. However, it is quite distant from the details of the budget process, much more so than the literature on voting procedures reviewed in section 1.3. Once the policymakers' incentives to be strategically ambiguous are well understood, one is left with the rather difficult task of understanding *how,* in reality, policymakers obfuscate the budget and what to do about it. The only paper that attempts to explicitly model the role of ambiguity and lack of transparency in the budget process is Milesi-Ferretti 1997. This author shows that politicians who want to run excessive deficits would choose nontransparent procedures, and the latter would help them achieve their (distorted) goals.

In practice a variety of tricks can serve the purpose of strategically influencing the beliefs and information of taxpayers/voters. For instance:

1. Overestimate the expected growth of the economy, so as to overestimate tax revenues, and underestimate the level of interest rates, so as to underestimate outlays. At the end of the fiscal year, the "unexpected" deficit can be attributed to unforeseen macroeconomic developments, for which the government can claim a lack of responsibility.

2. Project overly optimistic forecasts of the effect on the budget of various policies, so that, for instance, a small new tax is forecasted to have major revenue effects, thus postponing to the following budget the problem of a real adjustment.

3. Keep various items off budget, with a creative use of the budget of other public organizations not incorporated in the national budget.

4. Use budget projections strategically. For example, in all the discussions about future budgets, a key element is the "baseline." By inflating the baseline, politicians can claim to be fiscally conservative without having to create real costs for the constituencies. In this way, they create an illusion: they appear conservative in the eyes of the taxpayers, worried about the size of the budget, but they do not really hurt key constituencies with spending cuts. Clearly, this illusion cannot last forever, since adjustment rigorous only relative to inflated baseline in the end will not stop the growth of the debt. However, this procedure creates confusion and, at the very least, delays the electorate's realistic perception of the actual state of public finance.

5. Strategic use of multiyear budgeting. By announcing a, say, three-year adjustment plan in which all the hard policies occur in years two and three, politicians can look responsible and can buy time; then they can revise the next three-year budget policies to further postpone the hard choices.

Tanzi (1995) compares budget institutions in several OECD countries and emphasizes the role of transparency and how different countries show very different levels of it. This author relates the degree of transparency with the feasibility of expenditure control.[13]

---

13. Both Tanzi (1995) and Alesina, Mare, and Perotti (1996) argue that Italy has one of the least transparent procedures, if not the least transparent, in the OECD group of countries. These authors agree that lack of transparency has made expenditure control in Italy particularly difficult. In fact, Italy is an excellent test of Milesi-Ferretti's (1997) theoretical argument.

How to increase budget transparency is a difficult problem. We can think of three possibilities. The first and most commonly followed is a "legalistic" approach. That is, more and more rules and regulations are imposed on how the budget should be prepared, organized, and executed. This approach is unlikely to be successful: complicated rules and regulations provide fertile ground for nontransparent budget procedures. A second alternative is to create legislative bodies in charge of evaluating the transparency, accuracy, and projections of the government budget.[14] This approach is superior to the legalistic one, but it relies heavily on the political independence of this public body. This independence may be problematic, particularly in a parliamentary system where the government parties control a majority in the legislature. A third alternative, the most radical but the most effective, is to delegate to a respected private institution the task of verifying the accuracy and transparency of the budget process. In addition, the government budget should be based on an average of the economic forecasts of and projections derived by international organizations or private institutions, in order to avoid strategic manipulations of forecasts.

1.6 Budget Procedures and Fiscal Outcomes: Empirical Evidence

Von Hagen (1992) and von Hagen and Harden (1994) provide the first comprehensive empirical analysis of the effects of procedures on fiscal outcomes in European countries. They construct several indices, which are meant to rank fiscal procedures from the most hierarchical to the most collegial, using our terminology. Their sample is given by all the member countries of the European Community, and they focus on a wide range of information on budget procedures:

1. the government preparation of a budget
2. the legislative phase and the relationship between executive and legislature
3. the implementation phase
4. the degree of transparency of the budget
5. the existence of numerical targets (balanced-budget laws, etc.)
6. the existence of multiyear budgeting

They show that budget arrangements vary widely among EU countries, and this is encouraging for the theory, since debt/GNP ratios also are very different across these countries.

As for the government phase of budget preparation, they identify three types of procedures, which using our terminology we can call hierarchical, intermediate, and collegial. The key variable on which they focus is the relative position of the Treasury minister[15] vis-à-vis the spending ministers. Interestingly,

---

14. An example could be something like the Congressional Budget Office in the United States.
15. Or of the minister(s) responsible for the preparation of the budget.

Table 1.1   **Public Debt in OECD Countries**

	1965	1975	1990	1994
Australia	n.a.	n.a.	23.5	36.1
Austria	19.4	23.9	58.3	65.7
Belgium	67.5	61.1	128.5	135.0
Canada	58.8	43.1	73.1	95.6
Denmark	11.3	11.9	68.0	81.1
Finland	17.7	8.6	16.8	62.3
France	53.1[a]	41.1	43.4	54.7
Germany	17.3	25.1	43.4	51.5
Greece	14.1	22.4	77.7	119.0
Ireland	n.a.	64.4	97.4	92.3
Italy	35.4	60.4	106.4	123.9
Japan	0.0	22.4	66.0	75.6
Netherlands	52.2	41.4	78.8	79.1
Norway	47.0[a]	44.7	32.5	43.5
Portugal	n.a.	n.a.	68.6	70.5
Spain	n.a.	n.a.	50.3	68.2
Sweden	30.5	29.5	44.3	79.5
United Kingdom	81.8[a]	63.7	39.3	54.5
United States	52.1	42.7	55.7	63.0

Source: OECD.
Note: Debt is gross as a share of GNP.
[a]1970.

they argue that France and the United Kingdom are the clearest examples of the hierarchical procedural type. The "superiority" of the prime minister and the finance minister in France is formally established. In the case of the United Kingdom, the "superiority" of the Treasury is more de facto, and is based on seniority and accepted practice. Von Hagen and Harden (1994) write that "In France the strong position of the Prime Minister in budgetary matters is grounded in the constitution. . . . [T]he British Chancellor of the Exchequer . . . derives most of his power from seniority and historical convention, the British equivalent of constitutions law" (340). It is interesting to note that neither of these countries has a debt problem despite a very large public sector (France), and relatively low rate of economic growth in the last two decades (England). At the opposite extreme we find countries where the Treasury minister has no special status, including Ireland, Italy, Belgium, Greece, Luxembourg, and Portugal. The reader will recognize in the first three countries those that, at least until the early nineties, have had the highest debt/GNP ratios in the OECD, and in the other three countries cases of rapidly rising debt/GNP ratios (see table 1.1).

The authors also look at the structure of negotiations, ranking as more collegial countries where the negotiations are not bilateral between Treasury and each spending minister, but cabinet-wide. According to this indicator the most collegial countries are Greece, Ireland, and Spain, and the most hierarchical are France, the Netherlands, Portugal, and the United Kingdom.

As a matter of fact, it is not clear a priori which of the two procedures is more conducive to fiscal discipline. On the one hand, Alt and Chrystal (1981) argue, with an eye on the British case, that bilateral negotiations give an opportunity to individual spending ministers to "strike deals" with the Treasury so that, in the end, the budget is inflated by the accumulation of these bilateral deals since no spending minister has the opportunity or the desire to "attack" another spending minister's deal. On the other hand, multilateral negotiations create an opportunity for the spending ministers to form a coalition "against" the Treasury. Also, as von Hagen (1992) emphasizes, multilateral bargaining creates an opportunity for reciprocity between spending ministers, namely incentive to favor each other's spending programs. On balance, we agree with von Hagen (1993) that bilateral negotiations are more likely to encourage fiscal discipline than multilateral ones. However, Perotti and Kontopoulos (chap. 4 in this volume) reach inconclusive empirical results on a sample of OECD countries.

As for the legislative phase, these authors look at the restrictions on amendments, and at the agenda-setting power of the executive, that is, what the government can do to influence voting in the legislature. For example, they focus on what types of amendments are possible from the floor of the legislature and what the restrictions are (if any) on amendments that increase the deficit or the size of spending proposed by the government. Classifying countries along these dimensions is not always straightforward. For instance, France is a clear example of an authoritarian procedure. According to the authors, Italy, Greece, and Denmark "have procedures which are characterized by comparable degrees of openness."[16]

As for the implementation phase, they consider the degree of control that the Treasury minister has on spending, how easy it is to increase actual spending over the planned level, and how flexible are transfers of spending from one chapter to another. Interestingly, France appears, once again, as the country with the most restrictive procedures.

The transparency of the budget is measured by a variety of indicators, from responses to interviews (see von Hagen 1992, 71) to the existence of "special funds" in the budget, to the presentation of the budget in a single document, and so forth. Interestingly, Italy and Ireland, current and former high-debt countries, respectively, have the least transparent budgets.

Von Hagen (1992) finds support for what he calls the "structural hypothesis," namely that budgetary procedures that are more hierarchical (in our terminology) lead to greater fiscal discipline. This result is based on correlations

---

16. Actually, our reading of the Italian case is a bit different. Using their own criteria, we would have classified Italy at the very least in the intermediate group, if not in the hierarchical one. See Alesina, Mare, and Perotti 1996 for more discussion.

between various aggregate indices of budget procedures and fiscal policy measures in his sample of European countries. These indices summarize in numerical scale all the information discussed above, and they turn out to be strongly correlated with cross-country differences in debt/GNP ratios and budget deficits in the eighties. Von Hagen and Harden (1994) also consider other fiscal indicators of fiscal policy, such as debt sustainability, the growth of open-ended programs, and the role of fiscal policy in macroeconomic stabilization. Interestingly, concerning the last issue, they find that countries with more hierarchical institutions do not show worse performance in terms of output stabilization, despite their more fiscally conservative policies.[17]

These aggregate indices squeeze into a single number several different features of the budget process. Thus, different countries may receive similar aggregate values of the indices for very different reasons. For instance, in von Hagen's work, France and Germany have high indexes (high meaning more hierarchical procedures) for different reasons. In France the high value of the index is due mostly to the strong role of the prime minister and its voting rules; in Germany it is mostly due to the transparency of the budget and the inflexibility of implementation. On the other hand, Italy receives a low score mostly for the weak role of the Treasury minister and the lack of transparency of the budget; Belgium receives a low score because of its voting procedures.

De Haan, Moessen, and Volkerink (chap. 11 in this volume) make progress in disentangling the effects of different components of these indices in a sample of European countries. They conclude that the position of the minister of finance is especially important. Case studies can also shed light on which aspects of budget procedures are more important. Examples of research in this vein include Alesina, Mare, and Perotti 1996 on Italy; Campos and Pradhan (chap. 10 in this volume) on Australia and New Zealand; Courchene (chap. 12 in this volume) on Canada and Australia; Feld and Kirchgässner (chap. 7 in this volume) on Switzerland; and Wright 1997 on Japan, the United Kingdom, and Canada.

Several authors have also investigated the role of fiscal institutions in Latin America. Alesina et al. (1996) consider a sample of almost all the Latin American countries and construct an index of budget procedures on a hierarchical-collegial dimension, and on a transparent-nontransparent one. They use both the written legislation and a survey conducted by means of questionnaires answered by the budget director's office of each country. The index is related but far from identical to the one constructed by von Hagen for OECD countries. The index by Alesina et al. focuses on several critical aspects: (*a*) whether or not the budget is approved in the context of a binding macroeconomic program; (*b*) the role of the Treasury minister, de jure or de facto, as the agenda

---

17. This result is reminiscent of findings concerning central bank independence. Alesina and Summers (1993) show that in OECD countries more independent central banks show lower inflation without an increase in output variability.

setter in the budget process; (c) the relationship between the government and the legislature in the budget process; (d) the voting procedure in the legislature; and (e) various proxies for the degree of transparency of the budget. These authors find that for a sample from 1980 to 1993, more hierarchical/transparent procedures are associated with lower primary deficits in Latin America, after controlling for several economic determinants of the government budget. They also attempt to disentangle which aspects of the budget procedures are more important than others. For a variety of reasons, their results are not conclusive on this point; however, it would seem that a particularly important aspect is the fact that the budget outcomes (particularly the deficit) are discussed and decided in the context of a binding macroeconomic program for the year.

Gavin and Perotti (1997) and Stein, Talvi, and Grisanti (chap. 5 in this volume) provide vast and comprehensive assessments of several aspects of Latin America's fiscal performance in the last few decades. Among others, they emphasize issues of procyclicality of fiscal policy, composition of spending, relationship between central and local governments, and transparency of the budget. They conclude that institutions are important determinants of fiscal outcomes in this region. Jones, Sanguinetti, and Tommasi (chap. 6 in this volume) focus on Argentina and discuss the institutional relationship between central and provincial governments. This is indeed a critical factor for the maintenance of fiscal discipline in this country.

An important point that should receive further attention is the interaction of budget institutions with other political variables. One problem in pursuing this research is the number of degrees of freedom. Since this empirical work is almost exclusively cross-sectional in nature, one needs several countries in the sample to investigate several institutional characteristics, and their interaction together. Perotti and Kontopoulos (chap. 4 in this volume), Hallerberg and von Hagen (1997 and chap. 9 in this volume), and de Haan and Sturm (1994, 1997) have made some progress along this line, focusing on OECD country samples.

A vast related literature that can also shed light on the effect of budget procedures on outcome focuses on American states, which provide a sample with a large variance in institutional arrangement and fiscal performance. Several recent papers by Poterba (1994), Alt and Lowry (1994), Bayoumi and Eichengreen (1995), Bohn and Inman (1995), Inman (1996), Kiewiet and Szakaly (1996), and Alesina and Bayoumi (1996), among others, are particularly relevant for our discussion.[18]

For instance, Poterba (1994) focuses on fiscal shocks, namely the difference between planned and actual spending and revenues, due to a variety of unexpected random events. While many states cannot plan to run deficits, unexpected deficits as a result of fiscal shocks can and do materialize. American states have rather different provisions concerning state balance, that is, differ-

18. See also earlier work by von Hagen (1991).

ent budget laws. The Advisory Council on Intergovernmental Relations (1987) scales them from 1 to 10 in terms of how restrictive they are for the state budget balance. Poterba studies whether the different degrees of stringency of budget balance provisions affect the reaction of states to fiscal shocks. He finds that states with weak antideficit rules adjust spending less in response to positive deficit shocks than their counterparts with strict antideficit laws. More generally he concludes that "fiscal institutions affect the short-run patterns of taxes and expenditures" (801). Interestingly, Poterba also finds that adjustments to adverse fiscal shocks are less vigorous and prompt in states with divided government, where the governor does not belong to the party that holds a majority in the legislature. Alt and Lowry (1994), using a somewhat different approach and sample, reach very similar conclusions. They find that adjustments to fiscal imbalances are low in states with divided government and weak antideficit rules. Alesina and Bayoumi (1996) show that while restrictions on budget deficits enforce fiscal balance, they do not have observable costs on state product variability, for lack of fiscal stabilization.

Bayoumi and Eichengreen (1995) find that the response of deficits to income fluctuations is stronger in states with less stringent budget rules. These authors find that in states with tough rules, most of the budget adjustments occur on the spending side, suggesting that stringent rules are effective at containing spending. These authors make a distinction between those balanced-budget rules that require only a prospective or beginning-of-the-year balance and those that require an end-of-the-year balance. They find that soft, beginning-of-the-year constraints are much less effective than the tougher end-of-the-year ones at controlling deficits. These results are quite intriguing, and they relate to the issue of transparency discussed above. Clearly, beginning-of-the-year requirements leave open the possibility of strategic use of projections and accounting to make a budget look balanced in theory but not with realistic forecasts of revenues and spending needs.

Several other authors have studied the effects on state budgets of gubernatorial line-item veto. The latter does not impose caps on state spending or deficits but, at least theoretically, tilts the relative power in favor of the governor against the legislature in the budget process. As a result, in principle, the line-item veto should promote fiscal discipline. American states differ: many have the line-item veto, several do not. They also differ on what majority is required in the legislature to overcome a gubernatorial veto. Clearly, the higher the majority required, the stronger the governor's relative power. As pointed out in the survey by Carter and Schap (1990), the empirical effects of the line-item veto on state budgets are unclear. Holtz-Eakin (1988), for instance, finds that in the long run the presence of the line-item veto does not reduce spending or deficits. However, in the short run it has some effect, depending on the political context and, in particular, the party affiliation of the governor and the composition of the legislature. Alm and Evers (1991) describe similar findings and conclude that the line-item veto has a small negative effect on the level of spending in the case of divided state government. Similar results are reached by Bohn and Inman (1995).[19]

Broadly speaking, one is struck by the similarity of some of the results between American states and OECD countries. First, in both cases, budget deficits seem to be the result of delayed fiscal adjustments of fragmented governments (coalition governments in OECD countries, divided government in American states). Second, budget institutions influence budget outcomes in the expected direction. Third, perhaps more hierarchical institutions are particularly necessary and useful in situations of government fragmentation.

Also, one may note an analogy between the effect of budget institutions and government structure. Collegial institutions and fragmented governments do not cause budget deficits per se, but delay adjustments to fiscal imbalances that appear, for any reason. Thus, questions concerning both the timing of deficits and the cross-country differences can be answered by the interaction between, on the one hand, the shocks in the seventies, lower growth, and demographic factors that posed a heavy burden on social security systems and, on the other hand, certain budget procedures and fragmented government.

References

Advisory Council on Intergovernmental Relations. 1987. *Fiscal discipline in the federal system: National reform and the experience of the states.* Washington, D.C.: Advisory Council on Intergovernmental Relations.

Alesina, A., and T. Bayoumi. 1996. The costs and benefits of fiscal rules: Evidence from the U.S. states. NBER Working Paper no. 5614. Cambridge, Mass.: National Bureau of Economic Research.

Alesina, A., and A. Cukierman. 1990. The politics of ambiguity. *Quarterly Journal of Economics* 107:829–50.

Alesina, A., and A. Drazen. 1991. Why are stabilizations delayed? *American Economic Review* 81:1170–88.

Alesina, A., R. Hommes, R. Hausmann, and E. Stein. 1996. Budget deficits and budget procedures in Latin America. NBER Working Paper no. 5586. Cambridge, Mass.: National Bureau of Economic Research.

Alesina, A., M. Mare, and R. Perotti. 1996. The Italian budget procedures—analysis and proposals. Columbia University Working Paper.

Alesina, A., and R. Perotti. 1995a. Fiscal expansions and fiscal adjustments in OECD countries. *Economic Policy* 21 (October): 207–48.

———. 1995b. The political economy of budget deficits. *IMF Staff Papers* 42 (March): 1–31.

Alesina, A., and H. Rosenthal. 1995. *Partisan politics, divided government, and the economy.* Cambridge: Cambridge University Press.

---

19. An interesting closely related literature studies the effects of bond rating, and, more generally, of municipal bond market behavior on state balance sheets. See, in particular, Poterba and Rueben (chap. 8 in this volume) and the references cited there.

Alesina, A., and L. Summers. 1993. Central bank independence and macroeconomic performance: Some comparative evidence. *Journal of Money, Credit, and Banking* 25 (May): 151–62.

Alesina, A., and G. Tabellini. 1990. A positive theory of budget deficits and government debt. *Review of Economic Studies* 57:403–14.

Alm, J., and M. Evers. 1991. The line-item veto and state government expenditures. *Public Choice* 68:1–15.

Alt, J., and A. Chrystal. 1981. Electoral cycle, budget controls, and public expenditure. *Journal of Public Policy* 1:32–59.

Alt, J., and R. Lowry. 1994. Divided government, fiscal institutions, and budget deficits: Evidence from the states. *American Political Science Review* 88:811–28.

Arrow, K. 1951. *Social choice and individual values.* New Haven, Conn.: Yale University Press.

Baron, D. 1989. A non-cooperative theory of legislative coalitions. *American Journal of Political Science* 33:1048–84.

———. 1991. Majoritarian incentives, pork barrel programs, and procedural control. *American Journal of Political Science* 35:57–90.

Baron, D., and J. Ferejohn. 1989. Bargaining in legislatures. *American Political Science Review* 83:1181–1206.

Barro, R. 1979. On the determination of the public debt. *Journal of Political Economy* 87:940–71.

Bayoumi, Tamim, and Barry Eichengreen. 1995. Restraining yourself: The implications of fiscal rules for economic stabilizations. *IMF Staff Papers* 42 (March): 32–67.

Bohn, H., and R. Inman. 1995. Constitutional limitations and public deficits: Evidence from the US states. *Carnegie-Rochester Conference Series on Public Policy* 45: 13–76.

Buchanan, J., and R. Wagner. 1977. *Democracy in deficit.* New York: Academic Press.

Carter, J., and D. Schap. 1990. Line item veto: Where is thy sting? *Journal of Economic Perspectives* 4:103–19.

Chari, V. V., and H. Cole. 1993. A contribution to the theory of pork barrel spending. Federal Reserve Bank of Minneapolis Staff Report no. 156.

Chari, V. V., L. Jones, and R. Marimon. 1997. On the economics of split voting in representative democracies. *American Economic Review* 87:957–77.

Cukierman, A., and A. Meltzer. 1986. A theory of ambiguity, credibility, and inflation under discretion and rules. *Econometrica* 53:1099–1128.

de Haan, J., and E. Sturm. 1994. Political and institutional determinants of fiscal policy in the European Community. *Public Choice* 80:157–72.

———. 1997. Political and economic determinants of OECD budget deficits and government expenditures: A reexamination. *European Journal of Political Economy* 13: 322–36.

Emerson, M. 1988. *What model for Europe?* Cambridge, Mass.: MIT Press.

Ferejohn, J., and K. Krehbiel. 1987. The budget process and the size of the budget. *American Journal of Political Science* 31:296–320.

Fiorina, M., and R. Noll. 1978. Voters, bureaucrats, and legislators: A rational choice perspective on the growth of bureaucracy. *Journal of Public Economics* 9:239–54.

Gavin, M., and R. Perotti. 1997. Fiscal policy in Latin America. In *NBER macroeconomics annual,* ed. B. Bernanke and J. Rothemberg, 11–70. Cambridge, Mass.: MIT Press.

Grilli, V., D. Masciandaro, and G. Tabellini. 1991. Political and monetary institutions and public finance policies in the industrial democracies. *Economic Policy* 13: 341–92.

Hallerberg, M., and J. von Hagen. 1997. The budgetary process and the size of the budget: A reexamination. CEPR Working Paper. London: Centre for Economic Policy Research.

Holtz-Eakin, D. 1988. The line item veto and public sector budget. *Journal of Public Economics* 37:263–92.

Huber, J. 1992. Restrictive legislative procedures in France and in the United States. *American Political Science Review* 86:67–82.

Inman, R. P. 1996. Do balanced budget rules work? U.S. experience and possible lessons for the EMU. NBER Working Paper no. 5838. Cambridge, Mass.: National Bureau of Economic Research.

Kiewiet, R., and K. Szakaly. 1996. The efficacy of constitutional restrictions on borrowing, taxing, and spending: An analysis of state bonded indebtedness, 1961–1990. *Journal of Law, Economics, and Organization* 12:62–97.

Lucas, R., and N. Stokey. 1983. Optimal fiscal and monetary policy in an economy without capital. *Journal of Monetary Economics* 12:55–94.

Milesi-Ferretti, G. 1997. The good, the bad, and the ugly. Unpublished.

Mueller, D. 1978. *Public choice.* Cambridge: Cambridge University Press.

Niskanen, W. 1971. *Bureaucracy and representative government.* Chicago: Aldine Atherton.

Persson, T., and L. Svensson. 1989. Why a stubborn conservative would run a deficit: Policy with time in consistent preferences. *Quarterly Journal of Economics* 104: 325–45.

Poterba, J. 1994. State responses to fiscal crises: "Natural experiments" for studying the effects of budgetary institutions. *Journal of Political Economy* 102:799–821.

———. 1996. Do budget rules work? NBER Working Paper no. 5550. Cambridge, Mass.: National Bureau of Economic Research.

Premchand, A. 1983. *Government budgeting and expenditure control.* Washington, D.C.: International Monetary Fund.

Rogoff, K. 1990. Political budget cycles. *American Economic Review* 80:1–16.

Rogoff, K., and A. Sibert. 1988. Elections and macroeconomic policy cycles. *Review of Economic Studies* 55:1–16.

Roubini, N., and J. Sachs. 1989a. Government spending and budget deficits in the industrialized countries. *Economic Policy* 8:99–132.

———. 1989b. Political and economic determinants of budget deficits in the industrial democracies. *European Economic Review* 33 (May): 903–33.

Shepsle, K. 1979a. Institutional arrangements and equilibrium in multidimensional voting models. *American Journal of Political Science* 23:26–59.

———. 1979b. The role of institutional structure in the creation of policy equilibrium. In *Public policy and public choice,* ed. D. Rae and T. J. Eisinuier. Beverly Hills, Calif.: Sage.

Spolaore, E. 1993. Macroeconomic policy, institutions, and efficiency. Ph.D. diss., Harvard University.

Tabellini, G., and A. Alesina. 1990. Voting on the budget deficit. *American Economic Review* 80:37–49.

Tanzi, V., ed. 1991. *Fiscal policies in economies in transition.* Washington, D.C.: International Monetary Fund.

———. 1993. The political economy of fiscal deficit reduction. In World Bank, *Macroeconomics of public sector deficits.* Forthcoming.

———. 1995. International systems of public expenditures: Lessons from Italy. Paper presented to the Bank of Italy conference Public Expenditure Controls.

von Hagen, J. 1991. A note on the empirical effectiveness of formal fiscal restraints. *Journal of Public Economics* 44:99–110.

———. 1992. Budgeting procedures and fiscal performance in the European Communities. Economic Paper no. 96, Commission of the European Communities. October.

von Hagen, J., and I. J. Harden. 1994. National budget processes and fiscal performance. *European Economy: Reports and Studies* 3:311–418.

Weingast, B., K. Shepsle, and C. Johnsen. 1981. The political economy of benefits and costs: A neoclassical approach to distributive politics. *Journal of Political Economy* 89:642–64.

Wildasky, A. 1986. *Budget: A comparative theory of budgetary processes.* New Brunswick, N.J.: Transaction Books.

Wright, M. 1997. Illusion and reality in central government budgeting in Japan, the UK, and Canada, 1975–1997. Photocopy.

2 A Model of Endogenous Fiscal Deficits and Delayed Fiscal Reforms

Andrés Velasco

2.1 Introduction

Two striking facts characterize the recent fiscal policy of a number of countries. First, since 1973 there has been a pronounced and systematic increase in government spending and budget deficits (both measured as a percentage of GDP). This is true of both OECD economies and developing countries such as those in Latin America.[1] Second, in some cases fast debt accumulation has been allowed to go on unchecked for long periods of time, giving rise to a path that is inconsistent with intertemporal solvency. In some extreme cases, such as those of Mexico, Argentina, and Bolivia in the 1980s, drastic changes in spending and taxes were eventually required to restore solvency. In other serious but less dramatic cases—such as those of Belgium and Italy, where the public debt is above 100 percent of GNP and growing—lasting fiscal stabilization is yet to occur.

Neither feature is easy to reconcile with the neoclassical model (Barro 1979) that views debt accumulation as a way to spread over time the costs of distortionary taxation. While the neoclassical model fits the U.S. data reasonably well (Barro 1986), cyclical and intertemporal smoothing factors cannot fully account for the recent increase in peacetime deficits in OECD countries (Roubini and Sachs 1989).[2] Furthermore, the tax-smoothing model does not seem

Andrés Velasco is associate professor of economics at New York University and a faculty research fellow of the National Bureau of Economic Research.

1. On the OECD, see Alesina and Perotti 1994. The fiscal experience of a number of Latin American countries is also reported and analyzed in Tornell and Velasco 1995 and references therein. See also the essays in Larraín and Selowsky 1991.

2. In a recent paper, Bizer and Durlauf (1990) argue that U.S. tax rates do not seem to be a random walk, as implied by the theory. Rather, they find an eight-year cycle for tax changes, a feature suggestive of a political equilibrium.

to fit the budget data from developing countries (Edwards and Tabellini 1991; Roubini 1991).

Even harder to justify as the result of rational government action are the debt bubbles (and sometimes the accompanying inflation) that occur when stabilization is delayed, as discussed by Alesina and Drazen (1991). If the need for an eventual fiscal correction can be foreseen, nothing can be gained by waiting. This is especially true if distortionary taxes, especially inflation, are heavily used during the transition.

This paper develops a political-economic model of government behavior that can throw light on both of these puzzles. To do so, it goes beyond the standard model of a representative individual and a benevolent policymaker bent on maximizing the individual's welfare. It considers a society divided into several influential interest groups, each of which benefits from a particular kind of government spending. The government is assumed to be weak, in that each of the interest groups can influence fiscal authorities to set net transfers on the group's target item at some desired level. Hence, we have a case of "fragmented" fiscal policymaking.

This setup can be interpreted in one of several ways, all of which have counterparts in countries' recent experience. First, spending pressures may arise from sectoral ministers or parliamentary committees with special interests that overwhelm a weak finance minister. In a detailed set of studies of the European Community in the 1970s and 1980s, von Hagen (1992) and von Hagen and Harden (1994) conclude that budgeting procedures that lend the finance minister "strategic dominance over spending ministers" and "limit the amendment powers of parliament" are strongly conducive to fiscal discipline. The opposite arrangement often leads to sizable deficits and debts.[3] The three countries with weakest budgetary procedures (those with the weakest finance minister, most parliamentary amendments, etc.) had deficits that averaged 11 percent of GDP in the 1980s, while the three countries with the strongest procedures had deficit ratios of 2 percent. The accumulated public debt stocks were also very different between these two sets of countries.[4] Similar results are reported by Alesina et al. (1996) in their study of 20 Latin American and Caribbean countries. Using a methodology quite similar to that of von Hagen, they find that the 6 countries with the strongest fiscal processes had, between 1980 and 1993, fiscal surpluses that averaged 1.8 percent of GDP; the 7 countries with the weakest processes had deficit ratios of 2.2 percent over the same period.

---

3. More specifically, von Hagen (1992) constructs an index characterizing EU national budget processes on four grounds: (a) strength of the prime minister or finance minister in budget negotiations; (b) existence of overall budget targets fixed early on and limits on parliamentary powers of amendment; (c) transparency of the budget document; and (d) limited discretion in the implementation of the budget.

4. More generally, Roubini and Sachs (1989a,b) and Grilli, Masciandaro, and Tabellini (1991) have shown that among OECD countries, those with proportional representation systems and fractionalized parties tend to display high deficits and debt.

Second, spending may be set by decentralized fiscal authorities representing particular geographical areas. The cases of Argentina and Brazil are instructive.[5] They are both federal countries in which over the last two decades many spending responsibilities have been transferred to the subfederal level. Lacking sufficient revenues of their own and facing unclear rules, subfederal governments have systematically run deficits that de facto have become the responsibility of the federal authorities. There have generally been three mechanisms through which state and provincial entities could "pass on" their deficits: (a) borrowing from state development banks, which in turn could rediscount their loans at the central bank—in effect monetizing the subfederal deficits; (b) obtaining discretionary lump sum transfers from the federal government, generally requested around election time and after large debts had been accumulated; and (c) accumulating arrears with suppliers and creditors, which (for either legal or political reasons) were eventually cleared up by the federal authorities. Understanding that at least part of the cost would be borne by others, subfederal governments have been tempted to overspend and overborrow. Similar troubles affected the former Yugoslavia. They are also becoming increasingly severe in Russia, as Wallich (1992) and Sachs (1994) argue.

Third, transfers may be determined by money-losing state enterprises facing soft budget constraints—for instance in Mexico and Brazil in the 1970s or in Russia and some countries of Eastern Europe more recently. As Kornai (1979) emphasized, state firms have an incentive to pay excessive wages (thus simply reducing the profit stream that would go to the Treasury) and engage in large and risky investments (managers benefit from running larger firms but bear none of the investment risk). Bankruptcy is not a real threat, as government subsidies and bailouts from state banks often extend the life of distressed firms. Lipton and Sachs (1990), among others, have pointed out that this problem became increasingly acute with the decline of Communism and the beginning of transition. Holzmann (1991) estimates that in Eastern Europe during the 1980s budgetary subsidies to state enterprises averaged almost 10 percent of GDP.

The inefficiencies that arise when several groups or officials with redistributive aims have control over fiscal policy have been recognized in the literature. Weingast, Shepsle, and Johnsen (1981) and, more recently, Chari and Cole (1993) and Chari, Jones, and Marimon (1994) show that having the supply of local public goods financed with national or federal revenues creates incentives for pork barrel spending. Aizenman (1991) and Zarazaga (1993) have argued that if fiscal and/or monetary policy are decided upon in a decentralized manner, a "competitive externality" arises that gives the economy an inflationary

---

5. The case of Argentina is studied in Jones, Sanguinetti, and Tommasi 1997 and World Bank 1990a, b, and c and that of Brazil in Shah 1990 and Bomfin and Shah 1991. Stein, Talvi, and Grisanti (chap. 5 in this volume) discuss fiscal arrangements at the subnational level for all of Latin America and the Caribbean.

bias. What all these models have in common is that, because the benefits from spending accrue fully to each group, while the costs are spread over all groups, incentives are distorted and a "spending bias" emerges.

As Alesina and Perotti (1994) stress, however, the models in the literature so far are essentially static, focusing on the level of expenditures rather than on the behavior of debt and deficits.[6] This chapter by contrast, focuses on the dynamic aspects of fragmented fiscal policymaking in the context of an infinite horizon model. Fiscal authorities are confronted with an explicit intertemporal trade-off: high deficits today mean lower spending or higher taxes tomorrow. Does a divided government structure lead rational fiscal authorities to run debts and deficits that are "too high" in some well-defined sense? The model in section 2.3 below provides an affirmative answer to this question. If government net assets (the present value of future income streams minus outstanding debts) is the common property of all fiscal authorities, then a problem arises that is logically quite similar to the "tragedy of the commons" that occurs in marine fisheries or public grazing lands (Levhari and Mirman 1980; Benhabib and Radner 1992). Two distortions are present if n agents share the stock of the resource. First, each uses the whole stock and not one-nth of it as the basis for consumption or spending decisions. Second, the return on savings as perceived by one agent is the technological rate of return (the rate of interest or the rate of growth of natural resource stocks) minus what the other $n - 1$ agents take out. Hence, to the extent that savings depends positively on the rate of return, each agent undersaves (overspends in the case of fiscal policy, overexploits in the case of natural resources). This means that deficits are incurred and debts accumulated even in contexts where there is no incentive for intertemporal smoothing, so that a central planner guiding fiscal policy would run a balanced budget.[7] In short, the model exhibits a "deficit bias."

But any empirically plausible model must account not only for debt accumulation. After all, since the borrowing binge of the 1970s and 1980s many countries (particularly in Europe and Latin America) have drastically restructured their fiscal policies and curtailed debt growth. Indeed, the model of this paper can also account for fiscal stabilizations—that is to say, changes in fiscal policy that end the process of debt accumulation.

For that purpose I study trigger-strategy equilibria, in which interest groups coordinate on a zero-deficit path for spending and threaten to return to the excess-deficit path the period after a defection has been detected. Groups' payoffs depend on the outstanding stock of government debt. A fiscal stabilization

---

6. A partial exception is Chari and Cole 1993, who consider a two-period model.

7. Of course, this is not the only type of "political economy" explanation for the existence of budget deficits. An important explanation is provided by Persson and Svensson (1989), Tabellini and Alesina (1990), and Alesina and Tabellini (1990). In their models, society is divided into groups with different preferences (over the composition of government spending, for instance). Because current majorities know that in the future a different majority with different preferences may be in control of fiscal policy, those currently in power attempt to "bind" the actions of their successors by leaving them a large public debt.

may not be sustainable from low levels of debt (high levels of government net assets), but may become sustainable once debt reaches a sufficiently high level. The intuition for this result is simple. As debt grows and the government becomes poorer, the static efficiency gains associated with stabilization become more attractive relative to the payoff groups can obtain by continuing to transfer aggressively, until eventually low spending and stabilization become sustainable in equilibrium. Thus, the model suggests a rationale for the popular notion that "things have to get very bad before they can get better again." Or, in the sense of Alesina and Drazen (1991), the model can generate delayed stabilizations.

The paper is structured as follows. Section 2.2 sets up the basic model, while section 2.3 characterizes a simple Markov-Nash equilibrium of the dynamic game between the interest groups and derives the endogenous budget deficit. Section 2.4 introduces "trigger strategies," and section 2.5 characterizes the "switching equilibrium" that results in a delayed fiscal reform. Section 2.6 analyzes the effects of adverse shocks, while section 2.7 offers a summary and some conclusions.

2.2   The Basic Model

There are n symmetric groups, indexed by $i, i = 1, 2, \ldots, n$. Each can be thought of as a particular constituency or recipient of government largesse. Net transfers to group i—denoted by g_i—can be interpreted as subsidies to its members minus the taxes that group pays, or net spending on a public good that only benefits those in group i. Hence, g_i can be positive or negative, but there is a maximum negative transfer (tax), denoted by $\bar{g}$, that can be extracted from any group.

Any excess of expenditure over revenues can be financed by borrowing in the world capital market at a constant gross real rate R, which is exogenous given the assumption that the economy is small and open. Accumulated debts are a joint liability of all n groups, as would be the case with the national debt in any country. The government budget constraint therefore is

$$(1) \qquad b_{t+1} = Rb_t + y - z_t - \sum_{i=1}^{n} g_{it},$$

where y denotes exogenous nontax government revenue (e.g., income from state enterprises or transfers from abroad)[8] and b_t is the stock of the internationally traded bond held by the government at time t, which can be interpreted as the gross international reserves minus outstanding public debt—both earning or paying the interest rate R. The variable z_t represents a deadweight loss per period of time; conditions under which this cost is incurred are made explicit below.

---

8. This serves simply as a shift parameter, which is useful in section 2.6 below. Before that, nothing changes if it is simply set to zero.

As is usual in this kind of setting, we impose on the government the solvency condition

(2)
$$\lim_{t \to \infty} b_t R^{-t} \geq 0,$$

which simply ensures that debt does not grow without bound. Solving equation (1) as of any time t and imposing equation (2) yields

(3)
$$\sum_{i=1}^{n} \sum_{s=t}^{\infty} g_{is} R^{-(s-t)} \leq Rb_t + \left(\frac{R}{R-1}\right)y - \sum_{s=t}^{\infty} z_s R^{-(s-t)},$$

which has the standard interpretation that the present value of all net transfers as of t cannot exceed the value of the government's assets plus the present value of all of its net income (inclusive of possible deadweight losses). Adding $[R/(R-1)]n\overline{g}$ to both sides of equation (3) we obtain

(4)
$$\sum_{i=1}^{n} \sum_{s=t}^{\infty} (g_{is} + \overline{g})R^{-(s-t)} \leq R\left[b_t + \frac{y + n\overline{g}}{R-1} - R^{-1}\sum_{s=t}^{\infty} z_s R^{-(s-t)}\right] \equiv Rw_t,$$

where w_t can be interpreted as the maximum wealth the government can have, starting from assets b_t and given the expected sequence $\{z_s\}_{s=t}^{\infty}$. Notice from this definition that w_t must be nonnegative for the government to remain solvent: otherwise at some later point transfers would have to be below $-\overline{g}$, something that is infeasible given our assumptions.

How do groups interact in order to determine fiscal policy? The key assumption is that the central fiscal authority is weak, and that group i itself can determine (subject to a constraint made explicit below) the sequence $\{g_{it}\}_{t=0}^{\infty}$. While each group has many members, they act in a coordinated fashion (through a congressional leader or member of the cabinet, for example) in setting the level of net transfers g_{it}.

To ensure that the lack of coordination in ministers' actions does not lead to a violation of the solvency condition, it is necessary to impose a rule that prevents ministers' total desired net transfers from exceeding the maximum feasible amount. Suppose that after groups decide on their target transfers g_{it}, these are satisfied by the central fiscal authority (the finance minister or the president) as long as

(5)
$$g_{it} \leq (R/n)w_t, \quad \forall i \text{ and } \forall t.$$

Any minister whose desired net transfer violates equation (5) simply gets zero.[9] Application of this rule leads to $\sum_{i=1}^{n} g_{it} \leq Rw_t$ for all i and all t.

9. Note that this rule simply prevents solvency from being violated as a result of the lack of coordination among ministers. Why the government as a whole (represented by the finance minister or president) chooses to remain solvent—or not to default—is a question beyond the scope of this paper. I simply assume away the possibility of default, as does most of the literature on optimal fiscal policy. For important papers that study default explicitly in similar contexts, see Bulow and Rogoff 1989, Atkeson 1991, and Chari and Kehoe 1993a and b.

The leader of group i maximizes the objective function

$$(6) \qquad U_i = \sum_{s=t}^{\infty} \log(g_{is} + \overline{g})R^{-(s-t)}$$

with respect to g_{it} starting at each time $t > 0$, subject to equations (1), (2), and (5). Thus, groups' utility is an increasing function of the excess of the actual net transfer they receive over the minimum they could have received. I assume a logarithmic utility function in order to get closed-form solutions.

Equations (1), (2), (5), and (6) provide the setting for a dynamic game among the leaders of the n groups. Before constructing equilibria for that game, however, it is useful to ask about the level of transfers that would be chosen by a benevolent planner that maximized the joint welfare of all groups (with equal weights for each). It is easy to show that, because groups' subjective rate of time preference is equal to the world rate of interest, the planner would to each group to transfer one-nth of the government's permanent income. Thus,

$$(7) \qquad g_{it} = \frac{(R-1)b_t + y - \left(\dfrac{R-1}{R}\right)\displaystyle\sum_{s=t}^{\infty} z_s R^{-(s-t)}}{n},$$

which—if all n groups follow it—ensures that debt is constant if z_t is constant. This policy is used below as a benchmark with which to compare game outcomes.

Assume finally that, if and only if all groups agree to stabilize, the deadweight loss disappears:

$$(8) \qquad z_t = \begin{cases} 0 \text{ if } g_{it} = \dfrac{(R-1)b_t + y - \left(\dfrac{R-1}{R}\right)\displaystyle\sum_{s=t}^{\infty} z_s R^{-(s-t)}}{n} \quad \forall i \\[2em] z \text{ otherwise.} \end{cases}$$

Notice that if all groups follow the transfer policy in equation (7), then $z_t = 0$ for all t; as a result, debt is constant throughout. I will refer to such policies as being associated with "fiscal stabilization."

The assumption on the deadweight loss in equation (8) can be justified by the presence of static efficiency gains associated with stabilization. The suggested interpretation is that government resources are no longer wasted in dealing with lobbyists, in the spirit of Krueger (1974) and Bhagwati (1982). Alternatively, following Alesina and Drazen (1991), the net gain to government finances associated with stabilization could be interpreted as a switch to nondistortionary taxes or a lowering of tax collection costs, so that the government gets more revenue (net of costs) for each unit of output obtained from the private sector. Or, one could assume that stabilization produces a permanent increase in government income, perhaps in transfers from abroad intended to reward sound fiscal behavior. All that matters for the results below is that the gains from stabilizing extend beyond the dynamic benefits of curtailing net transfers and debt accumulation. In the interest of realism, I henceforth assume that $z < y$.

The timing of actions is as follows. The economy enters period t with government assets Rb_t. Government net transfers then take place, with the n groups simultaneously setting their transfers g_{it}. The deadweight loss then occurs according to equation (8).

I now characterize more formally the game among the groups and its corresponding equilibrium:

DEFINITION 1. *A strategy is a sequence* $\{g_{it}\}_{t=0}^{\infty}$ *for each player.*

DEFINITION 2. *An equilibrium for this game is represented by a set of strategies, one for each player, such that no group can improve its total payoff by a unilateral change in strategy at any point in the game.*

2.3 Endogenous Government Deficits

In this section I focus on simple Markovian strategies in which net transfers are a function of the state variable only, and temporarily assume away more complex behavior, such as trigger strategies, based on the previous history of the game.

Since the setting is log-linear, I construct an equilibrium in which each player uses policy rules such that actions are linear functions of the relevant state variable:

$$(9) \qquad g_{it} = \mu + \phi Rb_t,$$

where μ and ϕ are coefficients to be endogenously determined.

Suppose that starting at time t, group i expects that all other groups will employ rule (9) for all $s \geq t$. Then, debt evolves according to

$$(10) \qquad b_{t+1} = Rb_t[1 - (n - 1)\phi] - (n - 1)\mu + y - z_t - g_{it}.$$

Group i's best response is therefore the solution to the problem

$$(11) \qquad V(b_t) = \max_{g_{it}}\{\log(g_{it} + \bar{g}) + R^{-1}V(b_{t+1})\},$$

subject to equations (5) and (10). Using this best response, and using the fact that all groups are symmetric, one can endogenously determine the coefficients μ and ϕ.

The Euler equation that corresponds to problem (11) is

$$(12) \qquad g_{it+1} + \bar{g} = (g_{it} + \bar{g})[1 - (n - 1)\phi].$$

Suppose next that μ and ϕ are such that equation (7) does not occur in equilibrium (we will check later, of course, whether this supposition is self-confirming). It follows that in equation (10) we may replace z for z_t $\forall t$. As the appendix shows in greater detail, combining the resulting equation with equations (10) and (12), and imposing symmetry across all n groups we obtain

$$(13) \quad \mu = \frac{R(y - z) + (n - 1)\bar{g}}{1 + n(R - 1)} \text{ and } \phi = \frac{R - 1}{1 + n(R - 1)},$$

so that each group's policy rule is

$$(14) \quad g_{it} = \left(\frac{R}{1 + n(R - 1)}\right)\left[(R - 1)b_t + y - z + \left(\frac{n - 1}{R}\right)\bar{g}\right] \forall t$$

$$= \phi R w_t - \bar{g}.$$

Notice that $\phi R < R/n$, so that rule (5) is satisfied.

Clearly, the policy in equation (14) is a strategy in the sense of definition 1. It is also feasible, in that rule (5) is satisfied.[10] Then a set of such a strategies, one for each group, constitutes an equilibrium in the sense of definition 2: the strategies are best responses to themselves. The resulting Markov-Nash equilibrium is subgame perfect. That is because the strategies are specified as a function of the state (in this case debt), not of time. Hence, no group leader has an incentive to change strategies as a result of the mere passage of time.

Notice also that the policy rule in equation (14) does not correspond to the "stabilizing" net transfers rule in equation (7). Thus, given equation (8), the conjecture that $z_t = z$ $\forall t$ is confirmed.

Substituting equation (14) into equation (1), we obtain

$$(15) \quad b_{t+1} = \left(\frac{R}{1 + n(R - 1)}\right)b_t - \left(\frac{n - 1}{1 + n(R - 1)}\right)(y - z + n\bar{g}) < b_t,$$

where the inequality follows from the fact that $R/[1 + n(R - 1)] < 1$ as long as $n > 1$.

This result can also be expressed in terms of government wealth. It is the case that $1 - n\phi = 1/[1 + n(R - 1)]$. Using this result in equation (A5) we have

$$(16) \quad \frac{w_{t+1}}{w_t} = \frac{R}{1 + n(R - 1)} < 1.$$

Hence, w_t goes to zero only asymptotically, and solvency condition 2 in the text is satisfied.

Expressions (15) and (16) show two sides of the same result: there is an endogenously determined fiscal deficit, debt is accumulated and government wealth decreases over time: fragmented fiscal policymaking leads to a "deficit bias."

---

10. The solvency condition (2) is also satisfied, as I show below.

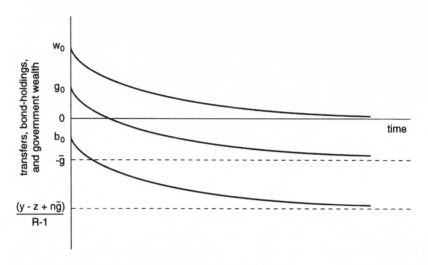

Fig. 2.1   Time path of deficits and related variables

How does the deficit bias depend on the number n of interest groups, and hence on the degree of fragmentation of the policymaking process? Since $\phi = (R - 1)/[1 + n(R - 1)]$, given policy rule (14) it is clear that each group's desired transfers are decreasing in n. However, total transfers ng_{it} are easily shown to be increasing in n. This is reflected in equation (16), which shows that the speed with which government wealth falls is also an increasing function of n. Hence, the larger the number of interest groups (the larger the degree of fragmentation in policymaking), the greater the deficit bias.

Figure 2.1 shows the behavior of transfers g_{it}, bond-holdings b_t, and government wealth w_t as a function of time.[11] The time path of transfers is particularly interesting: they are initially positive and large, fall as government wealth falls, and eventually become positive (that is, groups eventually begin paying taxes). In the limit, as time goes to infinity and government wealth goes to zero, taxes converge to their maximum feasible level $\bar{g}$.

The reason for this set of results—particularly the "deficit bias"—is simple. Property rights are not defined over each group's share of overall revenue or debt. A portion of any government wealth not spent by one group will be spent by the other group. Hence, there are incentives to raise net transfers above the collectively efficient rate. As in the "tragedy of the commons" literature, there is overconsumption and overborrowing.

Using equations (14) and (15) in equation (6), one can easily obtain the utility that each group obtains along this equilibrium path

---

11. Notice that initial bond-holdings can be positive or negative, as long as they are not so negative as to make initial wealth nonpositive. As drawn, initial bond-holdings are negative—that is to say, the government is a debtor.

$$
V^m(b_t) = \left(\frac{R}{R-1}\right)
$$
(17)
$$
\times \left[\log\{(R-1)b_t + y - z + n\bar{g}\} + \left(\frac{R}{R-1}\right)\log\left(\frac{R}{1+n(R-1)}\right)\right],
$$

where "m" stands for "Markov."

Consider now what is the utility that accrues to players if stabilization is achieved—that is, if transfer behavior accords with the planner's solution. If at time t each player were to agree to transfer according to equation (7), government debt would remain constant forever, and the corresponding value would be

$$
(18) \qquad V^s(b_t) = \left(\frac{R}{R-1}\right)\log\left(\frac{(R-1)b_t + y + n\bar{g}}{n}\right),
$$

where "s" stands for "stabilization." Comparing equations (17) and (18) we see that $V^s(b_t) > V^m(b_t)$ for any b_t. Relative to the stabilizing outcome, the path involving a fiscal deficit is characterized by two inefficiencies. First, an intratemporal one: lobbying imposes a deadweight loss, reflected in the fact that $z > 0$. Second, an intertemporal one: given that government nontax revenue is constant and the rate of discount is equal to the rate of interest, a benevolent planner maximizing a weighted average of the utility of both groups would never find it optimal to borrow. Here the groups borrow, purely for strategic reasons, and this results in lower utility for all players.[12]

2.4   Incentive Constraints and Debt Dependence

Can the two groups, acting in a decentralized manner, ever coordinate on a better outcome? Can they ever coordinate on stabilization, with net transfers at levels such that the fiscal deficit is eliminated and government debt growth stopped? To answer these questions, I focus on trigger strategy equilibria, and characterize equilibrium paths along which groups receive utilities that are at least as high as those that they could obtain by higher immediate net transfers and suffering retaliation later on.

DEFINITION 3. *A trigger strategy is an implicitly agreed upon net transfer path for each player, plus the threat of a reversion to the stationary Markov-Nash path forever the period after a defection takes place.*

Suppose the agreed-upon net transfers path is the stabilizing one, described above in equation (7).[13] If implemented starting from a level of debt b_t, such a

---

12. Notice that $\log n + [R/(R-1)] \log \{R/[1-n(R-1)]\} < 0$, so that $V^s(b_t) > V^m(b_t)$ even if $z = 0$, so that no intratemporal distortion exists.

13. Here I follow the tradition of the folk-theorem literature for repeated games—see, for instance, Fudenberg and Maskin 1986—and the dynamic game literature—Chari and Kehoe 1993a

path would yield utility as in equation (18). A group can always defect from the agreed-upon path, and will do so when the utility associated with defection is higher than that associated with the path.

What is the optimal defection? The nondefecting groups obviously continue to follow the policy in equation (7) during the period of defection. Given that starting the next period all will revert to the Markov-Nash path, the defecting group must solve

(19) $$V^d(b_t) = \max_{g_{it}}\{\log(g_{it} + \bar{g}) + R^{-1}V^m(b_{t+1})\},$$

subject to

(20) $$b_{t+1} = \gamma R b_t + \left[1 - \left(\frac{n-1}{n}\right)\right](y - z_t) - g_{it},$$

where $\gamma \equiv \{1 - [(n-1)/n]\,[(R-1)/R]\} < 1$, and to equation (5). Notice that in equation (19) $V^m(b_{t+1})$ is given by equation (17), and "d" stands for "defection." The solution to this problem is

(21)
$$g_{it} = \gamma[(R - 1)b_t + y - z] + \bar{g}\left(\frac{n-1}{R}\right)$$

$$= \gamma\left(\frac{R-1}{R}\right)Rw_t - \bar{g}.$$

Note that, since $\gamma\,[(R-1)/R] < 1/n$, condition (5) is satisfied: even when deviating and requesting relatively larger transfers, the deviating group attempts to get less than one-nth of available resources.

Using equations (19), (20), and (21), total utility from defecting when assets equal b_t can be written as

(22)
$$V^d(b_t) = \left(\frac{R}{R-1}\right)\log[(R-1)b_t + y - z + n\bar{g}]$$

$$+ \left(\frac{R}{R-1}\right)^2\log\left(\frac{R}{1 + n(R-1)}\right)$$

$$+ \left(\frac{R}{R-1}\right)\left[\log\gamma - \log\left(\frac{R}{1 + n(R-1)}\right)\right].$$

Notice that, as one would expect, $V^d(b_t) > V^m(b_t)$, for the expression in the second line of equation (22) is positive as long as $n > 1$. By cheating and

---

and b, Benhabib and Velasco 1996—in asking whether the first-best path (in this case the path with constant debt) can be sustained through trigger strategies. But clearly, in this model as in the earlier ones in the literature, one could also ask whether other, less desirable, outcomes can be sustained as well.

obtaining net transfers according to equation (21) at time t, while the remaining $(n - 1)$ groups adhere to the more frugal rule (7) during that period, group i increases its utility.[14]

We can now return to the question of whether the stabilizing, constant-debt path can ever be sustained. If both groups follow such a path, they receive utilities $V^s(b_t)$ as shown in equation (18). If a group defects, on the other hand, it receives $V^d(b_t)$, as shown in equation (22). Individual rationality dictates that the agreed-upon path will be followed if and only if $V^s(b_t) \geq V^d(b_t)$. Using equations (18) and (22), this is equivalent to

$$(23) \quad \log\left[\frac{(R - 1)b_t + y + n\bar{g}}{(R - 1)b_t + y + n\bar{g} - z}\right] \geq \frac{\log\left(\dfrac{R}{1 + n(R - 1)}\right)}{R - 1}$$
$$+ \log\left[n - (n - 1)\left(\frac{R - 1}{R}\right)\right].$$

When equation (23) is satisfied, stabilization becomes self-enforcing.

The only endogenous variable in equation (23) is the stock of government debt. There are two cases, given that the left-hand side of equation (23) is always positive and monotonically decreasing in b_t. First, if the right-hand side of equation (23) is negative, equation (23) is satisfied for all levels of debt. Second, if the right-hand side of equation (23) is positive, there is one level of debt for which equation (23) is satisfied with equality. Figure 2.2 plots $V^s(b_t)$ and $V^d(b_t)$ as a function of b_t in this second case. At low levels of debt, total utility from defecting exceeds total utility from stabilizing, but this situation is reversed as debt grows. The schedules cross once, at the point labeled b^*.

Individual rationality dictates that along an equilibrium path a group's utility must be at least as high as the utility associated with deviating from that path. In the second case above, condition (23) can be interpreted as revealing that this constraint binds at some levels of government debt but not at others. In particular, it binds at only low levels of debt: as long as the government is rich, groups are tempted to defect and consume as much as they can.

But incentives change with higher debt: because stabilization involves the elimination of the deadweight loss, the payoff associated with defecting falls more quickly than that associated with stabilization as debt rises. Put differently, the static gain associated with stabilizing becomes more desirable to groups as debt increases and the government becomes poorer. Only when the

---

14. In fact, the second line in equation (22) has a ready interpretation along these lines. The parameter $\gamma < 1$ is the share of government wealth left over after all other $(n - 1)$ groups have done their spending in the case of defection; the expression $R/[1 + n(R - 1)] = 1 - (n - 1)\phi$ is the share of government wealth left over after all other $(n - 1)$ groups have done their spending in the case of Markov-Nash behavior. The difference of the logarithm of the two is the welfare gain to group i of cheating on the other $(n - 1)$ groups.

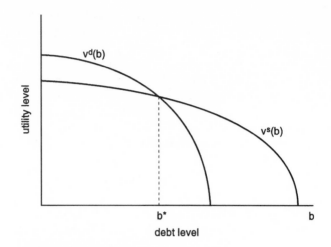

Fig. 2.2   Utility levels from stabilizing versus defecting

stock of debt is so high that the payoff associated with defection falls below that associated with stabilization does the latter become self-sustaining.

2.5   Delayed Stabilization

I have shown that stabilization may be sustainable from some levels of the stock of debt, but not from others. In particular, it could well be that the economy starts out at a level of debt sufficiently low such that stabilization is not possible. But it is not clear thus far whether and how the economy will get to the debt threshold where stabilization can be achieved. In what follows I characterize "switching equilibria" of the sort described by Benhabib and Radner (1992): groups follow an agreed-upon path until debt reaches a level such that it is individually rational to stabilize. At that point, a "switch" takes place and the fiscal deficit is eliminated. Because the necessary debt accumulation takes time, stabilization is "delayed," as in Alesina and Drazen 1991.

Just as in the case of simple trigger strategies, there are many paths for net transfers that are potentially sustainable. To keep matters simple, I focus on the case in which groups follow simple Markov-Nash transfer policies until the switch takes place.[15]

15. I have established that stabilization will occur when debt reaches b^*. Any set of spending policies that takes debt from b_0 to b^*, and that is sustainable through the threat of reversion to Markov if anyone deviates, will give rise to a switching equilibrium. There could be many such paths. More generally, it would be of interest to search for the best switching path; that would involve the difficult task of jointly choosing the best sustainable path to the switching point and after the switching point. To the best of my knowledge, there exist no general results characterizing this kind of "second best" equilibria. For some limited progress, see Benhabib and Rustichini 1991 and Benhabib and Velasco 1996.

DEFINITION 4. *A switching path is given by*

$$g_{it} = \begin{cases} \left(\dfrac{R}{1 + n(R - 1)} \right)\left[(R - 1)b_t + y - z + \left(\dfrac{n - 1}{R} \right)\bar{g} \right] & \text{if} \quad b_t < b^* \\[2em] \left(\dfrac{1}{n} \right)[(R - 1)b_t + y] & \text{if} \quad b_t \geq b^*. \end{cases}$$

DEFINITION 5. *A switching strategy consists of following the path in defini-tion 4 as long as no one deviates. If a deviation takes place, groups revert to Markov-Nash net transfers after one period. Hence, a switching strat-egy is nothing but a generalized trigger strategy.*

DEFINITION 6. *A switching equilibrium for this game is represented by a set of switching strategies, one for each player, such that no group can im-prove its total payoff by a unilateral change in strategy at any point in the game.*

To characterize such an equilibrium one must describe the behavior of the economy prior to reaching b^*. If all groups consume according to equation (14), it will take T periods to reach b^*, where T is the smallest number such that

$$(24)\ b_T = b_0 \left(\frac{R}{1 + n(R - 1)} \right)^T + \left(\frac{y - z + n\bar{g}}{R - 1} \right)\left[\left(\frac{R}{1 + n(R - 1)} \right)^T - 1 \right]$$

$$\geq b^*,$$

which is simply the solution to difference equation (15).

If stabilization takes place, equations (23) and (24) jointly determine the stock of debt and the time at which it will occur. In figure 2.3, equation (23) appears as the schedule RR and equation (24) appears as the schedule SS. Their intersection occurs at T and b^*.

As usual, to be an equilibrium this path must be such that the continuation value at every point of the trajectory (that is, the utility of behaving in a Markov-Nash fashion until b reaches b^* and stabilizing thereafter) must be at least as large as the value of defecting. Once $b \geq b^*$ this is indeed the case, by the definition of b^*. What about when $b < b^*$? In that case, a defecting group must solve

$$(25) \qquad V^d(b_t) = \max_{g_{it}}\{\log(g_{it} + \bar{g}) + R^{-1}V^m(b_{t+1})\}$$

subject to

$$(26) \qquad b_{t+1} = Rb_t[1 - (n - 1)\phi] + (y - z_t) - (n - 1)\mu - g_{it}$$

and to equation (5). But this is exactly the problem solved in computing the Markov-Nash equilibrium above. We know the corresponding solution is that

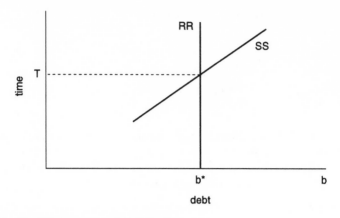

Fig. 2.3   Equilibrium time of stabilization

in equation (14). Hence, a group that—when confronted with the policy specified in definition 4 for the case of $b < b*$—chooses to maximize its current-
period utility, knowing that everyone will revert to Markov-Nash behavior in
the future, does exactly what definition 4 specifies. The path is therefore also
self-sustaining for the range $b < b*$.

The conclusion is that the strategies for each group contained in definition
5 do indeed constitute an equilibrium in the sense of definition 6: they are best
responses to themselves. The associated equilibrium has two phases. In the
first one, when debt is low, net transfers by groups are high, a fiscal deficit
occurs, and debt is accumulated. In the second, when debt reaches the relevant
threshold, net transfers fall, the deficit is closed, and debt accumulation ceases.
We therefore have a delayed stabilization or, more precisely, a delayed fiscal
reform.

2.6   The Effects of Economic Crises

The possibility of delayed fiscal stabilization places the economy in a
second-best situation, in which exogenous shocks can have unexpected effects
on welfare. Hirschman (1985), in the context of the Latin American experience, conjectured that adverse external shocks may prompt economic reforms
and thereby have unexpected beneficial effects. In the same vein, Drazen and
Grilli (1993) showed that an economic crisis may alter relative payoffs in such
a way as to reduce the equilibrium delay in implementing a stabilization program and thereby increase welfare. That paradoxical result also holds in the
present model.

For simplicity, identify an economic crisis with a permanent fall (as of time
0) in exogenous nontax revenue y. This could be interpreted, for instance, as

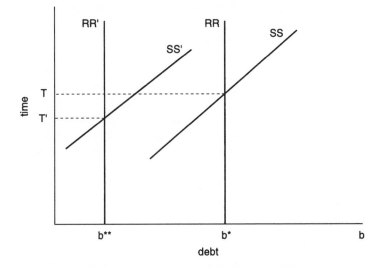

Fig. 2.4   Effect of shock to nontax revenue on time of stabilization

an adverse terms-of-trade shock that lowers the value of income from state enterprises (oil in Mexico or Indonesia, copper in Chile or Zambia).

Such a shock has two effects.[16] First, it lowers the debt threshold and the length of time that elapses before fiscal stabilization takes place. As can be seen in figure 2.4, both RR and SS shift to the left; the new intersection is such that both b^* and T fall.[17] Ceteris paribus, that raises groups' welfare: loosely, since the Markov-Nash path yields lower utility than does the stabilizing path, switching from one to the other at an earlier date must be good for welfare. But second, the permanent fall in y lowers total government resources available for making net transfers; ceteris paribus, that lowers groups' welfare.

Hence, the sign of the net effect is ambiguous, leaving open the possibility that the discounted utility that groups derive from government transfers could indeed rise as a result of the adverse shock!

2.7   Conclusions

Economists have spent much time and energy modeling the allocation of resources in those regions of the modern economy where the market system indeed does allocate resources. But there is a very large portion of such economies—the government sector—within which there are no private property rights, and where the allocation of resources does not follow market forces. If

16. Formal proofs of the statements that follow are available from the author upon request.
17. This is not obvious from the picture, but can be shown algebraically.

we move beyond the view of government as a monolithic entity that behaves like a single individual, economics must provide an account of how economic decisions are made among government groups, and how politics both frames and determines those decisions.

This paper suggests one of the simplest possible models of a government with many controllers and fragmented policymaking—one in which government net income is a "commons" from which interest groups can extract resources. This setup has striking macroeconomic implications. First, fiscal deficits emerge even when there are no reasons for intertemporal smoothing. Second, those deficits can be sometimes eliminated, but only after a delay during which government debt is built up. Thus, the model offers a plausible rationale for the tardiness in stabilizing that we often observe in real-life economies.

Appendix

Recall that in equation (4) in the text we defined the variable

$$
(A1) \qquad w_t \equiv b_t + \frac{y - z + n\bar{g}}{R - 1},
$$

expressed here for constant z_t. It follows from equation (A1) and budget constraint (1) in the text that

$$
(A2) \qquad w_{t+1} = Rw_t - \sum_{i=1}^{n} (g_{it} + \bar{g}).
$$

Using definition (A1), we can write the policy rule as

$$
(A3) \qquad g_{it} + \bar{g} = \phi R w_t.
$$

It follows that

$$
(A4) \qquad \frac{g_{it+1} + \bar{g}}{g_{it} + \bar{g}} = \frac{w_{t+1}}{w_t} = 1 - (n - 1)\phi,
$$

where the second equality comes from Euler equation (12) in the text.
Using equation (A3) in (A2) we have

$$
(A5) \qquad \frac{w_{t+1}}{w_t} = R(1 - n\phi).
$$

Combining equations (A4) and (A5) we have

$$
(A6) \qquad 1 - (n - 1)\phi = R(1 - n\phi),
$$

which implies $\phi = (R - 1)/[1 + n(R - 1)]$. This, together with definition (A1), reveals that $\mu = [R(y - z) + (n - 1)\overline{g}]/[1 + n(R - 1)]$, as it appears in the text.

References

Aizenman, Joshua. 1991. Competitive externalities and the optimal seigniorage segmentation. *Journal of Money, Credit, and Banking* 24:61–71.

Alesina, Alberto, and Allan Drazen. 1991. Why are stabilizations delayed? *American Economic Review* 81:1170–88.

Alesina, Alberto, Ricardo Hausmann, Rudolph Hommes, and Ernesto Stein. 1996. Budget institutions and fiscal performance in Latin America. NBER Working Paper no. 5586. Cambridge, Mass.: National Bureau of Economic Research.

Alesina, Alberto, and Roberto Perotti. 1994. The political economy of budget deficits. NBER Working Paper no. 4637. Cambridge, Mass.: National Bureau of Economic Research.

Alesina, Alberto, and Guido Tabellini. 1990. A positive theory of fiscal deficits and government debt. *Review of Economic Studies* 57 (3): 403–14.

Atkeson, Andrew. 1991. International lending with moral hazard and risk of repudiation. *Econometrica* 159:1069–90.

Barro, Robert. 1979. On the determination of the public debt. *Journal of Political Economy* 87:940–71.

———. 1986. U.S. deficits since World War I. *Scandinavian Journal of Economics* 88:195–222.

Benhabib, Jess, and Roy Radner. 1992. Joint exploitation of a productive asset: A game theoretic approach. *Economic Theory* 2:155–90.

Benhabib, Jess, and Aldo Rustichini. 1991. Social conflict, growth, and inequality. Working paper no. 1-46, C. V. Starr Center for Applied Economics, New York University. September.

Benhabib, Jess, and Andrés Velasco. 1996. On the optimal and best sustainable taxes in an open economy. *European Economic Review* 40:135–54.

Bhagwati, Jagdish. 1982. Directly unproductive profit-seeking (DUP) activities. *Journal of Political Economy* 90:988–1002.

Bizer, Daniel, and Steven Durlauf. 1990. Testing the positive theory of government finance. *Journal of Monetary Economics* 26:123–41.

Bomfin, A. N., and Anwar Shah. 1991. Macroeconomic management and the division of powers in Brazil: Perspectives for the 1990s. World Bank Working Paper no. 567.

Bulow, Jeremy, and Kenneth Rogoff. 1989. Sovereign debt: Is to forgive to forget? *American Economic Review* 79:43–50.

Chari, V. V., and Harold Cole. 1993. A contribution to the theory of pork barrel Spending. Federal Reserve Bank of Minneapolis Staff Report 156.

Chari, V. V., Larry Jones, and Ramón Marimón. 1994. On the economics of split voting in representative democracies. Paper presented at the Conference on Political Economy, New York University, May.

Chari, V. V., and Patrick Kehoe. 1993a. Sustainable plans and debt. *Journal of Economic Theory* 61:230–61.

———. 1993b. Sustainable plans and mutual default. *Review of Economic Studies* 60:175–95.

Drazen, Allan, and Vitorio Grilli. 1993. The benefits of crises for economic reforms. *American Economic Review* 83:598–607.

Edwards, Sebastian, and Guido Tabellini. 1991. Explaining fiscal policies and inflation in developing countries. *Journal of International Money and Finance* 10:S16–S48.

Fudenberg, Drew, and Eric Maskin. 1986. The folk theorem in repeated games with discounting or with incomplete information. *Econometrica* 54:533–54.

Grilli, Vittorio, Donato Masciandaro, and Guido Tabellini. 1991. Political and monetary institutions and public financial policies in the industrial democracies. *Economic Policy* 6:341–92.

Hirschman, Albert. 1985. Reflections on the Latin American experience. In *The politics of inflation and economic stagnation,* ed. L. Lindberg and C. Maier. Washington, D.C.: Brookings Institution.

Holzmann, Robert. 1991. Budgetary subsidies in centrally planned economies in transition. IMF Working Paper 91/11. April.

Jones, Mark, Pablo Sanguinetti, and Mariano Tommasi. 1997. Politics, institutions, and fiscal performance in the Argentine provinces. Universidad de San Andrés, June. Photocopy.

Kornai, Janos. 1979. Demand versus resource-constrained systems. *Econometrica* 47:801–20.

Krueger, Anne. 1974. The political economy of the rent-seeking society. *American Economic Review* 64:291–303.

Larraín, Felipe, and Marcelo Selowsky. 1991. *The public sector and the Latin American crisis.* San Francisco: ICS Press.

Levhari, David, and Leonard Mirman. 1980. The great fish war: An example using the Cournot Nash solution. *Bell Journal of Economics* 11:322–34.

Lipton, David, and Jeffrey Sachs. 1990. Creating a market economy in Eastern Europe: The case of Poland. *Brookings Papers on Economic Activity,* no. 1:75–133.

Persson, Torsten, and Lars Svensson. 1989. Why a stubborn conservative would run a deficit: Policy with time-inconsistent preferences. *Quarterly Journal of Economics* 104:225–45.

Roubini, Nouriel. 1991. Economic and political determinants of budget deficits in developing countries. *Journal of International Money and Finance* 10:S49–S72.

Roubini, Nouriel, and Jeffrey Sachs. 1989a. Government spending and budget deficits in the industrial countries. *Economic Policy* 8:100–132.

———. 1989b. Political and economic determinants of budget deficits in the industrial democracies. *European Economic Review* 33 (5): 903–33.

Sachs, Jeffrey. 1994. Russia's struggle with stabilization: Conceptual issues and evidence. Paper presented at the World Bank's Annual Conference on Development Economics, April.

Shah, Anwar. 1990. The new federalism in Brazil. World Bank Working Paper no. 557. December.

Tabellini, Guido, and Alberto Alesina. 1990. Voting on the budget deficit. *American Economic Review* 80:37–49.

Tornell, Aaron, and Andrés Velasco. 1995. Exchange rate–based and money-based stabilization with endogenous fiscal policy. NBER Working Paper no. 5300. Cambridge, Mass.: National Bureau of Economic Research.

von Hagen, Jürgen. 1992. Budgeting procedures and fiscal performance in the European Communities," Economic Paper no. 96, Commission of the European Communities, October.

von Hagen, Jürgen, and Ian Harden. 1994. National budget processes and fiscal performance. *European Economy: Reports and Studies* 3:311–418.

Wallich, C. 1992. Fiscal decentralization: Intergovernmental relations in Russia. Studies of Economies in Transformation, paper no. 6, World Bank.

Weingast, Barry, Kenneth Shepsle, and Christian Johnsen. 1981. The political economy of benefits and costs: A neoclassical approach to redistributive politics. *Journal of Political Economy* 189:642–64.

World Bank. 1990a. *Argentina: Reforms for price stability and growth.* World Bank.

———. 1990b. *Argentina: Provincial government finances.* World Bank.

———. 1990c. *Tax policy for stabilization and economic recovery.* World Bank.

Zarazaga, Carlos. 1993. Hyperinflations and moral hazard in the appropriation of seigniorage. Working Paper 93-26. Federal Reserve Bank of Philadelphia, November.

3 Consumption Smoothing through Fiscal Policy in OECD and EU Countries

Adriana Arreaza, Bent E. Sørensen, and Oved Yosha

3.1 Introduction

There is wide agreement that large government budget deficits are undesirable. The main argument is that a deficit forces the government to borrow, raising interest rates and crowding out private-sector investment. Furthermore, accumulated government debt constitutes a potentially unfair burden on future generations and reduces a country's credit rating on international markets.

Despite these obvious drawbacks, most governments run substantial deficits. Deficit spending may be partly driven by a desire to smooth the distortion of taxes needed to finance government consumption over time (Barro 1979) but, as stressed by Velasco (chap. 2 in this volume), the magnitude of budget deficits since the early seventies has been too large to be explained by such intertemporal tax smoothing. Recently, a literature has developed seeking to explain the formation of government deficits as a consequence of a coordination failure among spending ministers or political parties (in the "tragedy of the commons" sense), or as a consequence of excessively short planning horizons of governments who do not expect to remain in office (e.g., Hallerberg and von Hagen, chap. 9 in this volume; Velasco, chap. 2 in this volume). In either case, the government does not internalize the full social cost of deficit spending, which

Adriana Arreaza is a Ph.D. student in the Economics Department at Brown University. Bent E. Sørensen is assistant professor of economics at Brown University. Oved Yosha is senior lecturer at the Berglas School of Economics, Tel Aviv University.

The authors thank Charles Goodhart for encouraging them to investigate risk-sharing patterns in Europe and Alex Cukierman, Manfred Neumann, Assaf Razin, and conference participants for helpful comments. Sørensen acknowledges financial support from the Watson Institute, Brown University, and thanks Tel Aviv University for its hospitality. The authors gratefully acknowledge financial support through a Salomon Grant from Brown University, a grant from the Armand Hammer Fund for Economic Cooperation in the Middle East, and a United States National Science Foundation grant. Hyung-Kwon Chung, Sara Dawes, and Lisa Wu provided excellent research assistance at various stages of the project.

results in deficits that are larger than what is socially optimal.[1] In other words, large deficits may be a consequence of "fiscal sinning," reflecting deficiencies in the political decision-making process rather than long-run optimal planning. In some countries, there are legal restrictions on the size of the deficit for various levels of government. The effectiveness of such restrictions has been studied by, for example, Poterba (1994), Bohn and Inman (1996), and Poterba and Rueben (chap. 8 in this volume).

Government deficits may serve to reduce the variability of consumption over time if, for example, the government has better access to foreign credit markets than the private sector. Among the authors who have focused on the cyclical properties of government deficits, Gavin and Perotti (1997) have pointed out that deficits have been countercyclical in OECD countries, contributing to the stabilization of consumption over the business cycle,[2] whereas in Latin America government deficits have been procyclical (see also Gavin et al. 1996). Sørensen and Yosha (1998) have recently found that government budget deficits play a central role in smoothing consumption among OECD and EU countries. They report, for the period 1966–90, that there is virtually no cross-country income smoothing (income insurance) among OECD countries, and that the only operative mechanism for smoothing gross domestic product (GDP) shocks is through borrowing and lending. They estimate that about 40 percent of shocks to GDP are smoothed on average at the one-year frequency through this channel, with about half the smoothing achieved through government budget deficits and half through corporate saving (dividend smoothing). At the three-year frequency all the smoothing is achieved through government budget deficits, with only 25 percent of shocks to GDP absorbed.

To obtain a more complete picture of government consumption smoothing mechanisms, we measure the amount of smoothing achieved through various components of the deficit. For EU countries, we find that, at the one-year frequency, about 13 percent of shocks to GDP are smoothed on average via government consumption, 18 percent of shocks are smoothed via government transfers, and about 5 percent are smoothed via government subsidies, while taxes do not smooth consumption. The results for OECD countries are very similar.[3] Taxes actually dis-smooth consumption, that is, they increase less than proportionately with output, which may be due to institutional rigidities in the tax system or to increased tax evasion during booms. If excessive deficits are a result of political expedience, with deficits increasing sharply in recessions

1. The "tragedy of the commons" is a classic example of such an outcome. When economic agents possess a common resource—the grass in the commons, or a marine fishery as in Levhari and Mirman 1980—they tend to deplete the resource too quickly.

2. Evidence regarding the countercyclicality of U.S. federal debt since the 1920s is provided by Barro (1979).

3. These findings are consistent with results reported by Gavin and Perotti (1997). The main advantage of our method for studying this issue is that it allows us to estimate the fraction of shocks to GDP absorbed through each fiscal component.

but not rapidly reversed in booms, then the government deficit will absorb a larger fraction of negative shocks than of positive shocks. We examine this issue, finding that government consumption smooths positive and negative output shocks equally. Government transfers provide more smoothing of negative shocks among EU countries but not among OECD countries, which probably reflects a higher commitment to social insurance in EU countries.

Next, we investigate the relation between the level of the government deficit and the amount of consumption smoothing achieved through (government and private) saving. The level of the deficit may affect the ability of the government to use the deficit as a tool for smoothing consumption. For example, governments that during recessions provide many public services and distribute transfers generously, but tax moderately, may find it hard to reverse this pattern in booms due to institutional rigidities or political pressure. It is, therefore, conceivable that high deficits are associated with little, not much, government consumption smoothing. The level of the government deficit may also affect the ability of the private sector to smooth consumption since government borrowing may crowd out private-sector borrowers who face high interest rates or credit constraints. To investigate these issues empirically, we split our sample into high- and low-deficit countries, finding no evidence in support of such effects. There seems to be no trade-off between high government deficits in a country and the ability to smooth consumption via saving in that country.

Hallerberg and von Hagen (chap. 9 in this volume) find that fiscal institutions have a significant impact on the level of the public sector deficit. We ask whether the amount of smoothing via deficits differs according to the type of budgetary institution that determines government fiscal policy, using the classification of Hallerberg and von Hagen, to whom we are grateful for kindly providing us the data. We find that in countries where there is "delegation" of power (e.g., to a strong finance minister) or where fiscal targets are negotiated effectively by coalition members, consumption smoothing via government consumption and government transfers is considerably higher (although smoothing via government subsidies is smaller). This result is not driven by the effect of budgetary institutions on the level of the deficit since there is no apparent statistical relation between the level of the deficit and the amount of consumption smoothing in a country. We interpret this finding as evidence that effective budgetary institutions can accomplish efficient consumption smoothing via government deficit spending *and* lower average deficits.

Our findings have implications for the evaluation of the Maastricht guidelines requiring countries wishing to join the European Monetary Union (EMU) to reduce the yearly deficit to less than 3 percent of GDP and national debt to less than 60 percent of GDP. Sørensen and Yosha (1998) suggested that since much of the smoothing among EU countries is achieved via government lending and borrowing (with all the smoothing achieved via this channel at the three-year frequency), the Maastricht fiscal straitjacket should be relaxed, at least until capital markets are sufficiently integrated to carry out this role, as they do in the United States (see Asdrubali, Sørensen, and Yosha 1996). In light of the evidence suggesting that a large deficit is not necessary for better consumption smoothing in a country (including consumption smoothing via the deficit itself), we must qualify our criticism of the Maastricht guidelines by stressing that average deficits must be kept low, but that governments should be allowed, temporarily, to run high deficits during recessions.

We realize that the enforcement of such guidelines is tricky, for example, due to potential time inconsistency in the policy of the European Commission with regard to governments that run persistent deficits,[4] and since capital and credit markets may not generate effective sanctions to ensure fiscal discipline. We nevertheless believe that it is important to have a clear view regarding the "ideal" fiscal policy that combines the benefits from long-run fiscal discipline with the benefits from government consumption smoothing in an incomplete markets environment.[5]

In the next section we briefly describe the channels through which income and consumption smoothing occur among regions or countries, and describe the methodology for measuring the fraction of shocks to GDP smoothed through each channel. In section 3.3 we update the main regression of Sørensen and Yosha (1998) to the sample used here, and then present our results regarding patterns of smoothing through fiscal policy. Section 3.4 concludes.

3.2   Income and Consumption Smoothing among OECD and EU Countries

We begin by reviewing the channels through which regions and countries smooth output shocks. Government fiscal policy is but one such channel. It is not obvious that governments should use fiscal policy to smooth shocks to GDP since, in principle, consumption can be smoothed through transactions by individuals and corporations on markets. It can be argued, though, that if markets fail to provide income and consumption smoothing, governments can step in, borrowing and lending internationally on behalf of the country's citizens to help smooth national consumption. This, however, may slow down the development of financial markets. In light of these considerations we believe that it is useful to perform the analysis of the consumption-smoothing role of government fiscal policy in a more general framework where other forms of income and consumption smoothing are analyzed. We therefore begin by presenting such a framework, developed in Asdrubali, Sørensen, and Yosha 1996.

---

4. For example, due to the political cost or the ex post nonoptimality of imposing sanctions on countries in recession.

5. For further discussion of EMU-related fiscal issues, see Goodhart and Smith 1993, Inman and Rubinfeld 1994, and Eichengreen and von Hagen 1995.

3.2.1   Channels of Income and Consumption Smoothing among Countries

There are several mechanisms for smoothing income and consumption among regions or countries. Individuals in one country can hold claims to output produced in other countries. For example, if institutional investors (e.g., pension funds) in a country invest internationally, income in that country will comove with the output in other countries. Similarly, if financial intermediaries in one country lend to borrowers in other countries, the flow of interest payments smooths income in the lending country. We refer to this mechanism as income smoothing (or risk sharing) through cross-border ownership of productive assets. It consists mainly of cross-country income smoothing via capital income flows, but, more generally, it also includes labor income flows.

Similarly, international transfers smooth income if the net transfers to a country are larger during (country-specific) recessions. Of course, the motivation for having an international tax-transfer system need not be related to income smoothing, but a tax-transfer system designed to redistribute income across countries or to finance multinational projects may contribute to international income smoothing. The empirical implication of income smoothing, whether through capital markets or via international transfers, is that cross-country income variability will be lower than cross-country output variability.

Intertemporal consumption smoothing—through saving and dis-saving—also contributes to intercountry consumption smoothing. Individuals in one country can increase or decrease their saving in response to income shocks, adjusting the amount of domestic investment or transferring funds across country borders with the help of financial intermediaries. Similarly, corporations can retain more or less profits in response to profitability shocks. The retained profits can be invested in physical assets in the country where the corporation operates, or in financial assets; the funds may then finance investment in the home country or in other countries. In any event, the empirical implication is that cross-country consumption variability will be lower than cross-country income variability.

Intertemporal consumption smoothing through government saving and dis-saving has precisely the same effect. During recessions the government runs a large deficit, borrowing internationally, and during booms it runs a surplus (or a smaller deficit), reducing its stock of debt (or the growth rate of its debt).[6] The government can run a countercyclical deficit by adopting a countercyclical expenditure policy, a countercyclical transfers and subsidies policy, or a procyclical tax policy. These forms of government consumption smoothing have the same empirical consequence, namely, to reduce cross-country consumption variability.

Cross-country income smoothing via factor income flows is reflected in the

---

6. In practice, the government may borrow domestically, crowding out private-sector borrowers who are forced to raise money internationally. The final result is the same.

National Accounts data as the difference between GDP and gross national product (GNP). The difference between the GNP and GDP of a country is precisely the net flow of capital and labor income to that country (see Atkeson and Bayoumi 1993). Net international transfers are measured as the difference between Disposable National Income (DNI) and National Income (NI).[7] Consumption smoothing is manifested in the National Accounts as the difference between disposable income, DNI, and total (private and government) consumption, $C + G$.

Patterns of capital depreciation may also contribute to cross-country income smoothing. In the National Accounts, depreciation is responsible for the discrepancy between GNP and NI. As depreciation is calculated according to fixed accounting rules, and since the capital-output ratio is typically countercyclical, depreciation in the National Accounts data will constitute a larger fraction of output in recessions and a smaller fraction in booms, resulting in higher cross-sectional variance of NI with respect to GNP (dis-smoothing).[8]

3.2.2 Measuring the Fraction of Shocks Smoothed through Various Channels

We begin with a benchmark—perfect consumption smoothing and full risk sharing. Risk is fully shared within a group of countries if the consumption of a country comoves with the aggregate consumption of the group, but does not comove with country-specific shocks.[9] Denote the period t total (private and public) per capita consumption of the representative consumer of country i by $C_t^i + G_t^i$, and the period t per capita aggregate GDP of the entire group of countries by GDP_t. Then, when individuals have the same constant elasticity utility functions and are equally impatient across countries, full risk sharing implies that

$$(1) \qquad\qquad C_t^i + G_t^i = k^i \text{GDP}_t,$$

where k^i is a country-specific (time and state of the world invariant) constant representing the strength of country i's claim to output in the risk-sharing ar-

---

7. The National Accounting concepts we use are those of the OECD National Accounts publications. These concepts differ slightly from those in the United States Statistical Abstract. For example, the Abstract defines Net National Income as Net National Product minus indirect taxes plus subsidies, whereas in the OECD National Accounts publications Gross National Income is obtained from Gross National Product by adding and subtracting only *international* taxes and transfers.

8. Real capital depreciation may be affected by economic activity. For example, there may be more capital depreciation during booms due to more intense utilization of productive capacity. Such effects are not likely to be reflected in the National Accounts data.

9. See, e.g., Cochrane 1991, Mace 1991, Obstfeld 1994, and Townsend 1994. For extensions of the basic framework, see, e.g., Canova and Ravn 1996 and Lewis 1996. A comprehensive survey of research on international diversification is provided in Lewis 1995 and Obstfeld and Rogoff 1996. Recent related contributions can be found in Leiderman and Razin 1994. For microstudies of risk sharing, see, e.g., Altug and Miller 1990 and Hayashi, Altonji, and Kotlikoff 1996. For an estimation of welfare gains from risk sharing, see, e.g., van Wincoop 1994 and Tesar 1995 for OECD countries, and Sørensen and Yosha 1996 for U.S. states.

rangement. In other words, when risk is fully shared, consumption in each country is a country-specific fixed proportion of aggregate output.[10]

The derivation of equation (1) can be found in most of the references in note 9 and is, therefore, omitted. It should be stressed, though, that expected utility maximization by the representative consumer in each country is part of this derivation, and for equation (1) to hold it is necessary that, for each country, the marginal utility of consumption in period t be equal to the expected marginal utility in period $t + 1$. Full risk sharing thus implies perfect consumption smoothing for each country, in the standard Euler equation sense.

Returning to our discussion of the channels of income and consumption smoothing among countries, we think of consumers in each country progressing gradually from their endowment (no intertemporal smoothing nor intercountry risk sharing) toward full risk sharing and perfect consumption smoothing, that is, toward the allocation in equation (1), which may or may not be eventually achieved. The first level of smoothing is income smoothing (income insurance) through international factor income flows. In theory, full risk sharing may be achieved already at this level of smoothing, in which case $GNP_t^i = k^i GDP_t$ with no further need for income or consumption smoothing. If full risk sharing is not achieved at this level, there is scope for further income smoothing through international transfers. If full risk sharing is not achieved after the second level of income smoothing, there is scope for consumption smoothing, that is, borrowing and lending by individuals, corporations, or the government.[11] Then, after all channels of income and consumption smoothing have been exhausted, equation (1) may or may not hold. Even if equation (1) does not hold, it is still of interest to estimate the incremental amount of smoothing that is achieved through the various channels. We now describe how the estimation is carried out.

Consider the identity

$$GDP^i = \frac{GDP^i}{GNP^i} \frac{GNP^i}{NI^i} \frac{NI^i}{DNI^i} \frac{DNI^i}{C^i + G^i}(C^i + G^i),$$

where all the magnitudes are in per capita terms, and i is an index of countries. The national accounting identities that are relevant here are GNP = GDP + net factor income, NI = GNP − capital depreciation, DNI = NI + international transfers, $C + G$ = NI − net saving.

If there is smoothing through net factor income flows, namely, income smoothing via cross-country ownership of productive assets, then GDP^i/GNP^i

---

10. This formulation assumes that private and public consumption are perfect substitutes. It is also assumed that GDP shocks are exogenous, which is a reasonable assumption at relatively short time horizons. At longer horizons, income and consumption smoothing patterns may affect the cross-country correlation of GDP shocks, as argued by Frankel and Rose (1998).

11. It may not be optimal for consumers to fully smooth shocks to income (i.e., output shocks that were not insured) if these shocks are highly persistent. Lack of consumption smoothing therefore need not imply any imperfections of credit markets.

should vary positively with GDP^i. Similarly, if depreciation of capital further smooths income, then GNP^i/NI^i should vary positively with GDP^i. If net transfers from abroad, for example, transfers from EU institutions, contribute to income smoothing, then NI^i/DNI^i should vary positively with GDP^i. If saving further smooths total consumption, then $DNI^i/(C^i + G^i)$ should vary positively with GDP^i. Finally, to the extent that not all the shocks to GDP^i are smoothed, $C^i + G^i$ will be positively correlated with GDP^i.[12]

The cross-sectional smoothing of income shocks may involve cross-border flows of funds as in the case of factor income flows and international transfers, or it may not, as in the case of domestic investment or capital depreciation. Accounting capital depreciation of a country's capital stock is not sensitive to GDP fluctuations since it is approximately a predetermined proportion of the capital stock that itself does not vary much with shocks to GDP. Therefore, the ratio of accounting capital depreciation to GDP will typically decline when a country is hit by a positive shock and rise in response to a negative shock, with the result that capital depreciation typically contributes to cross-sectional dissmoothing of shocks to output.

To obtain a measure of smoothing, we use the above identity

$$GDP^i = \frac{GDP^i}{GNP^i} \frac{GNP^i}{NI^i} \frac{NI^i}{DNI^i} \frac{DNI^i}{C^i + G^i}(C^i + G^i),$$

that holds for any given year in the sample. To stress the cross-sectional nature of our derivation, we suppress the time index. Now take logs and time differences, multiply both sides by $\Delta\log GDP^i$ (minus its mean), and take the cross-sectional average, obtaining the following variance decomposition:[13]

$$\begin{aligned}
\text{var}\{\Delta\log GDP^i\} = \ &\text{cov}\{\Delta\log GDP^i, \ \Delta\log GDP^i - \Delta\log GNP^i\} \\
&+ \text{cov}\{\Delta\log GDP^i, \ \Delta\log GNP^i - \Delta\log NI^i\} \\
&+ \text{cov}\{\Delta\log GDP^i, \ \Delta\log NI^i - \Delta\log DNI^i\} \\
&+ \text{cov}\{\Delta\log GDP^i, \ \Delta\log DNI^i - \Delta\log(C^i + G^i)\} \\
&+ \text{cov}\{\Delta\log GDP^i, \ \Delta\log(C^i + G^i)\}.
\end{aligned}$$

Dividing by $\text{var}\{\Delta\log GDP^i\}$ we get $1 = \beta_f + \beta_d + \beta_\tau + \beta_s + \beta_u$, where β_f is the ordinary least squares estimate of the slope in the cross-sectional regression

---

12. Due to the more limited availability of data for U.S. states, Asdrubali, Sørensen, and Yosha (1996) considered the following channels for smoothing shocks to gross state product: "capital market smoothing," which is income smoothing through cross-state factor income flows, depreciation, and corporate saving; "federal smoothing," which is income smoothing through interstate taxes and transfers by the U.S. federal government; and "credit market smoothing," which refers to consumption smoothing through personal and state government saving.

13. In this equation "var$\{X\}$" and "cov$\{X,Y\}$" denote the statistics $1/N \sum_{i=1}^{N}(X^i - \bar{X})^2$ and $1/N \sum_{i=1}^{N}(X^i - \bar{X})(Y^i - \bar{Y})$, respectively, where N is the number of countries in the sample.

of $\Delta\log$ GDP^i $-$ $\Delta\log$ GNP^i on $\Delta\log$ GDP^i, β_d is the slope in the cross-sectional regression of $\Delta\log$ GNP^i $-$ $\Delta\log$ NI^i on $\Delta\log$ GDP^i, and similarly for β_τ and β_s. β_u is the coefficient in the cross-sectional regression of $\Delta\log(C^i + G^i)$ on $\Delta\log$ GDP^i. We interpret the β coefficients as the incremental percentage amounts of smoothing achieved at each level, and β_u as the percentage of shocks not smoothed. If $\beta_u = 0$, there is full risk sharing and the remaining coefficients sum to 1. Otherwise, they sum to less than 1. We do not constrain any of the β coefficients, at any level, to be positive or less than 1. Therefore, if there is dis-smoothing at some level, it will be reflected in a negative value of β.

At the practical level, the following (panel) equations are estimated:

$$\Delta\log\text{GDP}_t^i - \Delta\log\text{GNP}_t^i = \nu_{f,t} + \beta_f\ \Delta\log\text{GDP}_t^i + \varepsilon_{f,t}^i,$$

$$\Delta\log\text{GNP}_t^i - \Delta\log\text{NI}_t^i = \nu_{d,t} + \beta_d\ \Delta\log\text{GDP}_t^i + \varepsilon_{d,t}^i,$$

$$(2) \qquad \Delta\log\text{NI}_t^i - \Delta\log\text{DNI}_t^i = \nu_{\tau,t} + \beta_\tau\ \Delta\log\text{GDP}_t^i + \varepsilon_{\tau,t}^i,$$

$$\Delta\log\text{DNI}_t^i - \Delta\log(C_t^i + G_t^i) = \nu_{s,t} + \beta_s\ \Delta\log\text{GDP}_t^i + \varepsilon_{s,t}^i,$$

$$\Delta\log(C_t^i + G_t^i) = \nu_{u,t} + \beta_u\ \Delta\log\text{GDP}_t^i + \varepsilon_{u,t}^i,$$

where $\nu_{.,t}$ are time-fixed effects. The inclusion of time-fixed effects is crucial, since with time-fixed effects the β coefficients are weighted averages of the year-by-year cross-sectional regressions.[14] The time-fixed effects capture year-specific impacts on growth rates, most notably the impact of the growth in aggregate EU (or OECD) output. To take into account autocorrelation in the residuals we assume that the error terms in each equation and in each country follow an AR(1) process. Since the samples are short, we assume that the auto-correlation parameter is identical across countries and equations. We further allow for country-specific variances of the error terms. In practice, we estimate the system in equation (2) by a two-step generalized least squares (GLS) procedure. Unless we explicitly say otherwise, we use differenced data at the yearly frequency.

3.3   Consumption Smoothing through Fiscal Policy among OECD and EU Countries: Empirical Results

The data are from the OECD National Accounts, Detailed Tables (vol. 2), 1996 diskettes. For the series we need, there are consistent data for the majority of countries for the period 1971–93.

For the sake of consistency, and as a robustness check, we update here the relevant analysis in Sørensen and Yosha 1998 using differenced data for 1971–

---

14. See Asdrubali, Sørensen, and Yosha 1996, note 5, for an explicit formula.

Table 3.1   **Channels of Income and Consumption Smoothing (percent)**

	EU8 1971–93	EU11 1980–93	OECD14 1971–93	OECD17 1980–93
Factor income (β_f)	−1	−3	−1	−1
	(1)	(2)	(1)	(1)
Capital depreciation (β_d)	−8	−8	−8	−9
	(1)	(1)	(1)	(1)
International transfers (β_τ)	3	5	2	3
	(2)	(2)	(1)	(1)
Saving (β_s)	50	37	48	46
	(5)	(5)	(3)	(4)
Not smoothed (β_u)	56	69	59	62
	(4)	(5)	(3)	(3)

Note: EU8: Austria, Belgium, Denmark, Finland, France, Greece, Germany, United Kingdom. EU11: EU8 + Italy, Netherlands, Sweden. OECD14: EU8 + Australia, Canada, Iceland, Japan, Switzerland, United States. OECD17: OECD14 + Italy, Netherlands, Sweden. Fraction of shocks absorbed at each level of smoothing. Standard errors in parentheses. β_f is the GLS estimate of the slope in the regression of $\Delta \log \text{GDP}^i - \Delta \log \text{GNP}^i$ on $\Delta \log \text{GDP}^i$, β_d is the slope in the regression of $\Delta \log \text{GNP}^i - \Delta \log \text{NI}^i$ on $\Delta \log \text{GDP}^i$, and similarly for β_τ and β_s. β_u is the coefficient in the regression of $\Delta \log (C^i + G^i)$ on $\Delta \log \text{GDP}^i$. We interpret the β coefficients as the incremental percentage amounts of smoothing achieved at each level, and β_u as the percentage of shocks not smoothed.

93. In table 3.1 we display the estimated percentages of shocks to GDP smoothed through each channel, among OECD and EU countries. The results are very similar to those in Sørensen and Yosha 1998.[15] It is immediately apparent that there is negligible income smoothing through factor income flows, among EU as well as OECD countries. This finding is fully consistent with the Feldstein and Horioka (1980) puzzle and with the "home bias" puzzle (French and Poterba 1991; Tesar and Werner 1995).[16] There is also very little smoothing via international transfers, resulting in almost no income smoothing among OECD and EU countries.

The only operative smoothing mechanism is consumption smoothing through saving. For the period 1971–93 it amounts to 48 percent of shocks to GDP for OECD countries and 50 percent of shocks for EU countries. Furthermore, Sørensen and Yosha (1998) estimated the fraction of shocks smoothed by the main components of national saving, and found that personal saving contributes nothing to cross-country consumption smoothing, corporate saving absorbs 23 percent of shocks to GDP at the one-year frequency but provides no smoothing at the three-year frequency, while government saving absorbs about 25–30 percent of shocks at both frequencies. A plausible interpretation is that the longer differencing period captures the response of changes in in-

---

15. The estimated coefficients do not sum to 100 percent because of rounding.
16. See Gordon and Bovenberg 1996 for a recent contribution on this issue.

come and consumption to longer-lasting shocks to GDP. Thus, in a bad year, corporations decrease (on average) the fraction of earnings they retain (to avoid a sharp decrease in distributed profits), but over longer horizons corporations do not change the fraction of earnings retained. By contrast, governments respond to temporary as well as to longer-lasting shocks by adjusting the budget deficit in response to fluctuations in GDP.

As a further robustness check, we decompose Δlog GDP into a predicted part and an unpredicted part. As predictors we use lagged Δlog GDP and lagged Δlog WORLD GDP (two lags of each). We then estimate equation (2) using the fitted value and the innovations as regressors (each separately, in place of Δlog GDP), finding that the estimated coefficients are similar for the predicted and the unpredicted components of changes in GDP.[17]

We turn to a more detailed analysis of the patterns of consumption smoothing via government fiscal policy, which is our focus in this paper. Due to data availability, the countries included vary somewhat across regressions. They are listed in the notes to the various tables. In all regressions for the OECD group we excluded Luxembourg and Mexico.

3.3.1 Smoothing through Fiscal Components: Tax Smoothing or Consumption Smoothing?

Table 3.2 displays the average size (across countries and across years) of the main components of the budget for the general government sector (central + local government). Most notable is the larger fraction of GDP allocated to government transfers (mainly social security benefits and social assistance) in EU countries in comparison to the entire OECD group, although also taxes are higher on average among the EU countries.[18]

Table 3.3 displays averages across countries of simple country-by-country time series correlations of government budget components with GDP. These correlations do not control for aggregate (world) output fluctuations and exhibit high variation across countries, but are nevertheless suggestive. It is apparent that government transfers and subsidies are acyclical or countercyclical and, therefore, are likely to play a major role in cross-country consumption smoothing, particularly in EU countries, where government transfers on average are larger relative to GDP. Furthermore, transfers and subsidies are substantially more countercyclical in the later sample period, suggesting that the

---

17. The amount of income smoothing via factor income flows of both types of shocks is not significantly different from zero, the amount of income smoothing via international transfers varies from 1 to 5 percent of shocks and is precisely estimated, and the fraction of shocks smoothed through saving varies from 29 to 46 percent, which is qualitatively similar to the results displayed in table 3.1.

18. We stress that transfers and taxes in tables 3.2–3.7 refer to within-country (not intercountry) transfers, subsidies, and taxes. Intercountry net transfers vary roughly proportionally with GDP (table 3.1).

Table 3.2   The Size of Fiscal Components (percentage of GDP)

	EU8 1971–93	EU11 1980–93	OECD14 1971–93	OECD18 1980–93
Government consumption	19	20	18	19
	(3)	(4)	(4)	(4)
Government transfers	17	20	15	16
	(4)	(5)	(4)	(6)
Government subsidies	3	3	2	3
	(1)	(1)	(1)	(1)
Government indirect taxes	15	15	13	14
	(2)	(2)	(3)	(4)
Government direct taxes	25	28	23	25
	(5)	(6)	(5)	(7)

Note: EU8: Austria, Belgium, Denmark, Finland, France, Greece, Germany, United Kingdom. EU11: EU8 + Italy, Netherlands, Sweden. OECD14: EU8 + Australia, Canada, Japan, Norway, Switzerland, United States. OECD18: OECD14 + Iceland, Italy, Netherlands, Sweden. The sample periods for Norway are 1969–91 and 1978–91. For each country we calculated the mean over time of each fiscal component. For each group the mean of these means is displayed in the table and the standard error of the means is displayed in parentheses. Government transfers do not include interest payments, subsidies, and transfers to the rest of the world.

Table 3.3   The Cyclicality of Fiscal Components (correlation with GDP)

	EU8 1971–93	EU11 1980–93	OECD14 1971–93	OECD18 1980–93
Government consumption	.23	.32	.26	.32
	(.20)	(.34)	(.17)	(.34)
Government transfers	−.07	−.14	−.13	−.20
	(.29)	(.39)	(.26)	(.41)
Government subsidies	.06	−.13	.06	−.11
	(.27)	(.30)	(.27)	(.29)
Government indirect taxes	.68	.60	.66	.62
	(.18)	(.24)	(.15)	(.20)
Government direct taxes	.41	.52	.48	.58
	(.14)	(.30)	(.20)	(.26)

Note: EU8: Austria, Belgium, Denmark, Finland, France, Greece, Germany, United Kingdom. EU11: EU8 + Italy, Netherlands, Sweden. OECD14: EU8 + Australia, Canada, Japan, Norway, Switzerland, United States. OECD18: OECD14 + Iceland, Italy, Netherlands, Sweden. The sample periods for Norway are 1969–91 and 1978–91. For each country, we calculated the correlation of the growth rate of every fiscal component with the growth rate of GDP. The mean of these correlations is displayed in the table and the standard error (across countries) of the correlations is displayed in parentheses.

macroeconomic insurance role of these budget components has increased in recent years.

Table 3.4 displays the fraction of shocks to GDP absorbed by various components of the general public budget. We measure the fraction of shocks smoothed via government consumption by estimating the coefficient in the

Table 3.4   **Smoothing by Fiscal Components (percent)**

	EU8 1971–93	EU11 1980–93	OECD14 1971–93	OECD18 1980–93
Government consumption	13	8	14	13
	(2)	(2)	(1)	(1)
Government transfers	19	19	17	18
	(2)	(2)	(1)	(1)
Government subsidies	4	6	3	4
	(1)	(1)	(1)	(1)
Government indirect taxes	−3	−4	−2	−3
	(2)	(2)	(1)	(1)
Government direct taxes	−15	−2	−9	−5
	(5)	(6)	(3)	(3)

Note: EU8: Austria, Belgium, Denmark, Finland, France, Greece, Germany, United Kingdom. EU11: EU8 + Italy, Netherlands, Sweden. OECD14: EU8 + Australia, Canada, Japan, Norway, Switzerland, United States. OECD18: OECD14 + Iceland, Italy, Netherlands, Sweden. The sample periods for Norway are 1969–91 and 1978–91. Fraction of shocks smoothed via fiscal components. Standard errors in parentheses. For example, smoothing through government consumption is measured by estimating the coefficient in the panel regression (with time-fixed effects) of $\Delta \log \text{DNI}^i - \Delta \log(\text{DNI}^i + \text{government consumption}^i)$ on $\Delta \log \text{GDP}^i$. If DNI + government consumption is less correlated with GDP cross-sectionally than DNI, then the coefficient will be positive, reflecting the fraction of shocks to DNI absorbed by government consumption. The coefficient in the regression of $\Delta \log \text{DNI}^i - \Delta \log(\text{DNI}^i + \text{government transfers}^i)$ on $\Delta \log \text{GDP}^i$ measures the fraction of shocks smoothed via government transfers and similarly for government subsidies. The coefficient in the regression of $\Delta \log \text{DNI}^i - \Delta \log(\text{DNI}^i - \text{taxes}^i)$ on $\Delta \log \text{GDP}^i$ measures the fraction of shocks smoothed via taxes (government direct or indirect taxes, according to the case).

panel regression (with time-fixed effects) of $\Delta\log \text{DNI}^i - \Delta\log(\text{DNI}^i + \text{gov-}$ ernment consumption^i) on $\Delta\log \text{GDP}^i$, that is, we measure the fraction of the cross-sectional variance of GDP absorbed by government consumption. If the cross-sectional correlation of (DNI + government consumption) with GDP is lower than the cross-sectional correlation of DNI with GDP, then the coefficient in this regression should be positive, measuring the fraction of shocks to GDP absorbed by government consumption. The coefficient in the regression of $\Delta\log \text{DNI}^i - \Delta\log(\text{DNI}^i + \text{government transfers}^i)$ on $\Delta\log \text{GDP}^i$ measures the fraction of shocks smoothed via government transfers. Similarly for government subsidies. The coefficient in the regression of $\Delta\log \text{DNI}^i - \Delta\log(\text{DNI}^i - \text{taxes}^i)$ on $\Delta\log \text{GDP}^i$ measures the fraction of shocks smoothed via taxes (government direct or indirect taxes, according to the case).[19]

The results in table 3.4 bear out the above conjecture regarding the consumption-smoothing role of government transfers, which are, indeed, the central mechanism providing consumption smoothing, although substantial

---

19. In relation to the decomposition displayed in table 3.1, the fraction of shocks smoothed by components of the government budget are a further decomposition of the fraction of shocks smoothed via saving.

consumption smoothing is also achieved through government consumption. Even though government consumption varies positively with GDP (table 3.3), it tends to vary less than proportionately with GDP, which reduces the correlation of $C + G$ (total consumption) with GDP, thereby contributing to consumption smoothing. It is worth noting that although government transfers constitute a smaller fraction of GDP compared to government consumption (table 3.2), transfers provide more consumption smoothing since they are less correlated with GDP.[20]

Subsidies also smooth consumption, slightly more in EU countries than in the entire OECD group, and somewhat more in the later sample, as one might expect from table 3.2. It is worth noting that a small and countercyclical component, such as subsidies, can smooth consumption significantly. Direct and indirect taxes dis-smooth consumption. That is, taxes vary less than proportionally with GDP. When income increases by 1 percent, taxes typically increase by less than 1 percent (some taxes, for example taxes on property, may not depend on income in the short run). The amount of dis-smoothing from direct taxes is declining over time, reflecting that direct taxes have become closer to being proportional to income at the annual frequency. Interestingly, the amount of consumption smoothing provided by indirect taxes and subsidies taken together is close to zero. We may be picking up here cross-subsidization among different groups within countries (e.g., indirect energy taxes that help finance subsidies to farmers), while the overall consumption smoothing effect of these two fiscal components appears to be close to zero.

An important consequence of the results in table 3.4 is that consumption smoothing via government deficits is achieved through government consumption, transfers, and subsidies, not through taxes. Barro's (1979) tax-smoothing theory predicts that (if income shocks are transitory, which they may not be) optimal public finance requires that taxes be proportional to income (a constant average tax rate). In our metric, this implies that taxes should provide no consumption smoothing. Our finding that the smoothing is provided only by government consumption, transfers, and subsidies is, therefore, consistent with tax-smoothing theory, although the slight dis-smoothing of shocks by taxes may be an indication of institutional rigidities that result in an average tax rate that is not constant.

Table 3.5 displays the amount of smoothing contributed by fiscal components over three-year horizons. The main finding is that government transfers provide more consumption smoothing over longer horizons and that direct taxes provide less dis-smoothing at the three-year horizon in the EU.[21]

---

20. Sørensen and Yosha (forthcoming), in their analysis of federal insurance mechanisms for U.S. states, use the ratio of the fraction of output shocks smoothed by a fiscal component to the size of that component as a crude measure of its effectiveness in providing income smoothing.

21. Sørensen and Yosha (forthcoming) find that Social Security benefits in the United States smooth about the same fraction of shocks at different frequencies, but that personal income taxes provide considerably more smoothing at the three-year frequency than at the one-year frequency.

Table 3.5   **Smoothing by Fiscal Components (percent): Three-Year Differenced Data**

	EU8 1971–93	OECD14 1971–93
Government consumption	12	10
	(3)	(2)
Government transfers	26	19
	(3)	(2)
Government subsidies	2	1
	(1)	(1)
Government indirect taxes	−3	−2
	(3)	(2)
Government direct taxes	5	−5
	(9)	(5)

Note: EU8: Austria, Belgium, Denmark, Finland, France, Greece, Germany, United Kingdom. OECD14: EU8 + Australia, Canada, Japan, Norway, Switzerland, United States. The sample period for Norway is 1969–91. Fraction of shocks smoothed via fiscal components. Standard errors in parentheses. See the note to table 3.4.

3.3.2   Positive versus Negative Shocks

In tables 3.6 and 3.7 we examine whether fiscal components smooth shocks in an asymmetric fashion, for example, contributing more to consumption smoothing in bad times.[22] For each level of smoothing, we estimate two β coefficients, one for negative shocks and one for positive shocks. To measure smoothing in good and bad times we estimate the panel regression

$$(3) \quad \Delta \log \mathrm{DNI}_t^i - \Delta \log(\mathrm{DNI}_t^i + X_t^i)$$

$$= v_t + \beta D_t^i \, \Delta \log \mathrm{GDP}_t^i + \beta^*(1 - D_t^i)\Delta \log \mathrm{GDP}_t^i + u_t^i,$$

where $D_t^i = 1$ if in year t the country i growth rate of GDP is above the average growth rate (across years) of country i's GDP, and $D_t^i = 0$ in years when the GDP growth rate of country i is below average. β estimates the fraction of shocks absorbed by the generic component X in good times, and similarly for β^* in bad times. The variable X denotes government consumption, government transfers, government subsidies, indirect taxes, and direct taxes, respectively, where taxes are measured with a negative sign.

For OECD countries (table 3.6) there is no visible asymmetry in consumption smoothing through fiscal components, but for EU countries (table 3.7) we see that transfers tend to contribute more to smoothing in recessions. It is, therefore, plausible that the large government transfers in EU countries, driven perhaps by generous social insurance policies, play an important role in generating large government deficits, since increases in transfers during recessions are not easily reversed during upturns. Our result is, of course, only suggestive,

---

22. These regressions do not correct for autocorrelation.

ITHACA COLLEGE LIBRARY

Table 3.6   **Smoothing by Fiscal Components in OECD Countries (percent): Negative versus Positive Shocks**

	Positive Shocks		Negative Shocks	
	OECD14 1971–93	OECD18 1980–93	OECD14 1971–93	OECD18 1980–93
Government consumption	13	12	13	13
	(2)	(2)	(2)	(2)
Government transfers	18	18	17	19
	(2)	(2)	(2)	(2)
Government subsidies	3	4	3	5
	(1)	(1)	(1)	(1)
Government indirect taxes	−2	−1	−2	−4
	(2)	(2)	(2)	(2)
Government direct taxes	−10	−6	−8	−4
	(4)	(5)	(5)	(5)

Note: OECD14: Australia, Austria, Belgium, Canada, Denmark, Finland, France, Germany, Greece, Japan, Norway, Switzerland, United Kingdom, United States. OECD18: OECD14 + Iceland, Italy, Netherlands, Sweden. The sample periods for Norway are 1969–91 and 1978–91. Fraction of shocks smoothed via fiscal components. Standard errors in parentheses. For example, smoothing through government consumption is measured by estimating the coefficients in the panel regression (with time-fixed effects) of $\Delta \log DNI^i - \Delta \log(DNI^i + $ government consumption$^i)$ on $\nu_t + \beta\, D_t^i\, \Delta \log GDP_t^i + \beta^* (1 - D_t^i)\, \Delta \log GDP_t^i + u_t^i$, where $D_t^i = 1$ if in year t the country i growth rate of GDP is above the average GDP growth rate of country i, and $D_t^i = 0$ in years when the GDP growth rate of country i is below average. β estimates the fraction of shocks absorbed by government consumption in good times, and β^* the fraction absorbed in bad times.

Table 3.7   **Smoothing by Fiscal Components in EU Countries (percent): Negative versus Positive Shocks**

	Positive Shocks		Negative Shocks	
	EU8 1971–93	EU11 1980–93	EU8 1971–93	EU11 1980–93
Government consumption	12	10	13	8
	(2)	(3)	(3)	(3)
Government transfers	17	19	23	22
	(2)	(3)	(3)	(3)
Government subsidies	3	5	5	6
	(2)	(2)	(2)	(1)
Government indirect taxes	−1	−2	−3	−2
	(3)	(4)	(2)	(3)
Government direct taxes	−10	−2	−17	−1
	(7)	(10)	(8)	(8)

Note: EU8: Austria, Belgium, Denmark, Finland, France, Greece, Germany, United Kingdom. EU11: EU8 + Italy, Netherlands, Sweden. Fraction of shocks smoothed via fiscal components. Standard errors in parentheses. See the note to table 3.6.

and further research on this issue is necessary before drawing firm conclusions.[23]

3.3.3   Consumption Smoothing and the Deficit Level

We ask whether there is a relation between the level of the deficit and the amount of consumption smoothing achieved via saving. Large government deficits may render private sector and government consumption smoothing more difficult since in countries with a large government deficit, cross-country borrowing is very expensive, perhaps due to a lower credit rating on international financial markets.

In tables 3.8–3.10 we examine whether there is a relation between large government deficits[24] and the amount of consumption smoothing achieved through the government deficit and through private saving. We split the sample into two groups according to the average deficit level over the sample for each country, with the same number of countries in each group.[25] We run the panel regression (3) where the dummy variable is constructed such that $D_t^i = 1$ for all the years in the sample if country i is in the high-deficit group; if not, $D_t^i = 0$, and the generic variable X is either the government deficit or the negative of private saving. The coefficients β and β^* measure the fraction of shocks to GDP smoothed for high- and low-deficit countries, respectively.

There is no evidence that the level of the deficit affects the amount of consumption smoothing provided through the deficit or through private saving. For the EU countries during 1971–93 (table 3.8), the point estimates indicate that smoothing through the government deficit is higher for low-deficit countries, but for the OECD group (table 3.9) there is more smoothing in high-deficit countries. The conflicting point estimates, as well as the high standard errors, give no evidence for a relation between the size of the average deficit and the amount of consumption smoothing obtained via the deficit.

From both tables, it appears that the amount of smoothing through the government deficit has increased during the 1980s, while smoothing through private saving has decreased during the same period. The overall amount of consumption smoothing does not show any systematic differences between the full sample and the 1980–93 sample. Over three-year horizons (table 3.10) only a small fraction of income shocks are smoothed by private saving (the point estimates are even negative for low-deficit countries) with all consumption smoothing being done by the government—confirming similar results in Sørensen and Yosha 1998.

23. See Gavin and Perotti 1997, which displays similar results.
24. All the reported results are for general government deficits. The results are similar when central government deficits are used.
25. In regressions where the number of countries is odd, we include one more country in the high-deficit group.

Table 3.8   **Consumption Smoothing (percent) through Government Budget Deficits and Private Saving: High versus Low Deficit (EU countries)**

	EU8, 1971–93		EU11, 1980–93	
	High Deficit	Low Deficit	High Deficit	Low Deficit
Government saving	16	34	35	34
	(8)	(9)	(9)	(8)
Private saving	37	14	−3	8
	(9)	(9)	(10)	(9)
Total saving	53	48	32	42
	(7)	(6)	(7)	(8)

Note: EU8: Austria, Belgium, Denmark, Finland, France, Greece, Germany, United Kingdom. EU11: EU8 + Italy, Netherlands, Sweden. Fraction of shocks smoothed. Standard errors in parentheses. We run a panel regression analogous to that in table 3.6. If country i is in the high-deficit group, then $D_t^i = 1$ for all the years in the sample; if not, then $D_t^i = 0$. The coefficients β and β^* measure the fraction of shocks to GDP smoothed for high- and low-deficit countries, respectively. The coefficients for government saving and private saving and have been adjusted to add up to the corresponding coefficient for total saving.

Table 3.9   **Consumption Smoothing (percent) through Government Budget Deficits and Private Saving: High versus Low Deficit (OECD countries)**

	OECD14, 1971–93		OECD17, 1980–93	
	High Deficit	Low Deficit	High Deficit	Low Deficit
Government saving	29	20	40	31
	(5)	(6)	(6)	(5)
Private saving	28	14	12	6
	(6)	(6)	(6)	(6)
Total saving	57	34	52	37
	(4)	(5)	(5)	(6)

Note: OECD14: Australia, Austria, Belgium, Canada, Denmark, Finland, France, Germany, Greece, Iceland, Japan, Switzerland, United Kingdom, United States. Relative to the OECD14 sample of table 3.6, Iceland is included and Norway is dropped, due to availability of data. OECD17: OECD14 + Italy, Netherlands, Sweden. Fraction of shocks smoothed. Standard errors in parentheses. See note to table 3.8.

3.3.4   Consumption Smoothing and Fiscal Institutions

Hallerberg and von Hagen (chap. 9 in this volume) found that appropriate budget institutions play an important role in limiting budget deficits. Controlling for various political economy variables that may affect the deficit level, they found that countries where the budgetary process is governed by explicit targets negotiated by coalition members and in countries where power regarding fiscal matters is delegated to a strong party or person (e.g., a strong finance minister), deficits are significantly lower.

We ask whether the institutions examined by Hallerberg and von Hagen (chap. 9 in this volume) contribute to more consumption smoothing via the

Table 3.10   Consumption Smoothing (percent) through Government Budget Deficits and Private Saving: High versus Low Deficits, Three-Year Differenced Data, 1971–93

	EU8		OECD14	
	High Deficit	Low Deficit	High Deficit	Low Deficit
Government saving	34	53	36	32
	(14)	(10)	(11)	(7)
Private saving	12	−5	10	−2
	(9)	(10)	(9)	(7)
Total saving	46	48	47	30
	(15)	(7)	(7)	(6)

Note: Samples are described in notes to tables 3.8 and 3.9. Fraction of shocks smoothed. Standard errors in parentheses. See the note to table 3.8.

budget, or if the fiscal discipline that they provide comes at a cost in terms of less ability to smooth income shocks. Using their data, we split the sample into two groups (of unequal size), with "targets or delegation" countries in one group and the rest of the countries in the other group, estimating the amount of smoothing via fiscal components in each group (using the method explained above). The interesting finding (table 3.11) is that countries in the "targets or delegation" group clearly achieve more consumption smoothing through government consumption and government transfers, suggesting that the institutions that facilitate fiscal discipline also facilitate consumption smoothing via the budget.

Subsidies smooth consumption significantly more in countries outside the "targets or delegation" group.[26] A potential explanation is that countries without strong institutional constraints on the budget process are less able to resist lobbying efforts by industrial and agricultural interests seeking subsidies in recessions.

Another interesting finding is that the total amount of consumption smoothing via saving is very similar across the two groups; namely, there is more consumption smoothing by the private sector in countries that are not in the "targets or delegation" group, compensating for the lower amount of consumption smoothing via the budget. This suggests that there may be some sort of "Second Moment Ricardian Equivalence," that is, more consumption smoothing through government budget deficits crowds out consumption smoothing by households and corporations. This conjecture requires, no doubt, further scrutiny.[27]

Finally, there seems to be more dis-smoothing through direct taxes in coun-

26. Closer inspection of the data reveals that these countries allocate a larger fraction of GDP to subsidies and that subsidies in all these countries vary countercyclically with GDP.
27. The crowding-out phenomenon may be due to the fact that high central-government borrowing makes it harder for the private and local government sectors to obtain credit. If true, this is probably more pronounced in bad times.

Table 3.11   **Smoothing by Fiscal Components (percent): The Role of the Budgetary Process, EU 1980–93**

	Targets or Delegation	
	No	Yes
Government consumption	−2	12
	(4)	(2)
Government transfers	10	22
	(4)	(2)
Government subsidies	10	4
	(2)	(1)
Government indirect taxes	−5	−3
	(5)	(3)
Government direct taxes	7	−10
	(9)	(8)
Total saving	40	35
	(8)	(7)

Note: "No": Countries without fiscal targets or delegation (Belgium, Greece, Italy, Sweden). "Yes": Countries with fiscal targets or delegation (Austria, Denmark, Finland, France, Germany, Netherlands, United Kingdom). Fraction of shocks smoothed via fiscal components. Standard errors in parentheses. We run a panel regression analogous to that in table 3.8. For "Yes" countries $D_t^i = 1$ for all the years in the sample, and for "No" countries $D_t^i = 0$. The coefficients β and β^* measure the fraction of shocks to GDP smoothed for each group, respectively.

tries with "targets or delegation," but this result is somewhat tentative, being marred by very large standard errors.

3.4   Concluding Remarks

Our results have the following implications for the Maastricht guidelines: Since governments provide a large fraction of consumption smoothing, the restrictions on the government deficit should be relaxed to allow governments to run large deficits in recessions. Since large average deficits do not make it easier for governments to smooth consumption, our results do not provide any arguments for relaxing the restrictions on government average debt levels. Wise fiscal policy can combine the benefits from long-run fiscal discipline with the benefits from government consumption smoothing, and our results provide some evidence that proper fiscal institutions will allow countries to achieve this goal.

Of course, there are substantial benefits to consumption smoothing via government fiscal policy only because income insurance on international capital and labor markets, and through international transfers, is practically nonexistent. The optimal long-run solution is probably to encourage the development of private markets for intercountry risk sharing. An important step in this direction is to allow institutional investors in EU countries, such as pension funds and life insurance companies, to invest freely in other countries. Other steps that should contribute to international income smoothing are reductions of international banking transaction costs (to which a common currency may contribute) and harmonization of bank regulations across countries. These measures should increase the cross-country mobility of savings deposits and facilitate international diversification of private, corporate, and institutional asset portfolios. As capital market integration approaches the degree of integration of U.S. markets (see Asdrubali, Sørensen, and Yosha 1996), the need for consumption smoothing through government fiscal policy will be substantially reduced.

References

Altug, Sumru, and Robert A. Miller. 1990. Household choices in equilibrium. *Econometrica* 58:543–70.

Asdrubali, Pierfederico, Bent E. Sørensen, and Oved Yosha. 1996. Channels of interstate risk sharing: United States, 1963–90. *Quarterly Journal of Economics* 111: 1081–1110.

Atkeson, Andrew, and Tamim Bayoumi. 1993. Do private capital markets insure regional risk? Evidence from the United States and Europe. *Open Economies Review* 4:303–24.

Barro, Robert. 1979. On the determination of the public debt. *Journal of Political Economy* 87:940–71.

Bohn, Henning, and Robert Inman. 1996. Balanced-budget rules and public deficits: Evidence from U.S. states. *Carnegie-Rochester Conference Series on Public Policy* 45:13–76.

Canova, Fabio, and Morten Ravn. 1996. International consumption risk sharing. *International Economic Review* 37:573–601.

Cochrane, John H. 1991. A simple test of consumption insurance. *Journal of Political Economy* 99:957–76.

Eichengreen, Barry, and Jürgen von Hagen. 1995. Fiscal policy and monetary union: Federalism, fiscal restrictions, and the no-bailout rule. CEPR Discussion Paper Series no. 1247. London: Centre for Economic Policy Research.

Feldstein, Martin, and Charles Horioka. 1980. Domestic savings and international capital flows. *Economic Journal* 90:314–29.

Frankel, Jeffrey, and Andrew Rose. 1998. The endogeneity of the optimum currency area criteria. *Economic Journal* 108:1009–25.

French, Kenneth, and James Poterba. 1991. Investor diversification and international equity markets. *American Economic Review: Papers and Proceedings* 81:222–26.

Gavin, Michael, Ricardo Hausmann, Roberto Perotti, and Ernesto Talvi. 1996. Managing fiscal policy in Latin America and the Caribbean: Volatility, procyclicality, and limited creditworthiness. Working Paper 326. Inter-American Development Bank, Washington, D.C.

Gavin, Michael, and Roberto Perotti. 1997. Fiscal policy in Latin America. In *NBER macroeconomics annual 1997,* ed. B. Bernanke and J. Rothemberg. Cambridge, Mass.: MIT Press.

Goodhart, Charles, and Stephen Smith. 1993. Stabilization. *European Economy: Reports and Studies* 5:419–55.

Gordon, R., and L. Bovenberg. 1996. Why is capital so immobile internationally? Possible explanations and implications for capital income taxation. *American Economic Review* 86:1057–75.

Hayashi, Fumio, Joseph Altonji, and Laurence Kotlikoff. 1996. Risk-sharing between and within families. *Econometrica* 64:261–94.

Inman, Robert, and Daniel Rubinfeld. 1994. The EMU and fiscal policy in the New European Community: An issue for economic federalism. *International Review of Law and Economics* 14:147–61.

Leiderman, Leonardo, and Assaf Razin, eds. 1994. *Capital mobility: The impact on Consumption, investment, and growth.* New York: Cambridge University Press.

Levhari, David, and Leonard Mirman. 1980. The great fish war: An example using the Cournot Nash solution. *Bell Journal of Economics* 11:322–34.

Lewis, Karen. 1995. Puzzles in international financial markets. In *Handbook of international economics,* ed. Gene Grossman and Kenneth Rogoff. Amsterdam: North Holland.

———. 1996. What can explain the apparent lack of international consumption risk sharing? *Journal of Political Economy* 104:267–97.

Mace, Barbara J. 1991. Full insurance in the presence of aggregate uncertainty. *Journal of Political Economy* 99:928–56.

Obstfeld, Maurice. 1994. Are industrial-country consumption risks globally diversified? In *Capital mobility: The impact on consumption, investment, and growth,* ed. Leonardo Leiderman and Assaf Razin. New York: Cambridge University Press.

Obstfeld, Maurice, and Kenneth Rogoff. 1996. *Foundations of international macroeconomics.* Cambridge, Mass.: MIT Press.

Poterba, James. 1994. State responses to fiscal crises: The effects of budgetary institutions and politics. *Journal of Political Economy* 102:799–821.

Sørensen, Bent E., and Oved Yosha. 1996. Income and consumption smoothing among US states: Regions or clubs? Working paper, Brown University and Tel Aviv University.

———. 1998. International risk sharing and European monetary unification. *Journal of International Economics* 45:211–38.

———. Forthcoming. Federal insurance for US states: An empirical investigation. In *Globalization: Public Economics Policy Perspectives,* ed. Assaf Razin and Efraim Sadka. New York: Cambridge University Press.

Tesar, Linda. 1995. Evaluating the gains from international risk sharing. *Carnegie-Rochester Conference Series on Public Policy* 42:95–143.

Tesar, Linda, and Ingrid Werner. 1995. Home bias and high turnover. *Journal of International Money and Finance* 14:467–92.

Townsend, Robert. 1994. Risk and insurance in village India. *Econometrica* 62:539–91.

van Wincoop, Eric. 1994. Welfare gains from international risk sharing. *Journal of Monetary Economics* 34:175–200.

4 Government Fragmentation and Fiscal Policy Outcomes: Evidence from OECD Countries

Yianos Kontopoulos and Roberto Perotti

4.1 Introduction

This paper investigates on a yearly panel of 20 OECD countries the role of fragmentation in decision making as a determinant of fiscal outcomes.

In very broad terms, fragmentation arises when several agents or groups participate in the fiscal decision-making process, each with its own interests and constituency to satisfy, and each with some weight in the final decision. To participate in the majority, each group demands a share in the budget; as all groups do this, the end result is a high level of expenditure or a large deficit.[1]

At this level of generality, the view that fragmentation is responsible for the high levels of expenditure and deficits observed in industrialized countries in the last 25 years is widely held in both academic and policy circles. Yet, when it comes to empirically testing this notion, one quickly realizes that conceptually fragmentation can take many forms, and each concept can be measured in many ways. Some theoretical guidance is needed.

As we argue in Kontopoulos and Perotti 1997, fragmentation of the fiscal policy decision-making process is closely related to the notion of internalization of the costs of fiscal policy. High expenditure and possibly high deficits result when *individual* policymakers do not fully internalize the costs of *aggre-*

Yianos Kontopoulos is a currency strategist at Merrill Lynch, Pierce, Fenner & Smith Inc. Roberto Perotti is professor of economics at Columbia University and a research associate of the Centre for Economic Policy Research, London.

This paper was written while Yianos Kontopoulos was at Columbia University. The views expressed here are solely those of the authors. The authors thank seminar participants at the Columbia University Political Economy Workshop for comments on an earlier version of the paper. Yianos Kontopoulos gratefully acknowledges financial support from the Onassis Foundation.

1. In its basic form, this intuition has been first formalized in the static "common pool" models of Weingast, Shepsle, and Johnsen (1981) and Shepsle and Weingast (1981), and subsequently extended in numerous papers. See Alesina and Perotti 1995 and Velasco 1995 for a survey of this literature.

gate expenditure and the associated taxation. This occurs because the expenditure proposed by each agent in the majority can be closely targeted to the group he or she represents, while revenues with their distortionary costs can be spread over a large number of groups.

Two key factors determine how much each agent in the majority internalizes the costs of the fiscal outcome: the number of decision makers participating in the process and the rules that govern the aggregation of preferences, that is, the set of procedures whereby a final decision is arrived at. As the number of decision makers gets larger, each will pay a smaller share of the revenue costs of each dollar of expenditure he or she proposes; the marginal cost of expenditure to each policymaker falls, and in equilibrium each will propose a higher expenditure. As a result, aggregate expenditure will also increase. The budget process is the second important determinant because it determines the game played by decision makers. For example, if the finance minister sets the total *size* of expenditure first, theoretically he or she is in a position to better internalize the costs of aggregate expenditure, and individual policymakers can only bargain over the *distribution* of this expenditure. At the other extreme, if the budget is just the sum of bids made by individual ministers, without any coordination from the top, the degree of internalization of the costs of expenditure will be at a minimum.

In this paper, we focus on the first determinant, the number of decision makers. As we show in Kontopoulos and Perotti 1997, conceptually there are two very different interpretations of this notion, depending on the basic decision-making unit one assumes. In one interpretation, the emphasis is on the legislative side of the fiscal decision-making process. In this case, the elementary unit could be the individual legislator. An empirically more relevant rendition of this interpretation would view the party in the ruling coalition as the basic decision-making unit, on the ground that—for the purposes of fiscal decision making—a party is a more or less cohesive entity representing the interests of specific groups. Thus, the first measure of fragmentation we use is simply the number of parties in the coalition, which we also call *coalition size*.

The second interpretation emphasizes the executive side of the fiscal decision-making process. Hence, the elementary unit is a spending minister. The rationale is that each spending minister participates in the formulation of, and makes demands on, the overall budget. Thus, the second measure of fragmentation we use is the number of spending ministers, which we also call *cabinet size*.

Conceptually, we see no a priori reason to privilege the first, "legislative" interpretation over the second, "executive" interpretation. In fact, all the models that apply to the former—in particular, the seminal "common pool" models of Weingast, Shepsle, and Johnsen (1981) and Shepsle and Weingast (1981) and their numerous extensions—can be applied, with a simple relabeling of variables, to the latter.

Yet without exception, all the existing empirical literature has focused on the first, "legislative" interpretation of fragmentation, and almost invariably on a very specific variant of this notion. In a seminal contribution, Roubini and Sachs (1989a,b) focused on the effects of a variable that can be termed "government weakness," assigning progressively higher scores to single-party majority, small coalition, large coalition, and minority governments. Based on a sample of 20 OECD countries over the period 1960–85, they concluded that deficits do tend to be positively associated with this variable. In subsequent research, Edin and Ohlsson (1991) found that practically all this effect was due to minority governments. Still later, de Haan and Sturm (1994) concluded that, over the period 1982–95, even this effect does not seem to be robust. Much of the difference in these findings seems to be due to considerable differences in the coding of several governments in several countries.

We see three main shortcomings in this exclusive emphasis on the notion of government weakness. First, this measure has a weak theoretical underpinning, and it can be unrelated to the notion of fragmentation. For instance, it is not clear that a minority government with many parties should be regarded as more fragmented than a single-party majority government. Second, it can be highly subjective: witness the large discrepancy in the classification between, say, Roubini and Sachs (1989b) and de Haan and Sturm (1994). Third, it neglects entirely any notion of "executive" fragmentation.

Thus, throughout this paper, we try to use measures of fragmentation with a well-defined theoretical counterpart, and as objectively measurable and quantifiable as possible. Armed with these measures, we explicitly test the two interpretations of the notion of fragmentation—"legislative" and "executive"—against each other.

As we first showed in Kontopoulos and Perotti 1997, executive fragmentation appears to be extremely important—both economically and statistically—as a determinant of fiscal outcomes. By contrast, legislative fragmentation, in its various forms—government weakness and coalition size—seems to be much less important and robust. These conclusions are of potential policy relevance because the size of a cabinet is typically not a constitutional issue, and in fact it can vary considerably over time within each country. By contrast, the size of a coalition is typically the result of historical traditions and of the whole structure of the political process—such as the electoral system—which are often deeply grounded in the constitutional framework and in the historical and cultural background of a country, and therefore are much less likely to be amenable to change.

Because of their potential policy relevance, it is important to check the robustness of our basic results. This is particularly so because the conclusions of the literature in the tradition of Roubini and Sachs have proved to be extremely sensitive to the sample of countries, the sample period, the specification, the form of the government weakness variable (whether as separate dummy variables or a single variable), the form of the fiscal policy variables (whether as shares of GDP or logarithms of real variables, whether in levels or differences, etc.), to the point that hardly any definite conclusion can be drawn with any reasonable degree of confidence.

Thus, in this paper we conduct an extensive sensitivity and robustness analysis of our basic results on "legislative" and "executive" fragmentation. As a consequence, we must necessarily narrow the scope of our empirical investigation. As mentioned above, we exclude from the present investigation the role of *procedural* fragmentation, that is, of the set of rules that constitute the budget process. The effects of procedural variables have been studied on panels of OECD countries by de Haan and Sturm (1994), Hallerberg and von Hagen (chap. 9 in this volume), and Kontopoulos and Perotti (1997), with mixed conclusions. One reason for these inconclusive results is that the budget process varies very little over time, so that it is very difficult to estimate its effects given the small cross-sectional dimension of the panel of OECD countries.[2] We also exclude from our investigation the role of fragmentation over time, that is, the effects of government instability and of the frequency of government turnovers. Grilli, Masciandaro, and Tabellini (1991) show that this variable seems to be positively associated with budget deficits, although here also there are considerable problems of definition, measurement, and robustness.[3]

Our main finding is that the relationship between executive fragmentation (i.e., cabinet size) and fiscal outcome is indeed very robust during the seventies and early eighties. In the following period, it is legislative fragmentation (i.e., coalition size) that is more strongly related to fiscal outcomes, although this relationship is somewhat less robust. We argue that these differences across the two periods make sense, given the different types of shocks policymakers faced.

The organization of the chapter is as follows. In the next section we briefly describe our data set. Section 4.3 introduces the basic estimation framework and discusses some key aspects of it. Section 4.4 presents the basic regressions. In section 4.5, we perform a number of robustness and sensitivity tests on our benchmark regressions. Section 4.6 concludes.

4.2   The Data

Our database includes 20 countries and covers the period 1960–95.[4] In this section, we describe the fiscal and political variables.

All the budget data we use refer to the general government and come, with a few exceptions mentioned later, from the OECD Economic Outlook and National Income Account data sets. The available data sets contain several gaps,

2. The empirical literature on the effects of procedural variables in U.S. states is much larger, and growing. For a survey, see Poterba 1994 and Inman 1996.

3. Estimating the effects of fragmentation over time poses problems similar to those of procedural fragmentation: the frequency of government turnover must be measured over time, and therefore one essentially ends up with cross-sectional estimates.

4. The countries are Australia, Austria, Belgium, Canada, Denmark, Finland, France, Germany, Greece, Ireland, Italy, Japan, Netherlands, Norway, Portugal, Spain, Switzerland, Sweden, United Kingdom, and United States.

mainly due to the shift from the old to the new system of national accounts in many OECD countries during the seventies. We combine the two sets of data to fill most of the gaps without sacrificing comparability of the data. In a few country-years, the two data sets mentioned above were supplemented with data from two other sources: the Revenue Statistics of OECD Member Countries, and EUROSTAT's National Income Accounts. Both these data sets also follow the guidelines of the new system of national accounts and are usually identical to the other two sources when they overlap. Perotti 1998 contains more details on the construction of this data set. As a result of these amendments, the data set contains consistent series on the primary deficit and all its major components covering all the years 1960–95 for all the 20 countries in the sample, with the exception of 23 country-years.

To preserve the comparability of the definitions both over time and across countries, our definition of the primary deficit is slightly different from the conventional one. We define the primary deficit as the difference between expenditure and taxes, net of all net property income. On the expenditure side, property income comprises mainly interests, but on the revenues side it also comprises items like rents and the "operating surplus" of the government that are normally included in the definition of the primary deficit. These items seem to be less consistently defined across countries, and the breakdown between interest and other property income is not available before 1970. We also exclude capital transfers paid by the government from the expenditure side, and current and capital transfers received by the government on the revenue side. These three items have a rather spotty coverage in the databases that we use, particularly for the 1960s and for some countries, so that their inclusion would have introduced substantial breaks in the series and in the consistency of the definitions; in any case, these items are typically very small and therefore are unlikely to affects our results substantially.[5] In addition, there is no reason to expect that their exclusion biases the year-to-year movements in fiscal outcomes—on which we focus in our paper—in any particular direction.

We used three principles in constructing our political data. First, because we have a precise definition of fragmentation, we concentrate on measuring its two interpretations—"legislative" and "executive"—as directly as possible; that is, we try to construct the variable that most immediately captures each component of the definition of fragmentation. Second, while some element of subjectivity is unavoidable when political variables are involved, we focus on quantifiable measures as much as possible. In classifying these governments, we rely exclusively on external sources (from the political science literature mostly) that were also cross-checked several times. Third, we exert a specific effort to match the political variables with fiscal data by tracking the investiture date and thus the duration of the governments, so that we can establish an accurate connection between the institutional framework and the fiscal policy outcome.

---

5. Recall that our fiscal variables refer to the general government, and therefore all intergovernmental transfers—which can be substantial—are consolidated in our figures.

To classify governments, we must first define them. With annual data, it is not always obvious how to associate the fiscal outcome of a given calendar year with a specific type of government. We follow two criteria. First, we exclude all governments with a duration of less than 60 days, under the assumption that they are too short-lived to have any influence on fiscal outcomes. Second, we pay particular attention to the month of investiture of a government. Because of the long decision and implementation lags, a new government that is formed toward the end of a year is most likely irrelevant for the fiscal results of that year. Hence, we assume that only governments that were formed before the beginning of August of any given year have any significant impact on the fiscal outcome of that year. Obviously, this cutoff point is somewhat arbitrary; hence, we also run our regressions with three different cutoff dates (June, July, September). Since the results are robust to these variations, we present only one set of results in order to economize on space. When there is more than one government before August, all lasting longer than two months, we average the characteristics of the governments of that year, with weights equal to the duration of each government.[6]

In the following two subsections, we briefly describe the construction of the two political variables.

4.2.1   Number of Parties in Coalition (NPC)

As we discuss above, one key criterion in our investigation is to use a direct and unambiguous measure of the two notions of fragmentation that we are investigating. The measure of coalition size that most closely matches its definition is just the total number of parties in the coalition, which we denote "NPC."

The primary source for this variable is Woldendorp, Keman, and Budge 1993, a special issue of the *European Journal of Political Research* (EJPR) with a wealth of information on each government in parliamentary democracies in the postwar period. The data set has been updated annually. The United States, Greece, Portugal, and Spain are not covered in the EJPR database;[7] the first, because it is a presidential system; the latter three, because in the initial parts of the period they were not run by democratic regimes. For these countries, we used the *Europa Yearbook* (EY), an annual publication with information on each country in the world and its government.

4.2.2   Number of Spending Ministers (NSM)

The most immediate measure of the notion of cabinet size that descends from the discussion in the introductory section is simply the number of spending ministers. We construct this variable as the sum of the following ministers: (i) industry, trade, or ministers with related or subdivided competencies like

6. In another robustness exercise we also ran the bulk of our regressions with a data set that included all governments irrespective of their duration and averaged (weighted) their characteristics in each year. This somewhat agnostic procedure did not significantly alter any of our results.

7. The annual updates cover these countries.

foreign trade, commerce, and state industries (if not attributed to public works—see next); (ii) public works, infrastructure, or ministers with related or subdivided competencies like (public) transportation, energy, post, telecommunications, merchant marine, civil aviation, national resources, construction (if not specifically attributed to housing—see below), urban development, and so forth; (iii) defense; (iv) justice; (v) labor; (vi) education; (vii) health; (viii) housing; (ix) agriculture. We also add all ministers with economics portfolios: (x) finance or ministers with related or subdivided competencies like First Lord of the Treasury, budget, taxation, and so on; (xi) economic affairs or ministers with related or subdivided competencies like (regional) economic planning or development, or small business.

The primary source for this variable is Woldendorp, Keman, and Budge 1993. However, because this source also reports, under each portfolio, all the ministers that held the same portfolio sequentially due to government reshuffles, to avoid overcounting portfolios we cross-checked each entry with the annual volumes of the *Europa Yearbook*.

4.3 Setting up the Basic Framework

Before we can start estimating the effects of fragmentation, we need to discuss the basic approach to estimating the model. Some of this discussion follows Kontopoulos and Perotti 1997; therefore we will keep it at a minimum here.

Our basic specification is of the following form:

$$X_t - X_{t-1} = \alpha_0 + \alpha_1 NPC_t + \alpha_2 NSM_t + \alpha_3 NPC_t*DY_t$$

(1)
$$+ \alpha_4 NSM_t*DY_t + \alpha_5 DY_t + \alpha_6 DU_t + \alpha_7 INFL_t$$

$$+ \varepsilon_t,$$

where X_t is a fiscal policy variable, which can be the deficit, total expenditure, or total revenues; DY_t is the rate of growth of GDP; DU_t is the change in the unemployment rate; $INFL_t$ is the rate of inflation of the consumer price index; NPC_t and NSM_t are the two indices of fragmentation, and are defined as the number of parties in the coalition and the number of spending ministers, respectively; NPC_t*DY_t and NSM_t*DY_t represent the interaction of these two indices with the rate of growth of GDP.

Since the early contributions, virtually all empirical investigations have focused on the effects of political and institutional variables on the *deficit*. Yet, the theoretical case for an effect of fragmentation on expenditure is much stronger than for the effects on the deficit. For instance, in the static common pool models à la Weingast, Shepsle, and Johnsen (1981) the budget is obviously balanced. Hence, any effect of fragmentation must be on both expenditures and revenues, with no effect on the deficit.

One might think that the basic intuition of the effects of fragmentation should be easily generalizable to the dynamic case. Indeed, Velasco (1995) develops a dynamic extension of a "common pool" model where, as the number of decision makers increases, the deficit increases. But this is the result of the specific functional forms assumed in the model, and there is no general intuition for the overall sign of the relationship between the number of policymakers and the deficit in the models.[8] In fact, Lane and Tornell (1996) present a slightly different dynamic extension of a "common pool" model, where the relationship between the number of decision makers and the deficit is nonlinear. Thus, in dynamic "common pool" models the presumption that fragmentation leads to higher deficits does not seem to lend itself to an easy and general formalization. Spolaore (1993) is just about the only contribution we are aware of where there is a direct relationship between the number of decision makers and the deficit, although only in response to a negative shock. The context, however, is slightly different—a combination of the Alesina and Drazen (1991) "war of attrition" model and of the Tabellini and Alesina (1990) "strategic motive" for deficit.

This discussion suggests estimating the effects of fragmentation on expenditure and revenues separately: even in theory, fragmentation might not manifest itself in the deficit, but only in expenditure, and limiting the investigation to the deficit might lead to very misleading conclusions. In addition, disaggregating the deficit into revenues and expenditure sheds considerable light on the channels by which fragmentation affects fiscal outcomes.

This brief theoretical discussion implies that, under the null hypothesis we test, $\alpha_1 > 0$ and $\alpha_3 > 0$ when the dependent variable is expenditure: virtually all theories would imply this hypothesis. When the dependent variable is revenues, however, the existing theories offer much less guidance. Indeed, both a positive and a negative value for α_1 and α_3 can be rationalized in this case. As a consequence, when the dependent variable is the deficit, we expect α_1 and α_3 to be positive or 0.

In equation (1), the two political variables, NPC and NSM, appear also interacted with the rate of growth of GDP, DY. The interactive terms capture the plausible, but rarely tested, notion that political and institutional factors might be particularly important, as determinants of policies, in "difficult" times. This notion, which is part of the conventional wisdom of policymaking, has been formalized in Drazen and Grilli 1993 and also plays a role in Spolaore 1993 and Velasco 1995; more discursive treatments and short historical discussion are in, among others, Bruno and Fischer 1993 and Tommasi and Velasco 1996. The hypothesis we test is that fragmentation is particularly "bad" for fiscal policy in "difficult" times: hence, we expect $\alpha_2 < 0$ and $\alpha_4 < 0$ when the dependent variable is expenditure or the deficit.

Our basic specification also includes a number of macroeconomic variables—DY_t, DU_t and $INFL_t$. There are two reasons for this: first, to capture

8. Personal communication to the authors.

the effects of the macroeconomic environment on expenditure, via automatic mechanisms like unemployment subsidies, and on revenues, because, for instance, of the progressivity of income taxes. Second, these economic variables capture the reaction function of the policymaker. When the dependent variable is aggregate expenditure, we expect $\alpha_5 < 0$, $\alpha_6 > 0$, and $\alpha_7 < 0$; when the dependent variable is revenues, we expect $\alpha_5 > 0$, $\alpha_6 < 0$, and $\alpha_7 > 0$. These are all intuitive signs for these coefficients, and we comment on them more extensively in Kontopoulos and Perotti 1997.

All regressions in the benchmark specification also include a full set of country and year dummies, whose role we study extensively in section 4.5.

Finally, all the fiscal policy variables we use in this paper are cyclically unadjusted and are expressed as changes in GDP shares. In Kontopoulos and Perotti 1997, we use cyclically adjusted fiscal variables. There are advantages and disadvantages in both strategies. In testing the effects of political and institutional factors, presumably one is interested only in the noncyclical changes in fiscal policy. This calls for using cyclically adjusted figures only if (i) political and institutional variables are correlated with cyclical conditions, and (ii) controlling for GR, DU, and INFL is insufficient, for instance because the elasticity of fiscal outcomes to growth differs across countries. On the other hand, cyclically adjusted figures are provided by international organizations only from 1973 at the earliest, and there is no commonly accepted methodology to cyclically adjust fiscal outcomes, so that all figures involve a large degree of subjectivity and may well involve some additional noise. In addition, using unadjusted GDP shares allows us a more direct comparison with existing results, since this is the definition that has been used in most of the literature.

4.4 Basic Results

Table 4.1 illustrates the basic results. Throughout the table, the dependent variables are the first differences in the ratio of deficit and expenditure to GDP. Table 4.1 delivers three main messages. First, disaggregating the deficit into expenditure and revenues is crucial. Looking at the first two columns, displaying regressions on the whole sample, it is clear that NSM is an important and very significant determinant of the deficit, and that its effects occur almost exclusively via aggregate expenditures.[9] By contrast, by looking only at the deficit one would fail to detect any significant effect of NPC; this is because NPC affects both expenditures and revenues in the same direction, although it is significant only in the expenditure regression. Note that this finding might help explain many negative results in recent papers, like those of de Haan and Sturm (1994), who mostly focused on the eighties and early nineties and failed to detect any significant effect of the "government weakness" variable.

---

9. Obviously, the coefficient of all variables in the revenue regression is exactly equal to the coefficient in the expenditure regression less the coefficient in the deficit regression.

Table 4.1   Fragmentation and the Determination of Fiscal Outcome

	ΔDEF 1960–95 (1)	ΔEXP 1960–95 (2)	ΔDEF 1960–73 (3)	ΔEXP 1960–73 (4)	ΔDEF 1974–83 (5)	ΔEXP 1974–83 (6)	ΔDEF 1984–95 (7)	ΔEXP 1984–95 (8)
NPC	.06	.12	.07	.16	–.03	–.02	.50	.29
	(0.80)	(2.15)	(0.39)	(1.26)	(–0.21)	(–0.20)	(2.92)	(2.27)
NSM	.15	.18	–.04	.01	.23	.24	.00	.06
	(3.19)	(4.88)	(–0.47)	(0.08)	(2.22)	(3.25)	(0.63)	(0.63)
NPC*DY	–.01	–.02	–.01	–.02	.05	.00	–.04	–.04
	(–0.45)	(–2.22)	(–0.22)	(–0.85)	(1.76)	(0.14)	(–1.65)	(–2.00)
NSM*DY	–.02	–.01	–.02	–.02	–.03	–.02	–.01	.01
	(–2.64)	(–2.12)	(–1.45)	(–1.82)	(–2.21)	(–1.58)	(–0.29)	(0.66)
DY	.10	–.12	.14	–.02	.06	–.21	–.08	–.38
	(1.07)	(–1.67)	(0.86)	(–0.18)	(0.36)	(–1.61)	(–0.34)	(–2.27)
DU	.44	.09	.49	.13	.28	–.00	.38	.00
	(5.60)	(1.52)	(2.35)	(0.85)	(1.73)	(–0.02)	(3.14)	(0.03)
INFL	–.07	–.02	–.12	–.03	–.13	–.12	–.04	–.05
	(–3.24)	(–1.42)	(–2.40)	(–0.96)	(–2.57)	(–3.19)	(–0.64)	(–1.11)
R^2	.31	.57	.08	.46	.30	.59	.39	.59
N	641	641	207	207	195	195	239	239

Note: NPC: number of parties in coalition; NSM: number of spending ministers; DEF: primary deficit (see text for precise definition); EXP: primary expenditure; REV: primary revenue; DY: rate of growth of GDP; DU: change in unemployment; INFL: rate of change of CPI. All fiscal variables are first differences of their shares in GDP. All regressions include year and country dummies.

Second, there is indeed some evidence that both NPC and NSM are more important in bad than in good times. At zero GDP growth, an extra party in the coalition adds on average 0.12 percent of GDP per annum to aggregate expenditure; but this effect increases by 0.02 percent of GDP for any percentage point of negative GDP growth, so that at 5.0 percent negative growth an extra party in the coalition is associated with an increase in aggregate expenditure by 0.22 percent of GDP. Similarly, at zero GDP growth an extra spending minister adds 0.18 percent of GDP per annum to aggregate expenditure, and 0.23 percent at 5.0 percent negative growth. These are substantial numbers, if one considers that in the sample the number of parties in the coalition ranges from one to five, and the number of spending ministers from 5 (in Switzerland) to 18 (in Italy).

Third, disaggregating the whole 1960–94 period into its three main decades is also of crucial importance. As one would expect, political and institutional variables have very little effect on fiscal policy in the 1960s, a decade characterized by more or less stable growth and little fiscal action in most countries of the sample. The two subsequent decades show much more action, but in very different ways. In the seventies, the coefficient of NSM is positive and highly significant in both the deficit and expenditure regressions, while the coefficient of NPC is virtually 0. In the 1980s, exactly the opposite is true (in addition, the coefficient of NPC is negative in the revenue regression, so that the coefficient in the deficit regression is virtually double that in the expenditure regression).

This difference between the last two decades is striking, and it is so significant that it is unlikely to be due to chance alone. We believe the interpretation lies in the nature of the fiscal shocks in the two decades. In the seventies, the problem common to all countries was how to best contain the growth of expenditure in response to an external negative shock. In the eighties, the main shock to fiscal policy was internal, and the dividing line was between those countries that engaged in large discretionary consolidations and those that did not. The decision to engage in a fiscal consolidation is largely political and requires a cohesive government agreeing on such a fundamental decision. Consequently, one would expect coalition size to play a particularly important role in the last decade. By contrast, in the seventies the goal—containing the growth of expenditure—was common in all countries: how well a country could attain it depended, among other things, on how the executive decision-making process was organized. Hence, one would expect cabinet size to matter particularly in this decade.

These are the three basic results of our approach. In the next section, we start exploring their robustness. Because, as we have shown, virtually nothing is significant in the regressions for the sixties, from now on we will concentrate mostly on the last two decades.

4.5   Robustness and Sensitivity

4.5.1   The Role of Country and Time-Fixed Effects

In table 4.2, we explore the role of country and year dummies. This is a particularly important issue given our sample and the nature of the estimation problem. The macroeconomic shocks that influence fiscal outcomes are likely to be highly correlated across countries. Year dummies can then parcel out the effects of these shocks if the latter are only partially captured by the macroeconomic variables we control for—GR, DU, and INFL. Perhaps even more important is the role of country-fixed effects. On the right-hand side of our regressions we have several political and institutional variables, which are arguably highly correlated with unobservable and time-invariant cultural and historical country-specific characteristics. If the latter also affect the rate of growth of expenditure and revenues, it is extremely important to control for country-fixed effects in order to eliminate this source of endogeneity bias.

The first four columns of table 4.2 display deficit and expenditure regressions with time-fixed effects only. This has rather drastic effects on the estimated coefficients. In the seventies, the coefficient of NSM remains highly significant in both regressions, but its point estimate is cut to about a half. In the eighties, the coefficient of NPC falls much more drastically in both size and significance, and it is now very far from being statistically significant.

In the next four columns of table 4.2, only country-fixed effects are present. Now even the coefficient of NSM in the seventies becomes insignificant, while the coefficient of NPC in the eighties remains significant, although only in the deficit regression.

These results clearly highlight the importance of controlling for time- and country-fixed effects in our regressions. From now on, all our regressions will include both.

4.5.2   Outliers

Before making further inference from the results we have obtained, it is important to make sure that they are not unduly influenced by the inclusion of individual countries, always a real possibility in panels with a small cross-sectional component like the present one. To address this issue, we started by reestimating all our regressions excluding one country at a time. The results of this procedure, reported in table 4.3, reveal a considerable difference between the robustness of the effects of cabinet size and coalition size.

The first panel reports the maximum p-values of the coefficients of NPC, DY*NPC, NSM, DY*NSM in the main regressions, the corresponding point estimate, and the country whose exclusion leads to the maximum p-value of that coefficient. From our previous analysis, we are particularly interested in the coefficients involving cabinet size in the seventies, and the coefficients involving coalition size in the eighties. As one can see, no single country has an overwhelming influence on the coefficients and their significance. The exclu-

Table 4.2   The Role of Time- and Country-Fixed Effects

	ΔDEF 1974–83 (1)	ΔEXP 1974–83 (2)	ΔDEF 1984–95 (3)	ΔEXP 1984–95 (4)	ΔDEF 1974–83 (5)	ΔEXP 1974–83 (6)	ΔDEF 1984–95 (7)	ΔEXP 1984–95 (8)
NPC	−.06	.05	.04	.06	.07	.14	.37	.16
	(−0.70)	(0.76)	(0.46)	(0.91)	(0.43)	(1.03)	(2.11)	(1.16)
NSM	.12	.13	−.03	−.03	.15	.14	.16	.16
	(2.73)	(3.64)	(−0.50)	(−0.75)	(1.34)	(1.68)	(1.25)	(1.62)
NPC*DY	.04	−.02	−.04	−.04	.01	−.02	−.04	−.04
	(1.40)	(−0.72)	(−1.69)	(−2.11)	(0.47)	(−0.78)	(−1.50)	(−1.88)
NSM*DY	−.03	−.02	−.01	.01	−.02	.00	−.02	.00
	(−2.74)	(−2.09)	(−0.35)	(0.78)	(−1.29)	(0.00)	(−0.94)	(0.14)
DY	.17	−.06	−.06	−.37	−.04	−.34	.00	−.35
	(1.07)	(−0.46)	(−0.27)	(−2.26)	(−0.20)	(−2.27)	(0.00)	(−1.99)
DU	.27	.06	.38	.07	.22	−.03	.35	.05
	(1.91)	(0.58)	(3.34)	(0.82)	(1.34)	(−0.23)	(3.10)	(0.61)
INFL	−.06	.01	−.03	−.02	−.04	.02	−.01	.01
	(−2.45)	(0.30)	(−1.20)	(−0.83)	(−0.80)	(0.50)	(−0.16)	(0.26)
R^2	.33	.55	.39	.57	.10	.41	.33	.53
N	195	195	239	239	195	195	239	239

Note: Columns 1 to 4: only year dummies; columns 5 to 8: only country dummies. See also note to table 4.1.

Table 4.3   Sensitivity Analysis of the Country Sample

Dependent variable Period	ΔDEF 1974–83		ΔEXP 1974–83		ΔDEF 1984–95		ΔEXP 1984–95	
Coefficient	NSM (1)	NSM*DY (2)	NSM (3)	NSM*DY (4)	NPC (5)	NPC*DY (6)	NPC (7)	NPC*DY (8)
Maximum p-value, Individual Significance								
Coefficient estimate	.21	−.02	.24	−.01	.42	.00	.22	−.02
Maximum *p*-value	0.10	0.07	0.01	0.61	0.02	0.36	0.11	0.52
Country excluded	FRA	IRE	FRA	CHE	FIN	DNK	FIN	FIN
Maximum p-value, Joint Significance								
Coefficient estimate	.19	−.03	.24	−.02	.42	−.03	.22	−.03
Maximum *p*-value		0.05		0.02		0.07		0.33
Country excluded		BEL		FRA		FIN		FIN
Greece, Portugal, Spain, United States Excluded								
Coefficient estimate	.18	−.03	.19	−.02	.28	−.02	.14	−.02
p-value	0.10	0.02	0.01	0.04	0.11	0.41	0.26	0.31
p-value, joint		0.03		0.01		0.27		0.44
Greece, Portugal Excluded								
Coefficient estimate	.20	−.03	.20	−.02	.32	−.03	.19	−.03
p-value	0.05	0.03	0.00	0.04	0.06	0.22	0.13	0.11
p-value, joint		0.02		0.00		0.14		0.17

Note: First panel: each column reports the maximum *p*-value (second line) and the corresponding point estimate (first line) of the coefficient indicated at the top of the column, out of the 19 regressions estimated by dropping one country at a time. The third line reports the country excluded. Second panel: same as in the first panel, except that the reported maximum *p*-value is that of a test of a joint significance of the two coefficients. Third panel: Greece, Portugal, Spain, and United States excluded. Fourth panel: Greece, Portugal excluded. See also note to table 4.1.

sion of France causes the p-value of the coefficient of NSM in the deficit regression of the seventies to become significant only at the 10 percent level, and so does the exclusion of Finland to the coefficient of NPC in the expenditure regression of the eighties. But the coefficient of NSM in the expenditure regression of the seventies and the coefficient of NPC in the deficit regression of the eighties are always well below the 5 percent significance level. The point estimates of the relevant coefficients are also remarkably close to the benchmark estimates of table 4.2.

The picture is slightly different for the interactive terms. The exclusion of just one country makes the coefficient of NSM*DY in column 4 or the coefficient of NPC*DY in column 8 lose its statistical significance, with p-values of .61 and .52, respectively. Although we report only the highest p-value, corresponding to the exclusion of Finland, the interactive term NPC*DY becomes insignificant when just one of several other countries is excluded.

Although the interactive terms do appear to be sensitive to the inclusion of individual countries, one could argue that what matters is really the joint significance of the coefficients of the fragmentation variable and its interactive term. The second panel of table 4.3 reports maximum p-values for tests of the joint significance of the two coefficients listed at the top of the table, together with the associated excluded country. The coefficients of NSM and NSM*DY are always jointly significant, with a maximum p-value of .05. By contrast, when Finland is excluded, the coefficients of NPC and NPC*DY have a joint significance level of about .07 and .33 in the deficit and expenditure regressions. Thus, the analysis of the joint significance gives a considerably more robust impression than the analysis of the individual coefficients.

Recall that, in constructing our data set of political and institutional variables, for four countries—Greece, Portugal, Spain, and the United States—we had to use a different source than for all the others. In addition, one could question the inclusion of the first three countries, on the ground that they were not democracies until the mid-1970s, and of the United States, on the ground that it is not a parliamentary regime and therefore the notion of coalition size is somewhat less clear cut. The criticism concerning Greece, Portugal, and Spain hardly applies to the regressions we have presented, since they cover the period 1974–95, and therefore include very few years of nondemocratic regime in these countries. However, the role of these countries still warrants further investigation, albeit for a different reason: the fiscal data of Greece and Portugal are widely regarded to be somewhat less reliable than those of the other countries, particularly in the early part of the sample.[10]

When the basic benchmark regression is estimated without the four countries (see the third panel of table 4.3), one finds that the coefficients of NSM and NSM*DY are robust, but once again the coefficients of NPC are much less so: both the coefficient estimates and their significance drop drastically.

---

10. For instance, Portugal revalued its gold reserves in the mid-1970s, causing a large change in the deficit.

On further investigation, one finds that this result is mostly due to precisely the two countries mentioned above: Portugal and Greece. It is sufficient to exclude these two countries (as in the last panel of table 4.3) for the *p*-value of NPC in both the expenditure and deficit regressions to rise to .06 and .23, respectively, and for the *p*-value for the joint significance of NPC and NPC*DY to rise to .14 and .17.

Whether these are considered gross violations of the benchmark results with the whole sample is largely a subjective matter. Two countries represent more than 20 percent of the sample, and they might contain useful information that should not be wasted. Nevertheless, a conservative conclusion from this preliminary robustness analysis is that the role of cabinet size appears much more robust than the role of coalition size, in particular as concerns the asymmetric role of fragmentation in good and bad times.

4.5.3   Alternative Definitions of the Dependent Variables

In tables 4.4 and 4.5 we explore the robustness of our results to alternative constructions of the fiscal variables on the left-hand side. Some sensitivity to the specific construction of the dependent variables has emerged in the literature on government weakness.[11] In addition, in a large part of the existing literature the dependent variable is defined as the change in net or gross debt, rather than the deficit or its components.

We start in table 4.4 by considering three alternative constructions of the aggregate expenditure variable on the left-hand side, and in all cases we focus on aggregate expenditure in the last two decades, where, as we have seen, most of the action is concentrated. In the first two columns the dependent variable is in levels, and we obviously control for the lagged value of the dependent variable on the right-hand side.[12] Not surprisingly, given the very high persistence of the data, the coefficient of the latter is very close to 1, with only a marginal change in the coefficients of the variables of interest, NSM in the seventies and NPC in the eighties.

In the next two columns, the dependent variable is defined as the change in the real per capita values of expenditure divided by the previous year's real per capita GDP. One advantage of this procedure is that it eliminates movements in the dependent variable that are due exclusively to changes in GDP. For instance, suppose in year *f* the government takes no action on expenditure. Still, if there is a fall in GDP, the change in the expenditure/GDP ratio would show a substantial increase in the dependent variable, although the government did not intend to make any change to its expenditure policy.[13]

---

11. De Haan and Sturm (1994) survey these results.

12. As is well known, including both a lagged dependent variable and country-fixed effects in panel regressions generates inconsistent estimates. We do not address this problem here.

13. Because the numerator—particularly when the variable in question is revenues—is also sensitive to changes in GDP, this definition of the dependent variable makes even more sense when the fiscal variables are cyclically adjusted: see Kontopoulos and Perotti 1997.

Table 4.4   **Sensitivity Analysis of the Expenditure Definition**

	ΔEXP 1974–83 (1)	ΔEXP 1984–95 (2)	ΔEXP 1974–83 (3)	ΔEXP 1984–95 (4)	ΔEXP 1974–83 (5)	ΔEXP 1984–95 (6)
NPC	−.03	.42	−.05	.27	−.14	.66
	(−0.23)	(2.58)	(−0.36)	(1.88)	(−0.38)	(1.74)
NSM	.35	.04	.28	.12	.84	.27
	(3.68)	(0.30)	(3.30)	(1.07)	(3.48)	(0.91)
NPC*DY	.01	−.09	.02	−.03	.06	−.06
	(0.25)	(−3.62)	(0.86)	(−1.49)	(0.91)	(−1.14)
NSM*DY	−.02	.01	−.02	−.00	−.05	−.01
	(−1.49)	(0.29)	(−1.59)	(−0.15)	(−1.53)	(−0.35)
DY	−.32	−.40	.07	.08	.19	.29
	(−1.89)	(−1.85)	(0.47)	(0.44)	(0.46)	(.59)
DU	.08	.20	−.05	−.04	−.06	−.10
	(0.49)	(1.72)	(−0.41)	(−0.37)	(−0.14)	(−0.39)
INFL	−.13	−.16	−.12	−.05	−.35	−.16
	(−2.86)	(−2.94)	(−2.49)	(−0.09)	(−2.98)	(1.29)
EXP_{t-1}	.23	.81				
	(24.19)	(30.21)				
R^2	.99	.99	.32	.17	.38	.15
N	195	234	224	239	195	239

Note: Columns 1 and 2: dependent variable is level of expenditures, EXP_t, instead of first difference; columns 3 and 4: dependent variable is the change in the real, per capita values of expenditure divided by the previous real, per capita GDP; columns 5 and 6: dependent variable is the change in the logarithm of expenditures. See note to table 4.1.

As one can see, once again the basic picture remains unchanged relative to the benchmark estimates of table 4.1, even though the coefficient of NPC in the eighties is no longer significant at the 5 percent level. Exactly the same conclusion applies to the last two columns of table 4.4, where the dependent variable is defined as the change in the logarithms of aggregate expenditure. Thus, overall table 4.4 confirms both the robustness of the coefficient of NSM in the seventies, and the picture of a somewhat less robust coefficient of NPC in the eighties.

In table 4.5 the dependent variable is the change in the debt/GDP ratio. In principle, the overall budget deficit should correspond exactly to the change in net debt. In practice, the difference between the two measures can be substantial, for many reasons. One can argue that the change in net debt better captures the overall stance of fiscal policy as it is actually realized, independently of how it is recorded in the official accounts. This is presumably the motivation for using this variable in Roubini and Sachs 1989a,b. On the other hand, one can also argue that the flow variable, the deficit, better captures the developments in fiscal policy that are under the control of the current policymaker; for instance, the net debt differs from the deficit because of, among other things, changes in arrears. In addition, to evaluate net debt directly (rather than from

Table 4.5   Sensitivity Analysis of the Fiscal Deficit Definition

	ΔDEBT 1960–95 (1)	ΔDEBT 1974–83 (2)	ΔDEBT 1984–95 (3)	ΔDEBT 1960–95 (4)	ΔDEBT 1974–83 (5)	ΔDEBT 1984–95 (6)
NPC	−.23	−.62	.46	.18	−.34	1.36
	(−0.95)	(−1.71)	(1.06)	(0.68)	(−0.91)	(2.97)
NSM	.15	−.15	.31	.11	−.06	.05
	(0.93)	(−0.61)	(0.93)	(0.60)	(−0.24)	(0.14)
NPC*DY	.00	.09	.00	−.08	.00	−.13
	(0.11)	(1.20)	(0.02)	(−1.72)	(0.01)	(−1.88)
NSM*DY	−.05	−.06	−.07	−.01	−.01	−.03
	(−1.72)	(−1.54)	(−1.46)	(−0.19)	(−0.27)	(−0.56)
DY	.47	.24	.86	−.05	−.18	.31
	(1.37)	(0.49)	(1.39)	(−0.14)	(−0.42)	(.48)
DU	.46	−.02	.75	.90	.62	1.02
	(1.98)	(−0.06)	(2.51)	(3.80)	(1.71)	(3.18)
INFL	−.28	−.26	−.46	−.17	−.39	−.30
	(−3.28)	(−2.28)	(−2.36)	(−2.25)	(−3.67)	(−1.94)
R^2	.33	.37	.40	.32	.45	.39
N	381	157	188	423	163	239

Note: Columns 1 to 3: dependent variable is change in the *net* debt/GDP ratio; columns 4 to 6: dependent variable is change in the *gross* debt/GDP ratio. See also note to table 4.1.

the flow) one must measure changes not only in liabilities but also in the assets of the government, often a highly speculative exercise, with the result that the amount of noise is likely to be much higher than for the deficit. Finally, using the change in net debt rather than the deficit causes a drastic fall in the number of observations available for our regressions—a total of 381 in the first column of table 4.5, against the 641 of the deficit regression in the first column of table 4.1.

In fact, when we use the change in the net debt/GDP ratio we find that the coefficients of both NPC and NSM lose all significance in the whole sample and in each of the last two decades (columns 2 and 3 of table 4.5). In view of our previous discussion, we believe these results simply suggest that one should not use the net debt/GDP ratio as a dependent variable in this kind of regression.

Some authors (e.g., de Haan and Sturm 1994) also use the change in the *gross* debt/GDP ratio as dependent variable. The advantages of this variable are that it is slightly more widely available than net debt, and especially that it avoids the type of measurement problems involved in any measure of government assets. On the other hand, the change in gross debt does not correspond to *any* meaningful variable under the control of the policymaker: theoretically, any change in gross debt is consistent with a given deficit, and vice versa. Columns 4 to 6 of table 4.5 report estimates with the change in the gross debt/GDP ratio as the dependent variable. We still find mostly insignificant coefficients everywhere, except the coefficient of NPC in the last decade, which is positive, significant, and extremely large. In fact, the point estimate is suspiciously large, which in our view reinforces our position on the problems with this variable. As an example, the OECD data on gross debt that we use imply a change in the gross debt/GDP ratio of 20.5 percent in 1993 in Finland, a figure that we find it hard to attribute any macroeconomic significance to since in the same year the measured budget deficit was only 5.8 percent of GDP. This and other similar values in the nineties in several countries contribute to the implausible estimate of 1.26 for the coefficient of NPC in the last decade.

Once again, in view of the lack of theoretical motivation for the use of gross debt, and in view of the serious measurement problems it involves, we consider these results mostly as a warning against using this variable.

4.5.4   The Definition of Difficult Times

One novelty in our approach is a systematic investigation of the importance of political factors in periods of macroeconomic distress. In the basic results of table 4.1 we found some support for the notion that fragmentation is a particularly important determinant of fiscal outcomes in difficult times. Table 4.6 explores the robustness of this finding.

In the first two columns, we interact NPC and NSM with a measure of the GDP gap rather than with the rate of growth of GDP. This variable, provided by the OECD, measures the percentage deviation of GDP from some measure of potential output. The results confirm the usual pattern—the coefficients of NSM in the 1970s are much more robust than the coefficients of NPC in the 1980s. In the former case, the interactive term if anything becomes more significant; in the latter case, both coefficients of NPC become insignificant.

Columns 3 and 4 present a different specification. We now divide the sample into "good" and "bad" times; the former are defined as years where growth was more than one standard deviation above the country-specific average; the latter as all other years. We then allow for a different coefficient for NSM and NPC in "bad" and in "good" times. The results broadly confirm our previous findings: in the expenditure regression in the 1970s, only NSM is significant, and there is virtually no difference in the coefficients of this variable in "bad" and "good" times. In the expenditure regression in the 1980s, the coefficient of NPC is significant only in bad times, confirming the earlier result that there seems to be a significant role of NPC in bad times.

4.6   Conclusions

Our main purpose in this chapter was go beyond existing investigations of the effects of political variables on fiscal outcomes by distinguishing and testing two alternative notions of fragmentation, which have equal theoretical status. To do so, we strove to define all our variables quantitatively, so that we could measure them as objectively as possible.

Table 4.6   Sensitivity Analysis of the Definition of Difficult Times

	ΔEXP 1974–83 (1)	ΔEXP 1984–95 (2)	ΔEXP 1974–83 (3)	ΔEXP 1984–95 (4)
NPC	.01	.25		
	(0.10)	(1.61)		
NSM	.20	.10		
	(2.20)	(0.87)		
NPC*DY	−.00	−.00		
	(−0.46)	(−0.14)		
NSM*DY	−.00	−.00		
	(−1.74)	(−0.68)		
NPC*GOOD			−.08	.15
			(0.49)	(−1.14)
NPC*BAD			.10	.36
			(.46)	(−0.35)
NSM*GOOD			.22	.08
			(0.00)	(−1.14)
NSM*BAD			.21	.04
			(0.01)	(−0.35)
DY	.00	.00	−.32	−.36
	(1.46)	(0.82)	(0.00)	(.59)
DU	.45	.54	.04	.03
	(2.62)	(4.64)	(0.76)	(−0.39)
INFL	−.03	.02	−.11	−.05
	(−0.73)	(0.38)	(0.00)	(1.29)
p-value, difference between NPC*GOOD and NPC*BAD			0.34	0.05
p-value, difference between NSM*GOOD and NSM*BAD			0.01	0.15
R^2	.36	.36	.59	.59
N	185	228	195	239

Note: Columns 1 and 2: DY is the GDP gap from potential output, OECD definition; columns 3 and 4: GOOD is a dummy variable with a value of 1 for years with growth more than one standard deviation above the country-specific average; BAD is a dummy capturing all other years; columns 3 and 4: values in parentheses are probability values of the t-statistics. See note to table 4.1.

Of the two notions, the first one is fairly traditional, although we measure it differently from the existing literature and identify fragmentation with the number of parties. The second is new in the literature and identifies fragmentation with the number of spending ministers.

Our empirical investigation reveals that this distinction was worthwhile: the number of spending ministers has a strong and very robust effect on expenditure, particularly during the period that includes the large macroeconomic shocks of the seventies and early eighties. The number of parties in the coalition has also a statistically significant association with expenditure, but it appears only in the last decade and it seems also to be far less robust.

We believe our results are plausible and have one potentially important policy implication. The size of the ruling coalition is the result of the electoral system and of the characteristics of the whole political system; for these reasons, even if one found that coalition size is an important determinant of fiscal outcomes, realistically this finding would have limited policy implications because its causes would be very hard to modify.

By contrast, typically the number of spending ministers is not fixed in the constitution, and within certain limits it is unlikely to be a politically charged issue. In fact, in many circumstances reducing the number of spending ministers is likely to be a very popular move, with the public at large if not with the party apparatus. Thus, our findings suggest that reducing the number of spending ministers could be a feasible and even popular institutional reform with a potentially significant impact on expenditure.

References

Alesina, A., and A. Drazen. 1991. Why are stabilizations delayed? *American Economic Review* 81:1170–88.

Alesina, A., and R. Perotti. 1995. The political economy of budget deficits. *IMF Staff Papers* 42 (March): 1–31.

Bruno, M., and S. Fischer, eds. 1993. *Lessons of economic stabilization and its aftermath.* Cambridge, Mass.: MIT Press.

de Haan, J., and T. E. Sturm. 1994. Political and institutional determinants of fiscal policy in the European Community. *Public Choice* 80:157–72.

Drazen, A., and V. Grilli. 1993. The benefits of crises for economic reforms. *American Economic Review* 83:598–607.

Edin, P., and H. Ohlsson. 1991. Political determinants of budget deficits: Coalition effects versus minority effects. *European Economic Review* 35:1597–1603.

Grilli, V., D. Masciandaro, and G. Tabellini. 1991. Political and monetary institutions and public financial policies in the industrial countries. *Economic Policy* 13:341–92.

Inman, R. P. 1996. Do balanced budget rules work? U.S. experience and possible lessons for the EMU. NBER Working Paper no. 5838. Cambridge, Mass.: National Bureau of Economic Research.

Kontopoulos, Y., and R. Perotti. 1997. Fiscal fragmentation. Columbia University. Photocopy.

Lane, P., and A. Tornell. 1996. Power, growth, and the voracity effect. *Journal of Economic Growth* 1 (2): 213–41.

Perotti, R. 1998. Fiscal policy in good times and bad times. Columbia University. Photocopy.

Poterba, J. 1994. State responses to fiscal crises: The effects of budgetary institutions and politics. *Journal of Political Economy* 102:799–821.

Roubini, N., and T. D. Sachs. 1989a. Government spending and budget deficits in the industrialized countries. *Economic Policy* 8:99–132.

————. 1989b. Political and economic determinants of budget deficits in the industrial democracies. *European Economic Review* 33:903–38.

Shepsle, K., and B. Weingast. 1981. Political preferences for the pork barrel: A generalization. *American Journal of Political Science* 25 (1): 96–111.

Spolaore, E. 1993. Policy making systems and economic efficiency: Coalition governments versus majority governments. European Centre for Advanced Research in Economics. Photocopy.

Tabellini, G., and A. Alesina. 1990. Voting on the budget deficit. *American Economic Review* 80:37–49.

Tommasi, M., and A. Velasco. 1996. Where are we in the political economy of reform? Journal of Policy Reform 1 (April).

Velasco, A. 1995. The common property approach to fiscal policy. New York University. Photocopy.

Weingast, B., K. Shepsle, and C. Johnsen. 1981. The political economy of benefits and costs: A neoclassical approach to redistributive politics. *Journal of Political Economy* 89:642–64.

Woldendorp, T., H. Keman, and I. Budge. 1993. A compilation of political data on industrialized parliamentary democracies. *European Journal of Political Research* 24:1–120.

5 Institutional Arrangements and Fiscal Performance: The Latin American Experience

Ernesto Stein, Ernesto Talvi, and Alejandro Grisanti

5.1 Introduction

During the last decade, Latin America has made substantial progress on the fiscal front. After a prolonged period of growing government and lack of commitment to fiscal discipline, which resulted in high stocks of debt and high inflation during the second half of the 1980s, expenditures and deficits were significantly reduced. Although the improvement in the fiscal accounts was widespread throughout the region, there is still a great deal of variety across countries with regard to fiscal performance. For the 1990s, public sector deficits in countries in the region have ranged from more than 10 percent of GDP in Guyana and Suriname, to a surplus of 2.2 percent in Jamaica. The differences also remain very important in terms of expenditure levels and stocks of public debt.

A less well known characteristic, which distinguishes countries in Latin America from the industrialized countries, is the highly procyclical response of fiscal policy: in general, public expenditures increase and tax rates decline during expansions, and the opposite happens during recessions. Unlike the progress made in other aspects of fiscal performance, the procyclicality of fiscal policy is still a lingering problem in the region, as the recent experiences of Argentina and Mexico illustrate. Both countries had to engineer very large fiscal adjustments in the midst of the severe recessions that followed the Mexican devaluation of December 1994. While management of fiscal policy over

Ernesto Stein is research economist in the Office of the Chief Economist at the Inter-American Development Bank. Ernesto Talvi is the director of CERES. Alejandro Grisanti is a Ph.D. candidate in the Department of Economics at the University of Pennsylvania and is currently working in the Office of the Chief Economist at the Inter-American Development Bank.

The authors thank Ricardo Hausmann, Rudolf Hommes, Torsten Persson, James Poterba, Carmen Reinhart, and Jürgen von Hagen for useful discussions during the preparation of this paper. Arnaldo Posadas provided excellent research assistance.

the business cycle has been procyclical in every country in the region, as in the case of deficits and expenditures, there are also significant differences across countries in this regard.

The great variety of fiscal experiences among fairly homogeneous groups of countries is not unique to Latin America. Within the OECD countries, for example, debt ratios currently range from less than 40 percent to more than 120 percent of GDP. Total deficits vary from close to zero, to more than 10 percent of GDP. Purely economic factors seem insufficient to explain these very large differences in fiscal outcomes across countries. For this reason, several recent studies have explored whether political-institutional factors may contribute to explain these cross-country differences in fiscal performance.

One strand of this literature has emphasized the importance of political variables such as the type of government (whether single-party majority, coalition, or minority), the durability of government, and the polarization of the political system on fiscal performance. The evidence, drawn mostly from OECD countries, is generally supportive of the idea that differences in political variables can explain differences in fiscal performance, although the specific political variables that are relevant vary across different studies.[1]

A second strand of this literature emphasizes the role of budgetary institutions on fiscal outcomes. As with the political variables, until recently this literature had focused on the OECD countries. Von Hagen (1992) and von Hagen and Harden (1995) find that budget institutions have a significant impact on debt ratios and on deficits in the countries of the European Union. In turn, Eichengreen (1992), Alt and Lowry (1994), and Poterba (1994), among others, have studied the effects of fiscal restraints on fiscal outcomes for the case of the U.S. states, reaching qualitatively similar conclusions. Alesina, Hausmann, Hommes, and Stein (1996) have recently extended this line of research to developing countries. They find evidence that, in Latin America, budgetary institutions have had an important effect on primary deficits. Similar findings are reported by Jones, Sanguinetti, and Tommasi (chap. 6 in this volume), in their study of Argentine provinces.

This paper explores the links between institutional arrangements and fiscal performance in Latin America. We consider four measures of performance, namely, the size of the public sector, fiscal deficits, the size of the public debt, and the degree of procyclicality of fiscal policy in response to business fluctuations; and two institutional dimensions, namely, electoral systems and budgetary procedures.

The next section presents a stylized description of fiscal performance in Latin America. Section 5.3 describes the main characteristics of electoral systems in Latin America and evaluates the impact of electoral institutions on political outcomes. We find that systems that rely on proportional representation, as opposed to plurality systems, tend to generate a greater number of

1. See, for example, Roubini and Sachs 1989; Grilli, Masciandaro, and Tabellini 1991; Roubini 1991; and Alesina and Perotti 1995.

effective political parties and less congressional support for the governing party. Section 5.4 describes the main characteristics of budgetary procedures in Latin America and presents an index of budgetary institutions, based on Alesina et al. 1996, that is subsequently used in the empirical analysis. Section 5.5 evaluates the impact of institutional arrangements on fiscal performance. We find that countries with a large district magnitude and a large number of effective parties tend to have larger governments and larger deficits and to respond more procyclically to the business cycle. We also find that budget procedures that include constraints on the deficit, introduce hierarchical elements into the budget process, and are more transparent lead to lower deficits and lower debt. By hierarchical procedures we mean those that tend to concentrate more power in the finance minister, vis-à-vis other ministers, and in the executive vis-à-vis the legislature. Finally, we explore the interactions between electoral systems and budgetary institutions. In contrast to the findings of Hallerberg and von Hagen (chap. 9 in this volume) for the European countries, we do not find evidence that strong budgetary institutions can neutralize the potentially adverse fiscal consequences of proportional representation on fiscal deficits and debt. Section 5.6 concludes.

5.2   The Fiscal Performance Variables: Evidence from Latin America

This section briefly describes the stylized facts on fiscal performance in Latin America in four different dimensions: the size of the public sector, the size of fiscal deficits and public debt, and the business cycle response of fiscal policy. When appropriate we also report industrial country information on fiscal performance for the purpose of comparison. Rather than relying on readily available central government data, we work in most performance dimensions with data corresponding to the consolidated public sector, which includes the central government, the social security system, public enterprises, and local governments. We think this comprehensive definition of government is more appropriate for the present study. Central government data would, for example, underestimate the size of highly decentralized governments such as Argentina, Brazil, and Colombia, where nearly half of all expenditures are carried out by state and local governments. Given the lack of coverage of existing sources of public-sector data, we constructed a data set for 1990–95, based on the Recent Economic Development reports of the IMF, for 26 countries in Latin America and the Caribbean, those which are members of the Inter-American Development Bank.[2]

5.2.1   The Size of the Public Sector in Latin America

In contrast to the OECD countries, where the size of government has grown dramatically and uninterruptedly in the last 35 years from an average of 26.6

---

2. The countries included in our data set are those that appear in table 5.1.

percent of GPD in 1960 to 49 percent of GPD in 1995, its evolution has been uneven in Latin America. Latin American governments grew very rapidly through the seventies and early eighties, collapsed in the late eighties in the aftermath of the debt crisis, and have remained fairly stable since the beginning of the nineties. The average size of government—as measured by the expenditures of the consolidated public sector—stands today at 28 percent of GDP, slightly over half the size of their OECD counterparts.

Except for notable exceptions, such as Japan and the United States, which have significantly smaller governments than the rest of the OECD countries, and Sweden and Denmark, which have significantly larger governments, the dispersion among OECD countries is relatively small. In contrast, in Latin America there are wide differences across countries in government size, ranging from 12 percent of GDP in Guatemala and Haiti to numbers in excess of 40 percent of GDP in Belize, Guyana, Nicaragua, and Suriname. The average government expenditure of the consolidated public sector for each country in 1990–95 is presented in table 5.1. The second column in the table (G') presents a measure of government expenditure that excludes social security and interest payments.

The observed disparity in government size within Latin America and between Latin America and the OECD countries is related in part to the level of income per capita. The size of government in the lowest income quartile in Latin America averages 20 percent of GDP, compared to 30 percent of GDP in the highest and 48 percent of GDP in the OECD countries. In other words, richer countries tend to have larger governments.[3]

5.2.2   Fiscal Deficits and Public Debt

With a few exceptions, standard measures of public debt do not suggest that Latin American governments are highly indebted when compared to the industrial countries. The median of public debt as a percentage of GDP is in fact lower in Latin America (55 percent) than in the OECD (65 percent).[4] However, the debt-to-GDP ratio is not necessarily the most adequate metric to measure the extent of countries' indebtedness. The ratio of public debt to total revenues of the public sector might be a better indicator. In fact, the ratings of Latin American bonds are highly correlated with the debt-to-revenues ratio: the Baa-rated countries had at the end of 1996 a debt level equivalent to 1.2 years of revenues, while the B-rated countries had a debt level equivalent to 2.1 years of revenues.[5] Measured by this standard, Latin America is still highly

3. As we shall see later, in addition to income per capita, the degree of openness of an economy to international trade, the degree of indebtedness, and the age distribution of the population are other important determinants of the size of government.

4. We report here the median rather than the average due to the existence of outliers in Latin America, such as Nicaragua and Guyana, two small countries that are very highly indebted. For the OECD countries, the median and the mean are virtually the same. The average for Latin American countries is reported in table 5.1.

5. The same association can be found in the case of subnational governments in the United States and Canada.

Table 5.1   **Fiscal Performance in Latin America (average 1990–95)**

Country				Performance Variables			
	G	G'	Surplus	Primary Surplus	Debt/GDP	Debt/Revenues	Procyclicality
Argentina	0.32	0.22	−0.03	−0.00	0.59	2.03	0.29
Bahamas	0.24	0.19	−0.02	0.01	0.11	0.51	
Barbados	0.35	0.23	0.02	0.06			0.28
Belize	0.45	0.41	−0.06	−0.04	0.35	0.96	
Bolivia	0.30	0.25	−0.04	−0.01	0.84	3.59	0.28
Brazil	0.31	0.24	0.00	0.03	0.47	1.48	0.56
Chile	0.23	0.15	0.02	0.03	0.26	1.02	0.60
Colombia	0.26	0.20	−0.00	0.03	0.31	1.17	0.31
Costa Rica	0.24	0.20	−0.01	0.03	0.76	3.26	0.80
Dominican Republic	0.18	0.16	−0.01	0.00	0.53	3.42	0.16
Ecuador	0.26	0.22	−0.02	0.03	0.87	3.38	0.21
El Salvador	0.18	0.15	−0.02	−0.00	0.34	2.40	0.60
Guatemala	0.12	0.11	−0.01	0.01	0.24	2.05	0.53
Guyana	0.47	0.34	−0.16	−0.03	4.82	12.59	
Haiti	0.12	0.12	−0.05	−0.05			
Honduras	0.31	0.24	−0.05	0.01	1.11	4.36	0.37
Jamaica	0.31	0.21	0.02	0.12	0.93	2.63	0.49
Mexico	0.26	0.20	0.00	0.05	0.31	1.19	0.81
Nicaragua	0.40	0.38	−0.06	−0.03	6.96	26.03	NA
Panama	0.28	0.17	−0.00	0.05	0.97	3.53	0.67
Paraguay	0.15	0.12	0.02	0.03	0.24	1.39	0.67
Peru	0.16	0.11	−0.02	0.01	0.78	5.81	0.82
Suriname	0.41	0.35	−0.12	−0.08	0.88	3.93	NA
Trinidad and Tobago	0.30	0.24	0.01	0.06	0.45	1.46	0.59
Uruguay	0.30	0.15	−0.02	−0.01	0.37	1.23	0.53
Venezuela	0.31	0.26	−0.06	−0.01	0.57	2.11	0.86
Mean	0.28	0.22	−0.03	0.01	1.00	3.81	0.52
Median	0.29	0.21	−0.02	0.01	0.55	2.25	0.55

Sources: G, G', surplus, primary surplus, and debt: own calculations based on the recent economic developments, IMF. Procyclicality: Talvi and Vegh 1996.

Note: G is the total expenditures of the consolidated public sector in proportion of GDP. G' excludes social security expenditures and interest payments. Government surplus is measured by the surplus of the consolidated public sector in proportion of GDP. Primary surplus is total surplus minus interest payments. Government debt is measured by the total debt of the consolidated public sector in proportion of GDP and in proportion of government revenues. Procyclicality is the correlation coefficient between the cyclical component of government consumption and the cyclical component of output over the period 1970–95.

indebted. Public debt represents 2.25 years of revenues for the typical Latin American country and only 1.5 years for the OECD countries, where debt levels have grown substantially in recent years.

These regional generalizations hide a wide variety of situations within Latin America. Table 5.1 shows the debt-to-GDP ratio and the debt-to-revenues ratio for Latin American countries. Debt levels as a percentage of GDP vary from a low of less than 25 percent of GDP in the Bahamas, Paraguay, Guatemala, and Chile, to nearly five and seven times GDP in the cases of Guyana and Nicaragua. Several countries, such as Honduras, Panama, and Jamaica, have debt ratios of around 100 percent of GDP.

The ordering of debt levels as an indicator of past fiscal behavior should be interpreted with caution. Past accumulation of debt may be an imperfect measure of past fiscal behavior in Latin America, since in high-inflation countries it may underestimate the extent to which lack of fiscal discipline was pervasive in the past. Many countries in the region implicitly defaulted on their debt obligations through repeated episodes of surprise devaluations and inflation that significantly reduced the real value of nominal debt commitments. The tendency to resolve the fiscal problems generated by persistent deficits and debt accumulation through traumatic adjustments in the exchange rate and the price level may distort the ordering of countries when the stock of debt is used to assess the extent of lack of fiscal discipline.

In recent years, Latin America has undergone a substantial fiscal consolidation. The average fiscal deficit of the region has declined from 9 percent of GDP in the early 1980s to less than 2.6 percent of GDP in the 1990s. Furthermore, the number of countries that have fiscal deficits under 3 percent of GDP is currently 16, compared to only 4 in the early eighties.

Differences across Latin American countries are also substantial with respect to deficits: in the first half of the 1990s the deficit of the consolidated public sector was greater than 5 percent of GDP in Belize, Haiti, Honduras, Nicaragua, and Venezuela, and reached double digits in Guyana and Suriname, while Jamaica, Paraguay, Barbados, and Chile had surpluses in excess of 1.5 percent of GDP.

5.2.3   The Business Cycle Management of Fiscal Policy

The business cycle response of fiscal policy in Latin America has been at odds with both the established theory and the experience of industrial countries. According to standard Keynesian prescriptions, the government should either increase spending or reduce tax rates during recessions in order to stimulate aggregate demand and partially prevent the economy from underemploying resources for prolonged periods of time. During expansions the government must do the opposite in order to "cool off" the economy and contain inflationary pressures.

According to the neoclassical tradition (see, for example, Barro 1979 and Lucas and Stokey 1983), spending programs and tax rates should be set on the basis of long-run considerations and should not respond to business cycle movements of the economy; that is, fiscal policy should not be used for demand management purposes. During expansions, when both economic activity and tax revenues are high, the budget surplus should improve and debt should be retired, while during recessions, when both economic activity and tax collection are low, the budget surplus should decline and any resulting deficit should be financed by issuing debt. Put differently, the stock of debt should act as a buffer to prevent inefficient changes in either government spending programs or tax rates.

What does the evidence show? While fiscal policy in industrial countries appears to be broadly consistent with the neoclassical prescriptions, in Latin American countries, government spending and tax rates are highly procyclical; that is, government spending increases and tax rates fall during expansions and the opposite occurs during recessions. The behavior of fiscal policy in Mexico and Argentina in the aftermath of the December 1994 Mexican crisis is a recent and clear illustration of the procyclical nature of fiscal policy in Latin America: in spite of tumbling into very steep recessions in 1995 both countries implemented equally severe fiscal adjustments that resulted in spending cuts and increases in tax rates.[6]

Table 5.1 presents evidence on the business cycle properties of government consumption in Latin America, which we use as an measure of procyclicality of fiscal policy. We measure these cyclical properties as the correlation between the cyclical component of government consumption and the cyclical component of output, for the period 1970–95.[7] In contrast to the G-7 countries, where government consumption is not correlated with output over the cycle, it is highly procyclical in Latin America: the average correlation is .52 (see Talvi and Vegh 1996).

For the region as a whole, the behavior of fiscal policy is puzzling, both in terms of the existing body of theory and when compared to the G-7 countries. Naturally, there are important disparities in the degree of procyclicality of the countries in the region. While Argentina, Barbados, Bolivia, the Dominican Republic, and Ecuador display a relatively low degree of procyclicality, Costa Rica, Mexico, Peru, and Venezuela display a very high degree of procyclicality with correlation coefficients in excess of .8. In contrast to the G-7 countries, however, no single country in Latin America exhibits a negative correlation between government consumption and output.

Talvi and Vegh (1996) have suggested a possible explanation for this puzzle. The procyclical fiscal behavior may be an optimal response of the government, given the difficulty of saving fiscal resources during booms, due to the political pressures to increase public spending that occur in times of plenty. The fact

---

6. For recent evidence on the procyclicality of fiscal policy in Latin America see Gavin et al. 1996; Talvi and Vegh 1996; and Gavin and Perotti 1997.

7. This measure of procyclicality is the same one used in Talvi and Vegh 1996.

that procyclicality is not observed in OECD countries is a result of the lower volatility of the tax base. In this case, political pressures to spend will be relatively unimportant, as budget surpluses, even during good times, do not deviate much from their average levels.

In summary, there is a wide diversity within Latin America in the four dimensions of fiscal performance we have reviewed. In the next sections we exploit this diversity to assess the role of institutional arrangements, that is, electoral systems and budgetary processes, in accounting for the observed differences in fiscal performance.

5.3   The Institutional Variables: Electoral Systems

A large body of economic research has tested the empirical relevance of political variables on fiscal performance. Most of the literature concentrates on the impact of political variables on fiscal deficits and debt accumulation as measures of performance. Roubini and Sachs (1989), working with a sample of industrial countries, find evidence that countries characterized by governments with short average tenures and by the presence of many political parties in the ruling coalition tend to have larger deficits, particularly during periods of macroeconomic stress, when fiscal adjustments are necessary. A reexamination of Roubini and Sachs (1989) by Edin and Ohlsson (1991) finds that it is minority governments rather than majority coalition governments that affect budget deficits. Roubini (1991), using a sample of developing countries, finds that an index of political instability, measured by the frequency of government changes, appears to lead to larger deficits. Grilli, Masciandaro, and Tabellini (1991) test the impact on debt accumulation of three political characteristics: the type of government, that is, single-party majority, coalition, or minority; the durability of government; and an indicator of polarization as measured by significant changes in government. They find that lack of fiscal discipline is almost exclusively limited to proportional-representation systems and that the one feature that appears to be responsible is the shorter duration of governments. Alesina and Perotti (1995) analyze the anatomy of fiscal adjustments in the OECD and find that permanent improvements are mainly implemented via cuts in expenditures, while temporary improvements are carried out almost exclusively via tax increases. They also find that coalition governments often try to make substantial fiscal adjustments, but they are much less likely to carry out the expenditure cuts that make an adjustment successful.

Many of the political characteristics explored by the literature are, in a more fundamental sense, shaped by the electoral system, that is, the set of rules under which members of parliament and the executive are elected in a representative democracy. We therefore start this section by characterizing electoral systems in Latin American countries and then explore the links between those electoral systems and political outcomes.

How do we characterize electoral systems? There is consensus among electoral-system experts that the two most important dimensions of an electoral system are the electoral formula and the district magnitude (see Lijphart 1994). There are three main types of electoral formulas: first-past-the-post, or plurality, systems (where only one representative is elected per district and all seats go to the winner); proportional-representation systems (where the seats are distributed in proportion to the votes obtained according to some allocation rule); and mixed systems, which combine features of both.

The polar characterization of proportional-representation (PR) and plurality systems (PL) is less clear-cut in practice. Some PR systems have few seats to be allocated per district and hence cannot achieve much proportionality in the representation. District magnitude (DM) simply measures the average number of representatives elected per district. Plurality systems can then be redefined as those that have a district magnitude of 1, while systems become more proportional as the DM increases. Hence, district magnitude is a more continuous representation of the electoral systems contained between the two polar cases of pure PL or PR.

Lijphart (1994) presents evidence for the industrial countries that indicates that proportional-representation systems with large district magnitude, that is, where the number of representatives elected per district is large, tend to encourage multiparty political systems and coalition or minority governments. By contrast, first-past-the-post systems tend to produce two-party systems, majority governments, and a higher degree of disproportionality, that is, a larger deviation between the parties' shares of the seats in relation to their share of the votes. Furthermore, proportional-representation systems tend to have governments with shorter tenures than single-party majority governments (see Roubini and Sachs 1989 and Grilli, Masciandaro, and Tabellini 1991).

The previous evidence implies that other things being equal, PL or low-DM systems are likely to have governments with stronger support in the legislature and therefore are likely to be more decisive. Furthermore, they are likely to have more stable governments, that is, governments with longer tenures. To the extent that these arrangements generate two-party systems, there is likely to be a competition to capture the political center, and hence it is also likely that parties will be less ideologically polarized. However, these three characteristics come at the cost of a higher degree of disproportionality of the political system. By contrast, high-DM systems are more likely to produce weaker governments, because with a larger number of parties it is harder to ensure control of the legislature. Furthermore, coalition governments tend to have a shorter duration because, after all, they are formed by competing parties.[8] Finally, the increased number of parties might make the center a less attractive political strategy and hence may deliver wider ideological distances between the likely winners of an election. In summary, the strength or weakness of the govern-

---

8. For evidence on electoral systems and the durability of governments see, for example, Roubini and Sachs 1989 and Grilli, Masciandaro, and Tabellini 1991.

ment, the durability of government, and the polarization of the political system are all potential channels through which the electoral system can impact fiscal performance.

Next we describe the characteristics of electoral systems in Latin America. We then show that electoral systems are instrumental in shaping political outcomes such as the number of parties represented in the legislature and the likelihood that the executive enjoys a majority in the legislature or will have to form coalitions or govern with weak support in the legislature. In section 5.5, we present evidence that electoral systems have a meaningful impact on fiscal performance.

5.3.1   Electoral Systems in Latin America

Latin America has a large variety of electoral systems. However, proportional representation (PR) is by far the most common system: 15 out the 26 countries that form our sample have proportional-representation systems, 6 (the Bahamas, Barbados, Belize, Haiti, Jamaica, and Trinidad and Tobago) have first-past-the-post or plurality systems (PL), and 5 (Chile, Mexico, Panama, Peru, and Venezuela) have mixed systems (M) that combine features of both PR and PL in different ways (see table 5.2). For example, in Mexico and Venezuela some candidates for the lower house are elected under the PL system, while others are elected using the PR system. In Panama, legislators are elected by PL or PR depending on the electoral circuit in which they run. In Chile and Peru, candidates are presented in lists, but voters can cast a preferential vote for one of the candidates and the candidates with the largest number of preferential votes are selected within the list.

Seventeen countries have two-tier or bicameral systems, while nine countries have only one-tier or unicameral systems. Unicameral systems are predominantly observed in countries with PR systems, while all PL systems are bicameral. The basic rationale for two-tier systems is to combine the advantages of a close voter-representative contact characteristic of smaller districts with the advantages of greater proportionality and minority representation offered by larger districts (see Lijphart 1994).

District size, the average number of representatives elected per district, varies considerably across countries. PL systems have district sizes that are small in absolute value (less than 2) and smaller in every case than any PR or M system. Among PR or M systems district size for the lower house varies from 2 in Chile and 3.2 in Ecuador to more than 10 in Argentina, Bolivia, Mexico, and Brazil. The variety in district size is even greater in the upper house, ranging from 2 in Chile to 102 in Colombia, where the whole country constitutes a single district.

Past colonial links appear to be important determinants of electoral systems in Latin America. English- or French-speaking countries—with the exception of Guyana—have PL systems, low district magnitude, low effective number of parties, and, in general, majority governments. The rest of the countries have—whether they speak in Spanish, Portuguese, or Dutch—PR or M systems.

Table 5.2   Electoral Institutions and Political Outcomes

| | Electoral Institutions | | | | | | | Electoral Outcomes | | |
| | Legislative | | | | | Executive | | Legislative | | Executive |
Country	Legislative Electoral Formulas	Number of Legislative Chambers	Lower/ Single House District Magnitude	Higher House District Magnitude	Average District Magnitude	Presidential vs. Parliamentary Systems	Number of Rounds	Absolute Number of Parties in Lower House	Effective Number of Parties in Lower House	% of Legislative Seats Held by Head of Government's Party in Lower/ Single House
Argentina	PR	2	10.3	3.0	8.7	P	2	16	2.82	0.52
Bahamas	PL	2	1.0	n/a	1.0	Pa	n/a	2	1.34	0.85
Barbados	PL	2	1.0	n/a	1.0	Pa	n/a	3	1.84	0.68
Belize	PL	2	1.6	n/a	1.6	Pa	n/a	3	2.00	0.55
Bolivia	PR	2	14.4	3.0	12.5	P	2	8	3.71	0.40
Brazil	PR	2	19.0	3.0	16.8	P	2	18	8.16	0.38
Chile	Mix	2	2.0	2.0	2.0	P	2	8	4.95	0.58
Colombia	PR	2	5.0	102.0	42.1	P	2	2	2.24	0.57
Costa Rica	PR	1	8.1	n/a	8.1	P	2	5	2.30	0.49
Dominican Republic	PR	2	4.0	1.0	3.4	P	2	3	2.43	0.48
Ecuador	PR	1	3.2	n/a	3.2	P	2	13	5.21	0.23
El Salvador	PR	1	8.2	n/a	8.2	P	1	8	4.03	0.33
Guatemala	PR	1	6.9	n/a	6.9	P	2	7	2.72	0.54
Guyana	PR	1	43.4	n/a	43.4	P	1	4	2.14	0.54
Haiti	PL	2	1.0	1.0	1.0	P	2	8	1.46	0.82
Honduras	PR	1	7.1	n/a	7.1	P	1	3	2.03	0.55
Jamaica	PL	2	1.3	n/a	1.3	Pa	n/a	2	1.26	0.88
Mexico	Mix	2	16.6	4.0	14.0	P	1	4	2.29	0.60
Nicaragua	PR	1	8.1	n/a	8.1	P	1	10	2.74	0.45
Panama	Mix	1	1.8	n/a	1.8	P	1	12	4.06	0.46
Paraguay	PR	2	4.7	45.0	19.2	P	1	3	2.38	0.50
Peru[a]	Mix	2	4.8	2	4.0	P	2	13	2.91	0.56
Suriname	PR	1	5.1	n/a	5.1	Pa	n/a	8	5.36	0.47
Trinidad	PL	2	1.0	n/a	1.0	Pa	n/a	3	2.23	0.53
Uruguay	PR	2	5.2	31.0	11.4	P	1	4	3.30	0.32
Venezuela	Mix	2	8.8	2.0	7.6	P	1	5	4.73	0.24

Sources: Constitutional and legal texts, own calculations based on data by Wilfred Derksen.

Note: District magnitude is the average number of representatives elected per district. Average district magnitude is the weighted average (weighted by the number of representatives in each house) of the district magnitude of the lower and upper houses. The number of effective parties, Ns, is defined as $Ns = 1/\sum s_i^2$, where s_i is the proportion of representatives party i has in the lower house. Only one election has been held under the new rules.

[a] In Peru after the constitutional reform of 1993, there is only one electoral district and the congress has a single house.

Another important dimension of the electoral systems has to do with the way in which the executive is chosen. In presidential democracies the president is voted directly and has significant independent authority. By contrast, in parliamentary democracies the prime minister is accountable to the legislature. The manner in which the chief executive is chosen may have important consequences. On the one hand since only large parties have a realistic chance of winning the presidency and this advantage is likely to carry over to legislative elections, we expect, other things being equal, that presidential systems will have a smaller effective number of parties than nonpresidential systems of government. On the other hand, an independently elected chief executive might undermine party discipline: when the control of the presidency does not depend on parliamentary majorities, parties can afford greater internal dissent.[9]

In Europe, most countries have parliamentary democracies. The opposite is true in Latin America: 20 out of 26 countries are presidential democracies, and only 6 are parliamentary. All PL systems are parliamentary democracies (except Haiti), and all PR and M systems are presidential democracies (except Suriname).

The other dimension concerning the election of the executive in presidential democracies is whether there is only one round or two rounds of voting to elect the president. When there are two rounds of voting, unless a candidate wins the absolute majority in the first round, a second round is held. Of the 20 presidential democracies in Latin America, half have one round of voting to elect the president, the other half have two.

5.3.2   Electoral Systems and Political Outcomes

Proportional-representation systems with large constituencies, that is, where the number of representatives elected per district is large, allow a more exact mapping between the votes obtained by a party and the representation that party obtains in the legislature. A simple example may serve to illustrate the latter point. Consider an election in which the three main parties get 45 percent, 40 percent, and 10 percent, respectively. A first-past-the-post system, that is, a system that elects one representative per district with the winner taking all the seats, may create a very large majority. In fact, if the vote is homogeneously distributed throughout the country, the first party would win all congressional races and seats. A system of proportional representation that elects few representatives per district, for example two, would only allow the first two parties to obtain representation in the legislature, precluding the minority party with 10 percent of the vote from obtaining representation. By contrast, in a system of proportional representation where the number of representatives elected per district is large, for example 100, the smaller party will obtain 10 seats in the legislature. In fact, the two smaller parties may even be able to form a coalition and control the parliament.

---

9. See Rogowski 1987. Persson, Roland, and Tabellini (1997) argue that the lack of legislative cohesion of presidential systems may result in underprovision of public goods.

Proportional representation systems therefore allow a broader representation of the electorate. However, the inclusiveness of the PR system comes at a cost: the same electoral rules that allow a higher degree of proportionality are those that create the incentives for the system to produce a large number of parties. Figure 5.1 illustrates the relationship between the district magnitude, which measures the average number of representatives elected per district for 26 Latin American countries, and the number of effective parties that are represented in the legislature.[10] The difference between the absolute number of parties in the legislature and the effective number is that the latter weights each party by its share of the vote in the legislature. For example, if there are two parties represented in the legislature, one with 90 percent of the seats and the other with 10 percent, the effective number of parties will be 1.2 rather than 2. Only when the parties have an equal share of the seats in the legislature will the absolute and effective number of parties be the same.[11]

Electoral systems, by discouraging or encouraging the existence of a limited number or a large number of parties, affect the likelihood of having a single-party majority, a coalition, or a minority government. Figure 5.1 shows that in Latin America the percentage of the seats that the government enjoys in the legislature is very closely connected to the number of effective parties represented in parliament: the larger the number, the more likely it is that the government will have weak support in the legislature. The correlation coefficient between these two variables is .79.

There is another important dimension, concerning the election of the executive in presidential democracies, that may be relevant in determining the number of effective parties: whether there are one or two rounds of voting to elect the president. The two-round process, known as *ballotage,* is likely to encourage several parties to run in the first round and form electoral coalitions for the second round. As a result, the number of effective parliamentary parties is expected to be larger, other things being equal, with two rounds of voting than with one. There is some evidence of this effect in Latin America. The absolute number of parties is on average 10.5 in countries with two rounds of voting and 7 in countries with one. The corresponding figures for the effective number of parties are 3.7 and 3, respectively.

After discussing the role of budget institutions in the next section, in section 5.5 we will assess the importance of our two institutional dimensions on fiscal performance.

5.4   The Institutional Variables: Budgetary Institutions

As we mentioned in the introduction, there is a growing body of literature that links differences across economic units in fiscal performance to the nature

---

10. In two-tier systems the district magnitude for each country is the maximum between the lower and the upper house.

11. For details on the index that measures the number of effective parties see Lijphart 1994.

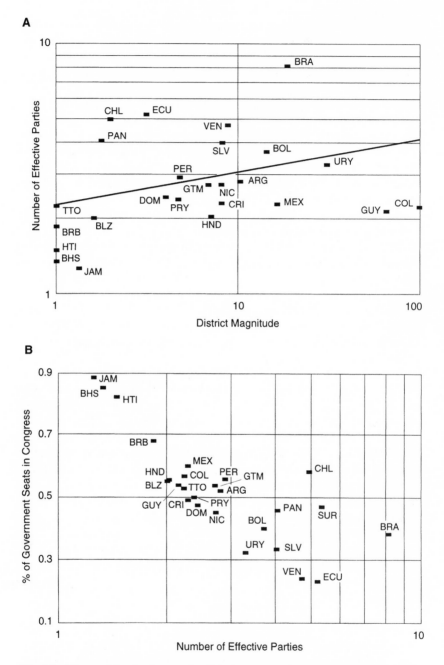

Fig. 5.1   Electoral institutions and political outcomes in Latin America

of their budget institutions. Until recently, this literature concentrated mainly on the experience of industrial countries. For example, von Hagen (1992) and von Hagen and Harden (1995) developed a comprehensive index of budget institutions for the countries in the European Union and found that these institutions have a significant impact on debt ratios and on deficits. Several authors, in turn, have studied the effects of fiscal restraints on fiscal outcomes for the case of the U.S. states, exploiting the differences across states regarding the stringency of their balanced-budget rules. Eichengreen (1992) finds that fiscal restraints have a significant and negative effect on deficits, as well as on state bond yields. Alt and Lowry (1994) find that states with stringent balanced-budget rules react more strongly to previous-year deficits. Qualitatively similar results are found by Poterba (1994), who also studied within-year adjustments to fiscal shocks.[12]

More recently, Alesina et al. (1996) have extended this line of research to the developing world: using data obtained through a survey of budgetary institutions in 20 Latin American countries, they find evidence that these institutions have an important effect on primary deficits.[13] In the present paper, we will use the budget institutions database created by these authors, but expand the focus to include not only effects on primary deficits, but on all the variables of fiscal performance described in section 5.2.

Following Alesina and Perotti (chap. 1 in this volume), we define budgetary institutions as the set of rules, procedures, and practices according to which budgets are drafted, approved, and implemented.

The government budget is the result of a collective decision-making process that involves a variety of agents from the executive and legislative branches of government: the finance minister, spending ministers, and members of the legislature. A very important characteristic of government programs is that they tend to generate benefits that are concentrated either geographically or sectorally. These programs, however, are typically financed from a common pool of resources. As a result of this asymmetry, those who benefit from a government program will fail to internalize the full cost of the program, since an important portion of the cost is borne by others. This externality inherent to the budget leads to a problem of overutilization of the common pool of resources, which the literature refers to as the commons problem. The fact that most of the agents involved in the budget negotiations represent either sectoral or geographical interests introduces spending and deficit biases into the process, which can compromise the achievement of fiscal discipline.

Legislators, for example, will push for programs that benefit their geographical constituencies, but are financed by the national taxpayer. Weingast, Shepsle, and Johnsen (1981) have studied this commons problem at the level of the

---

12. See also von Hagen 1991; Bohn and Inman 1995; and Eichengreen and Bayoumi 1994. For an excellent survey of this literature, see Poterba 1996.
13. Similar findings are reported by Jones, Sanguinetti, and Tommasi (chap. 6 in this volume), in a recent study of Argentine provinces.

legislature, showing that it can lead to excessive spending, as legislators fail to internalize the full cost of these programs. Velasco (chap. 2 in this volume) and von Hagen and Harden (1995) studied the commons problem within the cabinet. Spending ministers, who are subject to the pressures of sectoral interest groups, favor increases in programs for their departments, financed out of national resources. In a dynamic setting, this leads to excessive deficits and debt accumulation. This behavior of spending ministers is reinforced by the fact that their power within the government is usually perceived to be associated with the size of the budget they manage. In contrast to the rest of the participants in the budgetary process, finance ministers usually face the entire budget constraint. Moreover, since they have the ultimate responsibility for macroeconomic policy, they have better incentives to promote fiscal discipline.

Budget institutions matter because they can affect the "rules of the game" under which these agents interact, either by placing constraints on the whole budgetary process, or by distributing power and responsibilities among the different players, in ways that can affect outcomes in one direction or the other. If adequately designed, budgetary institutions can play a critical role in counterbalancing the spending and deficit bias that may otherwise prevail due to the incentives of some of the agents involved in the budgetary process.[14]

Budgetary institutions can be usefully divided into three different categories. The first are rules that impose *numerical constraints* on the deficit. Balanced-budget rules, such as the one recently considered and defeated in the U.S. Congress, are the best-known example of numerical constraints. As discussed above, evidence from the 50 U.S. states suggests that balanced-budget rules have significant effects on the size of the budget, on deficits, and on the reaction to fiscal shocks. However, these rules are, in general, very inflexible and do not allow for tax-smoothing policies. In addition, balanced-budget rules, as well as other numerical rules such as the Maastricht criteria for the European Union, may generate incentives for creative accounting in order to circumvent them, and can result in a less transparent process.[15]

Constraints on the deficit can take other forms. In most countries, governments prepare macroeconomic programs that include fiscal, monetary, and balance-of-payments targets consistent with expectations regarding key variables in the economy, such as the rate of growth and inflation. An alternative way to impose a constraint on the deficit is to require that the budget sent by the executive for discussion in the legislation be consistent with targets set in a previously approved macroeconomic program. Such a requirement may provide discipline to the budgetary process if the macroeconomic program clearly identifies limits on the size of the budget and its balance compatible with the achievement of other economic goals. Other possible constraints on the size of

---

14. For an in-depth discussion of the theoretical issues underlying the importance of budget institutions see von Hagen 1992 and Alesina and Perotti 1995.

15. This point has been made by Alesina and Perotti (1995).

the deficit are ceilings on government borrowing, usually set by the legislature before budget discussions. Some authors have proposed that borrowing ceilings be imposed by an independent agency, created specifically for this purpose.[16]

The second type of rules are *procedural rules* that govern the drafting of the budget by the executive, its discussion in the legislature, and its execution. While numerical rules impose constraints on all the agents involved in the budgetary process, procedural rules determine the way in which these agents interact, shifting the balance of power among the different agents in favor of one or the other. According to the procedural rules that organize the budgetary process, we can distinguish between more "hierarchical" and more "collegial" institutional arrangements. At the drafting stage, hierarchical rules are those that give considerable power to the finance minister in budget negotiations within the executive, limiting the prerogatives of the spending ministers. At the approval stage, hierarchical rules are those that set restrictions on the power of the legislature to modify the budget proposed by the executive, in particular with respect to the size of the budget and the deficit. At the execution stage, hierarchical rules are those that limit the initiative of the legislature to propose increases in the size of the budget once it has been approved. In contrast, collegial institutions provide a greater balance of power between the spending ministers and the finance minister during the drafting stage, and between the executive and the legislature during the approval and execution stages.

The third type of procedures and practices are those associated with the *transparency* of the budgetary process, that is, the extent to which the budget document provides an accurate representation of projected expenditures, revenues, and deficits. One issue regarding transparency is that the players involved do not always have an incentive to be truthful. If the government wants to hide a deficit, it might have incentives to overestimate the growth rate of the economy. On the other hand, a fiscally conservative finance minister might want to hide resources from the spending ministers and the legislature. Spending ministers, in turn, might want to misrepresent the composition of their budgets, knowing that the chances of obtaining more resources after the budget is approved are better for some items (such as their wage bill) than for others. Other issues of transparency include the existence of extrabudgetary items, hidden liabilities, and contingent liabilities, such as those derived from implicit or explicit guarantees by the central government to state and local governments, public enterprises, and the banking sector.

Alesina et al. (1996) used information collected through a survey to build an index of budgetary institutions for Latin America. The survey, which was responded to by budget directors from 20 countries in the region, provided

---

16. Von Hagen and Harden (1995) suggested the creation of such an agency, which they called the National Debt Board, for the European Union. Eichengreen, Hausmann, and von Hagen (1996) have made a proposal along similar lines, which they called the National Fiscal Council, specially tailored to the particular characteristics of Latin America.

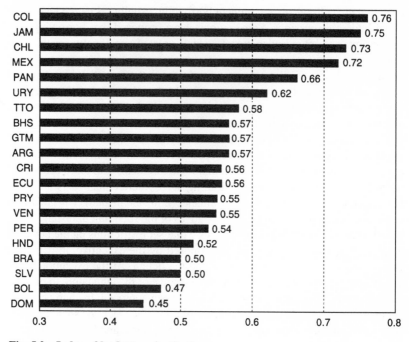

Fig. 5.2   Index of budgetary institutions

information on the extent to which budget institutions in the different countries impose numerical constraints on the deficit, have hierarchical rules in the different stages of the budgetary process, and transparent budgetary practices.

In this paper, we use an index of budget institutions based on the same survey, which is similar to the original one except for one factor: since our fiscal performance database covers the period 1990–95, we have adapted the index so that it represents, for each country, the nature of budgetary institutions for the same time period. This introduces some changes, as a number of countries have reformed some aspects of their budgetary institutions in recent years. The value of the index of budgetary institutions for each country is represented in figure 5.2.[17]

This index will be used in section 5.5 to assess the impact of budget institutions on aggregate fiscal performance.

5.4.1   The Question of Endogeneity

An important consideration regarding the effects of budget institutions on fiscal performance variables is related to potential endogeneity of the budget institutions variables. Alesina and Perotti (chap. 1 in this volume) discuss two

17. For a detailed description of the construction of the index, as well as information on the budget institutions of each country, see Alesina et al. 1996 and Hausmann and Stein 1996.

possible sources of endogeneity. First, budget institutions could be endogenous to past fiscal performance, that is, could be reformed as a result of poor past performance. Second, both the choice of budget institutions and the fiscal performance could in fact be explained by a third variable, which is omitted from the analysis.

Although Alesina and Perotti recognize that budget institutions are to a certain extent endogenous to past fiscal performance, these authors argue that, at least in the short run, it is reasonable to consider them as exogenous. The argument relies on the fact that institutional reform is costly, and therefore fiscal outcomes have to be very unsatisfactory before these reforms take place, which results in a strong status quo bias of these institutions.

A few countries in our sample have had reforms of their budget institutions, as measured by changes in our index, since 1980. Although our data set does not allow us to study the important issue of endogeneity in a systematic way, these changes can shed some light on the determinants of institutional reform. Out of the 20 countries in the sample there are only 2 that have implemented what we consider to be major budget reform, defined as changes of 0.15 or more in the value of our index, during this 15-year period. These two countries are Argentina and Peru.

In Argentina, changes in the budget process began in 1991, but were formalized by the Law of Financial Administration in 1992. Among the most important changes, the budget was made more inclusive, substantially reducing the importance of off-budget items; the macroeconomic program became a more important reference for the elaboration of the budget by the executive, and changes were made to the process of elaboration, through which the different ministries were given quantitative spending limits at the beginning of the process rather than just qualitative orientations, as was the case until then; during the approval stage, the legislature was restricted from proposing amendments that would increase the deficit; and the autonomy of state-owned enterprises to borrow was curtailed. Perhaps more importantly, for the first time since 1953, the budget of the year 1992 was presented and approved within the constitutionally set time frame, before the beginning of the year, a practice that has continued every year since then (see Makon 1995).

In Peru, reform occurred in 1990, in the early stages of President Fujimori's term. In this case, changes included elevating the status of the finance ministers over that of the spending ministers on budgetary matters, requiring consistency between the budget presented to the legislature and the macroeconomic program, and limiting the prerogatives of the legislature in proposing amendments to the budget that increase either the deficit or spending. In both countries, budget reform was not an isolated event, but rather part of wide-ranging reform packages implemented, particularly in the case of Argentina, by strong finance ministers.

Although these countries had important fiscal deficits during the late 1980s, this was a characteristic that was common to most countries in Latin America.

What sets Argentina and Peru apart during this period is the fact that they both suffered severe hyperinflations, which reached three-digit (monthly) levels.[18] The experience of Argentina and Peru provide support for the argument of Alesina and Perotti: institutions are costly to change, and tend to change in significant ways only when performance is very unsatisfactory. The fact that in Argentina the budget was not presented and approved in time for almost 40 straight years suggests that these institutions do have a strong status quo bias, even when they are not written into law.

An interesting case is that of Costa Rica, where reform of the budget institutions is currently under consideration. The proposed reform includes strengthening the authority of the finance minister and increasing the role for the macroeconomic program and the coverage of the budget. The cornerstone of the proposed reform, however, is a constitutional amendment that would require that public sector deficits not exceed 1 percent of GDP.[19] The main goal of the reform (and particularly of this constitutional amendment) is to put an end to the electoral budget cycle, a problem that is quite common in Latin America, but has become particularly serious in Costa Rica. In 1994, the last electoral year, the fiscal deficit reached 7 percent of GDP. The legislature began discussion of the reform in 1995, but the process of approval has not been completed yet, and approval is not expected before the 1998 elections. In the meantime, Costa Rica is experiencing the increase in public wages typical of the period leading to elections. Costa Rica, then, represents another example of the difficulty of reforming the budgetary institutions, at least in the short run.

The long-term evolution of the budget institutions in Colombia, studied by Hommes (1996), also offers examples of the permanence of budgetary rules. For example, the Constitution of 1886, which laid out the basis for the budget process, established that the government could increase expenditures during periods when the legislature was not in session, provided these increases were judged to be "unavoidable." As a result, the government would typically wait for the end of the sessions to increase expenditures, reducing the transparency of the budget. Similarly, a 1916 law established the priority of earmarked expenditures, reducing the flexibility of the budget. It was only with the Constitution of 1991 that these two rules were eliminated.

Throughout his paper, Hommes discusses the determinants of institutional reform in Colombia. While in a few cases reform followed a severe crisis (for example, in 1892), in most cases budget reform was simply implemented by

---

18. The other two countries that experienced very high inflation in the late 1980s and early 1990s were Brazil and Nicaragua. Brazil did not reform its budget institutions. We have no data on budget institutions in Nicaragua. However, the new government implemented a stabilization program, trade liberalization, and tax reform in 1991, which makes it likely that the budgetary process was reformed as well.

19. For an account of the political cycle in Costa Rica, and details on the proposed reform, see Rodriguez 1995. Currently, there are no countries in Latin America that have this type of numerical constraint.

a reformist official motivated by good management principles, and in some cases, imposed from outside the country.[20]

Regarding the second potential source of endogeneity, the question is whether it is the institutions that are having an effect, or whether these institutions simply reflect society's aversion to fiscal indiscipline, and it is these preferences of society and not the institutions themselves that are responsible for the differences across countries in fiscal performance. The argument that institutions are endogenous to the preference of voters is, of course, a plausible one. However, it is not clear that this has been the case in Argentina and Peru. In fact, Menem won his presidency by running a populist campaign, and only after being elected did he shift toward the implementation of market-oriented reforms, surprising both those who had voted for him and those who had not. In the case of Peru, Fujimori did not have an economic program during his campaign and ended up implementing the program of his electoral opponent, Vargas Llosa.

Other possible determinants of institutions are the preferences of particular interest groups, and the difficulty or ease with which these groups can exert pressure on policymakers. Posen (1995) has pointed out the importance of interest groups in the context of the literature on central bank independence, arguing that it is the preferences of the financial sector and the influence that this sector has on policymakers that matter for inflation, rather than the statutory independence of the central bank per se. Posen admits, however, that the time span under consideration is important in establishing whether institutions matter. While preferences and political forces determine outcomes in the long run, over short periods of time institutions may in fact matter.[21]

Even though we recognize the existence of potential sources of endogeneity, in this paper we treat budgetary institutions as exogenous. Given the time period under consideration, 1990–95, we do not think that the assumption of exogeneity is a serious shortcoming of this study.

5.5   Electoral Systems, Budget Institutions, and Fiscal Performance

In the previous sections we described fiscal performance in Latin America and the two institutional dimensions this paper is concerned with, namely, electoral systems and budgetary processes. We now proceed with the empirical analysis in order to evaluate whether these institutional dimensions are significant in explaining cross-sectional differences in fiscal performance in Latin America. In doing so, we face the problem of working with a small sample, which is sometimes reflected in lower levels of significance. We first analyze

---

20. This author reports that in 1923 Colombia was seeking foreign loans to finance public investment, and that "the foreign bankers pressed for reforms such as the creation of a central bank, adherence to the gold standard, and adoption of 'modern' budget procedures" (Hommes 1996, 9).

21. See discussion following Posen 1995.

the impact of electoral systems and budgetary processes on fiscal performance individually, and then explore the interactions between the two sets of institutions.

5.5.1   Electoral Systems and Fiscal Performance

In the empirical analysis we consider three attributes of the political system: the district magnitude, which is our main characterization of the electoral system, and two outcomes of the system, namely, the number of effective parties and the support of the governing party in the legislature. District magnitude enters the regressions in logs, as we believe its effects should be nonlinear.

Table 5.3 presents the regression results for government size. In the first three columns, the dependent variable is public sector expenditures (G). In columns 4 through 6, it is a measure of public expenditures that excludes social security and interest payments (G'). The reason for using this last measure is that it is often argued, at least for the OECD countries, that a large part of the explanation for cross-country differences in the size of government is given by the size of the social security sector.

As control variables, we used the level of debt at the beginning of the period, the degree of openness of the economy (measured as imports plus exports over GDP), and the proportion of the population above 65 years of age. Initial public debt is expected to have positive effects on total public expenditures through its effect on interest payments. It is not expected to have effects on G', so it was not included in regressions 4 through 6. Openness is expected to have positive effects on the size of government, following recent findings by Rodrik (1996).[22] The age variable is expected to have positive effects as well, only in the government size measure that includes social security expenditures (G). All controls had the expected sign and were significant in most regressions.

Following our discussion in section 5.3, we expect district magnitude and the number of effective parties to have positive effects on government size, and the proportion of legislative seats held by the government to have a negative effect on size. Table 5.3 shows that, in every case, political variables enter with the correct sign, although the levels of significance are not always high, a consequence in part of the small sample size. For total government expenditure G, only the number of effective parties is significant. The estimated coefficient indicates that the impact of electoral institutions on government size is potentially large in economic terms: a country with a number of effective parties equal to four is expected to have a public sector 4 percentage points of GDP larger than one where the effective number of parties is two. For the case of G', the number of effective parties is significant at the 10 percent level, while

---

22. Rodrik (1996) argues that the explanation for this empirical regularity is that open economies are exposed to significant external risk, and that a large government sector reduces the exposure to this risk.

Table 5.3   **Electoral Institutions and Government Size (cross-section regressions, average 1990–95)**

| | Government Size | | | | | |
| | G | | | G' | | |
Institutional Arrangements	(1)	(2)	(3)	(4)	(5)	(6)
District magnitude	0.0109 (0.0143)			0.0135 (0.0121)		
Number of effective parties		0.0204 (0.0107)			0.0177 (0.0101)	
Number of legislative seats			−0.0967 (0.1271)			−0.1521 (0.1005)
Controls						
Constant	0.1189 (0.0582)	0.0412 (0.0705)	0.1776 (0.0709)	0.1199 (0.0392)	0.0736 (0.0517)	0.2160 (0.0523)
Debt at 1989	0.0147 (0.0080)	0.0160 (0.0071)	0.0154 (0.0078)			
Openness	0.1163 (0.0488)	0.1494 (0.0492)	0.1217 (0.0510)	0.1172 (0.0413)	0.1406 (0.0432)	0.1257 (0.0412)
Population over 65 years	1.1655 (0.8204)	1.3718 (0.7586)	1.2786 (0.8159)			
R^2	0.34	0.44	0.34	0.21	0.27	0.25
DF	18	18	18	22	22	22
N	23	23	23	25	25	25

Sources: G, G' and debt: own calculations based on the recent economic developments, IMF. Effective number of parties and number of legislative seats: own calculations based on data by Wilfred Derksen. District magnitude: District magnitude. Openness and population over 65 years: World Bank indicators, 1995.

Notes: Standard errors are given in parentheses. G is the total expenditures of the consolidated public sector in proportion of GDP. G' excludes social security expenditures and interest payments. District magnitude is the logarithm of the average number of representatives elected per district. Number of effective parties is the number of political parties weighed by its share of the vote in the legislature. Number of legislative seats is the proportion of the seats that the executive enjoys in the legislature.

the proportion of seats held by the government is significant at the 15 percent level.[23]

Table 5.4 shows the effects of two of our political variables on public-sector surplus and on primary surplus.[24] In the case of primary surplus, we controlled for the initial level of debt. In columns 2 and 4, we restricted the sample to the 20 countries for which we have data on budget institutions, in order to be able to discuss later the effects of including both institutional dimensions together. The coefficients of all the political variables have the expected sign. District magnitude is marginally significant for surplus, while the number of legislative seats is significant for the primary surplus. Note that when the sample is restricted, district magnitude becomes a significant determinant of primary surplus, and the number of legislative seats becomes significant for the surplus as well.[25]

The coefficient for DM suggests that, here again, economic effects are important: a country with a PL system is expected to have budget surpluses 1.1 percent of GDP larger than countries with a PR system and a district magnitude of 3. The same difference in surplus should be expected between two countries with PR systems with DM of 3 and 9.[26] We also performed regressions for both of our debt measures, but we failed to find any significant relationship between any of the political variables and debt levels. We will discuss later how the effects of our political variables change once we account for the effects of budget institutions.

Table 5.5 presents the results for procyclicality, where volatility, defined as the standard deviation of real GDP growth for the period 1970–95, is used as a control variable. Following the arguments of Talvi and Vegh (1996), volatility is expected to have a positive effect on procyclicality.

The only political variable that was significant (at the 15 percent level) was district magnitude, which enters with a positive sign. The coefficient suggests that our measure of procyclicality is expected to be 0.08 higher in a country with a DM of 3 compared to a country with DM of 1.[27]

How can we interpret this result? One possible interpretation would be re-

23. When European countries are included in the empirical analysis in order to increase the sample size, the qualitative results do not change, but the precision of our estimates increases significantly. District magnitude, for example, becomes significant at the 10 percent level for total expenditures, and at the 5 percent level for G'.

Similar results were obtained when GDP per capita was used as a control instead of the age variable. These two variables are highly correlated, and GDP per capita lost significance when included in the regressions together with the age variable. In contrast, this last variable remained significant.

24. We excluded the effective number of parties to save space. This variable had the expected sign in all cases, but was never a significant determinant of the surplus.

25. The countries that are excluded from the sample in columns 2 and 4 are Barbados, Belize, Guyana, Haiti, Nicaragua, and Suriname. Together, these six countries represent less than 1 percent of Latin America's GDP.

26. Since $[\log(3) - \log(1)]*0.0103 = [\log(9) - \log(3)]*0.0103 = 1.099*0.0103 = 0.0113$.

27. More precisely, the difference between these countries will be $[\log(3) - \log(1)]*0.071 = 0.077$.

Table 5.4   Institutional Arrangements and Government Surpluses (cross-section regressions, average 1990–95)

Institutional Arrangements	(1)	(2)[a]	(3)	(4)[a]	(5)	(6)	(7)
				Total Surplus			
Constant	-0.0085	-0.0036	-0.0466	-0.0405	-0.0869	-0.0786	-0.0873
	(0.0134)	(0.0093)	(0.0282)	(0.0291)	(0.0292)	(0.0290)	(0.0292)
District magnitude	-0.0103	-0.0050				-0.0053	
	(0.0063)	(0.0043)				(0.0037)	
Number of legislative seats			0.0391	0.0557			0.0294
			(0.0519)	(0.0291)			(0.0309)
Budget institutions					0.1266	0.1288	0.1022
					(0.0492)	(0.0479)	(0.0556)
R^2	0.07	0.02	−0.02	0.12	0.23	0.27	0.23
df	24	18	24	18	18	17	17
N	26	20	26	20	20	20	20
				Primary Surplus			
District magnitude	-0.0075	-0.0099				-0.101	
	(0.0066)	(0.0057)				(0.0040)	
Number of legislative seats			0.0942	0.1139			0.0735
			(0.0495)	(0.0350)			(0.0338)
Budget institutions					0.2165	0.2179	0.1578
					(0.0588)	(0.0516)	(0.0597)
Controls							
Constant	0.0316	0.0308	-0.0292	-0.0580	-0.1239	-0.1014	-0.1307
	(0.0145)	(0.0206)	(0.0265)	(0.0243)	(0.0380)	(0.0345)	(0.0346)
Debt at 1989	-0.0045	0.0166	-0.0048	0.0382	0.0318	0.0240	0.0387
	(0.0036)	(0.0230)	(0.0034)	(0.0197)	(0.0183)	(0.0164)	(0.0169)
R^2	0.06	0.10	0.15	0.35	0.41	0.55	0.52
DF	21	17	21	17	17	16	16
N	24	20	24	20	20	20	20

Sources: Surplus, primary surplus, and debt: own calculations based on the recent economic developments, IMF. Effective number of parties and number of legislative seats: own calculations based on data by Wilfred Derksen. District magnitude: constitutional and legal texts. Openness and population over 65 years: World Bank indicators, 1995. Index of budgetary institutions: Alesina et al. 1996.

Notes: Standard errors are given in parentheses. Government surplus is measured by the surplus of the consolidated public sector in proportion of GDP. Primary surplus is total surplus minus interest payments. District magnitude is the logarithm of the average number of representatives elected per district. Number of effective parties is the number of political parties weighed by its share of the vote in the legislature. Number of legislative seats is the proportion of the seats that the executive enjoys in the legislature.

[a]Restricted sample, excludes countries that have no data on budget institutions: Barbados, Belize, Guyana, Haiti, Nicaragua, Suriname.

Table 5.5   **Institutional Arrangements and Procyclicality (cross-section regressions)**

Institutional Arrangements	Procyclicality
District Magnitude	0.0705
	(0.0449)
Controls	
Constant	−0.1067
	(0.2397)
Volatility	10.9069
	(3.9145)
R^2	0.23
df	17
N	20

Sources: Procyclicality and volatility: own calculations based on the international financial statistics, IMF. District magnitude: constitutional and legal texts.

Note: Procyclicality is measured by the correlation coefficient between the cyclical component of government consumption and the cyclical component of output over the period 1970–95. District magnitude is the logarithm of the average number of representatives elected per district. Standard errors are given in parentheses.

lated to the arguments in Talvi and Vegh 1996. As discussed above, these authors link the procyclical fiscal behavior of Latin American governments to a political distortion: the difficulty of saving during booms, given the spending pressures that would occur if governments were running large surpluses. As these authors suggest, and our results confirm, the impact of the political distortion is larger the larger the degree of volatility faced by the country. But the political distortion itself may depend on the electoral system in place. An electoral system that tends to produce stronger governments (such as the PL system, or a PR system with low district magnitude) can place these governments in a better position to resist the spending pressures. Although we do not want to push this argument too far, our district magnitude result does suggest that this might in fact be the case.[28]

In summary, although the results are not always strong in every performance dimension, the evidence suggests that electoral institutions are a significant determinant of fiscal performance in Latin America. Countries with a large district magnitude, a large number of effective parties represented in the legislature, and weak support for the governing party in the legislature tend to be

28. We did not find a significant effect of the proportion of legislative seats held by the government on procyclicality, which may appear to be a better indicator of the strength of government. However, we must note that this variable corresponds to the current composition of the legislature and may not reflect adequately the strength of government during the 25-year period for which we have measured procyclicality. In contrast, district magnitudes, which are characteristics of the electoral institutions, rather than the outcome of elections, tend to be much more stable over time and may be a better representation of the strength of governments throughout the period. This problem is less important in the case of the other performance variables, since the time period considered is 1990–95.

Table 5.6   **Institutional Arrangements and Government Debt (cross-section regressions, average 1990–95)**

Institutional Arrangements	Debt/GDP	Debt/Revenues
Constant	0.8302	5.8564
	(0.4334)	(1.8469)
Budget Institutions	−0.4750	−5.8919
	(0.7302)	(3.1118)
R^2	−0.03	0.12
df	18	18
N	20	20

Sources: Government debt: own calculations based on the recent economic developments, IMF. Index of budgetary institutions: Alesina et al. 1996.
Note: Government debt is measured by the total debt of the consolidated public sector in proportion of GDP and in proportion of government revenues. Standard errors are given in parentheses.

associated with higher levels of government expenditures, larger fiscal deficits, and a more procyclical response to the business cycle.

5.5.2   Budget Institutions and Fiscal Performance

As discussed in section 5.4, more transparent and hierarchical budgetary institutions, that is, institutions that promote a more comprehensive view of the costs and benefits of government activities, should result in a higher degree of fiscal discipline. Therefore we expect countries that have a high index of budgetary institutions (IBI) to display relatively smaller levels of spending, fiscal deficits, and public debt. However, the direction of the impact of budgetary institutions on procyclicality is unclear: while more hierarchical procedures may improve the ability of the government to resist spending pressures during booms, constraints that enhance credibility in the commitment to fiscal discipline may hamper the ability of the authorities to react in an efficient manner to shocks.[29]

We find that countries with a high IBI tend to have lower deficits and lower debt levels than countries with a low IBI. The deficit result is presented in table 5.4, column 5. The coefficient for budget institutions is significant at the 5 percent level for the case of overall surplus, and at the 1 percent level for the case of primary surplus. The debt regressions appear in table 5.6. The IBI is a significant determinant of debt levels when these are measured in proportion to their revenues, which, as discussed in section 5.2, is our preferred measure of debt. Figure 5.3 illustrates the association between the IBI and overall surplus, and between IBI and debt.

From a quantitative point of view the statistical relationship suggests that

---

29. For example, a period-by-period balanced-budget rule would preclude the authorities from running a budget deficit during recessions and would therefore make it unnecessary to run surpluses during expansions, resulting in a procyclical fiscal response.

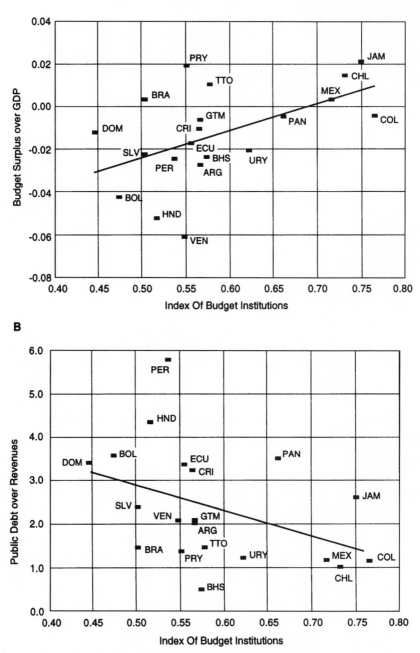

Fig. 5.3   Budget institutions and fiscal performance, 1990–95

the impact of budget institutions is large in economic terms. A country with an IBI of 0.45 is expected to have an average overall budget surplus 2.5 percentage points of GDP smaller, and a primary surplus 4 percentage points of GDP smaller, than that of a country with an index of 0.65.[30] A country with an IBI of 0.45 is also expected to have a debt-to-revenue ratio 1.2 years lower than a country with an IBI of 0.65. We did not find any significant impact of the IBI on government size and the degree of procyclicality.[31]

5.5.3   Electoral Institutions, Budget Institutions, and Fiscal Performance

The previous results offer very interesting possibilities for exploring the interactions between electoral systems and budgetary arrangements. We do this for the surplus and the primary surplus, the only dimensions of performance where both electoral institutions and budget institutions appear to be significant. Is it the case that countries with a high IBI governing the fiscal decision-making process can generate sound fiscal behavior whatever the electoral arrangements governing the political process? In Latin America, the answer appears to be negative.

In table 5.4, columns 6 and 7 present the results of the regressions where the effect of both institutional dimensions is considered together. The relevant comparisons are with the restricted sample regressions, in columns 2 and 4, respectively. When the overall budget surplus is used as a measure of fiscal performance, and IBI is included in the regressions, district magnitude gains some significance, while the number of legislative seats loses significance. When the primary surplus is used as the fiscal performance variable, the coefficient for DM remains unchanged, but the level of significance increases. In turn, the coefficient for the number of legislative seats drops slightly, but it remains significant at the 5 percent level. In sum, both political variables are significant determinants of primary surpluses when IBI is included in the regression. These results appear to contrast with those obtained by Hallerberg and von Hagen (chap. 9 in this volume) for European countries, who find that the existence of some form of centralization in the budget process, whether provided by a strong finance minister or by negotiated budget targets within the cabinet, rather than the electoral system, is the crucial determinant of fiscal performance.

5.6   Concluding Remarks

This paper has analyzed, for a sample of Latin American countries, the impact of two institutional arrangements, namely, electoral systems and budget-

---

30. The quantitative impact is even stronger if the primary budget surplus rather than the overall budget surplus is used to perform these calculations.

31. The empirical literature on budget institutions and fiscal performance has consistently found an impact of budget institutions on fiscal deficits and debt, but almost as consistently has failed to find an association with government size. This chapter is not an exception.

ary procedures, on four measures of fiscal performance, namely, the size of government, the size of budget deficits and public debt, and the degree of procyclicality in the response of fiscal policy to business cycle fluctuations. We find evidence that electoral systems characterized by a large degree of proportionality, that is, a large district magnitude, and by large degree of political fragmentation, tend to have larger governments, larger deficits, and a more procyclical response to the business cycle. We also find that more transparent and hierarchical budgetary procedures lead to lower deficits and debt. The effects of our institutional variables tend to be large in economic terms. Contrary to the findings of Hallerberg and von Hagen for European countries, we find no evidence that centralized budgetary arrangements neutralize the potentially adverse impact on fiscal deficits of a larger degree of proportionality of the electoral system.

References

Alesina, A., R. Hausmann, R. Hommes, and E. Stein. 1996. Budget institutions and fiscal performance in Latin America. NBER Working Paper no. 5586. Cambridge, Mass.: National Bureau of Economic Research.

Alesina, A., and R. Perotti. 1995. Fiscal expansions and fiscal adjustments in OECD countries. *Economic Policy* 21:207–48.

Alt, J., and R. Lowry. 1994. Divided government, fiscal institutions, and budget deficits: Evidence from the states. *American Political Science Review* 88:811–28.

Barro, R. 1979. On the determination of the public debt. *Journal of Political Economy* 87:940–71.

Bohn, H., and R. Inman. 1995. Constitutional limits and public deficits: Evidence from the US states. *Carnegie Rochester Conference Series on Public Policy* 45 (December): 13–76.

Edin, P., and H. Ohlsson. 1991. Political determinants of budget deficits: Coalition effects vs. minority effects. *European Economic Review* 35:1597–1603.

Eichengreen, B. 1992. *Should the Maastricht Treaty be saved?* Princeton Studies in International Finance, no. 74. Princeton: Princeton University Press.

Eichengreen, B., and T. Bayoumi. 1994. The political economy of fiscal restrictions: Implications for Europe from the United States. *European Economic Review* 38: 781–92.

Eichengreen, B., R. Hausmann, and J. von Hagen. 1996. Reforming fiscal institutions in Latin America: The case for a National Fiscal Council. Office of the Chief Economist, Inter-American Development Bank. Photocopy.

Gavin, M., R. Hausmann, R. Perotti, and E. Talvi. 1996. Managing fiscal policy in Latin America. Working Paper 325. Office of the Chief Economist, Inter-American Development Bank.

Gavin, M., and R. Perotti. 1997. Fiscal policy in Latin America. In *NBER macroeconomics annual*, ed. B. Bernanke and J. Rothemberg. Cambridge, Mass.: MIT Press.

Grilli, V., D. Masciandaro, and G. Tabellini. 1991. Political and monetary institutions and public financial policies in the industrial democracies. *Economic Policy* 13: 341–91.

Hausmann, R., and E. Stein. 1996. Searching for the right budgetary institutions for a volatile region. In *Securing stability and growth in Latin America,* ed. Ricardo Hausmann and Helmut Reisen. Paris: OECD-IDB.

Hommes, R. 1996. Evolution and rationality of budget institutions in Colombia. Working Paper 317. Office of the Chief Economist, Inter-American Development Bank.

Lijphart, A. 1994. *Electoral systems and party systems.* Oxford: Oxford University Press.

Lucas, R., and N. Stokey. 1983. Optimal fiscal and monetary policy in an economy without capital. *Journal of Monetary Economics* 12:55–94.

Makon, M. 1995. Instituciones presupuestarias en Argentina. Secretaría de Hacienda, Argentina. Photocopy.

Persson, T., G. Roland, and G. Tabellini. 1997. Comparative politics and public finance. Photocopy.

Posen, A. 1995. Determinations of central bank independence. In *NBER macroeconomics annual.* Cambridge, Mass.: MIT Press.

Poterba, J. 1994. State responses to fiscal crises: "Natural experiments" for studying the effects of budgetary institutions. *Journal of Political Economy* 102:799–821.

———. 1996. Do budget rules work? NBER Working Paper no. 5550. Cambridge, Mass.: National Bureau of Economic Research.

Rodriguez, E. 1995. El ciclo politico en Costa Rica. Photocopy.

Rodrik, D. 1996. Why do more open economies have bigger governments? NBER Working Paper no. 5537. Cambridge, Mass.: National Bureau of Economic Research.

Rogowski, R. 1987. Trade and the variety of democratic institutions. *International Organization* 41, no. 2:203–23.

Roubini, N. 1991. Economic and political determinants of budget deficits in developing countries. *Journal of International Money and Finance* 10:S49–S72.

Roubini, N., and J. Sachs. 1989. Political and economic determinants of the budget deficits in the industrial democracies. *European Economic Review* 33:903–38.

Talvi, E., and C. Vegh. 1996. Can optimal fiscal policy be procyclical? Office of the Chief Economist, Inter-American Development Bank and UCLA. Photocopy.

von Hagen, J. 1991. A note on the empirical effectiveness of formal fiscal restraints. *Journal of Public Economics* 44:199–210.

———. 1992. Budgeting procedures and fiscal performance in the European Communities. Economic Paper no. 96. Commission of the European Communities DG for Economic and Financial Affairs. October.

von Hagen, J., and I. Harden. 1995. Budget processes and commitment to fiscal discipline. *European Economic Review* 39:771–79.

Weingast, B., K. Shepsle, and C. Johnsen. 1981. The political economy of benefits and costs: A neoclassical approach to distributive politics. *Journal of Political Economy* 89:642–64.

6 Politics, Institutions, and Public-Sector Spending in the Argentine Provinces

Mark P. Jones, Pablo Sanguinetti, and Mariano Tommasi

This chapter contributes to the growing literature on the political and institutional determinants of fiscal outcomes by studying the behavior of public spending in the Argentine provinces since the return to democracy in 1983. Argentina is a federal republic with 23 provinces, and provincial finances play an important role in the overall fiscal picture of the country, with approximately 50 percent of total government expenditures occurring at the subnational level. The Argentine provinces possess a considerable amount of diversity in terms of their party systems, executive-legislative relations, and fiscal behavior, making Argentina an ideal laboratory for this type of study.

We begin in section 6.1 with a description of a vitally important aspect of Argentina's fiscal structure: its degree of vertical imbalance, by which a very large proportion of provincial spending is financed out of a common pool of tax revenues. Section 6.2 summarizes our theoretical approach, which emphasizes the common-property view of fiscal politics. Section 6.3 presents the main hypotheses, and section 6.4 contains the empirical analysis of the political determinants of provincial spending. Section 6.5 briefly studies the effect of budget institutions on provincial fiscal outcomes, while section 6.6 provides some concluding remarks.

Mark P. Jones is assistant professor of political science at Michigan State University. Pablo Sanguinetti is professor of economics at Universidad Torcuato Di Tella, Buenos Aires, Argentina. Mariano Tommasi is associate professor of economics at Universidad de San Andrés, Buenos Aires, Argentina.

The authors are indebted to Jorge Braga de Macedo, Arik Levinson, Robert Lowry, Jim Poterba, Jürgen von Hagen, Anne Case, Kim Rueben, Robert Inman, Alberto Porto, Marcelo Dabós, Hildegart Ahumada, Fernando Navajas, and seminar participants at Universidad de San Andrés, Universidad Torcuato Di Tella, Centro de Estudios para el Desarrollo Institucional, Universidad de La Plata, and the ZEI-NBER conference for helpful comments and suggestions. Juan Sanguinetti and Tamara Saront provided valuable assistance in the painstaking data collection process, as well as useful comments. Josefina Posadas provided first-rate research assistance.

6.1   Argentina's Federal Fiscal Structure

The Argentine constitution establishes that the federal government will employ tariffs on foreign trade to finance its expenditures, while provinces will finance themselves through taxes on production and the consumption of specific goods. Over time however, for both economic and political reasons, the national government became the main agent responsible for the collection of all taxes at the provincial level. The process by which these taxes, once collected, are then reallocated to the provinces has been the source of numerous conflicts and modifications.[1] Argentina's first national tax-sharing agreement (the Ley de Coparticipación Federal) dates from 1934.[2] Periodically, new laws have been written to regulate this distribution. The current law dates from 1988. Under this law the federal government retains 42 percent of these taxes, while 57 percent is distributed among the provinces, with the remaining 1 percent set aside to finance unforeseen crises in the provinces. The law also establishes the percentages of the secondary distribution and is supplemented by several other laws regulating the distribution and destination of a few specific taxes that finance a set of predetermined activities.

Argentina is the most decentralized country in Latin America in terms of public spending, with approximately 50 percent of total public spending occurring at the subnational level (Stein, Talvi, and Grisanti, chap. 5 in this volume). At the same time, Argentina has a high degree of vertical fiscal imbalance. During the period under analysis (1985–95, excluding 1989), an average of 80 percent of provincial expenditures were financed from the Ley de Coparticipación Federal (along with other transfer mechanisms), while an average of only 20 percent were financed from provincial revenues. The data in table 6.1 demonstrate that all of the country's 23 provinces on average financed less than half of their expenditures with provincial revenues, and nearly three-fourths financed less than one-fourth. Most of the transfers from the federal government are done on behalf of a delegation of tax authority from the provinces, in such a way that the use of 71 percent of the transfers is left to the discretion of the provincial governments (the remaining 29 percent of the transfers is earmarked for specific activities).

6.2   The Effect of Political and Institutional Variables on Public-Sector Spending: The Common Property Approach

We view the provincial fiscal accounts as the outcome of a multiagent game. The key players in our game are politicians interested in providing net benefits

1. For an analysis of Argentine fiscal federalism see Porto 1990.
2. These tax-sharing agreement laws define the share of taxes to be transferred from the central government to the provinces (i.e., the primary distribution) and the way in which these funds are to be allocated among the provinces (i.e., the secondary distribution).

Table 6.1   **Percentage of Provincial Expenditure Financed with Provincial Revenues, 1985–95**

Province	Percentage
Buenos Aires	49
Santa Fé	40
Córdoba	36
Mendoza	31
La Pampa	30
Entre Ríos	27
Neuquén	20
Salta	20
Tucumán	20
Río Negro	19
Tierra del Fuego	19
Jujuy	18
San Luis	18
Chubut	15
Misiones	14
San Juan	12
Santa Cruz	12
Corrientes	11
Chaco	11
Santiago del Estero	9
La Rioja	7
Catamarca	6
Formosa	5
23-province average	20

Source: Secretaría de Hacienda, Ministerio de Economía, Obras, y Servicios Públicos, República Argentina.
Note: Data from 1989 are excluded. For more information, see note 15 in the text.

to their constituencies. A substantial portion of these local or particularistic benefits are financed out of a common pool of taxes (current or future).

This common-property approach to fiscal politics was pioneered by Weingast, Shepsle, and Johnsen (1981), and extended by others such as Inman and Fitts (1990), Chari and Cole (1995), Campos and Pradhan (1996), and Velasco (1998). As is the case with any common resource, there is an overutilization of national wealth. Political economists know this process as "universalism," while the popular term in the United States is "pork-barrel politics."[3] In some versions, this generates suboptimal aggregate outcomes from the point of view of the political actors (e.g., legislators). In others, the outcome is suboptimal

---

3. The term "universalism" comes from Weingast (1979). The discussion in the text draws from Inman and Fitts (1990).

from the point of view of citizens due to fiscal illusion (Weingast, Shepsle, and Johnsen 1981), or to principal-agent problems in the relation between the people and their representatives (Tommasi 1998).[4]

We emphasize the common-pool problem at two levels, corresponding to the federal fiscal organization of Argentina described in the previous section. On the one hand, every province sees the aggregate national (present and future) taxing capacity as a common resource. On the other, each provincial legislator sees the provincial (and national) taxing capacity as a common resource. Political factors (such as the relations between the president and provincial governors and divided versus unified government) and budget institutions (such as costly borrowing procedures) act to exacerbate or mitigate the underlying problem.

In this chapter we focus on the impact of political factors on provincial public spending.[5] We emphasize spending and not provincial revenues because there are two countervailing forces in terms of the impact of politics on provincial fiscal revenues.

First, there is the standard "size" effect emphasized by Weingast, Shepsle, and Johnsen (1981), under the assumption of a balanced budget. This leads to the prediction that certain institutional configurations lead to higher spending *and* higher taxes than do other configurations. Second, as we emphasize below, in the Argentine case there are negative externalities across provinces that lead provincial governments to overspend and *under*tax (in the spirit of what Inman and Fitts [1990] call "tax expenditures"). Combining these two effects, we obtain clear-cut predictions from institutional and political variables to expenditure outcomes, while the implications for provincial revenues will depend on which effect dominates.

Within the common-pool view, individuals and institutions elected by regional representation (e.g., governors within the context of the nation, and legislators within the context of the province) have a greater tendency to act as free-riders on the collective good of fiscal prudence than individuals and institutions chosen from more encompassing constituencies (e.g., the president within the context of the nation and the governor within the context of the province). As stated before, we emphasize this hypothesis at two levels: in terms of the behavior of each province vis-à-vis the consolidated national fiscal accounts, and in terms of the provincial legislatures vis-à-vis the provincial executive branches.

---

4. Tommasi (1998) argues that agency slack is necessary for the suboptimality of fiscal outcomes. Otherwise, elected representatives should be able to reach an agreement on optimal fiscal policy. This pushes the collective action problem to the level of the citizens, via their control of elected officials.

5. In Jones, Sanguinetti, and Tommasi 1997a we focus on fiscal deficits.

6.3 Determinants of Provincial Public-Sector Spending: Three Hypotheses

Taking into consideration fiscal arrangements in Argentina, as well as the common-property approach just described, we develop three hypotheses regarding the political determinants of public-sector spending in the Argentine provinces. The first two hypotheses are tied to the partisan affiliation of the provincial governor. The third hypothesis is linked to the effect of the presence of divided versus unified government on fiscal behavior.

6.3.1 The Partisan Relationship between the Governor and the President

Within our common-pool view, the president, who is elected by a national constituency and who is held primarily responsible for macroeconomic outcomes, will have better incentives for fiscal conservatism than each provincial government. This should be especially the case in a country such as Argentina, where the vertical imbalance is severe (Stein, Talvi, and Grisanti, chap. 5 in this volume), with the provinces on average receiving nearly four-fifths of their revenue from the federal government.

The Argentine president has many instruments at his or her disposal with which to coerce provincial governments into behaving more in line with national fiscal objectives. We posit that, when the provincial governor is from the president's political party, the president has additional coercive resources stemming from his/her role as president of the political party (de jure and/or de facto) combined with the relatively high level of party discipline (stemming in large part from the high level of partisan control over the nomination process, the use of closed lists to elect legislators, and the high value of the party label) in Argentina's political parties.[6]

HYPOTHESIS 1. *Provinces where the governor is from the same political party as the president have lower per capita public-sector spending.*

This hypothesis could also be rationalized on the basis of Aizenman 1998, where the fiscal behavior of local authorities is determined as a game that includes *n* local governments, plus the central government. The central government uses some strategic variables in order to induce cooperative play from the local governments, as a way to mitigate the common-pool problem. Aizenman's model assumes that the electoral fortunes of governors are jointly tied to aggregate fiscal performance. It would be natural to extend his model to a multiparty environment, in which the electoral fortunes of governors from the president's party are more tied to aggregate macroeconomic performance than those of the opposition.[7]

6. For a discussion of the distribution of power within the Argentine political parties see Jones 1997.

7. We thank Osvaldo Schenone for bringing this point to our attention.

6.3.2   The Role of Ideology

Alt and Lowry (1994) demonstrate that in the U.S. states which political party controls the state government has an important influence on fiscal outcomes. For Alt and Lowry, the driving force behind this salient finding is the differential policy preferences of Democrats (high spending, high taxes) and Republicans (low spending, low taxes). Within their framework, political configurations and institutions move the actual outcome closer to one of the preferred points. Similar partisan differences in spending patterns among parties due to "ideology" have been detected in OECD countries by Kontopoulos and Perotti (chap. 4 in this volume).

In the Argentine context, we hypothesize that partisanship has an important influence on fiscal behavior, but that this influence does not stem from partisan ideological differences (as is the case in the United States). Instead, partisanship's salient effect is the product of the partisan linkage between the president and the provincial governors, combined with the relatively high degree of influence that the Argentine president has over fellow party members (e.g., governors). This influence contrasts quite markedly with the very weak level of control exercised by the U.S. president over same-party state governors.

Between 1983 and 1995 Argentine politics was dominated by two major national political parties: the Partido Justicialista (PJ) (i.e., the Peronist Party) and the Unión Cívica Radical (UCR).[8] In addition to these two national parties, provincial political parties, which effectively compete in only one province, have played a significant role in several provinces as either the dominant or number two party.

To our knowledge, we are the first to test for fiscal policy differences between Argentina's two national political parties. Historically, the PJ has been classified as a working-class party, while the principal base of UCR support has been identified as the middle class. This characterization, however, is somewhat misleading given the catchall and federal nature of the PJ and UCR, combined with the noteworthy policy shift that has taken place since 1989, during which time the governing PJ of President Carlos Menem implemented a series of far-reaching market-oriented reforms. In any event, it is our intuition that the key "political" variable is the one explained in section 6.3.1, and we hypothesize that the PJ and UCR will not show different inclinations to tax and spend, and thus that the partisan affiliation of the governor will have no significant independent effect on the level of provincial per capita public-sector spending.

---

8. Over the past decade the UCR has, however, experienced a marked decline in its electoral support, leaving the PJ as the only Argentine party with a significant presence in all of the country's 23 provinces and federal capital.

HYPOTHESIS 2. *Provinces governed by Peronist and Radical governors do not differ in their level of per capita public-sector spending.*

6.3.3   Divided Government

One of the most prominent political factors hypothesized to influence fiscal behavior is the presence or absence of divided government (Alt and Lowry 1994; Cox and McCubbins 1997; McCubbins 1991; Poterba 1994). In theory, we would expect budget deficits to be larger under divided than under unified government, due to the greater difficulties faced by the executive in getting his/her budget through the legislature. Under unified government the governor is more likely to be able to rely on a solid partisan contingent in the legislature approving his/her budget. This is particularly the case in systems where the level of party discipline is relatively high.

The U.S. and European literature has tended to emphasize the role of divided government in preventing fiscal adjustment following adverse shocks (e.g., Alt and Lowry 1994; Poterba 1994). The related mechanism, which we emphasize in this chapter, is that within each province governors have better incentives than the legislature for fiscal prudence, and unified government facilitates the governor's job.[9] This follows, at a different level, the same logic emphasized in hypothesis 1.

HYPOTHESIS 3. *Provinces where there is divided government have higher per capita public-sector spending than provinces where there is unified government.*

6.3.4   Other "Domestic" Political Variables

Other political variables are also hypothesized to influence public-sector outcomes. Bicameral (as opposed to unicameral) legislatures and larger legislatures (i.e., with more legislators), for example, are expected to result in higher levels of public-sector spending (Gilligan and Matsusaka 1995). Unfortunately, a bicameralism dummy variable and a variable that measures the size of the legislature (i.e., the number of legislators) are highly collinear with the provincial fixed-effects variables that we employ and are thus not included in this analysis. In future work, we will use other procedures (in particular substantively meaningful cross-sectional control variables) that will allow us to measure the independent effect of these and other variables, which at the intraprovince level are for the most part invariant across time.

---

9. This "level" effect also is emphasized in Alesina et al. 1996, and is the one that derives naturally from the work of Weingast, Shepsle, and Johnsen (1981) and Velasco (1998).

6.4 Empirical Analysis

6.4.1 Data and Variables

We employ a reduced-form model to analyze the determinants of per capita provincial public-sector spending.[10] The model is a reduced form of a system of equations used in Jones, Sanguinetti, and Tommasi 1997b and includes in the reduced form all of the independent variables utilized in the original revenue equation. The reduced form for provincial revenue was also analyzed, but as expected, there is no significant impact of the political variables on revenues.

We conduct this analysis using a pooled cross-section of the 23 Argentine provinces from 1985 to 1995. Out of the potential population of 253 provincial years (23 × 11), a total of 39 years are excluded, leaving a final analysis population of 214.[11]

In the analysis our dependent variable is annual per capita public-sector spending in the province (excluding interest payments).[12] As is the case with all of our monetary variables, the values are expressed in constant 1991 Argentine pesos.[13] The range for this variable is 279 to 4,886, while the mean and standard deviation are 994 and 696 respectively.

The basic economic (fiscal) model, subject to Argentine data limitations, employs the following control variables: NATIONAL TRANSFERS, ENERGY CONSUMPTION, UNEMPLOYMENT, LAGGED PRIMARY DEFICIT, along with variables measuring cross-sectional and temporal effects.

The variable NATIONAL TRANSFERS measures the amount of transfers per capita (in 1991 pesos) received by the province from the national govern-

10. The purpose of our study is to analyze the effect of political factors on provincial public-sector spending. As such, our units of analysis are the provincial years, with all provincial years weighted equally. If our goal were to analyze the determinants of aggregate fiscal outcomes in Argentina, then we would give more weight to those provinces where the most spending occurs. However, as this is not our goal, we do not include any weighted regression results in our analysis. We have run these regressions, which provide results that are relatively similar to those presented here, although of course they are in large part reflecting the variables' effects in the province of Buenos Aires, which accounts for 43 percent and 58 percent of the respective combined 23-province population and gross industrial production.

11. Twenty-two provincial years are excluded due to problems surrounding the coding of one of our influential variables for the year of 1989 (for more information see note 15). Six provincial years are excluded because during those years the province was under federal intervention. Four provincial years are excluded due to the lack of unemployment data. Seven years (1985–91) are excluded from the province of Tierra del Fuego, which, as a national territory, was under direct federal government control until nearly 1992. Tierra del Fuego achieved provincial status in 1990, but did not have a locally elected government until mid-December of 1991. The Federal Capital, Argentina's 24th district, was under direct federal government control between 1983 and 1996 and is therefore excluded from the analysis.

12. For more information on the sources of the data used here, see Sanguinetti and Tommasi 1997.

13. Following the adoption of the Law of Convertibility in 1991, the Argentine peso has been fixed at par with the U.S. dollar.

ment during the year. As explained in Jones, Sanguinetti, and Tommasi 1997b, it was included in the structural system alongside the (endogenous) provincial own fiscal revenues. The values for this variable range from 99 to 3,738, with a mean of 731 and a standard deviation of 566.

ENERGY CONSUMPTION is our proxy for provincial GDP, for which annual data for the entire population do not exist. The variable is measured as the number of megawatts per capita consumed in the province during the year. It ranges from 0.30 to 10.07, with a mean of 1.39 and a standard deviation of 1.79.

UNEMPLOYMENT is the percentage of the workforce that was unemployed in the province's capital city during the year.[14] The level of unemployment during this period ranged from 1.00 to 19.35, with a mean level of unemployment of 7.49 and a standard deviation of 3.47.

LAGGED PRIMARY DEFICIT is the provincial primary deficit per capita (in 1991 pesos), incorporating transfers on the revenue side, in the province during the previous year. It ranges from −289 (i.e., a surplus of 289 pesos per capita) to 550 (i.e., a deficit of 550 pesos per capita).

To test our three hypotheses we examine the effect of four political variables on the level of per capita provincial public-sector spending. PRESIDENT'S PARTY measures the partisanship of the governor in relation to that of the president. All years during which the governorship of a province was held by a member of the president's party are coded 1, while all other years are coded 0. During the period 1985–88 all provinces governed by the UCR are coded 1, while all others are coded 0. During the period 1990–95 all of the provinces governed by the PJ are coded 1 while all others are coded 0. In the analysis population of 214, 109 of the provincial years (51 percent) are coded 1. Of these 109 years, 86 come from the PJ administration of President Carlos Menem (1989–95), while the remaining 23 come from the UCR administration of President Raúl Alfonsín (1983–89).[15]

The second and third variables measure the partisan affiliation of the governor. For the variable UCR GOVERNOR, a 1 is assigned if the province was governed by a member of the UCR during the year being coded. For the variable PROVINCIAL PARTY GOVERNOR, a 1 is assigned if the province was governed by one of the country's center-right provincial parties (i.e., Acción Chaqueña in Chaco, the Movimiento Popular Fueguino in Tierra del Fuego, the Movimiento Popular Neuquino in Neuquén, the Pacto Autonomista Liberal in Corrientes, the Partido Bloquista in San Juan, and the Partido Renovador de

---

14. Two exceptions are the provinces of Buenos Aires and Santa Fé, from which more than one city is included.

15. On July 8, 1989, President Carlos Menem assumed office, five months prior to the date (December 10) on which the official transfer of power from President Raúl Alfonsín was constitutionally scheduled to take place. This early transfer occurred due to the severe economic, political, and social crisis facing the country. This year is excluded from the analysis as it is not possible to adequately code it for the PRESIDENT'S PARTY variable.

Salta in Salta). Both of these variables are measured as differences from the years in provinces that were governed by a PJ governor. Of the 214 provincial years included in the analysis, 141 were under a PJ governor, 39 under a UCR governor, and 34 under a provincial party governor.

The fourth variable is DIVIDED GOVERNMENT. Divided government is defined here as a situation in which the governor's party lacks a majority of the seats in the single house in unicameral systems and in both houses in bicameral systems.[16] We classify as unified government all other cases.[17] Years in which divided government existed are coded 1, while years in which there was unified government are coded 0. Of the 214 provincial years, divided government was present in 42 (18 percent), with unified government in the remaining 172 (82 percent).

Finally, included in the analysis are cross-sectional (i.e., provincial; 22 total) and temporal (i.e., year; 10 total) fixed-effects variables. For reasons of space the estimated coefficients and standard errors for these variables are not included in table 6.2.

6.4.2   Analysis

Table 6.2 provides the results of our analysis of the determinants of per capita public-sector spending in the Argentine provinces between 1985 and 1995. The first equation includes the four control variables along with the cross-sectional and temporal fixed-effects variables. The second equation retains the variables in the first equation, and adds the PRESIDENT'S PARTY and DIVIDED GOVERNMENT variables. Finally, the third equation adds the UCR GOVERNOR and PROVINCIAL PARTY GOVERNOR variables. The analysis below concentrates on the unrestricted equation (3).

The results in table 6.2 provide strong support for hypothesis 1. PRESIDENT'S PARTY has a prominent inverse effect on the level of per capita provincial public-sector spending. The estimated coefficient in equation (3) indicates that, all other things being equal, a province where the governor is from the same party as the president spends 65 pesos per capita less than a province where the governor is from an opposition party.

This finding supports our view, based on the common-pool theory, that governors who are copartisans of the president spend less than other governors. It also highlights the value of the common-pool theory, especially when analyzing units within a context where there is a severe vertical fiscal imbalance.

Hypothesis 2 is also supported to a considerable extent by the results in table 6.2. The weak positive result for UCR GOVERNOR indicates that, holding

---

16. Like Alt and Lowry (1994), we consider 50 percent a majority.

17. It would be possible to produce a finer classification. For instance, the case in which the governor faces opposition in both chambers may be a stronger form of divided government than the case in which he/she has a majority in one of the chambers ("split government" versus "split legislature" in the terminology of Alt and Lowry [1994]). We, however, have only seven instances of a split legislature in our population of 214.

Table 6.2   Determinants of Provincial Public-Sector Per Capita Spending

	Equation (1)		Equation (2)		Equation (3)	
Independent Variables	Estimated Coefficient	Standard Error	Estimated Coefficient	Standard Error	Estimated Coefficient	Standard Error
National transfers	0.795**	(0.051)	0.801**	(0.051)	0.788**	(0.049)
Energy consumption	17.040	(36.995)	30.120	(37.665)	47.325	(36.709)
Unemployment	0.138	(3.190)	−0.349	(3.168)	0.256	(3.057)
Lagged primary deficit	0.316**	(0.073)	0.295**	(0.073)	0.224**	(0.073)
President's party			−39.844*	(17.758)	−65.411**	(18.514)
Divided government			−23.550	(18.201)	−23.374	(17.845)
UCR governor					18.853	(25.247)
Provincial party governor					−129.840**	(33.163)
Constant	363.780**	(62.096)	371.490**	(61.635)	387.410**	(60.258)
Adjusted R^2	0.978		0.979		0.980	
Degrees of freedom	177		175		173	
N	214		214		214	

Note: White-type standard errors are employed.

*Significant at the .05 level for a two-tailed test.

**Significant at the .01 level for a two-tailed test.

other factors constant, there is no noteworthy difference in per capita spending between provinces that were governed by a member of the UCR and provinces that were governed by a member of the PJ.

The only noteworthy difference (which was not included in hypothesis 2) that exists is that between provinces that were led by a provincial party governor and those that were led by a PJ governor (or a UCR governor). Holding other factors constant, provinces run by a provincial party governor spent significantly less (130 pesos per capita) than provinces run by a PJ governor. This is an interesting finding that we plan to explore in future work.

The results in table 6.2 provide no support whatsoever for hypothesis 3. Not only does the presence of divided government fail to lead to a significant increase in per capita spending, but the negative estimated coefficient indicates that the presence of divided government actually reduces spending, albeit not at a significant level.

A possible explanation for the weak effect of the presence or absence of divided government on spending could be that whereas previous studies of this effect have analyzed governments with relatively closed fiscal environments (e.g., countries or the U.S. states), the Argentine provinces exist within an environment where there is a severe fiscal imbalance between the national and provincial governments. This fiscal imbalance in turn shifts the key determinant of provincial spending from intraprovincial factors to interprovincial factors, since the lion's share of potential revenues is located at the national level. Within this environment intraprovincial politics (e.g., divided government) is much less relevant for provincial fiscal behavior than is the interprovincial game between the provinces (as unitary actors) and the federal government.[18]

6.5   Fiscal Institutions and Provincial Public-Sector Spending

Alesina et al. (1996), Hallerberg and von Hagen (chap. 9 in this volume), von Hagen (1992), and von Hagen and Harden (1994) have emphasized the prominent effect that budgetary institutions have on fiscal behavior. Unfortunately, in Argentina there was little intraprovince budgetary institutions variance between 1985 and 1995. It was therefore not possible to include in our previous models a variable measuring the provinces' fiscal institutions.

However, given the potential relevance of budgetary institutions to provincial public-sector spending, as well as this volume's concern with budgetary institutions, we briefly analyze the link between budgetary institutions and spending in this section. Following a procedure similar to von Hagen (1992)

---

18. Future studies should explore the prediction that divided government at the subnational level would be a significant determinant of fiscal behavior only when vertical fiscal imbalances are small. See Stein, Talvi, and Grisanti, chap. 5 in this volume; and von Hagen and Eichengreen 1996 for further speculation on the interaction of vertical fiscal imbalances with fiscal politics more generally.

Table 6.3   **Provincial Fiscal Institutionalization and Provincial Fiscal Behavior**

Variables	Estimated Coefficient
Bivariate Regression (1). Fiscal Institutionalization Index and	−0.004
provincial fixed-effects coefficients (from equation [3])	(0.006)
Bivariate regression (2). Fiscal Institutionalization Index and	
average per capita provincial public-sector expenditures	−0.003
(for 1985–95)	(0.002)
Bivariate regression (3). Fiscal Institutionalization Index and	−0.772
average per capita deficits (for 1985–95)	(0.022)

Note: $N = 23$. In each bivariate regression the Fiscal Institutionalization Index is the independent variable. The standard errors are reported under the estimated coefficients in parentheses.

for Western European countries and Alesina et al. (1996) for Latin American countries, we utilized the provincial constitutions to construct an index of the level of fiscal institutionalization for the 23 Argentine provinces.[19] Using a 10-point scale (with 10 being the most fiscally institutionalized, and 0 the least) we coded provinces on the basis of the following six factors: (1) executive strength vis-à-vis the legislature in the elaboration of the budget, (2) the extent of limitations on provincial indebtedness, (3) the ability of the municipalities within the province to borrow money, (4) the autonomy/strength of provincial auditory agencies, (5) the incentives for fiscal prudence in the provincial-municipal tax-sharing agreement, and (6) the presence of promotional subsidies in the constitution. These six indicators were summed to create an index of fiscal institutionalization. This index has a potential range from 0 (least fiscally disciplined) to 60 (most fiscally disciplined). Its actual range is from 13 (Salta) to 45 (Mendoza).

Regression (1) in table 6.3 displays the results of the bivariate regression of the Fiscal Institutionalization Index on the estimated coefficients for the provincial (cross-sectional) fixed-effects variables from equation (3) in table 6.2. The Fiscal Institutionalization Index has a very weak effect on the provincial fixed-effects coefficients. This suggests that the lack of a fiscal institutions variable in our models of per capita provincial public-sector spending has no salient impact on the results that are shown in table 6.2. This premise is bolstered by the finding in regression (2) of table 6.3, where the estimated coefficient indicates that a province's budgetary institutions (i.e., the Fiscal Institutionalization Index) have a very weak effect on its level of per capita provincial public-sector spending during the 1985–95 period.

Finally, while this study does not analyze deficits, due to their importance in this literature we include in table 6.3 the result (see regression [3]) of the

19. Unlike this previous work, our index is based on a coding of written documents, not on reported procedures. For a detailed discussion of the methodology employed to create this index see Jones, Sanguinetti, and Tommasi 1997b.

regression of the Fiscal Institutionalization Index on the average per capita primary deficit in the provinces. The strong and significant estimated coefficient indicates a powerful inverse bivariate relationship between the fiscal institutions employed by the 23 provinces and the size of their per capita deficits, with greater levels of fiscal institutionalization leading to smaller deficits. This result corresponds with our previous work, which found the level of provincial fiscal institutionalization to have a potent effect on provincial fiscal behavior (Jones, Sanguinetti, and Tommasi 1997a). It is also consistent with many previous studies by von Hagen and others that have found budget institutionalization variables to have salient explanatory power for deficits, but not for spending.

6.6   Conclusion

This chapter applies the "political economy" approach to the study of fiscal performance in the Argentine provinces. Using a panel of the 23 provinces for the 1985–95 period, we find support for the common-property approach to fiscal policy. Given a high degree of vertical imbalance (i.e., a lack of correspondence between spending and taxing decisions at the local level), provincial governments tend to overexploit the common resource of national taxation. In this game, the federal government elected by a nationwide constituency has better incentives toward fiscal restraint. Given a relatively institutionalized party system and high degree of party discipline, presidents are able to "induce" lower spending by governors from their political party (thereby internalizing part of the fiscal externality).

The Argentine provinces provide a fertile and relatively unexplored ground for the study of the effects of institutions and politics on economic outcomes. In future work we will pursue three tasks. First, via the use of alternative quantitative methods we will include additional variables that were excluded in this analysis due to collinearity problems. Second, we will explore the fiscal impact of budget procedures in more detail. Third, we will engage in a more refined analysis of the link between institutions and expenditures by disaggregating expenditures in such a way that we will be able to distinguish public goods expenditures from particularistic expenditures.

The goal of this current and future research is to contribute to the improvement of general scholarly knowledge on the effect of political and institutional factors on fiscal behavior as well as to provide a better understanding of the determinants of fiscal outcomes in Argentina. In particular, we hope that this work will be of assistance to those currently engaged in the reform of Argentina's political and economic institutions at the national and provincial levels.

References

Aizenman, Joshua. 1998. Fiscal discipline in a union. In *The political economy of economic reforms,* ed. Federico Sturzenegger and Mariano Tommasi. Cambridge, Mass.: MIT Press.

Alesina, Alberto, Ricardo Hausmann, Rudolf Hommes, and Ernesto Stein. 1996. Budget institutions and fiscal performance in Latin America. NBER Working Paper no. 5586. Cambridge, Mass.: National Bureau of Economic Research.

Alt, James E., and Robert C. Lowry. 1994. Divided government, fiscal institutions, and budget deficits: Evidence from the states. *American Political Science Review* 88: 811–28.

Campos, Ed, and Sanjay Pradhan 1996. Budgetary institutions and expenditure outcomes: Binding governments to fiscal performance. World Bank Policy Research Working Paper no. 1646.

Chari, V. V., and Harold Cole. 1995. A contribution to the theory of pork barrel spending. Staff Report 156. Federal Reserve Bank of Minneapolis, Research Department.

Cox, Gary W., and Mathew D. McCubbins. 1997. Political structure and economic policy: The institutional determinants of policy outcomes. In "Political institutions and the determinants of public policy: When do institutions matter?" ed. Stephan Haggard and Mathew D. McCubbins. University of California, San Diego. Photocopy.

Gilligan, Thomas W., and John G. Matsusaka. 1995. Deviations from constituent interests: The role of legislative structure and political parties in the states. *Economic Inquiry* 33:383–401.

Inman, Robert P., and Michael A. Fitts. 1990. Political institutions and fiscal policy: Evidence from the U.S. historical record. *Journal of Law, Economics, and Organization* 6:79–132.

Jones, Mark P. 1997. Evaluating Argentina's presidential democracy: 1983–1995. In *Presidentialism and democracy in Latin America,* ed. Scott Mainwaring and Matthew Soberg Shugart. New York: Cambridge University Press.

Jones, Mark P., Pablo Sanguinetti, and Mariano Tommasi. 1997a. Institutions and fiscal outcomes: Evidence from the Argentine provinces, 1983–95. Universidad de San Andrés. Typescript.

———. 1997b. Politics, institutions, and fiscal performance in the Argentine provinces. Paper presented at the Centro de Estudios para el Desarrollo Institucional Conference on Democracy, Economic Reforms, and Institutional Design, Buenos Aires, June.

McCubbins, Mathew D. 1991. Party governance and U.S. budgets: Divided government and fiscal stalemate. In *Politics and economics in the eighties,* ed. Alberto Alesina and Geoffrey Carliner. Chicago: University of Chicago Press.

Porto, Alberto. 1990. *Federalismo fiscal: El caso Argentino.* Buenos Aires: Editorial Tesis.

Poterba, James. 1994. State responses to fiscal crises: The effects of budgetary institutions and politics. *Journal of Political Economy* 102:799–821.

Sanguinetti, Pablo, and Mariano Tommasi. 1997. The economic and institutional determinants of provincial budget outcomes: Argentina, 1983–1996. Inter-American Development Bank. Photocopy.

Tommasi, Mariano. 1998. Institutions and fiscal outcomes. *Desarrollo Económico* 38: 409–38.

Velasco, Andrés. 1998. The common property approach to the political economy of fiscal policy. In *The political economy of economic reforms,* ed. Federico Sturzenegger and Mariano Tommasi. Cambridge, Mass.: MIT Press.

von Hagen, Jürgen. 1992. Budgeting procedures and fiscal performance in the European Communities. Economic Paper no. 26. Commission of the European Commissions.

von Hagen, Jürgen, and Barry Eichengreen. 1996. Federalism, fiscal restraints, and European Monetary Union. *American Economic Review* 86 (2): 134–38.

von Hagen, Jürgen, and Ian J. Harden. 1994. National budget process and commitment to fiscal discipline. *European Economic Review* 39:771–79.

Weingast, Barry R. 1979. A rational choice perspective on congressional norms. *American Journal of Political Science* 23:245–62.

Weingast, Barry, Kenneth Shepsle, and Chris Johnsen. 1981. The political economy of benefits and costs: A neoclassical approach to distributive politics. *Journal of Political Economy* 89:642–64.

7   Public Debt and Budgetary Procedures: Top Down or Bottom Up? Some Evidence from Swiss Municipalities

Lars P. Feld and Gebhard Kirchgässner

7.1 Introduction

By the end of the eighties and early nineties government deficits and public debt in relation to GDP had increased to a higher level than before in nearly all OECD countries. Alesina and Perotti (1995) analyze this development of public debt in OECD countries and deduce two stylized questions that a theoretical explanation should capture: (i) Why are there large and persistent deficits in peacetime, and why now? (ii) Why do deficits and debt differ significantly between countries? The authors survey the existing theoretical explanations of public debt and establish that only a few political-economic models accord with the facts of increased public debt. The tax-smoothing theory of the government budget (see Barro 1979) that presents the government as a "benevolent social planner" maximizing the utility of a representative agent does not, for example, answer those two questions. It can explain neither the high public debt in the eighties nor the large cross-country differences, although it is compatible with the increase of debt as a result of the 1973–74 recession. Much the same holds with the fiscal illusion theory of Buchanan and Wagner (1977). However, similar verdicts can be brought forward against theories that rely on several political sources of time inconsistency,[1] partisan

Lars P. Feld is a research assistant at the University of St. Gallen, Switzerland. Gebhard Kirchgässner is professor of economics and econometrics at the University of St. Gallen, Switzerland.

The authors thank Marcel R. Savioz for helpful suggestions and for the correspondence with the French-speaking municipalities, as well as Sandra Elmer for providing the map of Switzerland and Robert Straw for editing the paper in English. The authors also acknowledge the very useful discussions and comments by W. Mark Crain, Bernard Dafflon, Guy Gilbert, Jürgen von Hagen, Claude Jean-Renaud, Jim Poterba, Philippe Thalmann, and Hannelore Weck-Hannemann. Without the cooperation of the administrations of 131 Swiss communities and 26 Swiss cantons and their answers to a survey, this study would not have been possible.

1. See, e.g., Alesina and Tabellini 1988.

theories,[2] and theories of intergenerational redistribution.[3] According to the analysis of Alesina and Perotti, there exist only two classes of models that are able to address the two stylized questions mentioned above: on the one hand, models in which governments use public debt strategically to commit future governments,[4] and, on the other hand, models of distributional conflict and "wars of attrition."[5]

Recently, Velasco (chap. 2 in this volume) has developed a dynamic model of government net assets as the common property of all fiscal authorities. Several interest groups or the different spending ministries attempt to get money from this common resource in order to finance policies benefiting the preferences of their group members or constituencies. Then a dynamic problem arises that is similar to the "tragedy of the commons" (see Hardin 1968). The problem of a fiscal commons consists in the fact that each of the n agents uses the whole stock of resources and not one-nth of it as a basis for consumption or spending decisions.

Given the facts of increasing public deficits and debt as a fiscal commons and the arguments brought forward that serious failures of political markets tend to create such deficits, two institutional possibilities to reduce deficits and debt may be proposed. Buchanan and Wagner (1977), for example, demand formal (constitutional) fiscal restraints. However, as the German example shows, formal fiscal restraints even on the constitutional level do not necessarily prevent federal public debt from growing.[6] Recently, several authors have analyzed the conditions that most probably lead to binding balanced-budget rules.[7] Bohn and Inman (1996) provide a comprehensive empirical analysis on the different designs of formal fiscal constraints. They find that in order to be effective deficit constraints must require a balanced budget at the end of the fiscal year, not just in prospect at the beginning (no-carry-over rule). Furthermore, balanced-budget rules must be grounded constitutionally rather than merely based on statutes. Another factor that matters is the enforcement of balanced-budget rules: Of the 36 U.S. states with a no-carry-over rule, the 15 whose supreme courts are appointed by the state's legislature or governor had larger deficits than the 21 states whose supreme courts are elected directly by the voters. Finally, the balanced-budget rule must be difficult to amend.

As von Hagen (1991) has shown for the U.S. states, formal fiscal restraints give incentives to policymakers to increase off-budget activities.[8] Thus, in con-

---

2. Tabellini and LaVia (1989) report empirical evidence that deficits in the United States were systematically larger under Democratic than under Republican administrations.

3. See Cukierman and Meltzer 1989 and Tabellini 1991.

4. See, e.g., Shachar 1993 or, for local governments, Rosenberg 1992.

5. See, e.g., Alesina and Drazen 1991, as well as Drazen and Grilli 1993.

6. Art. 115 (1) of the German Grundgesetz demands that, except for major macroeconomic disequilibria, federal net borrowing not be higher than investment expenditure of the federal level.

7. See Alesina and Bayoumi 1996; Alt and Lowry 1994; Eichengreen and von Hagen 1996; Poterba 1994, 1995a, 1995b; von Hagen and Eichengreen 1996; and the surveys in Poterba 1996, 1997.

8. For the ineffectiveness of constitutional limitations in the case of U.S. states see also Kiewiet and Szakaly 1996.

trast to this rather outcome-oriented institutional solution, von Hagen (1992) and von Hagen and Harden (1994, 1995) have analyzed whether budgetary procedures have an impact on the level of government expenditure and budget deficits. According to their results the following features reduce the spending bias: (i) a strong position of the prime minister or finance minister in the negotiation process of the budget within the government before the budget law has passed, or government negotiations producing a set of binding targets early in that process; (ii) a parliamentary process with strong limits on amendments, line-item voting on expenditures, and an "all-or-nothing" vote on the total size of the budget preceding the parliamentary debate; (iii) a large degree of transparency of the budget; (iv) a limited spending flexibility for the ministries and a strong position of the finance minister vis-à-vis the spending ministers in the execution process of the budget law. All in all, "top down" procedures work better than "bottom up" procedures.[9]

In these theoretical as well as empirical studies another institutional possibility of debt control has been neglected as an independent rule: Voters may have the possibility to vote on budget deficits in referenda. Buchanan (1958, 1987) supposed that democratic governments, either direct or representative, entail a bias for borrowing because voters favor current benefits but dislike taxes. Therefore he suggests constitutional constraints. Inman (1982) argued that fiscal limitations are potentially valuable policy tools when direct democratic review (or a Tiebout-like exit process) does not adequately control government behavior. Moak, however, considers direct democracy as the only reliable safeguard against excessive indebtedness (1982, 114). If voters acted as fiscal conservatives, as Peltzman (1992) in an empirical study of U.S. elections has impressively shown, they would be more reluctant to increase public debt. Indeed, because referenda and initiatives reduce the political leeway of the government, elements of direct democracy may also reduce the strategic use of public debt: governments and parties then have fewer opportunities to follow the special interests of their constituencies. More basically, the principal-agent problem inherent in (more or less) representative democracies becomes less severe once referenda and/or initiatives are available for citizens.[10]

Using Swiss (Pommerehne 1978, 1990) and U.S. data (Matsusaka 1995), researchers have derived empirical results concerning the relationship between direct democracy and the economy. First, government expenditure is—ceteris paribus—lower in direct than in representative democracy (see also Holcombe 1980). Second, the structure of public expenditure changes with respect to different institutional regimes. The existence of the initiative leads to a reduction in the state, as well as an increase in the local, component of state and local spending. Third, with respect to revenue composition direct democracies

---

9. De Haan and Sturm (1994) are able to confirm these results under ceteris paribus conditions for European Union (EU) member states during the eighties. These confirming results are, however, obtained by excluding Luxembourg from their panel data set.

10. See Matsusaka 1992; Matsusaka and McCarty 1997; as well as Romer and Rosenthal 1978, 1979.

rely more on charges than on broad-based taxes. Fourth, Pommerehne and Weck-Hannemann (1996) show that the willingness to finance government is higher in cantons with a direct than in those with a representative democratic system, indicating more efficient revenue collection. Fifth, some public goods are produced more efficiently in direct democracies than in representative democracies.[11] Sixth, economic performance, as measured by GDP per capita is—ceteris paribus—higher in those Swiss cantons with direct than in those with representative democracies (see Feld and Savioz 1997). Finally, Kiewiet and Szakaly (1996) show for a panel of the U.S. states from 1961 to 1990 that referendum approval of guaranteed debt is the most effective restraint on state borrowing.

In this paper, we thus attempt to find clues in the actual experience of Switzerland whether and which budgetary procedures have an impact on public debt. The variation in Swiss budgetary procedures and direct democratic decision making between municipalities and between states (cantons) is considerable. Switzerland is one of the few industrial countries (and presumably the only European one) where it is possible to study the effect of institutional differences on the level of government deficits and public debt. In section 7.2 the institutional variety of Switzerland is described. In section 7.3 a spatial model is outlined in order to illustrate the restrictions imposed on representatives by the voters in a referendum. An econometric model is developed and empirically estimated using data on Swiss municipalities in section 7.4. The paper finishes with some concluding remarks (sec. 7.5).

7.2 Budgetary Procedures at Swiss Subfederal Levels

Switzerland's constitution combines elements of direct democracy with a high degree of federalism. It consists of three governmental levels that establish strong fiscal competencies of the single states (cantons) and local government units. Although fiscal competencies of the different tiers of government are not the focus of this paper, they are worth mentioning. The main progressive taxes on personal and corporate income are state and local taxes. The cantons have the basic power to tax income and capital. The municipalities can levy a surcharge on cantonal direct and property taxes. The central government relies mainly on indirect (proportional) taxes, the general sales tax and specific consumption taxes like the mineral oil tax. There is, however, a small but highly progressive federal income tax, which amounts to 25 percent of total federal tax revenue in 1994, while the cantons and municipalities rely on income and property taxes for about 50 percent of their total revenue and 95 percent of their tax revenue. The federal income tax has a maximal marginal tax rate of 13.2 percent and an average tax rate of 11.5 percent. Owing to a

---

11. Pommerehne (1983) analyzes refuse collection in Swiss municipalities and shows that the costs of production are the lowest in direct democratic municipalities with a private supplier.

basic tax exemption, the highest 3 percent of income taxpayers pay 50 percent of the revenue of the federal income tax. The federal government can also rely on a source tax on income from interest, the so-called *Verrechnungssteuer.* There are systems of horizontal and vertical fiscal equalization, mainly consisting of matching grants, as well as regional policies. However, the system is not as generous as, for example, in Germany: The share of own revenue from all government revenue ranges from 65 percent to 99.8 percent in our sample of 137 Swiss municipalities.

Concerning elements of direct democracy, the Swiss constitution includes a constitutional initiative and obligatory and optional referenda on the federal level, but no legislative initiative. A constitutional initiative requires 100,000 signatures (2.2 percent of the voters in 1994), an optional referendum 50,000 signatures (1.1 percent of the voters in 1994). Since the share of required signatures from all votes has declined from 7.5 percent (1893) to 2.2 percent (1994) in the case of the constitutional initiative and from 4.7 percent (1879) to 1.1 percent (1994) in the case of the optional referendum, the number of executed initiatives and optional referenda has substantially risen during the last hundred years (Kleinewefers 1995). Only once, in 1977, after women's right to vote was established in 1971 (on the federal level), did voters increase the signature requirement in a referendum, bringing it back to its original time trend.

At the federal level, the Swiss political system continually developed toward a higher degree of direct democracy during the first hundred years after the constitution of 1848, which already established a constitutional initiative (on total revision of the constitution) and an obligatory referendum on constitutional changes.[12] Thürer (1992) argues that the development of direct democratic institutions at the central level in Switzerland follows a trend over time toward more popular participation. In 1874 the optional referendum on laws was introduced. In 1891 an initiative on partial revision of the constitution was established. In 1921 the referendum on international treaties (extended in 1977 to the joining of international organizations) and in 1949 an obligatory referendum on urgent, universally binding federal decisions were introduced in the constitution. Several attempts to introduce a legislative initiative at the federal level and thus to increase the possibilities for popular participation were rejected (1950, 1958, 1972). Most recently, a committee is collecting signatures for an initiative aimed at introducing a constructive referendum (a referendum with counterproposal) at the central level.

Since 1949 there have also been slight changes in the creation and use of

---

12. See Luthardt 1994. Sometimes direct democracy in Switzerland is attributed to the political self-organization of Swiss citizens in townships and villages by local assemblies comparable to the U.S. town meetings. The constitutional changes in the nineteenth century appear to have developed from the Middle Ages with elements of direct democracy carried over to modern times as the institutions of referendum and initiative. We start the description of the history of Swiss direct democracy in the nineteenth century, however, because it is more profoundly analyzed than the historical records of small villages in earlier times.

referenda and initiatives in the cantons and municipalities of Switzerland, although they are rather minor and do not always aim at more direct democracy. Referenda and initiatives are institutions with a widespread though varying use at those levels. On the state level, we find the whole spectrum from the classic assembly in some cantons, like the two Appenzell, Glarus, and Obwalden, to more representative democracies in others, like Neuchatel. The same dispersion is found at the local level. In some cantons and municipalities the obligatory and optional referenda include more issues than in others; some establish a legislative initiative in addition to the constitutional initiative, others do not.

Much the same holds with respect to budgetary procedures. Some cantons, like St. Gallen, rely on more stringent procedural rules than others. Some cantons allow for participation of voters in the budgetary process in a referendum on the budget draft, the tax rate, or the budget deficit. Other cantons give the secretary of finance a stronger position in the budgetary process, while yet others decide on the budget in a meeting of the heads of all spending departments. Thus, the question whether a "top down" or a "bottom up" budgetary procedure leads to more favorable results should become answerable in the Swiss institutional setting.

The focus of our analysis is on the local level only. Swiss municipalities have a much greater variation in budgetary decision-making processes than cantons do. Our data set includes 131 of the 137 largest Swiss towns and communities, whose population ranges between approximately 400,000 and approximately 3,000 persons.[13] Table 7.1 sketches the distribution of those municipalities within the 26 cantons and the percentage of the cantonal population that lives in them. Nearly 46 percent of the Swiss population lives in these 137 municipalities. Cantons that include relatively large towns like Zürich or typical city-states like Basel-Stadt or Genève have a higher municipal populational fraction in our data set. Small cantons that are situated in the mountainous areas and have a higher share of rural population are somewhat underrepresented. This sample selection also influences the variation and distribution of budgetary decision making since Swiss rural municipalities, for example, by having local assemblies, make more use of direct democratic decision making on the average than larger municipalities.[14]

Table 7.2 contains information on the extent of direct democratic budgetary decision making reported as the mean of the municipalities of the respective canton and descriptive statistics for the different language areas of Switzer-

13. We have not yet received data from the municipalities of Dübendorf (ZH), Baar (ZG), Onex (GE), Wetzikon (ZH), Cham (ZG), and Locarno (TI). These communities, which count only for 1.37 percent of the Swiss population, therefore had to be excluded from our sample.
14. One reason is that the larger the population of a community is, the smaller the benefits of participating and, therefore, the participation rate in local assemblies. (For empirical evidence in the canton Basel-Landschaft see Kirchgässner and Pommerehne 1978.) Correspondingly, on the state level, assemblies exist only in very small cantons, and they are sometimes contested today. Nevertheless, using the instruments of referenda and initiatives, direct democracy is also handled in large cantons or cities.

Table 7.1   **Population in Swiss Municipalities with Respect to Their State (Canton)**

State (Canton)	Number of Municipalities	Population in % of Population of the Canton
Zürich (ZH)	24	65.8
Bern (BE)	17	42.6
Luzern (LU)	7	47.8
Uri (UR)	1	24.2
Schwyz (SZ)	3	31.2
Obwalden (OW)	0	0.0
Nidwalden (NW)	1	18.8
Glarus (GL)	1	14.9
Zug (ZG)	3	56.9
Fribourg (FR)	3	23.4
Solothurn (SO)	3	21.5
Basel-Stadt (BS)	2	99.5
Basel-Landschaft (BL)	8	51.0
Schaffhausen (SH)	2	62.1
Appenzell a. Rh. (AR)	1	29.9
Appenzell i. Rh. (AI)	1	37.4
St. Gallen (SG)	8	37.6
Graubünden (GR)	4	29.6
Aargau (AG)	8	19.3
Thurgau (TG)	5	32.3
Ticino (TI)	4	22.7
Vaud (VD)	12	47.7
Valais (VS)	5	31.0
Neuchâtel (NE)	4	53.0
Genève (GE)	8	76.9
Jura (JU)	2	27.8

land. The first column reports whether there is an obligatory referendum, an optional referendum, or a local assembly on the budget draft. The second column indicates whether the tax rate is controlled by the voters in an obligatory referendum, an optional referendum, or a local assembly. The last column shows whether especially the budget deficit is controlled by the citizens in an obligatory referendum, an optional referendum, or a local assembly.

The latter information is graphically presented in figure 7.1, showing a map of Switzerland, the abbreviations for the cantons used in table 7.1, and the language border between the German and French (line 1) and the German and Italian (line 2) language areas of Switzerland. French-speaking Switzerland is the smaller area in the west of the map, while the Italian-speaking area consists of Ticino and parts of the canton of Graubünden in the south of Switzerland. Those cantons in which the majority of municipalities in our sample has no direct democratic decisions over the budget deficit are captured by the white (unshaded) area. Note that figure 7.1 does not capture direct democracy at the

Table 7.2   **Direct Democracy in Switzerland**

Canton	Mean of Cantonal Municipalities		
	Budget Draft[a]	Tax Rate[b]	Budget Deficits[c]
Zürich (ZH)	0.500	0.500	0.500
Bern (BE)	1.000	1.000	0.882
Luzern (LU)	1.000	1.000	0.714
Uri (UR)	1.000	1.000	1.000
Schwyz (SZ)	1.000	1.000	1.000
Obwalden (OW)			
Nidwalden (NW)	1.000	1.000	1.000
Glarus (GL)	1.000	1.000	0.000
Zug (ZG)	0.667	0.667	0.000
Fribourg (FR)	1.000	1.000	1.000
Solothurn (SO)	1.000	1.000	0.667
Basel-Stadt (BS)	0.000	0.000	1.000
Basel-Landschaft (BL)	0.250	0.250	1.000
Schaffhausen (SH)	1.000	1.000	1.000
Appenzell a. Rh. (AR)	1.000	1.000	0.000
Appenzell i. Rh. (AI)	0.000	1.000	0.000
St. Gallen (SG)	1.000	1.000	0.000
Graubünden (GR)	1.000	1.000	0.000
Aargau (AG)	1.000	1.000	0.000
Thurgau (TG)	1.000	1.000	0.600
Ticino (TI)	0.000	0.000	1.000
Vaud (VD)	1.000	1.000	1.000
Valais (VS)	0.200	0.200	0.800
Neuchâtel (NE)	0.000	1.000	0.000
Genève (GE)	1.000	1.000	1.000
Jura (JU)	1.000	1.000	1.000
All municipalities			
Mean	0.759	0.832	0.635
Median	1.000	1.000	1.000
Standard deviation	0.446	0.478	0.483
German speaking			
Mean	0.788	0.848	0.535
Median	1.000	1.000	1.000
Standard deviation	0.435	0.502	0.501
French and Italian speaking			
Mean	0.684	0.789	0.895
Median	1.000	1.000	1.000
Standard deviation	0.471	0.413	0.311

[a]$D = 1$ if the budget draft is controlled by the voters in an obligatory referendum, an optional referendum, or a local assembly.

[b]$D = 1$ if the tax rate is controlled by the voters in an obligatory referendum, an optional referendum, or a local assembly.

[c]$D = 1$ if the budget deficit is separately controlled by the voters in an obligatory referendum, an optional referendum, or a local assembly.

**Fig. 7.1   Cantons with majority of municipalities using referenda
on budget deficits**

cantonal level but the cantonal average of the municipalities concerning only
a single aspect of direct legislation. Figure 7.1 shows that the Latin-speaking
municipalities are more often directly controlled by the voters in the case of
the budget deficit than the German-speaking municipalities (mean$_G$ = 0.54
versus mean$_L$ = 0.90). As table 7.2 shows, however, German-speaking municipalities have more direct democracy with respect to the budget draft and the
tax rate than the French- and Italian-speaking municipalities. The mean of the
dummy variable on budget draft is 0.79 in German- and 0.68 in Latin-speaking
municipalities (mean of the 137 municipalities = 0.76), while the means of
the dummy on the tax rate are 0.85 and 0.79, respectively (mean of the 137
municipalities = 0.83).

In jurisdictions where voters are directly involved in the budgetary process,
they usually enter the process at the later stages. First, the budget is drafted in
the local executives either by the bureau of the secretary of finance or the
mayor or by the different spending bureaus. Second, it is discussed in the executive until a final budget draft is presented to the local parliaments (or directly
to the voters in a few cases). After the draft has passed the legislature and has
been amended by the executive according to the legislative requirements, it is
presented to the voters for final approval either after a proposal of the voters in

Table 7.3   Structure of Negotiations within Government

| | Mean of Cantonal Municipalities | | | |
Canton	General Constraint[a]	Agenda Setting[b]	Scope of Budget Norms[c]	Structure of Negotiations[d]
Zürich (ZH)	0.182	2.318	3.879	2.636
Bern (BE)	0.294	1.706	4.000	1.412
Luzern (LU)	0.000	1.714	4.000	1.143
Uri (UR)	0.000	2.000	4.000	2.000
Schwyz (SZ)	1.000	0.667	4.000	0.000
Obwalden (OW)				
Nidwalden (NW)	0.000	2.000	4.000	2.000
Glarus (GL)	0.000	1.000	4.000	0.000
Zug (ZG)	0.000	3.000	4.000	4.000
Fribourg (FR)	2.667	2.333	4.000	2.667
Solothurn (SO)	0.000	2.667	4.000	2.667
Basel-Stadt (BS)	0.000	2.500	4.000	3.000
Basel-Landschaft (BL)	0.125	2.125	4.000	2.250
Schaffhausen (SH)	0.000	2.000	4.000	1.000
Appenzell a. Rh. (AR)	3.000	1.000	4.000	2.000
Appenzell i. Rh. (AI)	0.000	1.000	4.000	2.000
St. Gallen (SG)	0.500	1.625	4.000	1.750
Graubünden (GR)	1.000	2.000	4.000	1.500
Aargau (AG)	0.500	2.250	4.000	2.250
Thurgau (TG)	0.000	2.000	4.000	0.800
Ticino (TI)	0.000	2.000	4.000	2.000
Vaud (VD)	0.417	1.750	4.000	1.833
Valais (VS)	2.400	2.000	4.000	2.000
Neuchâtel (NE)	0.000	2.250	4.000	2.500
Genève (GE)	2.143	2.714	4.000	1.714
Jura (JU)	0.500	2.500	4.000	3.000
All municipalities				
Mean	0.519	2.015	3.980	1.924
Median	0.000	2.000	4.000	2.000
Standard deviation	1.235	1.008	0.233	1.299
Range	4.000	4.000	2.670	4.000
German speaking				
Mean	0.333	1.968	3.972	1.874
Median	0.000	2.000	4.000	2.000
Standard deviation	1.023	0.983	0.274	1.331
Range	4.000	4.000	2.670	4.000
French and Italian speaking				
Mean	1.000	2.139	4.000	2.056
Median	0.000	2.000	4.000	2.000
Standard deviation	1.581	1.073	0.000	1.218
Range	4.000	4.000	0.000	4.000

[a]General constraint: no general constraint = 0; constraint on debt in relation to nominal GDP = 1; constraint on debt in relation to nominal GDP and deficit in relation to nominal GDP = 2; constraint on government spending in relation to nominal GDP or "Golden Rule" = 3; constraint on government spending and deficit in relation to nominal GDP = 4.

Table 7.3   (continued)

ᵇAgenda setting for budget negotiations: secretary of finance (SF) or "cabinet" collects bids from heads of departments = 0; SF or "cabinet" collects bids subject to preagreed guidelines = 1; "cabinet" decides on budget norms first = 2; SF proposes budget norms to be voted on by the "cabinet" = 3; SF or mayor determines budget parameters to be observed by heads of departments = 4.

ᶜScope of budget norms in the setting of agenda: expenditure or deficit = 0; specific budget targets = 1.33; specific together with overall limits on the budget size = 2.66; "broad," i.e., overall limits on the budget size = 4.

ᵈStructure of negotiations: all "cabinet members" involved together = 0; multilateral = 2; bilateral between heads of departments and SF = 4.

an optional referendum or because the budgetary process requires an obligatory referendum. In some municipalities, the budget deficit has to be approved by the voters separately; that is, the budget deficit is not only reported in the budget draft but also annexed on a different ballot sheet. Thus, the budget deficit has to be agreed upon by the voters in a way similar to the separate decision on tax rate changes.

We measure budgetary procedures of Swiss municipalities not only by the extent of direct democratic decision making on the budget, but also by more or less the same indices of procedures as von Hagen (1992, 69–74). Von Hagen builds a structural index and an index of long-term planning constraint that consists of five different items in the budgetary process: (i) the structure of negotiations within government, (ii) the structure of the parliamentary process, (iii) the informativeness of the budget draft, (iv) the flexibility of the budget execution, and (v) the long-term planning constraint. The information we received from the Swiss municipalities has not allowed us to get exactly the same information about the structure of parliamentary process and the flexibility of budget execution. Thus, the structure of negotiations within government is characterized in our data by the following issues, shown in table 7.3 as cantonal means of the municipalities and descriptives for the two Swiss language areas.[15]

The existence of a general constraint indicates that the draft begins with the statement of overall restrictions or targets on total spending, revenues, deficits, or government debt. General constraints are not used frequently as means to discipline municipalities in Switzerland. Only in the cantons of Fribourg, Appenzell Ausser Rhoden, Valais, and Genève are municipalities more strongly restricted by such formal constraints than in other cantons. In some of these cantons, municipalities facing severe budgetary problems get grants from the cantonal fiscal equalization scheme only if those local decision-making bodies agree to raise their local tax rates in order to reduce deficits and debt. This has been treated in the data underlying table 7.3 as the strongest general constraint. The agenda setting for budget negotiations reflects whether the initial budget

15. Information on the details of these indices is provided in the notes to tables 7.3–7.5.

guidelines are set by the mayor or secretary of finance or by the heads of the different departments. Agenda-setting power of a central authority in the budgetary process varies considerably between the municipalities and the different cantons. A particular pattern is observable only to a limited extent. The small cantons of Schwyz, Glarus, Appenzell Ausser Rhoden, and Appenzell Inner Rhoden have average values of their municipalities that are low, which indicates a weak role for the agenda setter. Agenda-setting power of the secretary of finance or the mayor is only slightly higher in Latin-speaking municipalities (mean = 2.14) than in German-speaking ones (mean = 1.97). The agenda may specify the scope of budget norms, that is, overall limits on the budget size, limits on spending or deficits, or it may determine specific budget targets together with one of the former limits. The scope of budget norms does not vary much over the municipalities in the sample except for the canton of Zürich. Subsequent negotiations may be structured bi- or multilaterally between the secretary of finance and the heads of the departments or contain the whole "cabinet." The structure of negotiations within government appears to be more centralized and "top down" in Latin-speaking municipalities (mean = 2.06) than in the German-speaking ones (mean = 1.87).

Table 7.4 contains information on the informativeness of the budget. It gives some answers on the budgetary treatment of special funds, that is, whether they are included in the budget or whether the municipality engages in considerable off-budget activities. The inclusion of special funds in the budget is higher in German-speaking (mean = 2.25) than in Latin-speaking Switzerland (mean = 2.00). Another interesting fact is that off-budget activities appear to be most prevalent in the municipalities of the two city cantons of Basel-Stadt and Genève. Basel-Stadt, for example, mixes up cantonal and municipal budgets such that a consistent separation between both becomes difficult. Furthermore, the table shows whether the budget is submitted in one comprehensive document or split up in different parts, for example, different documents for revenue and expenditure or for different policy domains, which make it difficult to estimate the overall effect of the budget and allow for common-pool problems. Particularly the municipalities of the smaller cantons, but also those from the cantons of Ticino, Basel-Landschaft, Schaffhausen, and Jura hardly submit any comprehensive document. After 1990, many of the Swiss municipalities introduced the so-called New Accounting Model, where the comprehensiveness of the budget document is a central requirement. Some municipalities introduced it earlier. This may also explain variations in this issue. Finally, table 7.4 contains information on the transparency of the budget. This is an overall judgment on the informativeness, for example, whether expenditures are broken down by function and administrative responsibility, or revenues are presented in a breakdown by source. This issue again reveals the differences in the introduction of the New Accounting Model in Swiss local budgets. Again, some municipalities, particularly in the German-speaking cantons, introduce these new requirements more slowly. The extent to which government loans to nongovernment

Table 7.4   Informativeness of the Budget Draft

Canton	Mean of Cantonal Municipalities		
	Special Funds[a]	One Document[b]	Transparency[c]
Zürich (ZH)	2.318	1.455	2.455
Bern (BE)	2.471	1.294	2.706
Luzern (LU)	2.429	1.714	2.857
Uri (UR)	2.000	0.000	2.000
Schwyz (SZ)	3.667	4.000	4.000
Obwalden (OW)			
Nidwalden (NW)	2.000	0.000	2.000
Glarus (GL)	2.000	0.000	2.000
Zug (ZG)	1.000	0.000	2.000
Fribourg (FR)	2.000	0.667	2.000
Solothurn (SO)	1.667	0.000	2.000
Basel-Stadt (BS)	0.500	2.000	3.000
Basel-Landschaft (BL)	1.750	0.000	1.750
Schaffhausen (SH)	2.000	0.000	2.000
Appenzell a. Rh. (AR)	2.000	0.000	2.000
Appenzell i. Rh. (AI)	2.000	0.000	2.000
St. Gallen (SG)	2.250	1.500	2.500
Graubünden (GR)	2.500	1.000	2.500
Aargau (AG)	2.375	1.500	2.750
Thurgau (TG)	2.600	1.600	2.400
Ticino (TI)	1.333	0.000	2.000
Vaud (VD)	2.750	2.000	3.000
Valais (VS)	2.000	0.000	2.000
Neuchâtel (NE)	2.250	1.000	2.000
Genève (GE)	0.571	2.857	3.429
Jura (JU)	2.000	0.000	2.000
All municipalities			
Mean	2.183	1.282	2.534
Median	2.000	0.000	2.000
Standard deviation	1.142	1.858	1.105
Range	4.000	4.000	4.000
German speaking			
Mean	2.253	1.200	2.484
Median	2.000	0.000	2.000
Standard deviation	1.081	1.831	1.080
Range	4.000	4.000	4.000
French and Italian speaking			
Mean	2.000	1.500	2.667
Median	2.000	0.000	2.000
Standard deviation	1.287	1.935	1.171
Range	4.000	4.000	4.000

[a]Special funds: not included in the budget draft (considerable off-budget activities) = 0; some special funds are included = 1; most special funds are included = 2; special funds are included, but annexed to budget draft = 3; special funds are included in the budget draft = 4.

[b]Budget submitted in one document or in different documents: no (different documents for revenue and expenditure or for different policy domains) = 0; in recent times submitted in one document = 2; submitted in one document = 4.

[c]Assessment of budget transparency, i.e., expenditures broken down by function and administrative responsibility or revenues presented in a breakdown by source: hardly transparent = 0; not fully transparent = 2; fully transparent = 4.

entities as well as links to national accounts statistics are revealed in the budget draft were reported only by a few municipalities and thus had to be skipped.

The municipalities have also provided some insight into the nature of long-term planning constraints at the local level. Table 7.5 contains some information on the existence of a multiannual target or projections of intertemporal guidelines of their budget plans, the length of the planning horizon, the kind of forecasts used—that is, on what basis these forecasts are derived, ad hoc, fixed, updated, or by using a macroeconomic model—and the degree of commitment that is connected to the multiannual plan. The commitment may only express political preferences and the willingness to make efforts to come close to these targets, without, however, being binding. The targets may also be only indicative in that they carry less weight than a political commitment. They may be part of a coalition agreement, only for internal orientation or more specific on total government revenue and expenditures. The long-term planning constraint shows that German-speaking municipalities are more constrained. The target exists more often, the nature of the forecast is more reliable, and the commitment connected with it is stronger. Only the planning horizon is longer in Latin-speaking Switzerland. However, again the municipalities of smaller cantons have less often introduced long-term planning constraints, as the figures for the municipalities of the cantons of Schwyz, Nidwalden, Zug, Appenzell Aussen Rhoden, and Appenzell Inner Rhoden show. Again, some of these differences are caused by differences in the introduction of the New Accounting Model, which does not require the introduction of long-term planning targets but recommends it as a basis for rational budgetary planning.

7.3   A Spatial Model

The budgetary process in Swiss municipalities with referendum approval of the budget deficit can be analyzed in a similar, but more stylized manner, as Inman (1997) does in a general paper. Consider a budget game where agents prefer different levels of budget deficits d up to a maximum limit on deficits d_{max} that is set by capital markets. Deficits that exceed d_{max} are not funded by the market. Suppose that the executive prefers a public deficit level d_e that is higher than the one preferred by parliament, d_p. The latter prefers deficits that exceed the deficit level preferred by the voters, d_v, such that $d_{max} > d_e > d_p > d_v$. The budgetary process outlined above corresponds to a multistage budget game illustrated by the following spatial model.[16]

The agents in figure 7.2 decide on two issues X_1 and X_2 that may represent two different spending categories. Let X_1 represent public infrastructure and X_2 public education spending. A movement along the axis corresponds to an increase in spending. The level as well as the structure of spending determines

---

16. The model develops Moser's (1996) and Feld's (1997) applications to the Swiss political system further and applies it to referenda on budget deficits.

Table 7.5   **Long-Term Planning Constraints**

	Mean of Cantonal Municipalities			
Canton	Target[a]	Horizon[b]	Forecast[c]	Commitment[d]
Zürich (ZH)	1.455	0.909	0.591	0.773
Bern (BE)	0.941	0.882	0.529	0.471
Luzern (LU)	2.857	1.571	1.857	1.571
Uri (UR)	4.000	0.000	1.000	2.000
Schwyz (SZ)	1.333	0.333	0.333	0.667
Obwalden (OW)				
Nidwalden (NW)	0.000	0.000	0.000	0.000
Glarus (GL)	4.000	3.000	1.000	2.000
Zug (ZG)	0.000	0.000	0.000	0.000
Fribourg (FR)	0.000	0.000	0.000	0.000
Solothurn (SO)	0.000	0.000	0.000	0.000
Basel-Stadt (BS)	0.000	0.000	0.000	0.000
Basel-Landschaft (BL)	0.500	0.500	0.375	0.250
Schaffhausen (SH)	0.000	0.000	0.000	0.000
Appenzell a. Rh. (AR)	0.000	0.000	0.000	0.000
Appenzell i. Rh. (AI)	0.000	0.000	0.000	0.000
St. Gallen (SG)	0.500	0.250	0.125	0.250
Graubünden (GR)	1.000	0.000	0.250	0.500
Aargau (AG)	1.000	0.500	0.375	0.500
Thurgau (TG)	1.600	0.400	0.400	0.800
Ticino (TI)	0.000	0.000	0.000	0.000
Vaud (VD)	0.000	0.000	0.000	0.000
Valais (VS)	0.800	0.400	0.200	0.400
Neuchâtel (NE)	3.000	1.750	0.750	1.250
Genève (GE)	2.857	2.143	0.714	1.429
Jura (JU)	2.000	1.000	0.500	1.000
All municipalities				
Mean	1.130	0.672	0.443	0.573
Median	0.000	0.000	0.000	0.000
Standard deviation	1.808	1.304	0.843	0.928
Range	4.000	4.000	3.000	3.000
German speaking				
Mean	1.137	0.642	0.484	0.589
Median	0.000	0.000	0.000	0.000
Standard deviation	1.814	1.320	0.909	0.951
Range	4.000	4.000	3.000	3.000
French and Italian speaking				
Mean	1.111	0.750	0.333	0.528
Median	0.000	0.000	0.000	0.000
Standard deviation	1.817	1.273	0.632	0.878
Range	4.000	3.000	3.000	2.000

[a]Multiannual target: no multiannual target = 0; multiannual targets on government spending or government revenue = 2; multiannual targets on total budget size = 4.

[b]Planning horizon (years): one year = 0; two years = 1; three years = 2; four years = 3; five years = 4.

[c]Kind of forecast used: ad hoc forecast = 0; fixed forecast = 1; updated forecast, but not based on a consistent macromodel = 2; updated forecast on the basis of a consistent macromodel = 3.

[d]Degree of commitment: internal orientation = 0; indicative = 1; weak political = 2; strong political = 3.

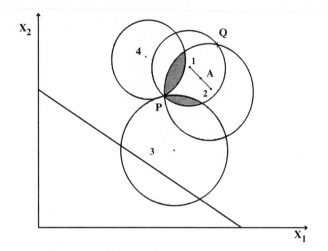

Fig. 7.2   The impact of referenda on the level of public deficits

the level of public deficits.[17] Suppose the budget is balanced if the combinations of X_1 and X_2 represented by the budget constraint are realized. Infrastructural and educational spending exceeding the budget constraint induces public deficits that are higher the farther away from the constraint a combination of X_1 and X_2 is located in the northeast of figure 7.2.[18] Agents have respective ideal or bliss positions represented by the points 1 to 4. For simplicity we assume that agents evaluate deviations from their bliss points equally, so there are common indifference circles around the bliss points. The interests of the government and the parliament differ from each other because they represent different constituencies. Suppose for example that government and parliament are elected in two separate election processes, like the U.S. Congress and the U.S. president, or the governments and parliaments of Swiss cantons and municipalities.[19] The interests of representatives and voters differ from each other because the decisions in municipal parliaments and governments differ among the different parties (ideologies). They may represent a smaller (or larger) fraction of constituent interests than is needed to gain a majority of voters in a referendum.

Suppose point P represents the status quo of a polity. In the jurisdiction,

17. The structure of spending increases the deficit level because local deficits can be incurred mainly in the capital budget, which contains investment in infrastructure to a larger extent than educational spending. This rule is enforced at the Swiss local level to differing degrees.

18. The maximal possible public deficit funded by the capital market, d_{max}, is not shown in figure 7.2 in order not to overload it. It would be located as a budget line in the northeast of point Q.

19. In this situation the government and the president are elected directly by the voters and not by the parliaments. A situation where there are two separately elected chambers like the Senate and the House in the United States or the Swiss Nationalrat and the Swiss Ständerat is also met by the assumptions of the model.

points 1 and 2 are the bliss points of the government and the parliament, respectively, while points 3 and 4 are the bliss points of two groups of voters that are necessary for a majority in a referendum on budget deficits. Point 1 thus corresponds to a public deficit of d_e and point 2 to a deficit of d_p, such that $d_e > d_p$. Suppose that the government is elected for four years and is not restricted by a referendum. The government and the parliament follow their own interests to the extent that political protest does not occur and this issue does not decrease reelection prospects dramatically. First, the government moves and proposes a budget with a deficit d_e. Second, the parliament moves and requires amendments that restrict the level of budget deficits to a point closer to d_p than d_e. The government and the parliament agree after the first two stages of the game to propose a budget deficit that is aimed at increasing deficits above the level of the status quo P. They would propose a combination of educational and infrastructural spending and thus a public deficit within the lens drawn by the points P and Q, that is, point A as a compromise. The interests of the two groups of voters 3 and 4 are not considered in this outcome because they do not have the possibility of exerting voice. If they can influence the outcome, voters will prefer the status quo P.

This can be seen from the following: If a referendum approval of public deficits were allowed as the final stage of the budget game, the representatives' proposal would only be accepted by the median voters of groups 3 and 4 as a majority of voters, if it were close enough to their bliss points. If only group 3 is necessary to gain a majority of voters, the possible outcomes of the game are reduced to the shaded lens in the lower half of figure 7.2. The group of voters represented by point 4 changes the possible outcomes to the shaded lens in the upper half of figure 7.2 close to the bliss point of the executive. If both groups are necessary to win a deficit referendum, the status quo P cannot be changed. The status quo P thus corresponds to d_v, such that $d_e > d_p > d_v$: A referendum prevents the government from implementing a self-interested spending policy inducing higher public deficits.[20] This model implies the following hypothesis:

HYPOTHESIS 1. *Budget deficits in a representative democracy without deficit referenda and a representative democracy with deficit referenda differ from each other to the extent that representatives are able to follow a self-interested fiscal policy.*

To the extent one follows Peltzman (1992) and Moak (1982) in their assessment that voters are fiscally conservative and prefer lower public deficits than representatives, one would expect that public deficits are lower in jurisdictions with deficit referenda than in those without referenda. To the extent one follows

---

20. In this spatial model it would also be possible to show the different impact of an optional and obligatory referendum as well as an initiative that shifts the agenda-setting power to the voters. In all these cases the ideal working of the direct democratic elements is assumed; i.e., referenda are costlessly possible.

Buchanan (1958, 1987) in his assessment of a bias of voters for borrowing, public deficits might even be higher in jurisdictions with deficit referenda than in those without referenda.

However, the impact of referenda on budget deficits and public debt does not necessarily have to rely on fiscal conservatism of voters and thus their preferences. If public budgets were common-property resources and public debt the policy outcome of a "tragedy of fiscal commons," as Velasco (chap. 2 in this volume) has shown, elements of direct democracy would reduce the danger of n agents overusing the fiscal commons. Remember the basic mechanism leading to a commons dilemma in budgetary decision making: The problem of a fiscal commons consists in the fact that each of the n agents uses the whole stock of resources and not one-nth of it as a basis for consumption or spending decisions. Each agent attempts to get an optimal level of resources out of the fiscal commons by optimizing according to his/her individual yield and individual costs. In a referendum situation agent n faces a different optimization problem. He/she can only decide how the level of the common fiscal resource is distributed among the different budgetary projects. Agent n faces the constraint that the other $n - 1$ agents extract fiscal resources as well and optimizes his/her profit by considering the actions of others. This reasoning implies hypothesis 2:

> HYPOTHESIS 2. *Budget deficits and public debt are lower in a representative democracy with deficit referenda than in a representative democracy without deficit referenda.*

7.4   An Econometric Model

All in all the arguments made above appear to indicate that direct democratic elements as well as a strong role of the finance minister reduce the possibilities of representatives incurring public debt. However, they do not give any insight into whether "top down" (strong finance minister) or "bottom up" (strong role of voters) budgetary procedures are more efficient in the reduction of public debt. In order to test this comparative relationship empirically we develop an econometric model inspired by the models of Roubini and Sachs (1989a, 1989b) and de Haan and Sturm (1994). The dependent variable is debt per capita.[21]

As higher income may reduce the level of public debt, mean income is introduced as an explanatory variable. Due to lack of local GDP data, mean income is defined by total taxable income divided by the number of taxpayers. Thus, it also makes sense to normalize public debt by using the number of taxpayers instead of the number of inhabitants as the population measure of the size of a

---

21. We use public debt instead of deficits because debt is the accumulated result of fiscal policies of the past and may thus enable us to indicate the longer-run influences of budgetary institutions, although the data set lacks a time dimension.

local community. This variable can itself also play a crucial role in the level of local public expenditure. However, its sign is ambiguous. On the one hand, more inhabitants will pay for public goods. This reduces cost per capita (taxpayer), and it should lead to a lower public debt per capita. On the other hand, due to economies of scale in their provision some public goods will be provided only in agglomerations. In this case, the overall level of public expenditure for the agglomeration might increase, and—ceteris paribus—public debt will rise.

Following Roubini and Sachs, the unemployment rate is included in the model. Higher unemployment might trigger higher public debt. The adverse shocks of high unemployment result in increasing deficits, and owing to the fact that net lending in booms rarely appears they also lead—in the long run—to a higher debt.

As pointed out above, the bequest motive as altruism between generations may not be sufficient to prevent the present generation of taxpayers from distributing wealth from future taxpayers by incurring public debt. As Cukierman and Meltzer (1989) as well as Tabellini (1991) have pointed out, the bequest motive becomes weaker the larger the spread in the personal income and/or wealth distribution. This is in line with a hypothesis by Meltzer and Richard (1981), who propose that the higher the ratio of average to median income, the higher the redistribution that is related to it. Thus, the higher this ratio is, the higher the relation between debt and income might be.

Additionally, the model contains some political variables. The first political variable that is included measures the strength of an executive government by introducing the number of coalition parties in the executive. Due to the fact that minority governments do not exist in Swiss municipalities, we avoid the queries made by Edin and Ohlsson (1991) with respect to the Roubini and Sachs coalition variable. As outlined above, the coalition variable is normally expected to have a positive sign; that is, the more political parties are involved in the executive, the higher the share of public debt. However, the existence of direct democratic decision-making rules at all Swiss government levels has led to grand coalitions in Switzerland. Although there is some variation between cantons and between municipalities, at least two of the three greatest political parties, often even all three, the SP (Social Democrats), the FDP (Liberals), and the CVP (Christian Democrats) are part of the executive. This kind of great consensus, called *Konkordanz* (concordance), renders the grand coalition rather normal. We thus would not expect this variable to have a significant impact. The second political variable follows the arguments of the partisan cycles models that left-wing parties are prone to incur a higher public debt. Thus, the share of left-wing parties in the executive should have a positive impact on the level of public debt.

Further political variables consist of the von Hagen indices on budgetary procedures. In contrast to the member countries of the EU, which were investigated by von Hagen (1992), only three of the five proposed items are available for Swiss municipalities. To avoid further aggregation problems, these items are introduced separately.[22] Since a strong position of the secretary of finance in the budget process is supposed to reduce the possibility that the different spending branches in the executive will overuse the fiscal commons, the index of the structure of negotiations within government is expected to have a negative sign. A strong secretary of finance would—ceteris paribus—reduce the level of public debt. A higher informativeness of the budget will reduce the time inconsistency problems mentioned by Alesina and Tabellini (1988), the information problems pointed to by Persson and Svensson (1989), and the fiscal commons problem as well. Therefore, the respective index should have a negative impact. Finally the index of the long-term planning constraint should also have a negative impact since it will also reduce time inconsistency problems.

The last political variable that is included in the model is a dummy variable for direct democracy. It takes on the value of 1 if the executive (or the parliament) is controlled by the voters because of an obligatory referendum, an optional referendum, or a local assembly on the level of the budget deficit, and 0 otherwise. This holds for 87 of our observations (local municipalities). Because of a budgetary referendum the fiscal commons problem is less severe. Deficit referenda lead to a lower level of public debt. Moreover, if voters are fiscally conservative, that is, if they weigh the future tax burden more heavily than the government and/or the parliament, the dummy variable for direct democracy should have a negative impact on the amount of public debt.

Since debt-servicing costs hardly vary between Swiss municipalities, we cannot use interest rates or some other indicator of the "cost of the debt."[23] Instead, one might use the tax rate for the median taxpayer as an indicator of the price a citizen has to pay for the public good. The higher the tax rate, the lower the level of public debt should be. However, in the political process people or political decision makers decide not only the size of public debt, but about several fiscal instruments. Hence, the tax rate is not an exogenously given variable. Public debt is rather the long-run result of fiscal policies, where decisions about expenditure and its financing are made. In Swiss local communities the latter consists of decisions about the tax rate and about revenue that is raised from other sources than taxes. This results in an (annual) surplus or deficit and finally in a certain amount of public debt. This implies, however, that we have a simultaneous decision in the budgetary process about (the planned values of) public debt, the tax rate, the share of own public revenue, and public expenditure.

22. Due to the large number of observations we do not have to aggregate the different indices to save degrees of freedom, as von Hagen (1992) had to do.
23. Although default risk may vary between different Swiss municipalities, neither public institutions nor the Swiss banks provide any data on it. As Bernard Dafflon indicated to us, both may even not have any reliable data since he was asked by Swiss banks to conduct a default risk assessment of municipalities of various cantons. Furthermore, depreciation rates of public capital goods are legally fixed in the different cantons and vary between municipalities. However, these data are not available to us.

Technically, the result is an econometric model with four equations that have to be estimated simultaneously. An estimation of the structural form is, however, impossible, because we do not have the necessary instruments due to the pure cross-section design of our data set. On the other hand, as the interesting political variables are strongly exogenous—there has been, for example, no change in the constitutional structure during the years preceding our analysis—the reduced-form estimates might even be more interesting because they represent the long-run effects of these variables. Thus, we estimate the reduced form of the system with the (logs of the) following variables:

Endogenous variables:

• public debt per taxpayer
• tax rate for the median taxpayer
• share of own government revenue from total revenue
• public expenditure per taxpayer

Exogenous variables:

• average taxable income
• unemployment rate
• number of taxpayers in the municipality
• ratio of average (mean) to median taxable income
• index of structure of negotiations within government
• index of informativeness of the budget
• index of long-term planning constraint
• a dummy variable that takes on the value of 1 if there is direct democratic decision making on the budget deficit and 0 otherwise
• share of leftist parties in the executive
• number of parties in the executive

We estimate this model using a Zellner-Aitken seemingly unrelated regression (SUR) with data for the 131 Swiss municipalities mentioned above for the year 1990.[24] As the sizes of these municipalities are rather different, instead of using ordinary least squares, we perform a weighted regression, using the square root of the number of taxpayers as weight.

The results are given in table 7.6. The main result is that the dummy for direct democratic decision making has a strong negative influence on the amount of public debt. Moreover, it has also significant impacts on the other variables in the system: direct democracy leads—ceteris paribus—to a higher tax rate of the median taxpayer, a higher share of own public revenue, and

---

24. Due to the fact that all explanatory variables are included in all equations the simultaneous estimates of the coefficients are the same as single equation estimates; only the estimates for the variances—and, thus, also the t-statistics—differ.

Table 7.6   Estimates of the SUR-Model for Public Debt, Median Tax Rate, Government Share of Own Revenue, and Public Expenditure

Dependent Variable	Log Public Debt per Taxpayer	Log Tax Rate of the Median Taxpayer	Log Share of Own Public Revenue	Log Total Public Expenditure Per Capita	Wald Coefficient Test
Constant	28.409	−11.177	−4.060	17.312	90.054***
	(6.19)	(−3.94)	(−5.18)	(4.86)	
Log of average taxable income	−2.059***	0.817***	0.340***	−1.753***	68.693***
	(−4.78)	(3.07)	(4.62)	(−5.24)	
Unemployment rate	0.351***	−0.172***	0.023	−0.047	35.443***
	(3.93)	(−3.12)	(1.52)	(−0.68)	
Log number of taxpayers	0.274***	−0.004	0.008	0.207***	71.429***
	(7.21)	(−0.16)	(1.22)	(7.01)	
Log ratio of average (mean) to median taxable income	4.781***	−1.672***	−0.206	5.128***	66.383***
	(5.06)	(−2.87)	(−1.28)	(6.99)	
Index of structure of government negotiations	−0.014	−0.019*	0.005*	0.018	12.893**
	(−0.87)	(−1.92)	(1.88)	(1.48)	
Index of budget informativeness	0.004	−0.013**	−0.003*	0.005	10.051**
	(0.46)	(−2.22)	(−1.69)	(0.66)	
Index of long-term planning constraint	−0.003	0.004	−0.003**	−0.019***	18.968***
	(−0.35)	(0.79)	(−2.02)	(−3.29)	
Dummy of referenda on budget deficits	−0.253***	0.143***	0.054***	−0.140**	37.163***
	(−3.13)	(2.86)	(3.89)	(−2.23)	
Share of leftist parties in the executive	−0.001	0.000	−0.001**	0.001	6.608
	(−0.44)	(0.18)	(−2.23)	(0.74)	
Number of parties in the executive	0.024	−0.043*	0.025***	0.042	17.056**
	(0.58)	(−1.69)	(3.58)	(1.32)	
R^2	0.254	0.166	0.256	0.360	
SER	0.482	0.287	0.079	0.295	
J.-B.	8.156**	0.541	1.722	653.123***	

Note: The numbers in parentheses are the absolute values of the estimated t-statistics. SER is the standard error of the regression, and J.-B. the value of the Jarque-Bera test on normality of the residuals. As weight we use the square root of the number of taxpayers.

***Significantly different from zero at the 1 percent level.

**Significantly different from zero at the 5 percent level.

*Significantly different from zero at the 10 percent level.

lower public expenditure. In contrast to that, none of the other political variables has any significant impact on the size of public debt. The von Hagen indices in particular do not influence the level of public debt at all.[25] This does not imply, however, that these other variables do not have any impact on the whole system: Wald tests for the impact on all four equations show a lack of significance only in the case of the share of leftist parties. The number of parties in the executive has a positive impact on the share of own public revenue, a negative impact on the median tax rate, and no impact on public debt and expenditure. This result is pretty surprising because grand coalitions are the rule rather than the exception in Switzerland. The index of structure of negotiations within government has a negative impact on the tax rate and a positive one on the share of own public revenue; the index of informativeness of the budget has a negative impact on both the tax rate and the share of own public revenue, whereas the index of long-term planning constraint has a negative impact on the share of own public revenue as well as public expenditure.

The log of average taxable income has a strong negative impact on public debt: the richer a local community, the less it has to rely on debt financing. Richer communities will also—ceteris paribus—have higher tax rates for the median taxpayer, a higher share of own public revenues, and—astonishingly—lower public expenditure per capita.[26] The higher unemployment, the higher is public debt and the lower the median tax rate. Neither the share of own public revenue nor public expenditure is significantly affected by unemployment. The population variable has a highly significant positive impact on government expenditure. Thus, the size of the community matters: A doubling of the number of taxpayers raises expenditure per capita by about one-fifth. This clearly reflects that—possibly due to economies of scale—the range of public services is larger in large than in small communities. Because there is no corresponding influence on the revenue side, this also results in significantly higher debt. The Meltzer/Richard–Cukierman/Meltzer variable also matters: the higher income inequality, the higher is public expenditure, the lower is the median tax rate, and, correspondingly, the higher is the public debt. Thus, a higher ratio of mean to median incomes induces higher intergenerational redistribution.

Given the fact that this estimate is a cross section for a share variable, the value of the multiple correlation coefficient might be acceptable: We can explain about 25 percent of the variance of the dependent variable in the debt equation. On the other side, it also clearly indicates that the explanation is far from being perfect. The possible factors that have been proposed in the literature and are included in this equation leave out some other, perhaps more important factors. This holds in a similar way for the other three equations.

25. A Wald test of the three von Hagen indicators gives $\chi^2 = 3.424$, of all five other political variables $\chi^2 = 4.224$. Both values are far away from any conventional significance level.

26. Similar (astonishing) results with respect to public expenditure have been derived by Guengant, Josselin, and Rocaboy (1997) for 36,143 French municipalities in 1991.

The Jarque-Bera statistic shows that the normality hypothesis has to be rejected for the estimated residuals in the debt equation at the 5 percent and in the expenditure equation even at the 1 percent significance level. In the debt equation, this is due to one outlier, the town of Wettingen. In the expenditure equation, we see three outliers: Basel, Lugano, and Altdorf. If we exclude these four observations from our sample, the coefficients of the variables as well as their significance remain largely unchanged. This indicates that our results are robust with respect to these outliers.

Up to now, we have only tested whether there is a significant difference with respect to direct and representative democracy in the constant term of our equation. However, it may well be the case that there are also differences in other coefficients that may lead to a significantly larger public debt in representative versus direct democracies. This might even be the case if we cannot find a structural break in this equation.[27] This can be checked if the model is first re-estimated for only the 84 communities with direct democracy and second the estimated coefficients are employed to simulate "theoretical" values for the 47 communities with representative democracy.[28]

The result is shown in figure 7.3. For the communities with representative democracy, the actual public debt is higher than the theoretical values in 32 of 47 cases: if we assume that an increase is equally likely as a reduction of debt per capita ($p = q = 0.5$), the probability that an increase occurs in not more than 15 municipalities is lower than 2 percent. The simulations show a (weighted) average public debt that is 45.2 percent lower than the actual one. If we calculate this in absolute terms, we get an average per capita debt that is lower by about sFr 10,000 than the actual one. Both of these values are strongly significantly different from zero.[29] But this result is mainly due to the large weight of Zürich, which actually has a rather high debt per capita. Nevertheless, if we exclude this observation, we still get the result that estimated average public debt is 23.8 percent lower than the actual one, and if we calculate this in absolute terms, we get a value of about sFr 4,500. Both of these values are again strongly significantly different from zero.[30] Given an average local public debt of sFr 20,400 per capita in Switzerland, this difference is not only statistically but also economically significant.

27. We performed Chow breakpoint tests for this system. If we test only for a break in the first equation within this system, we get a χ^2-statistic of 24.213 with 10 degrees of freedom, which is significantly different from zero at the 1 percent level. If we test for all coefficients in this equation without the constant term, the value of the test statistic is 13.922, which is not significant at the 10 percent level. If we test for a structural break in the whole system, we get $\chi^2 = 131.392$ with 40 degrees of freedom including the constant terms and $\chi^2 = 87.403$ with 36 degrees of freedom excluding the constant terms. Both results are highly significant.

28. Three of the 87 municipalities in our sample with direct democracy on budget deficits have not provided us with an answer on the survey.

29. The corresponding t-statistics in a weighted regression of the difference between actual and simulated values are 6.29 for the logarithmic and 7.24 for the absolute values.

30. If the observation of Zürich is excluded, the corresponding t-statistics in a weighted regression of the difference between actual and simulated values are 3.42 for the logarithmic and 4.87 for the absolute values.

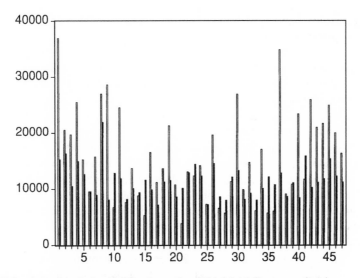

Fig. 7.3   Actual and simulated values of public debt (sFr per capita) in communities with representative democracy
Note: White: actual values. Black: simulated values.

7.5   Concluding Remarks

If we ask for the relative advantages of "bottom up" and "top down" procedures, the message of our empirical analysis is clear: The "bottom up" procedure incorporating direct democratic elements seems to be more promising for reducing public debt than a "top down" procedure. Elements of "top down" procedures that according to von Hagen (1992) have an impact in representative democracies have effects only on the median's tax rate, own revenue, and expenditure, but not on public debt. The voters themselves appear to care more about fiscal discipline than their elected representatives, even if there are no such constraints. The problem of fiscal commons is reduced due to the referendum approval of issuing new public debt. Our results are in line with those for the U.S. states reported by Kiewiet and Szakaly (1996), who have found that the referendum requirement poses a strong restriction on the issuance of guaranteed debt. The results point also in the same direction as Matsusaka's (1995) results for the impact of initiatives on public expenditures of the U.S. states. Referenda lead to lower public expenditures as well. However, our system estimates also indicate that taxpayers in municipalities with a deficit referendum are prepared to bear the cost of public goods to a larger extent than their parliamentary counterparts: the tax rate of the median taxpayer and the share of own revenue are higher in those municipalities.

On the other hand, the conventional story that left-wing politicians are more likely to increase government debt than their conservative counterparts has not been empirically supported. Accepting the evidence from representative democracies that supports this empirical finding, one might conclude that this typical "preference" of left-wing politicians, if it exists at all, can at least be neutralized by direct democratic rules: if the heads of the departments in local communities are directly elected by the citizens, as in most Swiss cities and towns, left-wing candidates might be forced to show the same or perhaps even stronger fiscal discipline to be (re-)elected by a majority of "nonleft" citizens than their centrist and right-wing competitors.

Our results, however, do not necessarily contradict the results of von Hagen (1992). One reason for the difference could be the small size of Switzerland as compared with most other European countries.[31] Of more importance, however, might be the fact that the Swiss direct democratic possibilities do not exist in the member countries of the EU. In the absence of such possibilities, it might well be the case that a budgetary "top down" procedure is to be preferred as a second-best solution. With respect to the future fiscal constitution of the EU a first best solution should be more eligible. Some aspects von Hagen (1992) captures with his indices, like a strong position of the finance minister or the informativeness of the budget, might be helpful, but the main impetus should be on following the Swiss example and implementing direct democratic institutions in the European Union, as has been demanded, for example, by Bernholz (1990) or by Feld and Kirchgässner (1996).

In this context, referenda may also serve their purpose in increasing the accountability of policy decisions. As Besley and Case (1995) have shown, electoral accountability in a representative democracy leads to a more favorable fiscal position of U.S. continental states than do gubernatorial term limits. A potential referendum on budget deficits additionally induces representatives to take the preferences of a majority of voters into account and thus increases accountability of policy decisions. The fact that, according to the evidence of Bohn and Inman (1996), of the 36 U.S. states with a no-carry-over rule, the 15 whose supreme courts are appointed by the state's legislature or governor have larger deficits than the 21 states whose supreme courts are elected directly by the voters, actually fits this conjecture pretty well.

References

Alesina, A., and T. Bayoumi. 1996. The costs and benefits of fiscal rules: Evidence from the U.S. states. NBER Working Paper no. 5614. Cambridge, Mass.: National Bureau of Economic Research.
Alesina, A., and A. Drazen. 1991. Why are stabilizations delayed? A political economy model. *American Economic Review* 81:1170–88.
Alesina, A., and R. Perotti. 1995. The political economy of budget deficits. *IMF Staff Papers* 42:1–31.

31. See von Hagen and Harden 1995 for such an argument.

Alesina, A., and G. Tabellini. 1988. Credibility and politics. *European Economic Review* 32:542–50.

Alt, J., and R. C. Lowry. 1994. Divided government and budget deficits: Evidence from the states. *American Political Science Review* 88:811–28.

Barro, R. J. 1979. On the determination of public debt. *Journal of Political Economy* 87:940–71.

Bernholz, P. 1990. Grundzüge einer Europäischen Verfassung: Ein Bundesstaat mit begrenzter Zentralgewalt. In *Argumente zur Europapolitik*, ed. Frankfurter Institut. No. 3, November, pp. 2–6.

Besley, T., and A. Case. 1995. Does electoral accountability affect economic policy choices? Evidence from gubernatorial term limits. *Quarterly Journal of Economics* 110:769–98.

Bohn, H., and R. P. Inman. 1996. Balanced-budget rules and public deficits: Evidence from the U.S. states. *Carnegie-Rochester Conference Series on Public Policy* 45: 13–76.

Buchanan, J. M. 1958. *Public principles of public debt.* Homewood, Ill.: Richard D. Irwin.

———. 1987. The constitution of economic policy. *American Economic Review* 77: 243–50.

Buchanan, J. M., and R. E. Wagner. 1977. *Democracy in deficit: The political legacy of Lord Keynes.* New York: Academic Press.

Cukierman, A., and A. H. Meltzer. 1989. A political theory of government debt and deficits in a neo-Ricardian framework. *American Economic Review* 79:713–32.

de Haan, J., and J.-E. Sturm. 1994. Political and institutional determinants of fiscal policy in the European Community. *Public Choice* 80:157–72.

Drazen, A., and V. Grilli. 1993. The benefits of Crises for Economic Reform. *American Economic Review* 83:598–607.

Edin, P. A., and H. Ohlsson. 1991. Political determinants of budget deficits: Coalition effects vs. minority effects. *European Economic Review* 35:1597–1603.

Eichengreen, B., and J. von Hagen. 1996. Fiscal policy and monetary union: Is there a trade-off between federalism and budgetary restrictions? NBER Working Paper no. 5517. Cambridge, Mass.: National Bureau of Economic Research.

Feld, L. P. 1997. Exit, voice, and income taxes: The loyalty of voters. *European Journal of Political Economy* 13:455–78.

Feld, L. P., and G. Kirchgässner. 1996. Omne agens agendo perficitur: The economic meaning of subsidiarity. In *Maastricht: Monetary constitution without a fiscal constitution?* ed. R. Holzmann, 195–226. Baden-Baden: Nomos.

Feld, L. P., and M. R. Savioz. 1997. Direct democracy matters for economic performance: An empirical investigation. *Kyklos* 50:507–38.

Guengant, A., J.-M. Josselin, and Y. Rocaboy. 1997. Spillover effects and congestion under alternative models of public goods provision: Evidence from French municipalities. Unpublished manuscript, University of Rennes.

Hardin, G. 1968. The tragedy of the commons. *Science* 162:1234–38.

Holcombe, R. G., 1980. An empirical test of the median voter model. *Economic Inquiry* 18:260–74.

Inman, R. P. 1982. The economic case for limits to government. *American Economic Review: Papers and Proceedings* 72:176–83.

———. 1997. Do balanced budget rules work? U.S. experience and possible lessons for the EMU. In *Quo vadis Europe?* ed. H. Siebert, 307–32. Tübingen: Mohr (Siebeck).

Kiewiet, D. R., and K. Szakaly. 1996. Constitutional limitations on borrowing: An analysis of state bonded indebtedness. *Journal of Law, Economics, and Organization* 12:62–97.

Kirchgässner, G., and W. W. Pommerehne. 1978. Gemeindegrösse und Stimmbeteiligung: Ein einfaches Regressionsmodell. *Schweizerische Zeitschrift für Soziologie* 4: 163–73.

Kleinewefers, H. 1995. "Verwesentlichung" der Politik durch die Einschränkung der direkten Volksrechte? Eine Auslegeordnung der Probleme und ein Vorschlag aus ökonomischer Sicht. Discussion paper, University of Fribourg, Fribourg.

Luthardt, W. 1994. *Direkte Demokratie: Ein Vergleich in Westeuropa.* Baden-Baden: Nomos.

Matsusaka, J. G. 1992. Economics of direct legislation. *Quarterly Journal of Economics* 107:541–71.

———. 1995. Fiscal effects of the voter initiative: Evidence from the last 30 years. *Journal of Political Economy* 103:587–623.

Matsusaka, J. G., and N. M. McCarty. 1997. Political resource allocation: The benefits and costs of voter initiatives. Unpublished manuscript, University of Southern California, Los Angeles.

Meltzer, A. H., and S. F. Richard. 1981. A rational theory of the size of government. *Journal of Political Economy* 89:914–27.

Moak, L. 1982. *Municipal bonds: Planning, sale, and administration.* Chicago: Municipal Finance Officers Association.

Moser, P. 1996. Why is Swiss politics so stable? *Swiss Journal of Economics and Statistics* 132:31–60.

Peltzman, S. 1992. Voters as fiscal conservatives. *Quarterly Journal of Economics* 107: 327–61.

Persson, T., and L. E. O. Svensson. 1989. Why a stubborn conservative would run a deficit. *Quarterly Journal of Economics* 104:324–45.

Pommerehne, W. W. 1978. Institutional approaches to public expenditure: Empirical evidence from Swiss municipalities. *Journal of Public Economics* 9:255–80.

———. 1983. Private versus öffentliche Müllabfuhr—nochmals betrachtet. *Finanzarchiv* 41:466–75.

———. 1990. The empirical relevance of comparative institutional analysis. *European Economic Review* 34:458–69.

Pommerehne, W. W., and H. Weck-Hannemann. 1996. Tax rates, tax administration, and income tax evasion in Switzerland. *Public Choice* 88:161–70.

Poterba, J. M. 1994. State responses to fiscal crises: The effects of budgetary institutions and politics. *Journal of Political Economy* 102:799–821.

———. 1995a. Balanced budget rules and fiscal policy: Evidence from the states. *National Tax Journal* 48:329–37.

———. 1995b. Capital budgets, borrowing rules, and state capital spending. *Journal of Public Economics* 56:165–87.

———. 1996. Budget institutions and fiscal policy in the U.S. states. *American Economic Review: Papers and Proceedings* 86:395–400.

———. 1997. Do budget rules work? In *Fiscal policy: Lessons from economic research,* ed. A. J. Auerbach, 53–86. Cambridge, Mass.: MIT Press.

Romer, T., and H. Rosenthal. 1978. Political resource allocation, controlled agendas, and the status quo. *Public Choice* 33:27–43.

———. 1979. Bureaucrats versus voters: On the political economy of resource allocation by direct democracies. *Quarterly Journal of Economics* 93:563–87.

Rosenberg, J. 1992. Rationality and the political business cycle: The case of local government. *Public Choice* 73:71–81.

Roubini, N., and J. D. Sachs. 1989a. Government spending and budget deficits in the industrial countries. *Economic Policy* 8:99–132.

———. 1989b. Political and economic determinants of budget deficits in the industrial democracies. *European Economic Review* 33:903–38.

Shachar, R. 1993. Forgetfulness and the political cycles. *Economics and Politics* 5: 15–25.

Tabellini, G. 1991. The politics of intergenerational redistribution. *Journal of Political Economy* 99:335–57.

Tabellini, G., and V. LaVia. 1989. Money, deficit, and public debt in the United States. *Review of Economics and Statistics* 71:15–25.

Thürer, D. 1992. Schweizerische Verfassungsordnung vor der Herausforderung durch die Europäische Integration. *Zeitschrift für Schweizerisches Recht* 1:73–106.

von Hagen, J. 1991. A note on the empirical effectiveness of formal fiscal restraints. *Journal of Public Economics* 44:99–110.

———. 1992. Budgetary procedures and fiscal performance in the European Communities. Economic Papers no. 96, Commission of the European Communities, October.

von Hagen, J., and B. Eichengreen. 1996. Federalism, fiscal restraints, and European Monetary Union. *American Economic Review: Papers and Proceedings* 86:134–38.

von Hagen, J., and I. J. Harden. 1994. National budget processes and fiscal performance. *European Economy: Reports and Studies* 3:311–418.

———. 1995. Budget processes and commitment to fiscal discipline. *European Economic Review* 39:771–79.

8   State Fiscal Institutions and the U.S. Municipal Bond Market

James M. Poterba and Kim Rueben

The effects of fiscal institutions on budget deficits, the level and composition of government spending, and the level of government indebtedness are topics of active interest in both economics and political science. Much of the motivation for ongoing research on these issues stems from the fiscal policy experience of developed nations during the last two decades, particularly the rise of substantial peacetime budget deficits. As policymakers have sought methods to reduce deficits and limit the growth of government debt, they have considered a range of possible changes in the institutional structure for fiscal policymaking. Because fiscal policy reforms are relatively rare at the national level, and because such reforms are likely to be correlated with other changes that may affect fiscal policy outcomes, it is difficult to develop empirical evidence on the effects of such institutional changes.

One alternative source of empirical evidence on the effects of budget rules involves comparisons of fiscal policy outcomes across different subnational governments in a federal system. We focus on the states within the United States. While states differ substantially in their incomes, tax bases, and levels of spending as a share of personal income, they operate in a homogeneous legal environment and face many of the same fiscal pressures. They nevertheless exhibit substantial disparities in their budgeting rules and fiscal policy institutions.

Studies of interstate differences in fiscal institutions and fiscal policy have

James M. Poterba is the Mitsui Professor of Economics at the Massachusetts Institute of Technology and director of the Public Economics Research Program at the National Bureau of Economic Research. Kim Rueben is a research fellow at the Public Policy Institute of California.

The authors are grateful to Anne Case and Robert Inman for comments, to Elizabeth Berko for research assistance, to the Chubb Corporation and especially to Thomas Swartz III for access to the Relative Value Study data, and to the National Bureau of Economic Research, the National Science Foundation (Poterba), and the Public Policy Institute of California for research support.

produced a growing body of evidence suggesting that fiscal institutions affect the size of state government, the incidence of fiscal deficits, and the level and composition of state borrowing. Rueben (1996) presents evidence of a negative correlation between tax and expenditure limits and state government spending as a fraction of state income. Alt and Lowry (1994), Bohn and Inman (1995), and Poterba (1994) document a negative correlation between state antideficit laws and the average size of state budget deficits. Bunche (1991), Eichengreen (1992), Kiewiet and Szakaly (1996), and von Hagen (1991, 1992) find that states with constitutional restrictions on the legislature's power to issue general-obligation debt issue less debt, and rely more heavily on revenue bonds and other "off-budget" debt, than states without restrictions on debt issue. These studies and others, summarized by Alesina and Perotti (chap. 1 in this volume), Inman (1996), and Poterba (1997), cast doubt on the view that fiscal institutions are simply "veils" that voters see through, with no ultimate effects on fiscal outcomes, and they suggest that changes in fiscal institutions can have real effects on policy choices.

Antideficit rules can affect measured deficits in two ways. First, they may lead to changes in the primary deficit because they constrain the actions, and the incentives, of fiscal policymakers. Second, they may affect the bond market's perception of the borrowing jurisdiction, and thereby affect the required interest rate on outstanding debt. Proponents of antideficit rules argue that such rules should result in lower interest payments, as bond market participants demand a lower risk premium as compensation for potential default.

While numerous studies have examined how fiscal institutions affect primary deficits, there is much less research on how financial markets react to differences in fiscal rules. There is a small literature, including studies by Eichengreen (1992), Goldstein and Woglom (1992), Bayoumi, Goldstein, and Woglom (1995), and Lowry and Alt (1997), on the correlation between fiscal institutions in the U.S. states and the interest rates on the bonds issued by these states. The present paper extends this research by examining a broader range of fiscal institutions, and by paying particular attention to the effect of tax and expenditure limits on borrowing costs. We also study bond market data for the 1973–95 period, a substantially longer sample than earlier studies, and one that includes the state fiscal crisis of the early 1990s.

The paper is divided into four sections. The first describes the conceptual model of bond market equilibrium that underlies our analysis and summarizes previous research on the link between fiscal institutions and borrowing costs. Section 8.2 describes the data on state-specific interest rates and state fiscal institutions that form the basis for this study, and it discusses a variety of issues surrounding specification and estimation. Section 8.3 presents our central findings on the link between fiscal rules and state borrowing costs. We present empirical results from a range of different regression models that explain the level of tax-exempt bond yields. Section 8.4 concludes, suggests several directions for future work, and discusses the key tradeoffs that are involved in selecting fiscal institutions.

8.1 Theoretical Framework and Previous Research

This section summarizes the model of tax-exempt bond yield determination that underlies our empirical analysis. It also presents a brief review of previous studies that have investigated the link between fiscal institutions and interest rates, and places the current research in perspective.

8.1.1 Theoretical Framework

We assume that the market for tax-exempt bonds clears by equating the after-tax return that a "marginal investor" can earn on tax-exempt bonds with the after-tax, risk-adjusted return that is available on a riskless taxable bond. If R_T denotes the taxable yield, and $R_{M,i}$ denotes the tax-exempt yield on bonds issued by state i, then asset market equilibrium requires that $R_{M,i}$ equal the after-tax taxable yield, plus a risk premium:

$$(1) \qquad R_{M,i} = [1 - \tau_{f,i}(B) - \tau_{s,i}(B_i)]R_T + \sigma_i(Z_i, X_i, B_i).$$

In this expression, $\tau_{f,i}$ denotes the marginal federal income tax rate on interest income for an investor in state i, B represents the aggregate stock of tax-exempt debt outstanding, B_i denotes the outstanding debt stock for state i, and $\tau_{s,i}$ denotes the marginal state income tax rate on interest received by residents of state i. By including state taxes in this expression we implicitly assume that the taxable bond is not a Treasury bond. The implicit assumption in this expression is that tax-exempt debt issued by state i is held only by investors who live in state i. There is usually a tax incentive for state residents to hold in-state tax-exempt bonds: many states tax out-of-state "tax exempt" interest, even though such interest is exempt from federal income taxation. While holding in-state debt may not be attractive from a portfolio diversification standpoint, we nevertheless assume that the tax benefits lead to such ownership patterns.

The outstanding stock of debt in state i, B_i, affects equilibrium yields in two ways. First, the size of B_i can affect the state marginal tax rate of the "marginal investor" holding the bonds issued by state i; we assume that B_i is not large enough to affect the marginal *federal* income tax rate at which the tax-exempt bond market clears. This change in the state marginal tax rate can affect the riskless after-tax return that the marginal investor earns on taxable bonds, and therefore the required return on state i's tax-exempt debt. In the simplest clientele models of capital market equilibrium, the first investor to hold tax-exempt bonds is the highest marginal tax rate investor, and an increase in the stock of tax-exempt debt outstanding leads progressively lower marginal tax rate investors to purchase these securities. Formally, $\tau'_{s,i}(B_i) < 0$. The size of this effect depends on the degree of progressivity in the state income tax schedule. If the state has a flat-rate income tax, then $\tau'_{s,i} = 0$. Even in these cases, changes in B_i may still affect required returns through a risk premium effect.

Second, the stock of outstanding debt can affect the risk premium demanded by investors holding state i's bonds. The second term in equation (1), the risk premium on tax-exempt debt issued by state $i(\sigma_i)$, depends on Z_i, a vector of state budget and tax institutions that affect the expected future supply of tax-exempt debt from state i and the probability of future payment of current interest obligations; X_i, a set of state-specific economic factors, such as the unemployment rate, that affect the probability that the state will be able to repay its obligations; and B_i, the outstanding stock of debt issued by state i. Although state defaults are rare, they have occurred. English (1996) and Ratchford (1941) discuss U.S. state defaults in the nineteenth century in some detail; most of these were the result of aggressive state borrowing to develop unprofitable canal systems in the 1830s and 1840s. The link between the outstanding debt stock and the risk premium is straightforward: for a given state economy, a larger debt burden corresponds to a greater risk of being unable to meet interest obligations. The link between economic conditions and the risk premium is also clear: for a given debt stock, the larger the economic base in the state, ceteris paribus, the lower the chance that the state will default. This is because a larger economy generates a larger tax base.

Fiscal institutions (Z_i) can affect the risk premium on state bonds for several reasons. Rules that make it more difficult for states to raise taxes increase the likelihood of future default on promised interest payments. Antideficit provisions in state constitutions and rules that limit the power of the legislature to issue new debt may affect the future supply of state debt, and therefore alter the chance that the future supply of debt will expand and drive down bond prices.

While the stock of debt outstanding can affect a state's risk premium, the stock of debt outstanding may also be *affected* by the prevailing interest rate on the state's bonds. Metcalf (1993) models the debt issue decisions of states, and finds that more debt is issued when interest rates are lower. Capeci (1994) presents a related empirical study of debt yields and debt issuance decisions by local governments. The interactions between the debt stock and the interest rate complicate our empirical analysis.

Most previous studies of fiscal rules and borrowing costs have included the outstanding debt stock in equations explaining the yields on state general-obligation bonds, but this leads to two problems. First, the stock of debt is endogenous, which means it is difficult to interpret the estimated coefficient on this variable. Second, because some of the variation in the stock of outstanding debt may be due to differences in fiscal institutions across states, controlling for interstate differences in debt outstanding may understate the potential effects of fiscal rules on borrowing costs. We estimate bond yield models with, and without, controls for the outstanding state debt stock as a way to investigate the importance of these effects.

If we were prepared to assume that fiscal institutions did not affect the risk premium on state bonds, then indicator variables for the presence of these institutions would provide instrumental variables that could be used to estimate a structural model of tax-exempt yield determination. The supply of debt from state i would depend on its fiscal institutions, but, without the risk premium effect, these institutions could be excluded from the demand equation for state *i*'s bonds. We could then estimate two-stage-least-squares models for state borrowing rates as a function of debt stocks and state economic conditions, recognizing the endogeneity of the debt stock. The estimate of the coefficient on the stock of debt in such a debt demand equation, in conjunction with first-stage estimates of how fiscal institutions affect state borrowing, could then be used to estimate the effect of fiscal institutions on state borrowing costs. Because we find statistical evidence against these identification assumptions, however, we pursue a reduced-form strategy in the estimation reported below.

8.1.2   Previous Research

There have been many previous studies of yield determination in the tax-exempt bond market. Most of these studies, which are surveyed in Fortune 1996 and Poterba 1989, compare an index of yields on tax-exempt bonds with the yields on Treasury bonds. The emphasis is therefore on explaining the time series variation in the relative yields on taxable and tax-exempt bonds. Other studies have considered the impact of state-specific factors on state and local borrowing costs, typically using data on the net interest cost (NIC) of specific bond issues. Examples of studies in this vein are Kidwell, Koch, and Stock 1984 and Lovely and Wasylenko 1992. Both of these studies explore the relationship between state income tax codes and state borrowing costs.

The present study is closely related to a number of previous investigations of the relationship between fiscal institutions and the borrowing rates faced by U.S. state governments. All of these studies analyze data from the Chubb Relative Value Study, but they focus on different sample periods. These data are now available for the period 1973–96, and we exploit the full data sample in our analysis.

The first studies of fiscal institutions and general obligation bond yields, by Eichengreen (1992) and Goldstein and Woglom (1992), relate the interest rate on general-obligation debt to an index of the strictness of state antideficit provisions compiled by the Advisory Council on Intergovernmental Relations (ACIR). Eichengreen (1992) examines the relationship between interest rates and (i) an indicator variable for whether the state can carry a deficit from one year to the next, and (ii) the ACIR index. For the 1985–89 period, he finds that both variables are correlated with the interest rates on general-obligation bonds. His estimating equations do not include any controls for state economic conditions. Goldstein and Woglom (1992) study the 1982–90 period, and they also find evidence that the ACIR index of deficit limits matters. They estimate that states with the most restrictive set of fiscal limits face interest rates five basis points lower than states with "average" limits.

The results in both of these studies are difficult to interpret because in addition to control variables for the level of state indebtedness and the observed state deficit, the regression specifications also include a measure of the rating on general obligation debt as reported by Moody's or another rating agency. Yet the state's credit rating, just like its borrowing cost, may depend on its fiscal institutions. If all of the information about future fiscal conditions that was associated with the presence of a fiscal limit is incorporated in the state's bond rating, and if bond ratings perfectly predict borrowing costs, then it would be possible for the state's borrowing rate to be uncorrelated with fiscal institutions, *conditional* on the state's bond rating, even if changes in fiscal institutions have important effects on borrowing costs. Capeci (1991) discusses the role of credit ratings and economic conditions in determining tax-exempt interest rates. Controlling for the state's bond rating in an interest rate equation can therefore mask the effect of the fiscal variables.

The most sophisticated study of bond yields to date is that by Bayoumi, Goldstein, and Woglom (1995). They analyze interest rate data for the 1981–90 period, and also conclude that fiscal institutions, as measured by the ACIR index, affect state borrowing costs. This study recognizes the potential endogeneity of the level of state debt, and it applies an instrumental variables strategy to estimate the effect of fiscal limits on borrowing costs. The instruments are a set of "year dummies," a set of state-specific demographic variables, and the trend growth rate in state product. Each of these variables could, under plausible modeling assumptions, be correlated with bond yields through channels other than their effect on the endogenous variables, so the ultimate success of this empirical strategy is open to question.

A final paper that explores the Chubb data, by Lowry and Alt (1997), is also concerned with the link between state fiscal institutions and interest costs. The novelty of this paper, however, is the investigation of how fiscal rules interact with economic conditions in determining bond yields. This study estimates statistical models in which the state's borrowing cost depends on the current level of the state deficit, and the interaction of this deficit with the state's fiscal rules. The key finding is that the bond market's reaction to a state deficit depends on whether or not the state has a balanced-budget requirement. States with balanced-budget rules experience smaller increases in their borrowing costs for a given deficit, measured using data from the Census of Governments. Lowry and Alt's (1997) findings, which are based on data for the 1973–90 period, suggest that capital market participants consider the presence of anti-deficit rules, and their interplay with state economic conditions, in pricing state general-obligation bonds.

The foregoing studies consider a limited range of fiscal institutions in analyzing the determinants of tax-exempt bond yields. Virtually all of the studies consider the ACIR index of state fiscal stringency, which provides a general guide to state antideficit provisions. Yet this index suppresses substantial variation in state fiscal rules. Bohn and Inman (1995), for example, examine the fiscal impact of nine different indicators of state fiscal stringency in their study of state deficit determination. They find that a number of more specialized variables, such as requirements for gubernatorial submission of a balanced budget, legislative passage of such a budget, and a referendum to approve new state debt issues, have distinct effects on budget outcomes. Their study suggests that it is possible to move beyond a single summary statistic for state fiscal stringency, and the present study therefore explores a broader menu of fiscal institutions than previous bond market studies.

The second important innovation in the current study is the use of the full data sample for the Chubb Relative Value Survey. Of the earlier investigations, only Lowry and Alt (1997) use data for the period before 1980, and none use data from the years since 1990. (This is not an indictment of methodology: several of the studies were completed before the post-1990 data were available.) The pre-1980 and post-1990 data may, however, provide important evidence on fiscal institutions and borrowing costs, since both of these periods were times of extreme fiscal stress for states. The New York City fiscal crisis of the mid-1970s, and the coincidence of an economic downturn and rising state spending needs that led to the state "fiscal crisis" of the early 1990s, are included in our sample period.

A final innovation is our consideration of the possible endogeneity of state fiscal institutions. The potential endogeneity arises from the fact that these institutions are not fixed, but can be changed by voters and legislatures. Besley and Case (1994) have argued that many of the policy differences across states, and within states over time, that are treated as exogenous in empirical research are in fact reflections of underlying voter tastes or economic conditions. It is therefore possible that fiscal institutions are simply a reflection of voter preferences, and as such, that the correlation between these institutions and fiscal policy outcomes just reflects an underlying correlation between voter tastes and fiscal policies. Rueben (1996) finds that the relationship between state fiscal institutions and state spending depends critically upon whether these institutions are treated as exogenous or endogenous. We address the potential endogeneity of fiscal institutions, with limited success, in our empirical work below. To anticipate our findings, we do not find any potential instrumental variables with significant explanatory power for fiscal rules, that is, variables that generate well-fitting "first stages" in a two-stage-least-squares setting. Treating the endogeneity of fiscal rules is therefore an issue that requires further work.

8.2   Data and Estimation Strategy

The estimation strategy we pursue is largely determined by the available data on state general-obligation bond yields. Our dependent variable, R_{it}, is the interest rate on 20-year general-obligation debt issued by state i as reported in the Chubb Insurance Company "Relative Value Survey." This survey, which has been carried out every six months since 1973, asks 20–25 sell-side bond traders at major brokerage houses that deal in tax-exempt bonds to estimate the current yields on general obligation bonds from 40 states. The states excluded from the sample—Arizona, Arkansas, Colorado, Idaho, Indiana, Iowa, Kansas, Nebraska, South Dakota, and Wyoming—are concentrated in the Midwest and Great Plains regions. The participants in the Chubb survey are asked to evaluate "hypothetical" general-obligation bonds that come due in 20 years, so reported differences in yields should not be attributable to differences in call provisions or other factors, but simply to the perceived riskiness of the state's general obligation debt. Swartz (1989) discusses the responsiveness of these estimated yields to state economic circumstances, and notes that over the time period that the survey data has been collected, there has been some tendency for more rapid incorporation of news into yield spreads. In particular, he claims that while changes in the Chubb values lagged changes in bond ratings in the early part of the sample, they often led rating changes in more recent years.

8.2.1 The Chubb Data and Model Specification

The Chubb survey reports the *relative* yield on a general-obligation bond issued by state i, compared with a similar bond issued by New Jersey. This means that rather than estimating models for the level of the tax-exempt bond yields on bonds issued by state i, we are estimating models for the difference between the yields on the bonds issued by two states, $R_{it} - R_{jt}$, where j denotes New Jersey. To explore the implications of this, we can difference equations like (1) for two states, i and j, and find

$$(2) \quad R_{M,i} - R_{M,j} = [\tau_{s,i}(B_i) - \tau_{s,j}(B_j)]R_T + \sigma_i(Z_i, X_i, B_i) - \sigma_j(Z_j, X_j, B_j).$$

Several terms involving the taxable bond yield, the federal marginal tax rate, and any other systematic factors such as the risk of federal tax reform that affect the yields of all states in the same way, drop out of the expression when we difference the two state yields.

To translate this equation into a form that we can estimate, we linearize equation (2), suppress the M subscript, and add a time subscript for the tax-exempt yields (hence $R_{M,j}$ becomes R_{jt}). This yields

$$(3) \quad \begin{aligned} R_{it} - R_{jt} &= (X_{it} - X_{jt})*\alpha + (Z_{it} - Z_{jt})*\beta + (B_{it} - B_{jt})*\gamma \\ &\quad + (\tau_{s,it} - \tau_{s,jt})*\delta + \theta_t + (\kappa_i - \kappa_j) + (\varepsilon_{it} - \varepsilon_{jt}). \end{aligned}$$

In this expression, R_{it} denotes the nominal interest rate on bonds issued by state i at time t, X_{it} denotes the set of state-specific economic and fiscal conditions that may affect borrowing costs, Z_{it} represents the vector of state budget and tax institutions that may affect the demand for state tax-exempt debt, B_{it} denotes the stock of state debt outstanding, and $\tau_{s,it}$ denotes the top state income tax rate in state i in year t. In some specifications we omit the debt stock variable, for the reasons described above.

The error term in equation (3) consists of three components: a time effect θ_t that captures period-specific shifts in the relative risk premium for New Jersey (state j) relative to all other states; the difference in two state-fixed effects, κ_i and κ_j, which captures the average difference between state-specific factors that affect the borrowing cost for state i and New Jersey (state j); and $\varepsilon_{it} - \varepsilon_{jt}$, which represents the difference in the state-specific error components at time *t*. Because most of the variation in fiscal institutions is across states but not across time within states, allowing for state-fixed effects substantially reduces the sample variation in fiscal rules. One important consequence of the data structure is that all of the independent variables need to be measured as deviations from the value for New Jersey.

While the use of survey methods rather than market prices to measure R_{it} raises questions about the reliability of the level of reported tax-exempt yields, our analysis focuses on *differences* in the yields on bonds for various states. Systematic errors in estimating the level of yields will therefore not contaminate the analysis. Previous work using these data, notably Bayoumi, Goldstein, and Woglom (1995), suggests that the yield spread between the highest yield and the lowest yield states responds to economic conditions, and that in recessions, when default risk rises, the range of yields in the Chubb survey increases substantially. By using the expanded data set we can also test how stable this relationship is over time.

The variables that we include in the X_{it} vector are the state unemployment rate, the level of real per capita income in the state, and state general fund revenues as a fraction of per capita income. State revenues are drawn from the U.S. Department of Commerce *State Government Finances* publications; state unemployment rates, population, and per capita income are from the Data Resources @MARKETS data file. We also include variables that proxy for the political climate in the state, on the grounds that such variables may provide information on the future evolution of state deficits. Our principal variable of this type is the Americans for Democratic Action (ADA) score for the state's Senate delegation; this should provide a general indication of the political ideology of the state.

We also include the highest state marginal income tax rate on interest income, as suggested by the equilibrium condition (1), in our regression models. This variable is collected from a review of state income tax forms, augmented with information from the State Tax Module of the NBER TAXSIM program. We lack detailed information on the state tax rates of the investors who own tax-exempt bonds, so we assume that all such investors face the state's highest marginal tax rate.

8.2.2 Measuring State Fiscal Institutions

We consider a range of variables on state fiscal institutions, $\{Z_{it}\}$, that may affect state borrowing costs. Briffault (1996) provides a useful introduction to the budget processes of the U.S. states. The first variable we consider is an index of state constitutional and legislative limits on deficit finance. This is the fiscal institution indicator that was analyzed in many of the studies described above. There is substantial heterogeneity in state balanced-budget rules. Only one state, Vermont, does not have a formal balanced-budget requirement. The balanced-budget requirements in the 49 states with such requirements can be broadly categorized into four groups, depending on the stage in the budget

Table 8.1   **State Fiscal Institutions**

State	Balanced-Budget Stringency	Debt Restriction	Year Passed Spending Limit	Year Passed Revenue Limit
Alabama	10	yes		
Alaska	6	yes	1982	
Arizona	10	yes	1978	
Arkansas	9	yes[a]		
California	6	yes[a]	1979	
Colorado	10	no	1992[b]	1992
Connecticut	5	no	1991	
Delaware	10	no		
Florida	10	yes[a]		1994
Georgia	10	yes		
Hawaii	10	yes	1978	
Idaho	10	yes	1980	
Illinois	4	no		
Indiana	10	yes		
Iowa	10	yes		
Kansas	10	yes[a]		
Kentucky	10	yes[a]		
Louisiana	4	no		1991[c]
Maine	9	yes[a]		
Maryland	6	no		
Massachusetts	3	no		1986
Michigan	6	yes[a]		1978
Minnesota	8	yes		
Mississippi	9	yes		
Missouri	10	yes[a]	1980	1980
Montana	10	none	1981	
Nebraska	10	yes		
Nevada	4	yes	1994[d]	
New Hampshire	2	none		
New Jersey	10	yes[a]	1976[e]	
New Mexico	10	yes		
New York	3	yes[a]		
North Carolina	10	none		
North Dakota	8	yes		
Ohio	10	yes		
Oklahoma	10	no	1985	
Oregon	8	yes[a]		
Pennsylvania	6	yes[a]		
Rhode Island	10	yes[a]	1992[f]	
South Carolina	10	yes[a]	1980	
South Dakota	10	yes		
Tennessee	10	no		
Texas	8	yes		
Utah	10	yes		
Vermont	0	yes		
Virginia	8	yes		

Table 8.1   (continued)

State	Balanced-Budget Stringency	Debt Restriction	Year Passed Spending Limit	Year Passed Revenue Limit
Washington	8	yes		1979
West Virginia	10	yes		
Wisconsin	6	yes		
Wyoming	8	yes		

Sources: Data on budget stringency rules and debt restrictions are from ACIR 1987 and Rafool 1997. Data on revenue and expenditure limits are from Rueben 1996.
[a]Requires a popular vote to approve debt issue.
[b]Passed a nonbinding spending limit in 1977.
[c]Adopted a nonbinding revenue limit in 1979.
[d]Passed a nonbinding spending limit in 1979.
[e]Spending limit expired in 1983.
[f]Nonbinding limit adopted in 1977.

process at which balance is required. In 44 states, the governor must submit a balanced budget. This is the weakest of the various balanced-budget requirements. In 37 of these states, the legislature must enact a balanced budget. These balanced-budget rules nevertheless allow for actual revenues and expenditures to diverge from balance if realizations differ from expectations. In 6 states, any unexpected deficit must be corrected in the next budget cycle. Finally, in 24 of the 37 states that require the passage of a balanced budget, there is a prohibition on deficit carry-forward into the next budget cycle. This represents the strictest antideficit rule.

Our data on balanced-budget rules are drawn from the Advisory Council on Intergovernmental Relations (hereafter ACIR) (1987) report on institutions that promote fiscal discipline in the states, updated using subsequent issues of the ACIR publication *Significant Features of Fiscal Federalism*. The ACIR index of budget stringency ranges between 0 (lax) and 10 (stringent). Table 8.1 reports this index. We use an indicator variable for whether this index is below 6 in our empirical work below. States with scores below 6 may have requirements that the governor propose or that the legislature pass a balanced budget, but they do not have stricter rules. States that require a balanced budget at the end of the fiscal year score 9 or 10 on the ACIR scale, and states that require a balanced budget over a two-year cycle receive an ACIR score of 8. Only 14 states receive ACIR scores of 6 or below.

We use the discrete indicator variable for the ACIR scores of 0 through 5, rather than the actual value of the ACIR score, because the latter imposes the same fiscal effect of one-unit changes at different levels of the ACIR scale, even though these differentials may be noncomparable. The indicator variable that we use, which was also analyzed in Poterba 1994, captures the key variation between states with lax and strict budgetary rules, but it downweights the small differences between states near either extreme. Our results are not sensitive to the cutoff that we use to define this indicator variable. In addition, while we focus on whether states have any restrictions on their budgetary outcome, we do explore the separate effects of these variables in some of our analysis below.

While an overwhelming number of states require budgets to be balanced during the current year, states in the Northeast and the upper Midwest are less likely to have stringent antideficit requirements. Many of the states outside those regions with less stringent budget rules, such as California, Nevada, and Louisiana, have more recently passed other fiscal constraints that restrict state revenue or expenditures. There is relatively little change within our sample period in state balanced-budget requirements.

The second fiscal institution that we consider is the ease with which the state can issue long-term general-obligation debt. The second column of table 8.1 lists the states that have some restriction on issuing general obligation debt. Ten states have no restrictions on debt issuance; of the other 40, 38 have constitutional restrictions on debt issue, and 2 have legislative limits. The most common restriction places a dollar limit on the amount of debt outstanding. This limit varies from $50,000 in Rhode Island and Oregon to $3 million in Alabama. In ten states—Arizona, California, Idaho, Kansas, Kentucky, Maine, Missouri, New Jersey, Pennsylvania, and Rhode Island—voters can override the constitutional restrictions on debt levels to issue additional debt. In 3 other states, including New York, voters are required to approve any debt issue. In another 3 states, issuing debt requires a supermajority vote in the state legislature. We define an indicator variable for all states with *any* type of debt restriction and include this indicator variable in our analysis below.

Finally, we consider whether a state has a state tax or expenditure limit (TEL). These laws typically limit the growth rate of general fund expenditures or revenues to the growth rate of personal income, or to some function of that growth rate. Rueben (1996) controls for the endogeneity of TEL passage and finds that states with tax or expenditure limits have lower growth rates in general fund revenues and expenditures. Shadbegian (1996), in a related study, shows that the impact of TELs can depend on the nature of these limits, as well as state economic conditions, such as the growth rate of personal income. Our analysis relies on Rueben's (1996) classification of "binding" state tax and expenditure limits. "Binding" limits are those that cannot be overridden by a simple legislative majority.

Most state limits on tax or expenditure growth were enacted during the "tax revolt" of the late 1970s, although some states have passed such legislation during the 1990s. Twenty-five states have instituted some form of limitation since 1976. The third and fourth columns of table 8.1 show the years in which revenue and expenditure limits were passed in various states. Some states have both tax and expenditure limits, and some states have enacted more than one tax or expenditure limit during the last three decades. A number of states have adopted nonbinding limits, and then adopted binding limits in later years.

From the standpoint of the tax-exempt bond market, limitations on revenues and limitations on expenditures may have different effects. Limits on the taxing authority of the legislature may increase the risk that future interest payments will not be covered by tax receipts. Limits on expenditures, which in many cases do not apply to interest outlays, are less likely to have adverse effects on the perceived riskiness of state bonds. If anything, expenditure limits may be perceived favorably by municipal bond participants, since such limits constrain the future expenditures that might compete with promised interest payouts. Thus we might expect that states with tax limits would face higher borrowing costs, while those with expenditure limits might face lower borrowing costs.

8.2.3   Estimation Issues

The primary estimation problem that we confront concerns the potential endogeneity of a state's outstanding debt level. We estimate reduced-form models with, and without, the outstanding debt level to evaluate the effect of this variable on the other coefficient estimates. We also instrument for current debt levels using a state's historical constitutional debt restrictions on debt issued, and using information on how difficult it is to change debt restrictions and other fiscal institutions. Unfortunately, these do not appear to be powerful instrumental variables: they do not explain a substantial fraction of the variation in state debt-to-income ratios.

A related concern involves the potential endogeneity of fiscal institutions themselves. There are two empirical strategies for addressing this endogeneity. The first involves controlling for some measure of voter preferences, such as the ADA score of elected officials. This reduces the potential for observed correlations between budget rules and fiscal outcomes to simply reflect a correlation of both of these variables with an omitted third variable, voter tastes for fiscal outcomes. While this approach has been used in a number of empirical studies of the relationship between fiscal rules and tax or expenditure outcomes, it has not been applied in studies of tax-exempt bond yields. The difficulty with this approach is that it is hard to find a set of control variables that completely capture the political tastes of state voters.

A second approach to the endogeneity problem involves modeling the evolution of budget rules and using variables that affect budget rules but not fiscal policy as instrumental variables in a simultaneous equations setting. This approach was developed by Rueben (1996). The difficulty with this approach is finding valid instruments that are correlated with the potentially endogenous fiscal institutions.

Table 8.2   Summary Statistics

Variable	Sample Mean	New Jersey
Interest rate on general-obligation bonds, relative	9.98	
to New Jersey (basis points)	(24.33)	
Unemployment rate (percentage points)	0.067	0.068
	(0.021)	(0.018)
Real per capita income (thousands of 1983	13.01	16.82
dollars)	(5.84)	(7.61)
Revenue/personal income	0.128	0.093
	(0.061)	(0.012)
State debt outstanding/personal income	0.086	0.088
	(0.074)	(0.059)
State marginal tax rate	0.065	0.035
	(0.042)	(0.021)
Lax antideficit rules (1 if ACIR < 6, 0 otherwise)	0.200	0.00
	(0.400)	(0.00)
Indicator for restrictions on debt issue	0.550	1.00
	(0.498)	(0.00)
Indicator for binding expenditure limit	0.142	0.304
	(0.350)	(0.460)
Indicator for binding revenue limit	0.057	0.000
	(0.231)	(0.000)
Indicator for legislature must pass balanced	0.060	0.00
budget	(0.238)	(0.00)
Indicator for requirement to correct deficit in	0.140	0.00
next budget cycle	(0.347)	(0.00)
Indicator for requirement to correct deficit in	0.140	0.00
current two-year cycle	(0.347)	(0.00)
Indicator for requirement to correct deficit in	0.580	1.00
current one-year cycle	(0.493)	(0.00)

Note: Sample means for the 1973–95 period, with standard deviations shown in parentheses. See text for further discussion.

8.3   Empirical Findings

We present summary statistics from our data set before presenting regression results. Table 8.2 reports sample means for principal variables that we include in our regression equations. The first column shows the sample mean for all states, and the second column shows the mean value for the state of New Jersey. The mean of the actual regression variables is the difference between the two columns.

The average differential between the tax-exempt bond yield for New Jersey and all other states in the sample is just under 10 basis points. Although table 8.2 does not show this, there are substantial interyear differences in the average value of this differential, presumably as a result of changes in New Jersey's fiscal situation relative to that of other states. The maximum annual value of this average spread was 21.7 basis points, in 1984, and the minimum was −7.9 basis points, in 1976. There is also time-related variation in the dispersion of tax-exempt bond yields. The year with the highest cross-sectional standard deviation of yield spreads was 1975, when this measure was 40.7. This was at a time when New York City's fiscal difficulties were affecting the tax-exempt bond market. The lowest cross-sectional standard deviation was in 1994, 9.2, a time of robust economic growth in most states.

Table 8.2 also presents summary information on other fiscal variables. The average state collects general fund revenue (total revenue less collections for state social insurance trusts) of 12.8 percent of personal income; this ratio is lower, 9.3 percent, for New Jersey. The average value of state debt as a share of state personal income is 8.6 percent, and New Jersey is very similar to the national average on this dimension. The ratio of debt to personal income is typically less than 10 percent, but in some states in some years, the debt burden is substantially higher. Delaware, Rhode Island, and Alaska all have outstanding debt of more than 25 percent of personal income. The average state top marginal income tax rate is between 6 and 7 percent, compared with 3.5 percent in New Jersey.

The bottom half of table 8.2 presents summary statistics on the indicator variables for fiscal institutions, which correspond to the budget rules that were described in table 8.1. The indicator variables for the last four variables measure different degrees of fiscal discipline in correcting budget deficits. The weakest variable is the one for legislative passage of a balanced budget. States that require the next fiscal measure, correction of a deficit within the next year's fiscal cycle, also require legislative passage of a balanced budget each year. The strictest states are those that require deficits to be corrected in the current annual budget cycle. Some states have biennial budget cycles, and the second-to-last variable indicates that the deficit must be corrected within the current biennial cycle.

Table 8.3 presents ordinary least squares (OLS) regression evidence on the association between fiscal rules, state fiscal conditions, and state borrowing rates. Each of the equations include control variables for the state unemployment rate, the level of per capita income in the state, state revenues as a share of personal income, state debt outstanding as a fraction of personal income, the top state marginal tax rate on interest income, and the ADA score for the state's senate delegation. The equation in the first column of table 8.3 shows the effect of using only these control variables to explain the relative yields on tax-exempt bonds. The results indicate that yields rise with the state unemployment rate and the level of debt relative to income, and that yields are lower when state revenue represents a higher fraction of personal income. These results also support the argument, developed in McKinnon 1997 and Bayoumi and Eichengreen 1994, that credit markets exert a disciplinary role on fiscal policy in the U.S. states. The coefficients on the other control variables are statistically indistinguishable from zero; this pattern persists in the other specifications that we estimate. This set of control variables can explain roughly one-third of the variation in the relative yield variable.

Table 8.3   State Fiscal Institutions and State Bond Yields

Variable	OLS (1)	IV (2)	OLS (3)	OLS (4)	OLS (5)
Unemployment rate	567.7	527.4	569.4	539.6	559.6
	(103.6)	(127.6)	(98.4)	(84.2)	(82.0)
Per capita income	1.56	0.56	0.94	0.78	−0.02
	(1.00)	(1.66)	(0.84)	(0.69)	(1.04)
Revenue/income	−72.7	−159.3	−34.7	−33.8	−41.7
	(25.0)	(134.2)	(28.2)	(25.3)	(25.3)
Debt/income	103.3	205.5	75.6	92.1	98.7
	(35.4)	(159.0)	(31.8)	(28.6)	(31.3)
State marginal tax	40.7	14.83	47.2	53.3	24.3
rate	(48.5)	(45.82)	(47.4)	(39.9)	(41.9)
Average ADA score	8.69	8.53	8.54	6.24	8.28
	(6.74)	(6.81)	(5.65)	(5.50)	(5.50)
Lax antideficit rules			13.30	8.42	
			(5.41)	(6.52)	
Limit on issuing				−5.38	−6.85
debt				(4.86)	(4.12)
Binding				−7.08	−5.75
expenditure limit				(3.59)	(3.57)
Binding revenue				17.61	14.01
limit				(6.63)	(6.57)
Legislature pass					−10.25
balanced budget					(8.99)
Correct deficit next					−11.58
cycle					(9.41)
Correct deficit this					−8.08
two-year cycle					(8.17)
Correct deficit this					−17.12
one-year cycle					(8.82)
Adjusted R^2	.35		.39	.44	.46

Note: Data are for 1973–95 for the 40 states covered in the Chubb Relative Value Survey and include 899 observations. Annual indicator variables are included in each regression, and all variables reported are differenced from the New Jersey value. Standard errors, which are in parentheses, control for across-state heterogeneity and within-state correlation. The state debt-to-income ratio is treated as endogenous in the equation reported in column 2, and state fiscal institutions are used as instrumental variables for this estimation.

One noteworthy but statistically insignificant coefficient is that on the state political ideology variable, the ADA score. This variable has a positive coefficient, implying that more liberal states pay more to borrow, but we cannot reject, at standard significance levels, the null hypothesis that this coefficient equals zero. This suggests that the omitted variable problems associated with failure to include a detailed set of variables capturing state political taste may not be critical.

The equation in the second column of table 8.3 includes the same explanatory variables as the equation in the first column, but it treats the state's debt-to-income ratio as an endogenous variable. We use the set of fiscal institutions, the variables in $\{Z_{it}\}$, as the set of excluded exogenous variables in the estimation. When the debt-to-income ratio is treated as endogenous, its coefficient doubles, but the standard error rises by a factor of five, and we would not reject the null hypothesis that the debt-to-income coefficients in the OLS and instrumental variables (IV) specifications are the same. The other coefficients also change between the two specifications, but given their large standard errors, it is again difficult to draw firm conclusions. We tested, and rejected, the null hypothesis that fiscal institutions only affect bond yields through their effect on the level of outstanding debt. The results therefore suggest that fiscal institutions do not provide a suitable set of instrumental variables for the debt-to-income ratio because they also affect bond yields *directly*.

The equation shown in the third column of table 8.3 returns to the OLS strategy of the first column, but it includes the indicator for lax fiscal rules along with the foregoing control variables. The results suggest that tighter antideficit rules are associated with lower borrowing rates. A state with weak antideficit rules, all else equal, faces a borrowing rate 13 basis points higher than a state with tough antideficit rules. This finding confirms the results in earlier studies using the Chubb data. This effect does not change significantly (it decreases by 1 basis point) if we redefine the lax antideficit rules to include states that can carry over a deficit but must correct it in the next budget cycle, that is, with ACIR scores of 0 through 6 rather than 0 through 5.

The equation in the fourth column of table 8.3 includes the indicator variable for antideficit rules as well as three additional variables: one for the presence of a debt limit, and two variables corresponding to binding expenditure and revenue limits. Adding these variables reduces the statistical significance of the coefficient on the antideficit rule variable, although this coefficient remains positive and greater than its standard error. The debt limit variable has a negative coefficient, consistent with the discussion above, but the coefficient is not statistically significantly different from zero. The expenditure limit variable has a negative and statistically significant effect on yields: states with binding expenditure limits face borrowing costs that average 7 basis points less than states without such limits. The presence of a binding revenue limit has a large and statistically significant positive effect on yields: the presence of such a limit raises a state's borrowing cost by almost 18 basis points. This finding represents an effect of fiscal institutions that has not been documented in previous work, and it suggests that bond market participants view revenue limits as institutions that raise the risk of default.

The equation in the last column of table 8.3 does not include the antideficit indicator variable. Instead, it includes a set of indicator variables for different degrees of stringency in the budget process. The omitted category in this equation is the set of states that have no balanced-budget rules (Vermont) or the relatively weak requirement that the governor submit a balanced budget (New York, Massachusetts, and New Hampshire). The first included category is states that only require their legislatures to pass a balanced budget. In these states bond yields are lower, by an average of 10 basis points, than in states where the only requirement is that the governor submit a balanced budget. This effect is statistically indistinguishable from zero, however.

The next three variables are indicator variables for progressively more stringent rules that require deficits to be corrected in specified time frames. States that require that deficits be corrected by the end of the next budget cycle also have lower borrowing costs than states with only gubernatorial submission requirements, but again, the effect is statistically indistinguishable from zero. States with the strictest requirements, namely the rule that deficits must be corrected within the *current* fiscal year, have borrowing costs that average 17 basis points below the costs of states in which governors are required to submit balanced budgets. This effect *is* statistically significant at standard confidence levels, and it suggests that much of the power of the "lax antideficit rules" variable is coming from the difference in borrowing costs in states with very strict, and all other, antideficit rules. When the expanded set of fiscal institution indicators is included in the regression specification, the explanatory power of the equation rises. The adjusted R^2 for the equation in the last column of table 8.3 is .46, compared with .44 for the equation in the penultimate column that excludes the detailed indicator variables on antideficit rules.

The equations reported in table 8.4 explore the possibility that the effect of fiscal institutions on borrowing costs is blunted by the inclusion of the debt-to-income ratio in the specifications shown in table 8.3. The equation shown in the first column illustrates the changes in the control variable coefficients when the debt-to-income ratio is deleted. The coefficient on the unemployment rate remains positive and statistically significant, but per capita income, which was insignificantly different from zero in the specifications shown in table 8.3, now becomes statistically significant and positive. Revenue as a percentage of income, which was *negative* in table 8.3, switches signs and becomes positive in table 8.4. The ADA score and the top marginal tax rate are statistically insignificantly different from zero in most of the estimates in table 8.4, as they were in table 8.3.

The sign pattern and the statistical significance of the coefficients on the fiscal institution variables is largely unaffected by exclusion of the debt-to-income ratio. This can be seen by comparing the coefficients in table 8.3 with those in table 8.4. The point estimate on the antideficit rule variable (column 2) rises slightly when the debt-to-income ratio is dropped from the specification. This is consistent with the notion that tight fiscal rules lower the value of the debt-to-income ratio, and that including this ratio in the estimating equation therefore captures some of the effect of these variables.

The equation shown in the third column of table 8.4 models the indicator of lax fiscal rules, the ACIR variable, as endogenous. This corresponds to our earlier discussion of the potential endogeneity of fiscal rules. The difficulty in treating fiscal rules as endogenous is that it is not clear what excluded exoge-

Table 8.4   **State Fiscal Institutions and State Bond Yields Excluding Outstanding State Debt Stock**

Variable	OLS (1)	OLS (2)	IV (3)	OLS (4)	IV (5)	OLS (6)
Unemployment rate	608.4	597.6	605.2	578.3	596.6	609.6
	(104.5)	(94.2)	(102.2)	(83.7)	(123.8)	(80.8)
Per capita income	2.56	1.53	2.26	1.46	0.35	1.02
	(0.95)	(0.81)	(2.20)	(0.68)	(3.98)	(0.96)
Revenue/income	14.7	31.7	19.6	45.2	60.2	43.8
	(23.6)	(24.3)	(40.3)	(20.1)	(78.4)	(23.3)
State marginal tax	66.8	66.3	66.7	74.7	68.3	40.4
rate	(48.9)	(47.1)	(47.4)	(39.0)	(46.9)	(43.0)
Average ADA	8.86	8.62	8.79	6.39	2.76	8.58
score	(7.08)	(5.67)	(6.77)	(5.67)	(10.68)	(5.77)
Lax antideficit		15.48	4.50	10.94	7.14	
rules		(5.07)	(28.42)	(6.43)	(43.92)	
Limit on issuing				−6.03	−26.78	−8.03
debt				(5.28)	(28.74)	(4.88)
Binding				−5.29	4.82	−3.96
expenditure limit				(3.89)	(44.62)	(3.83)
Binding revenue				15.87	21.76	12.26
limit				(6.63)	(52.96)	(6.56)
Legislature pass						−12.50
balanced budget						(8.18)
Correct deficit next						−15.94
cycle						(8.62)
Correct deficit this						−11.13
two-year cycle						(7.85)
Correct deficit this						−19.12
one-year cycle						(8.59)
Adjusted R^2	.32	.37		.41		.43

Note: Data are for 1973–95 for the 40 states covered in the Chubb Relative Value Survey and include 899 observations. Annual indicator variables are included in each regression, and all variables reported are differenced from the New Jersey value. Standard errors, which are shown in parentheses, control for across-state heterogeneity and within-state correlation. The endogenous variable in column 3 is the indicator for lax antideficit rules, and in column 5, all of the variables related to fiscal institutions are treated as endogenous. See text for further discussion of the excluded exogenous variables.

nous variables are available for use as instrumental variables. Such variables need to be correlated with current fiscal rules, but uncorrelated with the error term in equation (3).

The instrumental variables that we consider are related to the current or historical structure of the state political process. They involve constitutional or legal provisions that would make it more or less difficult to adopt fiscal rules, such as tax and expenditure limits or restrictions on state deficits. The five instrumental variables that we use are whether the state constitution permits statewide referenda to enact legislation (so-called direct-legislation states), whether voters can recall elected officials, whether the initial state constitution included limits on debt issuance, the "signature requirement" (the fraction of the state's voters that must sign a petition in order to place a policy proposal on a statewide ballot for referendum vote), and the year a territory became a state. It is sometimes argued, and the empirical evidence in Matsusaka (1995) suggests, that grassroots campaigns lead to support among voters for tax and expenditure limits, but that such support is much more difficult to generate in elected legislatures. If this is the case, then the direct legislation variable and the "signature requirement" should affect the chances of enacting a tax or spending limit. Similarly, one can argue that recall provisions increase the degree to which elected officials are responsive to voter preferences, and thereby affect the probability that legislatures will enact deficit limits, or tax or expenditure limits, conditional on a level of voter support for such measures. Magleby (1984) provides valuable background on the political consequences of various methods of implementing "direct democracy." The historical debt limit variable is largely determined by when the state was founded, since, as English (1996) explains, states whose constitutions were written after the state debt defaults of the 1830s and 1840s were more likely to place limits on debt. Finally, the year a state constitution was adopted is another way to pick up idiosyncracies in state constitutions that will affect the ease of adopting different fiscal institutions.

The estimates in the third column of table 8.4 are discouraging. While the IV estimates still yield a positive effect of weak antideficit rules on borrowing costs, the standard error of the coefficient estimate (28.42) is so large that a 95 percent confidence interval includes both the OLS estimate and a range of other values. The instrumental variables are "weak" in the sense that we find very imprecise estimates of the coefficient of interest; our instruments do not explain much of the variation in antideficit rules, even though, as Rueben (1996) finds, they do explain a substantial fraction of the variation in tax and expenditure limits.

Returning to OLS results that are similar to those in table 8.3, but that exclude the debt-to-income ratio from the specification, we find that the effect of a binding revenue limit, shown in table 8.4 column 4, is slightly reduced when we exclude the debt-to-income ratio from the specification. Column 4 presents OLS estimates including the variables for lax deficit rules, debt limits, revenue limits, and expenditure limits. The coefficients are broadly similar to those in table 8.3, where the debt-to-income ratio was included in the specification. The fifth column of table 8.4 presents an equation that treats all four of these fiscal institutions as endogenous. Just as with the IV estimates described above, however, the standard errors on all of the estimated coefficients rise substantially. It is not possible to draw any strong inferences from the IV estimates, except that the set of instruments that we have used has low power. Indeed, in first-stage regression equations relating the fiscal institutions to the instrument set, the only endogenous variable that the instruments are jointly statistically significant in explaining is that for a revenue limit.

The last column in table 8.4 shows another OLS equation, in this case estimated with the exhaustive set of fiscal institutional variables. There is no clear pattern of changes in the set of coefficients when compared with those in table 8.3. The estimated effect of the requirement that a deficit be corrected in the current annual budget cycle is larger than in the comparable equation in table 8.3 that included the debt-to-income ratio, but not by a large amount relative to the coefficient standard error. In general, the findings in table 8.4 do not suggest that the inclusion of the debt-to-income ratio has substantially altered the previous findings with regard to the impact of fiscal rules on borrowing rates.

The results from our basic specifications suggest that fiscal institutions affect state borrowing costs, and they provide new information on the types of fiscal rules that have the greatest impact. We now consider whether the impact of these fiscal rules depends on state economic conditions, as measured by the state unemployment rate. We do this by interacting three fiscal rules—the indicator for lax antideficit rules, and the indicators for tax and expenditure limits—with the state unemployment rate. This approach is related to Lowry and Alt's (1997) interaction of the state deficit with fiscal rules.

Table 8.5 presents the results of our unemployment-interaction analysis. The equation in the first column includes only the variable for lax antideficit rules, and this variable interacted with the unemployment rate. The effect of lax budget rules is not significantly affected by state economic conditions. We find similar results with respect to limits on the state legislature's authority to issue debt, as the results in the second column suggest. However, the equation in the second column also interacts the indicator variables for the presence of revenue and expenditure limits with the unemployment rate. While there is weak evidence that the effect of expenditure limits is accentuated in states with higher unemployment rates, there is a statistically significant, and substantively important, interaction effect between revenue limits and the state unemployment rate.

To illustrate this effect, contrast two states, one without a binding revenue limit, and one with such a limit. On average, the state without the revenue limit will face borrowing costs 10 basis points lower than the state with the revenue limit. Now consider a two-percentage-point increase in the unemployment rate in the two states. The estimates in table 8.5 suggest that there will be a 10-basis-point increase in the yield spread between the tax-exempt bonds issued by the two states. For each percentage point that the unemployment rate rises in a state with a binding revenue limit, the state bond yield rises by 5 basis points relative to the yield of a similar state without a revenue limit. This suggests that when state economic conditions deteriorate, revenue limits become a greater concern for bond market participants.

The data sample that we analyze is longer than that in previous studies of fiscal rules and borrowing costs. One advantage of this long sample is that we can examine whether the relationships described above are stable over time.

Table 8.5   State Fiscal Rules, Economic Conditions, and Bond Yields

Explanatory Variable	(1)	(2)	(3)
Unemployment rate	587.79	491.57	497.61
	(104.64)	(185.89)	(88.22)
Per capita income	1.54	1.33	1.32
	(0.81)	(0.66)	(0.66)
Revenue/income	32.06	52.82	−40.20
	(24.20)	(19.84)	(24.00)
State marginal tax rate	65.51	77.75	52.37
	(47.35)	(41.30)	(20.12)
Average ADA score	8.78	4.96	4.78
	(5.74)	(5.63)	(5.55)
Lax antideficit rules	15.56	12.90	12.74
	(5.04)	(6.99)	(6.90)
Lax antideficit rules*unemployment	57.26	68.00	
	(132.47)	(197.89)	
Limit on issuing debt		−4.95	−5.00
		(5.69)	(5.52)
Limit on issuing debt*unemployment		−9.35	
		(163.22)	
Binding expenditure limit		−4.54	−4.62
		(3.92)	(3.91)
Binding expenditure		−125.32	−127.34
limit* unemployment		(98.71)	(98.39)
Binding revenue limit		9.62	9.65
		(6.81)	(6.71)
Binding revenue		521.50	515.63
limit* unemployment		(264.91)	(224.35)
Adjusted R^2	.373	.427	.428

Note: Data are for 1973–95 for the 40 states covered in the Chubb Relative Value Survey and include 899 observations. Annual indicator variables are included in each regression, and all variables are differences from the New Jersey value. Standard errors, which are shown in parentheses, control for across-state heterogeneity and within-state correlation.

Table 8.6 presents four regression equations that address this issue. The equations in columns 1 and 2 correspond to column 2 in table 8.4, but the equation is estimated first for the 1973–89 sample period, and again for 1990–95. While the coefficients on several of the control variables differ across the sample periods, with a lower coefficient on the unemployment rate in the most recent subsample, for example, the coefficient on the indicator variable for lax antideficit rules does not change substantially across samples. An F-test of the hypothesis that all coefficients are the same in two sample periods would nevertheless reject the null of parameter constancy.

The third and fourth columns of table 8.6 present subsample estimates for the expanded equation, including revenue and expenditure limits. The results suggest one interesting pattern: the effect of binding revenue limits on state borrowing costs appears to be larger in the 1973–89 period than in more recent

Table 8.6   **State Fiscal Rules and Bond Yields: Are the 1990s Different?**

Explanatory Variable	1973–89 (1)	1990–95 (2)	1973–89 (3)	1990–95 (4)
Unemployment rate	654.68	350.56	609.21	355.96
	(103.46)	(79.97)	(94.20)	(89.57)
Per capita income	2.46	−0.50	2.15	−0.27
	(0.94)	(0.56)	(0.79)	(0.48)
Revenue/income	20.23	52.97	37.81	64.08
	(27.45)	(17.75)	(22.55)	(17.34)
State marginal tax rate	68.12	48.86	82.21	59.42
	(49.69)	(40.68)	(42.69)	(35.77)
Average ADA score	12.19	2.38	9.13	1.26
	(7.14)	(3.98)	(7.05)	(4.15)
Lax antideficit rules	15.03	18.98	10.45	16.95
	(5.79)	(3.39)	(7.69)	(3.65)
Limit on issuing debt			−7.40	−1.03
			(6.19)	(2.96)
Binding expenditure limit			−5.90	−4.70
			(5.23)	(2.44)
Binding revenue limit			25.19	4.63
			(9.65)	(2.93)
Adjusted R^2	.385	.511	.432	.543

Note: Data are for 1973–95 for the 40 states covered in the Chubb Relative Value Survey and include 899 observations. Annual indicator variables are included in each regression, and all variables are differences from the New Jersey value. Standard errors, which are shown in parentheses, control for across-state heterogeneity and within-state correlation. Regressions for 1973–89 include 680 observations, while those for 1990–95 have 219 observations. The F-statistic for equal coefficients in columns 1 and 2 is $F(9,858) = 7.42$, and $F(11,852) = 6.26$ for columns 3 and 4, so we reject the null of constant coefficients across the two time periods.

years. When we constrain the coefficients on the variables other than fiscal institutions to be the same for the entire sample, but interact the fiscal institution variables with a post-1990 dummy variable, the same findings emerge. The coefficient on the post-1990 dummy interacted with the indicator for a binding revenue limit is −23.2 (8.14), which suggests a much larger effect of this variable in the earlier part of the sample. The interpretation of this result is unclear. It may be that as more states have adopted revenue limits, bond market participants have become less concerned about the negative effect of these limits on state capacity to service debt. The rise of municipal bond insurance may also be a factor. This is an issue that requires further study.

In addition to the pre- and post-1990 sample divisions, we also explored the sensitivity of our findings to estimation on the "pre–New York City fiscal crisis" sample. We interacted an indicator variable for the pre-1975 period with our standard list of fiscal institutions. The results, which must be viewed with caution in light of the short sample period, suggest that the positive effect of debt restrictions on yields was greater in the years before 1975 than afterward, and that the effect of antideficit rules on borrowing costs was smaller in this period than subsequently. The effect of revenue and expenditure limits cannot be estimated for the pre-1975 period—there were no such limits. These results provide some support for the notion that bond market participants have become more interested in the role of fiscal institutions in the years since the New York City fiscal problem.

8.4   Conclusion and Future Directions

Our principal finding is that state fiscal institutions affect the required return that lenders demand when states enter the market for tax-exempt bonds. The effects that we uncover are substantively as well as statistically significant. A state with a binding tax limitation statute will face, on average, a borrowing rate between 15 and 20 basis points higher than a state without a tax limitation law. With long-term tax-exempt bond rates averaging something like five percentage points, borrowing cost differentials of this magnitude are not trivial. A state with an expenditure limitation law, in contrast, will face a borrowing rate that is several basis points lower than that of a state without any fiscal limits. Lenders appear to demand higher yields from states with tax limitation laws, presumably because such restrictions may make it difficult to raise taxes to pay interest in the future, while they appear to view spending limitation laws as favorable indicators of the state's future fiscal soundness.

We also confirm, with a longer data sample and somewhat more inclusive empirical model, previous findings that antideficit provisions in the state constitution have an important effect on borrowing costs. Those states with weak antideficit provisions face borrowing costs 10 to 15 basis points higher than similar states with stricter antideficit rules. Restrictions on state authority to issue long-term general-obligation debt are associated with lower borrowing costs, although the point estimates suggest weaker effects for these institutions than for some of the other fiscal rules considered above.

Our focus on the capital market as a way of obtaining evidence on the effects of fiscal institutions could be extended in several directions. One possibility would be to move beyond the use of interest rate differentials to analyze other market-based measures of state default risk. Studying how default insurance rates charged by municipal bond insurers are influenced by fiscal institutions would be one possible extension. This project would require detailed information on default insurance rates for state general obligation bonds, ideally at several different points in time. Our analysis could also be extended to the case of local rather than state governments. Hirsch's (1991) study of the net interest costs on California municipal bonds around the enactment of Proposition 13 provides some evidence that local bond yields are affected by changes in fiscal institutions. Yet another extension would focus on the short-run yield adjustments to economic news, and the effect of fiscal institutions on such adjustments. One could consider how unexpected state deficits that arise within a fiscal year raise borrowing costs for states with weak, and with strong, antideficit policies. Research of this type could complement the evidence in Poterba (1994) on the relationship between antideficit rules and short-run state fiscal adjustment.

Our results raise unanswered questions about why different states choose different fiscal institutions, and what trade-offs are involved in choosing one set of institutions or another. Research is just beginning on the general question of what the optimal fiscal constitution consists of; see Roubini 1995 for a discussion of these issues. With respect to state antideficit rules, there is a small, and as yet inconclusive, literature on how different fiscal rules affect state economic performance. Bayoumi and Eichengreen (1995) and Levinson (1997) find that states with more restrictive fiscal constitutions have higher output volatility, apparently as a result of less fiscal flexibility on the part of state government, while Alesina and Bayoumi (1996) do not find any evidence linking the stringency of state fiscal rules to the variability of state economic activity. With respect to tax and expenditure limits, there is evidence, for example Rueben 1996, that these rules affect the size of government in the state economy. These rules also have effects on state borrowing costs. These studies illustrate the type of research that is needed to identify the net benefits of different fiscal rules. Our findings suggest that voters in states that enact tighter fiscal rules benefit from lower borrowing costs; the unresolved question is what countervailing costs, or additional as-yet-unquantified benefits, these fiscal rules also produce.

References

Advisory Council on Intergovernmental Relations. 1987. *Fiscal discipline in the federal system: National reform and the experience of the states.* Washington, D.C.: Advisory Council on Intergovernmental Relations.

Alesina, Alberto, and Tamim Bayoumi. 1996. The costs and benefits of fiscal rules: Evidence from U.S. states. NBER Working Paper no. 5614. Cambridge, Mass.: National Bureau of Economic Research.

Alt, James E., and Robert C. Lowry. 1994. Divided government, fiscal institutions, and budget deficits: Evidence from the states. *American Political Science Review* 88: 811–28.

Bayoumi, Tamim, and Barry Eichengreen. 1994. The political economy of fiscal restrictions: Implications for Europe from the United States. *European Economic Review* 38:783–91.

———. 1995. Restraining yourself: Fiscal rules and stabilization. *IMF Staff Papers* 42 (March): 32–48.

Bayoumi, Tamim, Morris Goldstein, and Geoffrey Woglom. 1995. Do credit markets discipline sovereign borrowers: Evidence from U.S. states. *Journal of Money, Credit, and Banking* 27:1046–59.

Besley, Timothy, and Anne Case. 1994. Unnatural experiments: Estimating the incidence of endogenous policies. NBER Working Paper no. 4956. Cambridge, Mass.: National Bureau of Economic Research.

Bohn, Henning, and Robert P. Inman. 1995. Constitutional limits and public deficits: Evidence from the U.S. states. *Carnegie-Rochester Conference Series on Public Policy* 45 (December): 13–76.

Briffault, Richard. 1996. *Balancing acts: The reality behind state balanced budget requirements.* New York: Twentieth Century Fund Press.

Bunche, Beverly S. 1991. The effect of constitutional debt limits on state governments' use of public authorities. *Public Choice* 68 (January): 57–69.

Capeci, John. 1991. Credit risk, credit ratings, and municipal bond yields: A panel study. *National Tax Journal* 44 (December): 41–56.

———. 1994. Local fiscal policies, default risk, and municipal borrowing costs. *Journal of Public Economics* 53:73–89.

Eichengreen, Barry. 1992. *Should the Maastricht Treaty be saved?* Princeton Studies in International Finance, no. 74. Princeton, N.J.: Princeton University Press.

English, William. 1996. Understanding the costs of sovereign default: American state debts in the 1840s. *American Economic Review* 86:259–75.

Fortune, Peter. 1996. Do municipal bond yields forecast tax policy? *Federal Reserve Bank of Boston Review,* September/October, 29–48.

Goldstein, Morris, and Geoffrey Woglom. 1992. Market-based fiscal discipline in monetary unions: Evidence from the U.S. municipal bond market. In *Establishing a central bank: Issues in Europe and lessons from the United States,* ed. M. B. Canzoneri, V. Grilli, and P. R. Masson. Cambridge: Cambridge University Press.

Hirsch, Werner Z. 1986. Revenue limitation measures and their effects on municipal bonds: The case of California municipalities. In *Public Finance and Public Debt: Proceedings of the 40th Congress of the International Institute of Public Finance.* Detroit: Wayne State University Press.

Inman, Robert P. 1996. Do balanced budget rules work? U.S. experience and possible lessons for the EMU. NBER Working Paper no. 5838. Cambridge, Mass.: National Bureau of Economic Research.

Kidwell, David S., Timothy W. Koch, and Duane R. Stock. 1984. The impact of state income taxes on municipal borrowing costs. *National Tax Journal* 37:551–61.

Kiewiet, D. Roderick, and Kristin Szakaly. 1996. The efficacy of constitutional restrictions on borrowing, taxing, and spending: An analysis of state bonded indebtedness, 1961–90. *Journal of Law, Economics, and Organization* 12:62–97.

Levinson, Arik. 1997. Balanced budgets and business cycles: Evidence from the states. Department of Economics, University of Wisconsin. Photocopy.

Lovely, Mary E., and Michael J. Wasylenko. 1992. State taxation of interest income and municipal borrowing costs. *National Tax Journal* 45:37–52.

Lowry, Robert C., and James E. Alt. 1997. A visible hand? Bond markets, political parties, balanced budget laws, and state government debt. Department of Government, Harvard University. Photocopy.

Magleby, David B. 1984. *Direct legislation: Voting on ballot propositions in the United States.* Baltimore: John Hopkins University Press.

Matsusaka, John G. 1995. Fiscal effects of the voter initiative: Evidence from the last 30 years. *Journal of Political Economy* 103:587–623.

McKinnon, Ronald I. 1997. Monetary regimes, government borrowing constraints, and market-preserving federalism: Implications for the EMU. Stanford University. Photocopy.

Metcalf, Gilbert. 1993. Federal taxation and the supply of state debt. *Journal of Public Economics* 51:269–85.

Poterba, James M. 1989. Tax reform and the market for tax-exempt debt. *Regional Science and Urban Economics* 19:537–62.

———. 1994. State responses to fiscal crises: The effects of budgetary institutions and politics. *Journal of Political Economy* 102:799–821.

————. 1997. Do budget rules work? In *Fiscal policy: Lessons from economic research,* ed. A. Auerbach. Cambridge, Mass.: MIT Press.

Rafool, Mandy. 1997. State tax and expenditure limits. *State Tax Notes,* January 13, 115–35.

Ratchford, Benjamin U. 1941. *American state debts.* Durham, N.C.: Duke University Press.

Roubini, Nouriel. 1995. The economics of fiscal bondage: The balanced budget amendment and other binding fiscal rules. New York University. Photocopy.

Rueben, Kim S. 1996. Tax limitations and government growth: The effect of state tax and expenditure limits on state and local government. Public Policy Institute of California. Photocopy.

Shadbegian, Ronald J. 1996. Do tax and expenditure limitations affect the size and growth of state government? *Contemporary Economic Policy* 20:22–35.

Swartz, Thomas J., III. 1989. State general obligation trading values: Back to the future. *Municipal Analysts Journal,* August, 7–10.

von Hagen, Jürgen. 1991. A note on the empirical effectiveness of formal fiscal restraints. *Journal of Public Economics* 44:199–21.

————. 1992. Fiscal arrangements in a monetary union: Evidence from the United States. In *Fiscal policy, taxation, and the financial system in an increasingly-integrated Europe,* ed. Donald Fair and Christian de Boissieu. Dordrecht: Kluwer Academic Publishers.

9   Electoral Institutions, Cabinet Negotiations, and Budget Deficits in the European Union

Mark Hallerberg and Jürgen von Hagen

9.1   Introduction

Large government budget deficits are a concern in most OECD countries. In the United States, both major political parties, while differing on how to reach the goal of a balanced budget, have nonetheless agreed to make a balanced budget a top policy priority. Within the European Union, high budget deficits may soon affect a member state's ability to participate in monetary union—the Maastricht Treaty stipulates that governments with excessive debt levels, defined as yearly deficits of 3 percent of GDP and total debt burdens of 60 percent of GDP, should be excluded from participation in the common currency. One reason for a renewed commitment by politicians to reduce deficits is a recognition of the negative economic effects of chronic deficits and debt levels. They lead on average to higher interest rates, lower economic growth, a depreciated currency, and a restriction on spending on valued public services. States have had varying levels of success in keeping deficits low. Some, like Germany, Great Britain, and France, have managed to maintain relatively low deficit and debt levels, while others, such as Italy, Greece, and Belgium, have suffered chronic deficits and/or debt levels.

Two literatures in political economy argue that differences in political institutions explain much of the variation in the success of countries in their efforts to run small deficits. One group of authors considers how differences among electoral systems affect the size of budget deficits, while the second group concentrates on the governmental institutions that structure the formation of the yearly budget.

Mark Hallerberg is assistant professor in the Sam Nunn School of International Affairs at the Georgia Institute of Technology and codirector of the European Union Center of the University System of Georgia. Jürgen von Hagen is professor of economics at the University of Bonn, director of the Center for European Integration Studies, and a fellow of the Centre for Economic Policy Research, London.

Among the "electoral institutionalists," a consensus is beginning to emerge that treats proportional representation systems as a cause of high levels of public debt. Proportional representation (PR) systems are often considered inherently more unstable than pluralist electoral systems. Government ministers who expect to lose their positions soon after they gain them do not anticipate dealing with the consequences of their actions, and they willingly increase debt levels (Persson and Svensson 1989; Roubini and Sachs 1989; Tabellini and Alesina 1990; Grilli, Masciandaro, and Tabellini 1991; Hahm 1994; for a dissenting view on the stability of policies in PR systems, see Rogowski 1987). Others emphasize that coalition governments, which are common in PR systems, are less able to deal with negative shocks to the economy. Such governments face a prisoner's dilemma of whose ministry should suffer the budget cuts. Coalition partners may have enough power to block change, but not enough leverage to effect positive change on their own (Roubini and Sachs 1989; Alesina and Perotti 1995). PR systems also lead to greater polarization in the political system. If the party or parties in government anticipate that their opposition will someday assume power, they may seek to confine future governments by generating present debts, and the incentive to generate larger debts increases with political polarization (Tabellini and Alesina 1990).[1] In contrast, governments that emerge under a pluralist system are more decisive, the system discourages extremist parties, and the governments stay in power longer and are more stable. For all of these reasons pluralist electoral systems lead to lower levels of government debt.

While the theoretical work has sparked interest, the empirical support for this argument has been uneven. In a reconsideration of Roubini and Sachs's data set, Edin and Ohlsson (1991) find that minority governments, rather than PR states per se, are more likely to run large budget deficits. Alesina and Perotti (1995), while confirming a link between coalition governments and low success rates in the implementation of austerity programs in OECD countries, discover paradoxically that minority governments are the most fiscally responsible form of government, more fiscally responsible than even one-party majority governments. De Haan and Sturm (1994), in a pooled time-series analysis of European Community countries from 1981 through 1989, find no statistically significant relationship at all between the form of government and budget deficits.[2]

The "fiscal institutionalists" consider how budgetary institutions affect the size of deficits. During the formulation of the budget at the cabinet level (the government phase), a strong finance minister can force the decision makers to

---

1. Grilli, Masciandaro, and Tabellini also theorize that the existence of extremist parties in proportional representation systems should lead to higher levels of debt, but they do not find polarization to be statistically significant in their regressions.

2. De Haan and Sturm (1997) widen their study to include 21 OECD countries for the period 1982–92. They again find no significant relationship between the type of government and changes in gross debt.

consider the true benefits and costs of increased spending and taxation (von Hagen 1992; von Hagen and Harden 1994a, 1994b, 1996; Alesina et al. 1996; Hahm, Kamlet, and Mowery 1996). Similarly, negotiated spending targets for each ministry can also lead to smaller deficits (von Hagen 1992; von Hagen and Harden 1994a, 1994b, 1996). The approach examines the structure of other parts of the budget process as well, such as how parliament deals with the government's proposed budget, how the budget is implemented, and whether there are any ex post controls. While the statistical evidence in support of the effects of such institutions has generally been stronger,[3] this approach does not explain why some states choose a given budgetary institution and others do not.

In this paper, we argue that these two literatures complement one another. Electoral institutions matter because they restrict the type of budgetary institution at the governmental phase that a state has at its disposal. A strong finance minister is feasible in states where one-party governments are the norm, and such states usually have plurality electoral systems. In multiparty governments, which are common in states with proportional representation, the coalition members are not willing to delegate to one actor the ability to monitor and punish the others. Negotiated targets provide an alternative in multiparty governments. They will be credible, however, only if all the parties can monitor and punish each other. Since parties often lack the ability to provide one or the other of these functions, targets are harder to maintain successfully than a strong finance minister. This result explains why many electoral institutionalists find that PR states, on average, are more prone to run larger deficits. At the same time, since such states that do maintain negotiated spending targets will have deficits that are as low as plurality states with a strong finance minister, a general comparison of plurality states with PR states misses the effect of budgetary institutions.

We first develop a model of the budget process and show that the distinction between one-party and multiparty governments affects which institution, either a delegation of fiscal powers or commitment to negotiated targets, a country can use to reduce spending. Next, we consider one distinguishing feature of electoral systems, namely their effects on the likelihood of one-party or multiparty majority governments. The existing literature indicates that plurality systems are much more likely to have one-party governments than PR states. At the same time, PR states with a low average district magnitude (number of candidates per electoral district) are also more likely to have one party win a majority of votes and form a government.

The final section examines the use of such institutional constraints within the current 15 European Union states from 1981 through 1994. These states are of theoretical interest because economic shocks, which often have short-run consequences for a country's fiscal balance, should impact this group more

---

3. De Haan and Sturm (1994), in their comparison of different explanations for the size of the deficit, find von Hagen's (1992) institutional variable statistically significant.

or less equally. One can therefore provide a control for such external factors. From a policy perspective, these states are also of interest because of the Maastricht Treaty's provisions concerning yearly deficits and aggregate debt. If certain institutions have been effective in some states, they may provide a way for high-debt states to bring their fiscal policies in step with the Maastricht Treaty's guidelines. This section indicates a strong relationship between one-party majority government and the use of a strong finance minister on the one hand and multiparty governments and budgetary targets on the other. Pooled time-series regressions that are presented at the end of the paper indicate that the presence or absence of these constraints, rather than the electoral system per se, is the crucial variable that affects the size of the budget deficit. Not all of the states chose one of the institutions, and those that did so registered significantly lower yearly deficits and overall debt levels than those states that chose to forgo the institutional constraints.

9.2   The Budgeting Process within Cabinet Governments

In this section, we present a model of budgeting decisions in a cabinet government. We show that the structure of the bargaining process within the cabinet affects the size of the budget. If spending ministers are left to determine their own budgets, they will select amounts that are larger than what is collectively optimal for the government in power. The reason for this is that the budget process resembles a common-pool resource problem. Each minister determines the spending priorities of her department, but she does not consider the full marginal tax burden of an extra dollar of spending. Instead, each minister worries only about that part of the tax burden that her constituency must bear. An agriculture minister, for instance, will be most concerned about the services and goods she can provide to farmers and about the taxes that those farmers must pay. We then go on to discuss institutional mechanisms to remedy the resulting spending and deficit bias.

9.2.1   The Model

To make our point, we present a two-period model of budgeting in a cabinet government. Consider a government consisting of $i = 1, \ldots, n$ departments each headed by a spending minister. Government expenditures consist of transfers d_i to groups i in society. The government receives political support from these groups in return for the transfers. All transfers are paid out of a general revenue fund.

Revenues consist of taxes levied on all groups of society, and borrowing. Obviously, in a two-period model, all first-period borrowing must be repaid with interest in the second period. We assume that the government can borrow or lend at a fixed real interest rate, r. To capture the idea that the government borrows against future tax revenues, we assume that the government receives a predetermined (by past tax legislation) amount of tax revenues τ_1 in the first period. In the second period, the government receives an amount τ_2 of nontax revenue. In addition, it sets taxes endogenously to meet the intertemporal budget constraint. The tax system creates an economic loss, or excess burden of taxation, which depends on the amount of total taxation. Thus, budgeting involves a trade-off between the benefit from paying out more transfers in the first period and the cost of taxation in the second period.

The cabinet's collective utility function in period t is[4]

$$(1) \qquad U = \frac{1}{2}\sum_{t=1}^{2} \delta^{t-1}\left(\prod_{i=1}^{n} d_{i,t}^{\alpha_i}\right)^2 - \delta m\Gamma_2,$$

$$0 < \alpha_i < 1, \quad 0 < \delta \le \frac{1}{1+r} < 1.$$

In equation (1), the utility weights, α_i, indicate the share of transfers to group i the government wishes to pay out of a given budget. Later, we will assume that the differences among political parties can be expressed in terms of different α's: different parties favor different groups in society. We assume that the government's discount rate δ equals $1/(1 + r)$. Furthermore, m is the share of the excess burden from taxation falling on the government's constituency, and the excess burden of taxation is

$$(2) \qquad \Gamma_t = \eta T_t + \frac{\theta}{2}T_t^2.$$

Thus, the excess burden of taxation is positive, and the marginal cost of taxation increases with the level of taxation. For simplicity, we assume from now on that $i = 2$, so that $\alpha_2 = 1 - \alpha_1 = 1 - \alpha$, and that $\eta = 0$. The government's budget constraint over the two periods is

$$(3) \qquad \sum_{i=1}^{n}\left(d_{i,1} + \frac{1}{1+r}d_{i,2}\right) = \tau_1 + \frac{1}{1+r}(T_2 + \tau_2).$$

As a reference point, consider first the budgeting decisions made by a single actor maximizing equation (1) subject to equations (2) and (3). For our purposes, we need to consider only the first period level of spending, B_1, and deficit $B_1 - \tau_1$. The optimal decisions from the point of view of the cabinet as a group are

$$(4) \qquad B_1^c - \tau_1 = \frac{\theta m(\tau_2 - \tau_1) + \gamma\tau_1}{\theta m(1 + R) - \gamma}, \quad \gamma = \alpha^\alpha(1 - \alpha)^{1-\alpha}, \quad R = 1 + r.$$

---

4. In equation (1), we assume that the utility gained from transfers takes a Cobb-Douglas form, which implies that each group must get at least some positive transfer, that the marginal utility of transfers to a group is positive but declining, and that the government will want to divide any budget with constant shares α_i among the transfer recipients.

A sufficient condition for the government to borrow in the first period is that its revenue from sources not burdening its constituency is larger in the second period than in the first period, $\tau_2 > \tau_1$, and that the marginal cost parameter θ is sufficiently large, which we assume from now on. Two further parameters determine the size of the deficit in the first period, m, the weight of the cost of taxation in the budget, and γ. The latter implicitly describes the sharing rule of a given budget among the departments; the more uneven the government's preferences are, the larger will be its spending and deficit.

Consider next the budgeting decision of the spending ministers. A spending minister is responsible for the expenditures of her department, but in bidding for funds she takes into account only that part of the excess burden of taxation that falls on her constituency. This is reflected in the utility function

$$(5) \qquad U_i = \frac{1}{2} \sum_{t=1}^{2} \delta^{t-1} \left(\prod_{i=1}^{n} d_{i,t}^{\alpha_i} \right)^2 - \delta m_i \Gamma_2, \quad m_i = \frac{m}{n}.$$

In a completely decentralized budget process, each spending minister bids for and obtains the funds maximizing her utility given the bids of the other spending ministers. The resulting first-period deficit is

$$(6) \qquad B_1^d - \tau_1 = \frac{\theta m_i(\tau_2 - \tau_1) + \gamma \tau_1}{\theta m_i(1 + R) - \gamma} > B_1^c - \tau_1.$$

This illustrates the common-pool problem of budgeting. Individual spending ministers disregard the externality resulting from the common revenue fund and, hence, spend and borrow more than a single planner would. A large literature has developed examining the conditions under which the players will choose to cooperate with each other in such situations (Olson 1965; Hardin 1982; Ostrom 1990; Ostrom, Gardner, and Walker 1994). All of these solutions involve the use of selective punishments or incentives and the monitoring of the actors. In the next two sections we discuss institutional mechanisms to achieve a cooperative solution and reach budget decisions that are closer to the one that is collectively optimal for the government. The first approach involves delegation: one member of the government is vested with special strategic powers that allow him to achieve a cooperative solution. The second approach involves commitment to fiscal targets: playing a cooperative bargaining game at the outset of the budgeting process to agree on the main budgetary parameters allows one to reach the same goal.

9.2.2 Delegation: A Strong Finance Minister

With delegation, governments lend authority to a "fiscal entrepreneur," whose function is to assure that all actors cooperate. To be effective, this entrepreneur must have the ability to monitor the others, possess selective incentives that he can use to punish defectors and reward those who cooperate, and have some motivation to bear the costs of monitoring himself (Olson 1965; Frohlich and Oppenheimer 1978; Cox and McCubbins 1993). Among the relevant cabinet members, the finance minister often plays the role of this entrepreneur. His interests generally coincide with the general interests.[5] He has the responsibility to coordinate the formation of the budget, and, fair or not, the size of the budget deficit is often the principal indicator that others use to judge his effectiveness. He often also has only a trivial budget himself compared with other ministers, and he cannot "defect" in the prisoner's dilemma game being played in the cabinet. Finally, the finance minister's staff gives him the means to monitor the actions of the other ministries, and, since his prestige and hence his personal benefits depend on the effectiveness of his ministry, he has a private incentive to guarantee that the monitoring occurs. The only question is whether the finance minister has the power to offer selective incentives and/or punishments to the spending ministers.

To model delegation, assume that the finance minister serves as an agenda setter in the cabinet meeting where budget decisions are being made. Thus, the finance minister has the right to make the first proposal for the budget, and he has the power to constrain any amendments that the spending ministers might submit to his proposal. The finance minister's power as an agenda setter can be measured in terms of the utility his proposal must leave to the spending ministers in order not to be overruled. The stronger he is, the closer the outcome of these negotiations must be to his ideal budget. Formally, the finance minister will submit proposals for transfers d_i that maximize equation (1) under the constraint that each spending minister obtain sufficient utility. This can be modeled by assuming that the finance minister chooses d_i maximizing the weighted utility function

$$(7) \qquad U_{mf} = \beta U + (1 - \beta)U_i,$$

where β, $0 \le \beta \le 1$, is a measure of his bargaining power. The resulting first-period deficit is

$$(8) \qquad B_1^{mf} - \tau_1 = \frac{\theta m_{mf}(\tau_2 - \tau_1) + \gamma \tau_1}{\theta m_{mf}(1 + R) - \gamma}$$

$$< B_1^d - \tau_1, \quad m_{mf} = \beta m + (1 - \beta)m_i.$$

The larger the finance minister's agenda-setting power, the closer the deficit comes to the collectively optimal outcome, for at $\beta = 1$ the collectively optimal solution is achieved.

Spending ministers have reason to support a strong finance minister, as they obtain greater utility from the budget decision in equation (8) than from equation (6) provided that all members of the government adhere to that decision.

5. In order to keep actors straight, the finance minister will be referred to as "him," while the other ministers will be referred to as "her."

However, given that $n - 1$ spending ministers adhere to equation (8), it is optimal for spending minister n to defect from this decision and increase her spending if she can. Thus, in addition to agenda-setting powers, the finance minister needs enforcement powers to assure that equation (8) is implemented. Control devices like the requirement to obtain authorization for disbursing public funds during the fiscal year are examples of such enforcement powers.

9.2.3   Commitment to Fiscal Targets

With commitment, the government commits itself to a set of fiscal targets collectively negotiated at the start of the budgeting process. The emphasis here is on the multilateral nature of the negotiations, which implicitly forces all participants to consider the full tax burden created by additional spending. Using a Nash-bargaining solution, and assuming that all cabinet members have the same bargaining power, the first-period deficit becomes

$$(9) \qquad B_1^n - \tau_1 = \frac{\theta m (\tau_2 - \tau_1) + \gamma \tau_1}{\theta m (1 + R) - \gamma} = B_1^c - \tau_1.$$

Once again, the agreement reached in these negotiations must be enforced. A necessary condition for enforcement is the existence of a monitoring technology to detect potential defectors from the agreement. The commitment approach, therefore, requires that one member of the government, usually the finance minister, possesses sufficient screening power to control the spending ministers during the implementation of the budget.

9.2.4   Comparison of a Strong Finance Minister and Negotiated Targets

This discussion above suggests the availability of two institutional approaches, a delegation and commitment to negotiated budget targets, to overcome the deficit bias in public budgeting. The natural question then is, what determines the choice of governments between these two mechanisms? Here, we argue that the choice depends on the type of government. Specifically, we distinguish between single-party and multiparty governments. Delegation is the proper approach for single-party governments, but difficult for coalition governments. Commitment is the proper approach for coalition governments but more difficult to achieve for single-party governments.

Members of the same political party are likely hold similar political views. In terms of our model, members of the same party have the same utility weights α_i applying to the different groups of transfer recipients. The players therefore share the same views regarding the distribution of funds over the various departments, and conflicts of interest arise only from the common-pool problem.[6]

---

6. Laver and Shepsle (1994, 9–10), for instance, in summarizing the findings of the case studies in their edited volume, note that the distribution of portfolios among members of the same political party has little effect on the policies that the government adopts; much more important is the distribution of portfolios among different parties.

In a coalition government, in contrast, cabinet members are likely to have different views regarding the distribution of transfers over the groups of recipients. Agreement on a budget, therefore, involves a compromise between the coalition partners regarding the distribution of funds for a given budget size.

Delegating agenda-setting powers to the finance minister now becomes more difficult, as the latter necessarily is a member of one of the coalition parties himself. Delegation then creates a principal agent problem. The members of the other parties in the coalition must fear that the finance minister will abuse his strategic powers to shift the distribution of transfers in the budget toward his own preferred distribution, at the cost of the recipients favored more strongly by themselves. These members will, therefore, be reluctant to vest the finance minister with strong agenda-setting powers. But, as shown above, with limited agenda-setting powers the finance minister becomes unable to achieve the collectively optimal decision. The same principal agent problem does not arise in the case of commitment to fiscal targets, since the targets are negotiated by all cabinet members. Thus, coalition governments are more likely to opt for the commitment approach.

The second important distinction between the delegation and the commitment approach is in the scope and strength of the punishments and rewards a finance minister can use to assure the adoption of his proposal. During the budget negotiations, the finance minister's power must be backed up by the prime minister and, therefore, depends heavily on the prime minister's relative power in cabinet. The prime minister in one-party governments especially is the strongest member of the cabinet. The prime minister is the leader of the governing party, and this position reinforces her power within the cabinet. The prime minister also can often select cabinet members and can reshuffle her government.[7] Even in the United Kingdom, where the norm of "first among equals" is historically strong, a prime minister dictates the shape of her cabinet. If a given spending minister consistently presents unsatisfactory budgets, the prime minister can then replace her with someone who will develop more sympathetic policies. Finally, a prime minister can call a vote of confidence on a given issue which puts the very existence of the government at issue if a given minister does not support her position (Huber 1996). If the prime minister prefers that the party's ideal budget be reached, which should usually be the case, she will have identical preferences on the budget as the finance minister. She can then delegate her power to the finance minister, and the finance minister will represent a faithful "agent" of the prime minister.[8]

---

7. The prime minister does not have unlimited freedom, since the formation of a cabinet under a one-party government involves intraparty negotiations and agreements. Yet the prime minister does generally have some flexibility in deciding which faction will acquire which portfolio, as well as who will represent that faction in cabinet.

8. Lupia and McCubbins (1994) indicate that an agent will choose the principal's optimal policy if two conditions are met: the principal understands the implications of maintaining the current policy or accepting the agent's proposal, and the policy that is most favorable for the principal is

In coalition governments, the finance minister would lack the ability to insist on his proposal, because the prime minister cannot give him as much meaningful support as in the one-party case. The distribution of portfolios is, as far as the sitting prime minister is concerned, exogenously given, since agreement over forming the coalition determines which parties get which ministries. The prime minister cannot easily dismiss or otherwise discipline intransigent spending ministers from a different party, since that would be regarded as an intrusion into the internal party affairs of his coalition partners.

The third important dimension regards the scope of punishments for defecting from the agreed budget. In the one-party case, the ultimate punishment is dismissal from office. Such punishment is heavy for the individual minister who overspends, but generally light for the government as a whole. It is therefore relatively easy for the prime minister to enforce, and ministers who overspend can expect to be dismissed for the good of their political party. In the case of coalition governments, a defecting minister cannot be dismissed easily by the prime minister for the reasons mentioned above. The most important punishment mechanism here is the threat that the coalition breaks up if a spending minister reneges on the budget agreement. Overspending by an individual minister from one party in the coalition implies a redistribution of public spending away from the transfer recipients most favored by, and therefore implies a cost of political support for, the other parties in the coalition. This makes the threat of breaking up the coalition credible from the other parties' point of view. This suggestion is supported by the observation that fiscal targets are often part of the formal coalition agreement. Thus, punishment leads to the death of the government rather than the dismissal of a single individual. There are two important factors that affect the strength of this threat: the existence of alternative coalition partners, and, if a new coalition cannot be formed and new elections are necessary, the anticipation of electoral results.

If another partner exists with whom the aggrieved party can form a coalition, the threat to leave the coalition is clearly more credible. The number of parties in parliament is one obvious limit to the number of alternative coalition partners. Even among the parties that do exist, some may be undesirable for policy reasons or may not be considered *koalitionsfähig,* such as the Italian Communist Party. Other parties may simply be unexcludable from the coalition formation process. A party is "strong" according to Laver and Shepsle (1996) if it can veto every potential cabinet, and coalition partners may not be able to punish a party that occupies such a dominant position. Yet, to the extent that there are several possible coalitions, reputations will be important. Parties that

---

the one that the agent proposes. Especially in cases where spending cuts are needed, the prime minister can clearly see the implications of continuing spending at current levels or accepting the finance minister's negotiated settlement, and both principal and agent alike have the same interest to reduce the budget deficit. With both conditions met, the finance minister makes the same proposal the prime minister would have had she had better information.

are known not to keep coalition agreements will have problems finding partners, and as long as parties anticipate that none of them has a reasonable chance of winning an absolute majority of seats in the future, they will value the possibility of cooperation in the future. The threat of new elections may also scare a defecting party into meeting its targets, if this party must fear a defeat if elections are called.

For a single-party government, in contrast, the enforcement mechanism of the commitment approach is rather weak. To see this, consider a single-party government with weak prime and finance ministers. Assume that this government negotiated an agreement on a set of fiscal targets at the outset of the budget process and that an individual spending minister reneges on the agreement during the implementation phase. In this case, the other cabinet members cannot credibly threaten the defector with a dissolution of the government, since they would punish themselves by calling for elections. Absent a credible threat, the entire cabinet would just walk away from the initial agreement.

To summarize, we predict that coalition governments will typically choose commitment to fiscal targets and single-party governments will typically choose delegation of powers to a strong finance minister as a device to limit the deficit bias.

9.3 The Role of Electoral Systems

Electoral institutions strongly influence the likelihood of one party winning a majority of legislative seats and consequently having the ability to form a one-party majority government. One important factor is the number of parties; if there are few parties, there is a higher chance that one party can win an absolute majority, and an absolute majority is a virtual certainty in two-party systems. Several studies indicate that the number of effective parties in a given system is strongly and positively correlated with the number of representatives elected from each electoral district, known as district magnitude (Duverger 1954; Taagepera and Shugart 1989, 1993). Electoral systems with low district magnitudes distribute seats less proportionately than those with large district magnitudes, and lower proportionality usually favors larger parties. In Spain, for example, where the average district magnitude is just 6.73, the Socialist Party was able to win 44.3 percent of the popular vote in the 1986 national elections but 52.6 percent of the seats in the Congress of Deputies.[9] At the other extreme, the Netherlands has only one electoral district composed of 150 seats for the entire country, and a party that wins less than 1 percent of the national vote can gain seats in parliament. Other factors that affect proportionality include legal barriers that require a party to gain a certain percentage of

---

9. Mackie and Rose 1991, 397, 399. The average district magnitude figures are reported in Lijphart 1994, 22.

the national vote to win legislative seats, the method used to apportion seats, and whether or not a second allocation of seats is used to reduce disparities at the district level.[10]

Plurality systems, which elect only one representative per district, encourage a two-party system, and they are consequently most likely to have one-party majority governments. Proportional representation (PR) systems have more variation in their district magnitudes, though the magnitudes are always larger than those found in plurality systems. They tend to have a larger number of "effective" parties in parliament and are characterized by multiparty majority or either one-party or multiparty minority governments.[11] Empirical evidence has consistently supported this relationship—Arend Lijphart, for instance, found that from 1945 through 1980 plurality systems had on average 2.1 effective parties while PR systems had 3.8 effective parties (1984, 161).[12] Behind these figures is a result that should be emphasized and that will appear again shortly—the stronger the relationship between the proportion of seats won and the proportion of votes, the higher the number of effective parties. Thus, Spain's PR system, which sharply discriminates against small parties with its low district magnitude, should have fewer effective parties than the Netherlands, which has a high district magnitude.

Based on the plurality/PR distinction, what is the likelihood of one-party majority governments within the European Union? One unfortunate fact for comparison's sake is that only 2 of the 15 member states, Great Britain and France, have pluralist electoral systems. Yet, the variation in district magnitudes in PR systems does lead to some variation in the number of parliamentary parties as well.

Table 9.1 compares the political systems of the European Union countries. A few points require clarification. First, PR systems do not translate the percentage of votes directly into the percentage of seats, and smaller parties often cannot gain entry into the legislature. We noted previously that district magnitude affects the number of political parties possible, and a logical comparison would be between this figure and the likelihood of one-party government. Yet such a comparison would be somewhat misleading—as the second column in table 9.1 indicates, states sometimes have different district magnitudes at different levels of the allocation process. In addition, other factors including legal thresholds (such as Germany's requirement that a party win either 5 percent of the nationwide vote or three seats by plurality vote) and rules for the allocation of seats (use of D'Hondt, etc.) can also favor larger parties over smaller ones.

10. A succinct summary is found in Gallagher, Laver, and Mair 1992, 153–59.
11. A reasonable measure for the number of parties considers the strength of parties as well as their absolute number. The measure that will be used here is for the effective number of parties in parliament and is taken from Mark Laakso and Rein Taagepera, as quoted by Lijphart (1984, 68). It is calculated as $N = 1/\sum s_i^2$, where N equals the effective number of parties and s_i equals the proportion of seats party i possess in the legislature.
12. Other empirical studies that confirm this link include Lijphart 1994 and Taagepera and Shugart 1989 and 1993.

Table 9.1 Comparison of Electoral Systems within the European Union

State	System	District Magnitude	ENPP	Effective Threshold	Years in Lijphart Study	% One-Party Majority Government, 1945–90
Austria	2-tier PR, remainder transfers	20/91	2.42	2.6	1971–90	44
Belgium	PR	23	4.63	4.8	1946–87	17
Denmark	2-tier PR, adjustment seats	7/175	4.92	2	1964–88	0
Finland	PR	13	5.03	5.4	1945–87	0
France[a]	Plurality	1	3.5	35	1958–81	6
Germany (West)	2-tier PR, adjustment seats	1/497	2.95	5	1957–83	0
Greece	Reinforced PR	6	2.08	16.4	1974–85	95
Ireland	STV	4	2.79	17.2	1948–89	36
Italy	2-tier PR, remainder transfers	19/625	3.62	2	1958–87	0
Luxembourg	PR	14	3.3	5.1	1945–89	0
Netherlands	PR	150	4.59	0.67	1956–89	0
Portugal	PR	12	3.05	5.7	1975–87	33
Spain	PR	6	2.72	10.2	1977–89	58
Sweden	2-tier PR	11/350	3.4	4	1970–88	10
United Kingdom	Plurality	1	2.1	35	1945–87	99

Sources: All figures but those on one-party majorities come from Lijphart 1994, 17, 22, 31, 33–35, 44, 160–62; the one-party majority figures are based on Woldendorp, Keman, and Budge 1993. Greece, Portugal, and Spain were not democracies during the entire period, and the years covered are, respectively, 1974–90, 1975–90, and 1977–90. This data is published in various issues of the *European Journal of Political Research* and is based on the date of an election instead of the date of investiture used for the other countries. The Austrian, Irish, and Portugese data were not completely accurate in Woldendorp, Keman, and Budge 1993. The authors supplemented the Austrian and Portugese data themselves, while Jesse 1996, chapter 2, was used for Ireland, which includes the period 1951–90 here.

Note: PR corresponds to "proportional representation," *STV* to "single transferable vote," and *ENPP* to "effective number of parliamentary parties." District magnitude figures are rounded to the nearest whole number.

[a]The figures for France are just for its Fifth Republic, or 1958–90, and include the period 1986–88, when the country used a proportional representation system.

Arend Lijphart solves our problem of how to aggregate these institutional effects with his translation of such factors into an "effective threshold," which is the percentage of the national vote a party expects it must receive to gain any legislative seats.

Second, while France had a plurality system in all parliamentary elections but those held in 1986, its use of two rounds of voting increases the effective number of parties in parliament. Unless a given candidate wins an absolute majority in the first round, a second round of voting is held. This process encourages parties that ran candidates in the first round to form electoral coalitions for the second round. The predicted emergence of two strong blocks facing each other under plurality does still occur, however, since the UDF (Union pour la Démocratie Française) allies almost exclusively with the RPR (Rassemblement pour la République), while the Socialist Party works equally as often with the French Communist Party. France will therefore be treated as a one-party government in most cases later in this paper.

Table 9.1 confirms the general link among electoral institutions, the number of parties, and the likelihood of a one-party majority government for the European Union countries. The correlation between the effective threshold and the number of parties has the correct sign at $-.46$, and it jumps to $-.60$ if France is excluded from the sample. The most important figure is the correlation that links the occurrence of one-party majority governments with higher effective thresholds, and the correlation of .55 (.82 if France is excluded) indicates that this relationship is relatively strong. Since states that have low district magnitudes also have higher effective thresholds, this result indicates that plurality elections or PR systems with low district magnitudes are likely to have one-party majority governments. In contrast, PR systems with high district magnitudes usually have either multiparty majority governments or minority governments.

9.4   Comparison of Institutional Solutions

This section examines the choice of budgetary institutional tools within all European Union states. The statistical comparison, while unfortunately based on only 15 cases, nonetheless indicates a strong relationship between one-party governments and delegation solutions on the one hand and multiparty or minority governments and targets on the other. Table 9.2 summarizes the predicted institutions based on the prevalence of one-party majority government and the actual institutions that the countries used from 1981 to 1994, which are the years for which we have data available for all the current European Union member states. We expect that delegation to a strong finance minister develops in states where one-party majority governments are the norm. We therefore code the two states that had one-party government over 90 percent of the time, Greece and the United Kingdom, along with France as potential "delegation" states. The others are presumed to be able to use binding budgetary targets.

Table 9.2   Predicted and Actual Institutional Solutions, 1981–94

State	Predicted Institution	Actual Institution
Austria	Targets	Targets (1985–92)
Denmark	Targets	Targets (1982–94)
Finland	Targets	Targets
Ireland	Targets	Targets (1987–94)
Luxembourg	Targets	Targets
Netherlands	Targets	Targets
France	Delegation	Delegation
Germany	Targets	Delegation
United Kingdom	Delegation	Delegation
Belgium	Targets	No such constraint
Greece	Delegation	No such constraint
Italy	Targets	No such constraint
Portugal	Targets	No such constraint
Spain	Targets	No such constraint
Sweden	Targets	No such constraint

Source: Data for the incidence of targets and delegation are from von Hagen and Harden 1996.
Note: A state that almost always had one-party governments ($p > .9$) was coded with "delegation" as its predicted institution.

Of the three states expected to use delegation, France and the United Kingdom did, while Greece did not. However, Greece did not adopt an institutional solution to the problem of deficit bias at all. The United Kingdom is the only state in the sample that uses a pure plurality system in its parliamentary elections, and according to the theoretical discussion it is a good candidate for delegation. Indeed, the structure of the budget process at the governmental level follows this form. The prime minister is exceptionally strong and can reshuffle the cabinet as well as appoint ministers almost at will. The chancellor of the exchequer is generally regarded as second in power only to the prime minister, and he is given the power to negotiate one-on-one with spending ministers about their budget allocations. If there is a dispute between the finance minister and a given spending minister, it goes to a committee composed of senior ministers without portfolio for consideration and not to the full cabinet for resolution. These ministers do not have budgets of their own, and a logrolling situation in favor of the spending minister is not possible. Since the senior ministers are appointed to consider the general interests of the cabinet as well, they usually support the finance minister (von Hagen and Harden 1996).

Similarly, in France the prime minister and the finance minister together set budget targets for every spending ministry in the "framework letter" issued at the outset of the budgeting process. The finance minister then negotiates bilaterally with the spending ministers on adjustments to the size of their budgets, and the prime minister is the final arbiter of any disputes.

A similarly strong pattern emerges for the states where multiparty coalitions are common. Seven of the remaining twelve states predicted to use a commitment approach did so, while the remaining five opted for neither of the solutions. Five of the six states that did not use one of these institutions were predicted to choose targets. The sample size is too small to make any statistical comparison conclusive, but this high failure rate among states where one-party governments are not the norm is consistent with the argument presented here. Both the monitoring and punishment functions are presumably harder to execute in multiparty governments than in one-party governments.

The Netherlands has the most representative system in the European Union, and as a consequence has never had a one-party majority government during the postwar period. In contrast to her counterpart in the United Kingdom, the prime minister has little power. Negotiations among the parties during the formation of the coalition determine most items of importance, including the distribution of portfolios, and the prime minister consequently lacks the ability to remove defiant ministers. The prime minister also does not have the power to settle any disputes, and she votes in cabinet meetings only in cases of a tie. Instead of using a strong finance minister, the coalition negotiations inscribe into the coalition agreement explicit budgetary targets that constitute the fiscal contract among the parties. As expected, there are several institutional devices that promote the ability of parties to monitor each other's behavior. The legislature in particular serves an important oversight role. Committee jurisdictions are matched with specific ministries, and the committee chair is required to come from a different party than the one that provides the minister (Andeweg and Irwin 1993, 141). Parties also have the means to punish defectors. The same parties are likely to be potential coalition partners again, and, since there is little likelihood that any of them could win an absolute majority, the parties anticipate the need for a multiparty coalition government in the future. There is also competition among them for positions in the government: with the exception of a few extremist parties that receive almost no parliamentary seats, all of the parties are potential coalition partners, and a given party that breaks a coalition agreement can be excluded from future governments. It is therefore in a party's best interest to assure that it cultivates a reputation as a party that keeps its coalition agreements.

Germany is the difficult case in this sample. Germany's electoral system is based on a two-ballot structure that contains elements of both plurality and proportional representation, making a clear prediction difficult to begin with. During the postwar period a major party (the CDU/CSU or the SPD) always formed a coalition with a smaller partner (either the FDP or the DP) except during the grand coalition between the two large parties from 1966 to 1969. Although it has never had a one-party majority government, Germany also adopts a delegation approach. Thus, at a first glance, out of 15 cases only Germany went against our expectations. However, in previous elections coalition partners usually pledged a continuation of the coalition, if together they received enough votes, and the Green Party made it clear that it would enter a coalition only with the SPD. Thus, the number of "effective" parties was only two. To the extent that the coalition partners see their electoral fortunes as being one and the same, spending ministers regardless of party persuasion may prefer a strong finance minister who can deliver lower deficits. Note also that the German finance minister's role is restricted to one of a veto-player rather than an agenda setter, which implies that his ability to bias spending in favor of his party's preferences is much reduced (see von Hagen and Harden 1996).

The conduct of the coalition partners during the grand coalition supports out view. When the SPD and the CDU/CSU formed the coalition, they both anticipated that it would last no longer than through the national elections in 1969, and during the elections they campaigned vigorously against each other. The chancellor, Kurt Georg Kiesinger, was weak relative to other postwar chancellors, and the coalition parties negotiated most major decisions in the smaller Kressbonner Kreis composed of senior cabinet members from both sides. The finance minister during the time period, the Christian Social Union leader Franz-Josef Strauss, consequently did not have the freedom of action his predecessors had nor which his successors would have, and the coalition forced him to coordinate budget policy with the Social Democratic economics minister, Karl Schiller. Under such circumstances only budget targets were politically practical as a device to combat budget deficits, and indeed that is exactly what the coalition partners used. Schiller and Strauss together formulated the so-called Mifrifi *(Mittelfristige Finanzplanung),* which, among other things, detailed explicit spending targets for the coalition (Hildebrand 1984, 290). After the end of the grand coalition, Mifrifi is still practiced as required by law, but it has no practical importance.

9.5   Budgetary Institutions and Deficit and Debt Levels

The use of these institutions also contributed to sounder fiscal policies, although debt level comparisons should be treated with some caution. Von Hagen and Harden (1996) indicate that if states lack an institutional solution to the common-pool problem for any one of four characteristics of the budget process (the governmental, legislative, and implementation stages, as well as the informativeness of the budget draft), then budget deficits will be comparatively high. This paper examines the process for just one of the characteristics, the governmental stage, and hence the solutions discussed here will not by themselves always lead to lower deficits.

Nonetheless, even with these caveats figure 9.1 indicates a striking difference between the states that used either targets or strategic dominance and those that chose neither of the institutions. The graph displays yearly deficit data for the period 1990–94, which are the five most recent years for which we have data. The states with the institutions had a much lower average yearly budget deficit of −2.7, whose difference was statistically significant at the 1

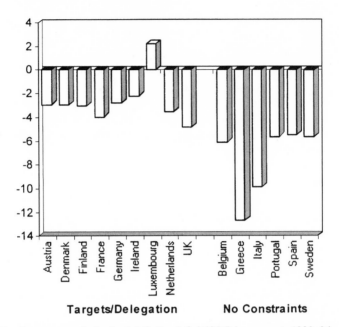

Targets/Delegation   No Constraints

Fig. 9.1   Average yearly budget deficits, deficit/GDP in percent, 1990–94
Source: OECD Economic Outlook (1995) and *OECD Economic Surveys, 1994–95: Belgium/ Luxembourg.*

percent level from the much higher average budget deficit of −7.6 for the states without the institutions. All of the "no institutional constraint" states had an average yearly deficit that was larger than the highest average yearly deficit among the states with one of the institutions, the United Kingdom.

Similar figures also exist for the net total debt burden that the states carried. Once again one must be careful with interpreting the figures, since the debt levels indicate cumulative fiscal policy decisions that extend beyond the period 1990–94. Yet one may also anticipate that, everything else being equal, over time the states with either targets or strategic dominance will be able to adjust more readily to fiscal shocks than states that lack such institutions, and that the total debt figures will reflect this tendency. Indeed, the average size of net debt burden in states without the institutions is almost twice as high at 87.0 percent of GDP in comparison to 53.5 percent of states with one of the two budget mechanisms, with the difference in means significant at the 6 percent level.

Of course, these comparisons are based on only five years, and they do not take into account other potentially important variables, such as changes in the economic health of a country or political variables such as possible partisanship effects or governmental instability. A more general claim of this paper is that the plurality/PR dichotomy is important because it affects the form of budgetary institutions that are politically feasible, but that it is the presence or absence of these institutions, rather than the plurality/PR distinction itself, that

Table 9.3   Comparison of Alternative Explanations for the Growth or Decline
                   of the Gross Debt Burden, 1981–94 (dependent variable: change in
                   the gross debt level as a proportion of GDP according to
                   Maastricht definitions)

Variable	Coefficient	Standard Error	*t*-ratio	Probability
Constant	3.6	0.81	4.45	0.0001
Change in debt $t-1$	0.30	0.05	5.62	0.0001
Change in GDP, real values	−0.90	0.16	−5.46	0.0001
Change in unemployment rate	0.76	0.28	2.71	0.01
Change in debt-servicing costs	−0.04	0.1	−0.38	0.70
Change in government	1.57	0.44	3.55	0.0005
2–3 party majority government	0.81	0.73	1.12	0.26
4–5 party majority government	0.40	0.88	0.46	0.65
Minority government	−0.52	0.86	−0.61	0.55
Left	−0.92	0.65	−1.43	0.15
Strong finance minister	−1.95	0.73	−2.67	0.01
Targets	−1.45	0.63	−2.30	0.02
R^2		53.9 percent		
R^2 (adjusted)		51.4 percent		

Sources: Data from European Commission 1995; de Haan and Sturm 1994; *European Journal of Political Research* (various years); Woldendorp, Keman, and Budge 1993; and von Hagen and Harden 1996.

Note: Diagnostics: A lagged dependent variable was added to eliminate significant autocorrelation. The Lagrange multiplier statistic did not reject the null hypothesis of homoskedasticity. A comparison of the group-effects model with the standard OLS regression also indicated the lack of country-specific effects.

affects the budget balance. How does the model presented here compare to other explanations?

Table 9.3 presents preliminary ordinary least square results from a panel data set for the 15 current members of the European Union from 1981 to 1994. Our list of variables generally follows those provided in Roubini and Sachs 1989 as well as in de Haan and Sturm 1994, 1997, with the important distinction that we add dummy variables for the presence or absence of a strong finance minister or budgetary targets.[13] There are two sets of variables. The first set of variables measure fluctuations in a given country's economy, and they are expected to have some impact on budget deficits regardless of the presence or absence of government policies meant to reduce public debt levels. Changes in gross domestic product should improve the budget situation, while increases in the unemployment rate are likely to add to the size of the deficit due to

---

13. There are also some differences in the countries and years covered in the respective studies. De Haan and Sturm base their regressions on the EC 12 from 1981 to 1989, while Roubini and Sachs consider 14 OECD countries from 1960 to 1985.

automatic payments of unemployment compensation. In addition, changes in real interest rates affect the size of interest payments on the debt, and, if the real interest rate is higher than the real growth rate, interest payments will generally cause an increase in the total debt level. We therefore include a variable for the net change in debt-servicing costs.[14] A lag for our dependent variable, which is the change in the debt level, is also included to reduce autocorrelation in the model.

The second set of variables covers some of the most frequently cited political explanations. Consistent with Grilli, Masciandaro, and Tabellini (1991), a change in government, which is defined as either one or more changes in coalition partners or the occurrence of an election, is expected to increase the size of government debt. Roubini and Sachs (1989) also argue that multiparty majority and all minority governments face a prisoner's dilemma of whose constituency should bear the brunt of budget cuts, with the dilemma becoming worse as the number of parties in the coalition increases. Following Edin and Ohlsson (1991), we include dummy variables for the number of parties in a majority coalition government (either two to three parties or four to five parties) and for the presence of minority governments, with a one-party government equal to the case where the two-to-three-party, four-to-five-party, and minority government dummies all equal zero. One would therefore anticipate that the presence of any of these dummies would positively affect the debt level, with coefficients that increase as one moves from two-to-three-party majority government to minority government.

The partisan hue of the government may also be important. The general expectation is that left-wing governments are more tolerant of larger budget deficits than right-wing governments. Yet previous empirical studies offer little guidance—Roubini and Sachs (1989) indicate that left-wing parties are associated with larger deficits, Alesina and Perotti (1995) pin the blame on center parties, while Borrelli and Royed (1995) consider right-wing governments the least able to control deficits. To keep this study comparable with Roubini and Sachs 1989 and de Haan and Sturm 1994, 1997, we code this variable as the percentage of cabinet seats held by left-wing parties in a given year. Finally, we include a dummy variable for the presence or absence of a strong finance minister or of targets.

The results of the regression are encouraging. The variables for the two budgetary institutions are both significant and have the correct sign. The more negative coefficient for a strong finance minister than for the budgetary targets also confirms the intuition that a strong finance minister is more effective in keeping the deficit lower than targets, other things being equal.[15] Section 9.2

---

14. We code this variable as (Nominal Long Term Interest Rate − Inflation Rate − Real GDP Growth Rate)*Debt Level ($t - 1$). We also coded it as d (Nominal Long Term Interest Rate − Inflation Rate − Real GDP Growth Rate)*Debt Level ($t - 1$), with no change in results.

15. We also did one minor recoding of the "targets" variable and did another regression run. In 1992–93 Belgium and Portugal negotiated convergence programs with the European Commission that they then put into place. These programs resemble commitment to targets. We therefore coded

argued that a strong finance minister reduces both the common-pool resource problem and the problem of budget-maximizing cabinet members, while targets combat just the former problem. These results fit that argument. All of the economic variables but the change in debt-servicing costs are also significant and have the anticipated sign.[16] This is to be expected—if fluctuations in the economy did not have some sort of impact on the budget, one would have reason to doubt the empirical results.

With the exception of changes to the government, other strictly political variables do not fare so well. The dummy variables for the contention that the form of government impacts the size of the budget are all insignificant, and the dummy for minority governments even has the wrong sign. The measurement for partisanship is also not significant, although its sign indicates that left-wing parties are more likely to reduce the size of the debt burden. Only a change in government has a significant impact on the growth of debt.

One interesting possibility is that there is an interactive effect among the budgetary institutions and a change in government. Countries with the proper institutions may be able to isolate their fiscal health from political instability. Table 9.4 presents results that include interactive terms for a change in government with a strong finance minister and with negotiated targets. The significance of the two institutions on their own disappears, although they continue to have an impact in the expected direction. More importantly, however, the interactive terms are both negative and significant. The regression indicates that, in years where there was a change in government, the aggregate debt burden grew by almost three percentage points of GDP. If those states also had one of the budgetary institutions, however, that effect was eliminated. Thus, the negative consequences of political instability appear to be neutralized if a country puts in place either delegation or commitment to negotiated budget targets.

9.6 Conclusions

The Maastricht Treaty's debt and deficit guidelines for states that want to join a future common currency may help to create a common interest in lower deficits in states where such a consensus has so far been lacking. Our statistical evidence indicates that the use of either delegation to a strong finance minister

---

Belgium and Portugal as having targets in 1993 and 1994. The results make the case for our institutional variables even stronger. The coefficients for both the Strong Finance Minister and Targets variables increased in size to -2.42 and -1.86 respectively while the standard errors stayed almost the same at .80 and .61. The results for the other variables change only trivially. We thank Jorge Braga de Macedo for bringing this issue to our attention.

16. This is the possibility that there is a simultaneity problem because the GDP term appears in some form on both sides of the equation. We therefore redid the regressions with a new indicator for the change in GDP as follows. We regressed the change in GDP in time t on GDP at $t-1$ as well as on the average change in GDP at time t within Europe. We then used the fitted values as our independent variable to measure the effects of economic growth. The results were virtually identical to those reported here.

Table 9.4   Consideration of the Interaction of the Change in Government with
                   Either a Strong Finance Minister or Budgetary Targets

Variable	Coefficient	Standard Error	t-ratio	Probability
Constant	2.85	0.84	3.39	0.0001
Change in debt $t-1$	0.32	0.05	6.07	0.0001
Change in GDP	-0.88	0.16	-5.40	0.0001
Change in unemployment rate	0.78	0.28	2.81	0.005
Change in debt-servicing costs	-0.02	0.1	-0.18	0.86
Change in government	2.86	0.63	4.51	0.0001
2–3 party majority government	0.71	0.73	0.98	0.33
4–5 party majority government	0.06	0.88	0.07	0.94
Minority government	-0.79	0.84	-0.93	0.35
Left	-0.59	0.65	-0.91	0.37
Strong finance minister	-0.81	0.86	-0.95	0.34
Targets	-0.32	0.77	-0.41	0.68
Change in government*Strong finance minister	-2.61	1.17	-2.22	0.03
Change in government*Targets	-2.34	0.99	-2.37	0.02
R^2	55.7 percent			
R^2 (adjusted)	52.8 percent			

Sources: See table 9.3 for data sources.
Note: The diagnostic results were virtually identical to the regression presented in table 9.3.

or commitment to negotiated budget targets can have a significant impact on the growth of the budget deficit. Such institutions are especially effective in keeping deficits down in countries where there is some political instability.

States that want to reduce their deficits should choose one of these budgetary institutions based on the form of government that they commonly experience, either one-party majority government or multiparty coalition government. One-party governments are most suitable for delegation, while multiparty governments have reason to rely on commitment. The comparison of the various systems and solutions that are now used indicates that, under certain circumstances, the use of a strong finance minister can be expanded to multiparty governments. The key is that all the parties in the government see their electoral fortunes as one, as in France and Germany. This indicates that delegation may soon be a viable solution for Italy. The new electoral system introduced in 1994, which relies on the plurality method for 75 percent of the seats in parliament, has led to two distinct constellations of parties. The presence of a center-left minority government indicates that targets may be the only feasible short-term solution, but if the electoral system continues to evolve and one of the two blocs can expect to win a majority of seats in future elections, a strong finance minister may become a better choice.

In other problem states with multiparty governments, such as Belgium and Portugal, a target-based approach will likely be the most practical route to solving the common-pool problem. Coalition partners have little reason to support a strong finance minister because they doubt that the finance minister will safeguard the collective interests of all. In such states it is important that targets be made credible, and further research is needed to determine how targets can be made credible when the threat of a coalition collapse is not a realistic deterrent.

References

Alesina, Alberto, Ricardo Hausman, Rudolf Hommes, and Ernesto Stein. 1996. Budget institutions and fiscal performance in Latin America. NBER Working Paper no. 5586. Cambridge, Mass.: National Bureau of Economic Research.

Alesina, Alberto, and Roberto Perotti. 1995. Fiscal expansions and adjustments in OECD countries. *Economic Policy* 21:207–48.

Andeweg, Rudy, and Galen Irwin. 1993. *Dutch government and politics.* London: Macmillan.

Borrelli, Stephen A., and Terry J. Royed. 1995. Government "strength" and budget deficits in advanced democracies. *European Journal of Political Research* 28: 225–60.

Cox, Gary W., and Mathew D. McCubbins. 1993. *Legislative leviathan.* Berkeley and Los Angeles: University of California Press.

de Haan, Jakob, and Jan-Egbert Sturm. 1994. Political and institutional determinants of fiscal policy in the European Community. *Public Choice* 80:157–72.

———. 1997. Political and economic determinants of OECD budget deficits and government expenditures: A reinvestigation. *European Journal of Political Economy* 13: 739–50.

Duverger, Maurice. 1954. *Political parties: Their organization and activity in the modern state.* New York: Wiley.

Edin, Per-Anders, and Henry Ohlsson. 1991. Political determinants of budget deficits: Coalition effects versus minority effects. *European Economic Review* 35:1597–1603.

European Commission. 1995. *Statistical annex of European economy.* November.

Frohlich, Norman, and Joe A. Oppenheimer. 1978. *Modern political economy.* Englewood Cliffs, N.J.: Prentice-Hall.

Gallagher, Michael, Michael Laver, and Peter Mair. 1992. *Representative government in Western Europe.* New York: McGraw-Hill.

Grilli, Vittorio, Donato Masciandaro, and Guido Tabellini. 1991. Political and monetary institutions and public financial policies in the industrial democracies. *Economic Policy* 6:341–92.

Hahm, Sung Deuk. 1994. The political economy of deficit spending: A cross comparison of industrialized democracies, 1955–1990. Photocopy.

Hahm, Sung Deuk, Mark S. Kamlet, and David C. Mowery. 1996. The political economy of deficit spending in nine industrialized parliamentary democracies: The role of fiscal institutions. *Comparative Political Studies* 29, no. 1:52–77.

Hardin, Russell. 1982. *Collective action.* Baltimore: Johns Hopkins University Press.

Hildebrand, Klaus. 1984. *Von Erhard zur Großen Koalition 1963–1969.* Stuttgart: Deutsche Verlags-Anstalt.

Huber, John. 1996. The vote of no confidence in parliamentary democracies. *American Political Science Review* 90, no. 2:269–82.

Jesse, Neal. 1996. The single transferable vote and Duverger's Law: Consequences for party systems and elections. Ph.D. diss., University of California, Los Angeles.

Laver, Michael, and Kenneth A. Shepsle. 1994. Cabinet ministers and government formation in parliamentary democracies. In *Cabinet ministers and parliamentary government*, ed. Michael Laver and Kenneth A. Shepsle, 3–14. Cambridge: Cambridge University Press.

———. 1996. *Making and breaking governments.* Cambridge: Cambridge University Press.

Lijphart, Arend. 1984. *Democracies: Patterns of majoritarian and consensus government in twenty-one countries.* New Haven: Yale University Press.

———. 1994. *Electoral systems and party systems: A study of twenty-seven democracies, 1945–1990.* Oxford: Oxford University Press.

Lupia, Arthur, and Mathew D. McCubbins. 1994. Who controls? Information and the structure of legislative decision making. *Legislative Studies Quarterly* 19, no. 3: 361–84.

Mackie, Thomas T., and Richard Rose. 1991. *The international almanac of electoral history.* 3d ed. London: Macmillan.

OECD Economic Outlook. 1995. 57 (June). Paris: OECD.

OECD Economic Surveys, 1994–95: Belgium/Luxembourg. 1995. Paris: OECD.

Olson, Mancur. 1965. *The logic of collective action.* Cambridge, Mass.: Harvard University Press.

Ostrom, Elinor. 1990. *Governing the commons.* Cambridge: Cambridge University Press.

Ostrom, Elinor, Roy Gardner, and James W. Walker. 1994. *Rules, games, and common pool resources.* Ann Arbor: University of Michigan Press.

Persson, Torsten, and Lars Svensson. 1989. Why a stubborn conservative would run a deficit: Policy with time inconsistent preferences. *Quarterly Journal of Economics* 325–46.

Rogowski, Ronald. 1987. Trade and the variety of democratic institutions. *International Organization* 41, no. 2:203–23.

Roubini, Nouriel, and Jeffrey D. Sachs. 1989. Political and economic determinants of budget deficits in the industrial democracies. *European Economic Review* 33: 903–38.

Taagepera, Rein, and Matthew Soberg Shugart. 1989. *Seats and votes: The effects and determinants of electoral systems.* New Haven: Yale University Press.

———. 1993. Predicting the number of parties: A quantitative model of Duverger's mechanical effect. *American Political Science Review* 87, no. 2:455–64.

Tabellini, Guido, and Alberto Alesina. 1990. Voting on the budget deficit. *American Economic Review* 80, no. 1:37–49.

von Hagen, Jürgen. 1992. Budgeting procedures and fiscal performance in the European Communities. Economic Papers no. 96, Commission of the European Communities.

von Hagen, Jürgen, and Ian Harden. 1994a. Budget processes and commitment to fiscal discipline. *European Economic Review* 39:771–79.

———. 1994b. "National budget processes and fiscal performance." *European Economy: Reports and Studies* 3:311–418.

———. 1996. Budget processes and commitment to fiscal discipline. IMF Working Paper.

Woldendorp, T., H. Keman, and Ian Budge. 1993. A compilation of political data on industrialized parliamentary democracies, 1945–1990. *European Journal of Political Research* 24:1–120.

10 Budgetary Institutions and the Levels of Expenditure Outcomes in Australia and New Zealand

J. Edgardo Campos and Sanjay Pradhan

10.1 Introduction

In recent years, there has been heightened concern about poor fiscal outcomes in both developed and developing countries. Governments have had to reduce aggregate public spending and deficits due to serious macroeconomic imbalances. At the same time, governments have had to focus attention on the composition of spending in deciding where to cut expenditures, that is, increase allocative efficiency. Moreover, many have recognized the need to address often serious problems with technical inefficiency in the use of budgeted resources (World Bank 1993). But while policymakers and researchers have recognized these three basic problems, for the most part they have not addressed them in an integrated manner. In particular, the interrelationships among these problems have not been systematically examined. Macroeconomists have focused on the control of aggregate spending and the deficit. Experts in public administration have worked predominantly on improving technical efficiency. And fiscal economists have concentrated on issues of allocative efficiency.[1]

Further, much of the work on these issues has not dealt with the underlying institutional arrangements that affect the outcomes. Indeed recently, there has been a flurry of work on the role of institutions in influencing aggregate fiscal discipline (Alesina et al. 1996; von Hagen 1992). But this work has not addressed the implications of these and other institutional arrangements on allocative and technical efficiency.

J. Edgardo Campos is senior economist at the Economic Development Institute of the World Bank. Sanjay Pradhan is sector leader of the Public Sector and Institutional Reform unit of the Eastern Europe and Central Asia Region of the World Bank.

1. The World Bank, for instance, has devoted enormous resources to carrying out public expenditure reviews to evaluate public expenditure allocations.

233

The relative lack of attention to coherence and institutional underpinnings stems in part from the absence of an analytical framework within which to evaluate a public expenditure management system. In this paper, we present such a framework. Specifically, we examine how institutional arrangements (i.e., the rules, norms, procedures) governing the budget process affect *incentives* governing the allocation and use of resources. Using theories from the new institutional economics to guide us, we identify key theoretical problems that underpin any public expenditure management system. We then construct a set of generic institutional arrangements each of which can potentially address one or more of the problems and link with each arrangement relevant accountability- and/or transparency-enhancing mechanisms. We categorize these arrangements and mechanisms according to their relative impact on three levels or categories of expenditure outcomes—the aggregate level of spending and the deficit, the composition of expenditures, and the technical efficiency in the use of budgeted resources. On the basis of this categorization, we are able to develop a parsimonious measure of the potential effectiveness of a system with respect to each of the three expenditure categories. We are then able to systematically examine key features of reform efforts, particularly the interlinkages, and are able to correlate the "quality" of public expenditure systems with expenditure outcomes.

Through our methodology, we are able to capture the principal changes that the radical reforms in New Zealand and Australia introduced. We are able to show that the New Zealand reforms have been geared to achieving aggregate fiscal discipline and enhancing technical efficiency, and that formal mechanisms for transparency and accountability have been central to these reforms. The data reveal that our measures, the slack coefficients, are correlated with expenditure outcomes (e.g., reduction in fiscal discipline and unit costs of service delivery). Our slack coefficients for Australia confirm that the thrust of the reforms was to focus attention on strategic priorities and achieve a significant shift away from central to line agencies as the source of savings in order to achieve aggregate fiscal targets. The result has been a dramatic reduction in the level of spending and deficits, and more significantly, large churnings in the composition of spending of a highly activity-specific nature.

This paper is divided into five sections. In the following section, we present the analytical framework and identify the key institutional arrangements that define the parameters of a public expenditure management system. We also construct indices to represent each of the key institutional arrangements, and we show how the indices can be used to derive three measures of the potential effectiveness of a system with respect to the three categories of expenditure outcomes. In section 10.3, we describe the pre- and postreform systems of New Zealand and Australia, apply the methodology developed in section 10.2 to derive the measures of potential effectiveness for each system, and correlate changes in these measures with changes in expenditure outcomes. We then compare the two postreform systems and derive some implications for the study of budgeting systems. In section 10.4 we discuss recent developments in the reforms in each country. We conclude the paper with a brief discussion of directions for future research in this relatively nascent area.

10.2   The Analytical Framework

Understanding the intricacies of a country's public expenditure management system is a complicated and demanding task. In this paper, we attempt to unravel the complications that arise in constructing an effective public expenditure management system, to present a methodology for characterizing the system parsimoniously without losing its essential features, and to undertake some correlations of system characterizations and expenditure outcomes. To organize our approach, we categorize expenditure outcomes according to three basic objectives that any system needs to achieve: (i) to instill *aggregate fiscal discipline,* (ii) to facilitate *strategic prioritization of expenditures across programs and projects,* and (iii) to encourage *technical efficiency in the use of budgeted resources,* that is, achieve outputs at the lowest possible cost.

Three distinct but interrelated theoretical problems impinge on the task of achieving the above objectives. The first has to do with what is known as the tragedy of the commons. Disparate claimants on government spending view the budget as a common resource pool into which they can dip with little or no cost. The second pertains to information revelation and "vote cycling" problems that primarily impede the strategic prioritization of expenditures across sectors and programs. The third involves information asymmetry and incentive incompatibilities within the government hierarchy (e.g., the principal-agent relationship between the central and line ministries), which can impede the efficient allocation and use of budgeted resources. Each of these problems can affect expenditure outcomes adversely. Each is inherently difficult to resolve. Together they present a formidable task.

To guide us in our analysis, we use theories from the new institutional economics to help us identify key institutional arrangements that can help address these problems. We describe each of these arrangements, explain briefly how they work, and indicate why they can help resolve one or more of these problems. From this, we are then able to piece together a set of institutional arrangements that can potentially make for an effective public expenditure management system.

Institutional arrangements, however, need not necessarily have any effect. For them to be binding, mechanisms that make adherence or nonadherence to these rules transparent and that hold the government and its ministries accountable for bad performance are necessary. *Transparency and accountability* mechanisms impose implicit costs on politicians and bureaucrats for violating rules and thus can make their commitment to the rules credible.

10.2.1   Aggregate Fiscal Discipline and the Tragedy of the Commons

Aggregate fiscal discipline is impeded by the so-called tragedy of the commons. There are many claimants to the budget, for example, interest groups, legislators, line ministries. Each has different preferences for the manner in which the budget is to be allocated, that is, the composition of spending, and each exerts pressure on the government to bias spending in the direction of their preferences. Given that taxes are collected from the general public, the tax burden of a claimant's spending priorities, which is spread across many groups and individuals, is likely to be considerably lower than the total social cost of the implied programs. On the other hand, the benefits accrue mostly to the claimant. Consequently, a claimant will always demand a level of spending on its desired programs that exceeds the level that is socially optimal.[2] For these reasons, constraints on the aggregate level of spending and deficits over the medium term become important. Absent any constraint, meeting the demands of disparate claimants is likely to result in large, unsustainable deficits that translate into an unstable macroeconomic environment—high inflation, high interest rates, burgeoning current account deficits—which can ultimately retard growth.[3]

Key institutional arrangements that can help mitigate the tragedy of the commons, together with associated transparency and accountability mechanisms are summarized in part 1 of table 10.1. The tragedy of the commons problem can be mitigated by introducing a medium-term macroeconomic framework into discussions of the budget, granting the central ministries a dominant position on decisions concerning aggregate spending, and by establishing formal constraints on spending and borrowing. A macroeconomic framework provides a basis for evaluating the implications of the public expenditure program for macroeconomic variables and gives the government a means to have claimants incorporate the real cost of inflation as well as implied changes in other macro variables into their decision calculus. It would be important, however, for all public expenditures, including extrabudgetary funds, to be included in the macroeconomic framework; in Ukraine in 1991 for instance, extrabudgetary funds accounted for about 12 percent of GDP and were not incorporated in the macro framework. To be effective, the macroeconomic framework needs to be supported by underlying institutional arrangements that ensure coordination among the key central agencies. For example in Thailand, the four central agencies—the Central Bank, the Budget Bureau, the Ministry of Finance, and the Planning Ministry—work closely to develop and monitor an internally consistent set of macro aggregates.

---

2. See Weingast, Shepsle, and Johnsen 1981 for a more detailed discussion of this issue.
3. This is consistent with the observation that macroeconomic crisis generally induces governments to confront and scale down the deficit (Haggard and Kaufman 1992).

Table 10.1   Key Institutional Arrangements and Expenditure Outcomes

Institutional Arrangements	Accountability	Transparency
1. Aggregate fiscal discipline		
A. Macro framework and coordination mechanisms	Ex post reconciliation	Published
B. Dominance of central ministries	Sanctions	Made public
C. Formal constraints	Openness of financial markets	Freedom of the press
D. Hard budget constraints		
E. Comprehensiveness of budget		
2. Prioritization		
A. Forward estimates	Reporting on outcomes	Published
B. Comprehensiveness of the budget	Ex post evaluations	Freedom of the press
C. Flexibility of line agencies	Hard budget constraint	Made public
D. Breadth of consultations	Technical capacity of parliament	Comprehensible
E. Use of objective criteria		
3. Technical efficiency		
A. Civil service pay and merit-based recruitment/promotion	Clarity of purpose/ task	Published
B. Managerial autonomy of line agencies	Chief executive tenure	Made public
C. Predictability of resource flow	Financial accounts, audits	Freedom of the press
	Client surveys	
	Contestability in service delivery	

Line ministries and other claimants have relatively parochial views on the budget. By virtue of their mandates and jurisdictions, the central ministries are better able to evaluate the big picture of which aggregate spending and macroeconomic trends are major components. Hence, the tragedy of the commons can also be mitigated by granting the central ministries dominance over aggregate spending. In Thailand, for instance, the four central agencies have had considerable autonomy and authority in setting aggregate fiscal targets; there have been only two years in the last few decades where the cabinet or the parliament has overridden their targets.

Given the nature of politics in many countries, however, this may not be enough. There will be constant pressure from claimants to expand the budget envelope. Establishing explicit rules that put specific limits on spending and borrowing and that impose penalties on overspending by line ministries can give the central ministries more leverage over claimants, that is, increase their bargaining power. In practical terms this means central ministries can refer to objective, predetermined rules to defend their decisions. Similarly, Indonesia's constitutional balanced-budget law prohibits the government from incurring any domestic borrowing.

In theory, then, aggregate fiscal discipline will depend upon (i) the existence of a medium-term expenditure framework based upon a consistent macroeconomic program; (ii) the relative dominance of the central ministries; and (iii) the existence of formal constraints on spending and deficits. But while such rules may exist on paper, they may not be binding. The following mechanisms can help improve accountability and/or transparency and thus impose political costs on politicians and bureaucrats for violating the rules: (i) reconciliation between ex ante and ex post aggregate spending and deficits; (ii) sanctions against overspending; (iii) publication and dissemination of the results to the public; and (iv) integration of all expenditures within the budget, including extrabudgetary funds. New Zealand offers the most dramatic example of accountability and transparency mechanisms that bind the government to aggregate fiscal discipline. The contract of the governor of the central bank is explicitly linked to inflation, and the contract of the minister of finance is linked to aggregate fiscal performance. Further, the government is legally required to commit itself to aggregate fiscal targets, and is legally bound to full and frequent disclosure. Open financial markets have exerted a disciplining force with the publication of this data. Similarly, Indonesia's balanced-budget law does not by itself exert a binding influence because while it prohibits domestic borrowing, it allows external borrowing; external discipline is in fact exerted by open capital accounts in Indonesia.

Indeed, *the openness of financial markets* represents a subtle mechanism that imposes accountability on the government for maintaining aggregate fiscal discipline. Open financial markets can potentially act as a disciplining device on the government even in the absence of other mechanisms. If the government decides to run a large deficit, institutional investors and fund managers may perceive this to imply macroeconomic problems down the road, such as inflation, devaluation, and so on, and thus may decide to pull their funds out and move them to other countries. Should this happen then the government is likely to confront a macroeconomic crisis, which would likely have serious political repercussions. In short, open financial markets make it politically costly for the government to run a large deficit.[4]

10.2.2 Strategic Prioritization, Transactions Costs, and Consensus Building

Given aggregate fiscal discipline, the second key challenge is how to prioritize competing claims on scarce resources. Once again, the underlying problem is the tragedy of the commons, which creates a tension among competing

---

4. Indeed, our preliminary explorations (Campos, Davoodi, and Pradhan 1995) into this issue suggests that more open financial markets tend to reduce the relative size of budget deficits (deficit-to-GDP ratio).

claims from individuals and groups. But there are two additional problems that make prioritization difficult: high transactions costs in getting feedback to and from civil society about how to map expenditures onto preferences, and information asymmetries within the government hierarchy characterized by the fact that line agencies possess better information about how best to allocate expenditures within their mandates.

Prioritization is fundamentally a political process. Politicians will set priorities based upon their understanding of the preferences of their constituencies: the key here is whether there are institutional arrangements that improve the quality of information needed to do this effectively. Key institutional arrangements and their associated transparency and accountability mechanisms, which can facilitate prioritization, are summarized in part 2 of table 10.1.

Invariably the tragedy of the commons will create demands in excess of the constraints. This raises the transactions costs of collective decision making within the political process because it creates a situation in which individuals and groups will strive to restructure coalitions in order to enlarge their share of a fixed pie.[5] This implies the need for institutional arrangements that help build consensus among the competing groups on the relative expenditure allocations.[6]

Consensus building requires information on what trade-offs are being made, including what everyone is having to give up and gain, together with a vision of future benefits that will derive from current sacrifices. Thus for prioritization, the most important arrangement is likely to be a process that articulates and seeks consensus over strategic outcomes that expenditures seek to achieve in the medium term and that links expenditure allocations with these strategic outcomes. This could include, for instance, a decision-making mechanism in the cabinet to decide upon strategic priorities informed by a system for comparing the medium-term costs of competing policies within a given hard budget constraint.

Line ministries have better information on how best to allocate resources within their sectors to achieve given objectives. Consequently, a complementary arrangement that would economize on transactions costs would be to give them the flexibility to determine what new programs to introduce and what existing programs to cut; that is, by allocating resources within their ceilings, information costs are reduced. For as long as line ministries can be held accountable for their performance (through reconciliations and ex post evaluations) and their performance is made transparent, they will tend to use the information they possess (but which central ministries and politicians do not) to allocate their ceilings to achieve their given objectives.

Australia offers the best example of such a priority-setting process. The process engenders strong focus on strategic outcomes that expenditure programs

---

5. Theoretically this refers to the problem of "vote" cycling (see McKelvey 1976).
6. On the U.S. Congress, see Weingast 1979; Krehbiel 1991; Shepsle 1979.

are seeking to achieve, and incorporates a medium-term expenditure framework that link allocations to the achievement of these outcomes. At the cabinet level, the process focuses on evaluating and setting strategic priorities based upon medium-cost estimates of spending and savings options identified by line agencies as well as by the cabinet. Line ministries are given a hard budget constraint consistent with these intersectoral priorities, but then given flexibility to reallocate resources within their portfolios. These medium-term costs of policies, called forward estimates, are rolled over into future budgets provided policies do not change. This lowers transaction costs and helps focus attention on changes in strategic priorities. Accountability is achieved through the hard constraint, reporting on results or outcomes, and a strong emphasis on ex post reconciliations and evaluations. Australia, for instance, publishes a reconciliation table with its budget showing the deviations between last year's forward estimates and this year's proposed allocations. This is accompanied by an explanation of the observed deviations. Australia also undertakes systematic ex post evaluations of its programs. Among developing countries, Colombia is launching the most ambitious program of ex post evaluations, and Malawi is attempting to institute a priority-setting process along the lines of Australia's.

A credible priority-setting process also requires that all expenditures be incorporated into the budget. In other words, the budget needs to be comprehensive. The existence of extrabudgetary funds and/or the exclusion of certain expenditure categories, for example, subsidies to public enterprises, is likely to weaken the ability of decision makers to allocate expenditures to achieve strategic outcomes. For instance, considerable earmarking of resources for particular expenditures in several Latin American countries (e.g., Colombia) effectively removes large chunks of expenditures from the prioritization process. Comprehensiveness or unity of the budget is perhaps the second most important arrangement for prioritization.

There is also a need to establish impersonal rules for evaluating the relative importance of programs and projects to complement the prioritization process. Since impersonal rules apply equally to every program and project, the government cannot be as easily accused of favoritism and thus is better able to defend itself against criticism. The use of economic cost-benefit analysis and incidence analysis are examples of such rules. The first can provide information on the net social gain, while the second can potentially make transparent who gains and who loses. These rules can thereby help claimants evaluate trade-offs more objectively and thus arrive at agreements more quickly.

To build a consensus, the decision-making process also needs to extract information about the preferences of different claimants, that is, determine the demand curve. Decisions have to be made about broad strategic priorities, for this determines ministerial objectives, ceilings, and allocations over the medium term. But again asymmetries in information between the government and claimants make this difficult. Consequently, there is a need for institutional arrangements that lower the costs of transmitting the information about social preferences to government and thus in determining broad strategic priorities.[7]

Broad consultations that involve representatives of claimants and that incorporate feedback and provide oversight at relatively low transactions cost can help arrive at strategic priorities. The most extensive, tractable form of such consultations is likely to involve parliamentary discussions of the budget. Parliamentarians represent some segment of the population as well as certain interest groups. Moreover, parliamentary committees and subcommittees generally evaluate specific components of the overall public expenditure program. So by exposing proposed public expenditure allocations to parliamentary scrutiny, feedback can be obtained on the appropriateness of the priorities and adjustments made accordingly.

In some countries, corporatist arrangements tend to complement if not dominate parliamentary procedures.[8] In such cases, representatives from various sectors in society become an important sounding board of the government. It is helpful if not necessary to create a forum through which these representatives can comment on and criticize budget proposals.[9] In any case, opinion surveys can help identify broad priorities that discussions with parliament and/or representatives of corporatist groups can refine.

Critical to the success of the demand-revealing (and thus consensus-building) mechanisms is a set of rules or criteria that introduces incentives for "shared sacrifice"; that is, claimants agree to smaller allocations within a constrained budget envelope. This suggests the need for commitment devices that insure claimants that their current sacrifices will result in future benefits and that each one will bear some part of the burden.[10] Hence, mechanisms that hold government accountable for allocating resources accordingly and making those allocations transparent become important. Unless claimants can be sure that the government will indeed allocate resources accordingly, they will be much less willing to support any proposed allocation, reducing the likelihood that a consensus can be reached.

Consensus building is really about creating institutional arrangements for claimants and the government to exploit potential gains from trade, that is, logrolling. Hence, for a consensus to emerge, arrangements that address logrolling problems are needed. There is by now a considerable literature on this in the context of the United States (see Shepsle and Weingast 1994 for a literature survey). However, much of this discussion is premised on the fact that

7. In practice what this has usually meant is for the cabinet to propose ministerial ceilings and intraministerial allocations and for broad consultations to inform the cabinet of changes that need to be made to conform more closely to preferences of claimants from civil society.

8. See Staniland 1985 for a definition and discussion of corporatism.

9. In Malaysia, for example, the Budget Dialogue Group, which consists of representatives from all major sectors including NGOs and industry groups, meets annually to discuss budget priorities for the coming year and to comment on the previous year's allocations.

10. See Campos and Esafahani 1996 and Campos and Root 1996 for a discussion of this issue.

individuals and groups are willing to behave according to the rules of the game. In much of the developing world, this cannot be presumed. The rules are not very transparent, and public officials are not held sufficiently accountable for their actions. Hence, politicians and public officials have very little incentive to behave according to the rules. This of course makes trades among different parties difficult since it creates an environment in which individuals may renege on agreements without fear of being penalized.

Increasing transparency and improving accountability make it more costly for politicians and public officials to violate rules and thus renege on agreements. Publishing the expenditure allocations and the agreed-upon (i.e., strategic) outcomes embodied in the expenditure plan and publicizing these (i.e., making the budget transparent) make it more difficult for both politicians and officials to alter things midstream without sufficient cause since they will have to defend any such action before the general public. Institutionalizing a process of reconciling actual expenditures of ministries with their annual budgeted allocations as well as reconciling their forward estimates with subsequent budget requests and publicizing all such reconciliations will induce the government to stick to the expenditure priorities (except when there are large exogenous shocks, and even then the government will have to provide a good explanation). Moreover, undertaking regular ex post evaluations of major ministerial programs and publicizing the results makes line ministries more responsive to producing the outputs that they have promised to produce over the medium-term period.

Closely linked to the above transparency and accountability mechanisms is the need to provide parliament with sufficient resources to hire and maintain a staff with the technical capacity to evaluate government programs and proposals. If parliament can adequately scrutinize government performance, then the government will be under more pressure to deliver on what it has promised in the expenditure plan.

In summary, institutional arrangements that can facilitate prioritization include (i) an expenditure planning process linked to the achievement of affordable outcomes, including a process to identify and discuss the medium-term costs of competing priorities at the cabinet level; (ii) flexibility for line agencies to make intrasectoral allocations; (iii) comprehensiveness of the budget; (iv) a process that allows feedback from claimants that inform priority setting; and (v) the use of objective criteria. Accountability and transparency mechanisms that can help bind the politicians and bureaucrats to the achievement of these strategic outcomes include (i) reconciliation of ex ante and ex post allocations; (ii) reconciliation of budgetary allocations with forward estimates; (iii) reconciliation of ex ante and ex post outcomes, including ex post evaluations; (iv) public dissemination of the results; (v) hard budget constraint to create incentives to prioritize expenditures; (vi) integration of all expenditures (e.g., extrabudgetary funds) into budgetary deliberations; and (vii) building the technical capacity of parliament.

10.2.3   Technical Efficiency and Incentive Incompatibilities

Assuming that an aggregate level and a prioritization of expenditures emerges from the above arrangements, there still remains the principal agent problem within the government hierarchy. Information asymmetries and incentive incompatibilities can impede the efficient delivery of public services by line agencies and their civil servants. Because of their closeness to the clients and their involvement in day-to-day operations in a specific sector or subsector, line ministries and their agencies possess superior information about how best to implement programs to achieve the intended results. It thus becomes imperative for the government to grant the line ministries a sufficient degree of managerial autonomy over the specific allocations and the responsibility to implement their respective budgets.

The capacity of line agencies for efficient delivery of services depends also on the predictability of the flow of budgetary resources. Unless a line agency can be certain of how much it is going to get over the fiscal year, it will not be able to make definite plans and therefore cannot make efficient allocations. For instance, in several African countries, the budget is remade during the year, and line agencies face considerable uncertainty in making their expenditure plans for the fiscal year. At the opposite extreme, the expenditure process in Australia with its requirement of automatically folding forward estimates (absent major policy changes) of line agencies into their annual budgets introduces a high degree of predictability.

Managerial autonomy and predictability will not produce desirable results unless the civil service in line agencies attracts competent individuals. A necessary requisite to do this is adequate compensation. In this regard, among the more critical arrangements is a compensation scheme that closely aligns public-sector with private-sector compensation. However this arrangement needs to be complemented by a merit-based recruitment and promotion system. Without such a system, competency will not be rewarded appropriately, which will affect the morale and thus the incentives of civil servants. The worst-case scenario is one in which promotions and recruitment are based solely on political connections and influence. In such cases, high salaries will tend to go to those who are most well connected, and civil servants will tend to concentrate on establishing such connections rather than on accomplishing their tasks efficiently.

Autonomy and competence of line agencies are necessary but not sufficient for technical efficiency. Indeed, there is no guarantee that the line ministries, despite their superior information, will implement their budgeted programs in ways that will achieve the intended results at the lowest possible cost. They could just as well use their budget inappropriately, for example, for personal or parochial gain. Hence, they have to be made accountable for the allocational decisions that they make, and for the efficient delivery of services. An appropriate balance between autonomy and accountability of the line agencies has to be struck. Accountability will depend upon (i) publication of financial accounts and with what lags; (ii) publication of financial audits and with what lags; (iii) the extent of oversight of financial accounts and audits by groups in civil society (e.g., parliamentary subcommittees); (iv) clarity of outputs of organizational units; (v) contestability in the delivery of outputs; (vi) tenure of agency heads; (vii) implicit or explicit performance contracts for agency heads and their employees; (viii) extent of performance audits and their publication; and (ix) the use of client surveys. The publication and general dissemination of their results, that is, making them transparent, will contribute further to the effectiveness of these arrangements.

To sum up, then, technical efficiency in the use of budgeted resources will depend upon the relative autonomy of line agencies and the extent to which they can be held accountable for performance, the predictability of resource flows into ministerial budgets, the competence of line agency bureaucrats, and the extent to which recruitment and promotion is based on merit. In part 3 of table 10.1, we present a capsule summary of the arrangements and accountability/transparency mechanisms that can help make government delivery of public services more technically efficient.

10.2.4   Interactions and Trade-offs among the Three Levels of Expenditure Outcomes

Above, we have summarized the institutional arrangements, transparency, and accountability mechanisms that can help achieve each the three basic objectives discussed above. Table 10.1 summarizes this matrix. This represents a diagnostic framework that can be used to analyze the impact of budgetary institutions on expenditure outcomes in particular countries.

In this regard, it is critical to underscore two central points: (i) there are interactions among the three levels of expenditure outcomes and their institutional arrangements; and (ii) budgeting systems face trade-offs among the levels of expenditure outcomes that they are geared toward. As the analyses below illustrate, how countries control aggregate spending affects the way they deal with budgetary allocations and the efficiency with which line agencies use their budgets, and conversely as well. These considerations induce trade-offs in terms of which category of expenditure outcomes to focus on. It is this emphasis on interactions and trade-offs that distinguishes our approach from other recent studies that have focused exclusively on institutional arrangements that contribute to aggregate fiscal discipline (e.g., Alesina et al. 1996; von Hagen 1992).

10.2.5   Constructing a Measurable Representation of a Public Expenditure Management System

To characterize a public expenditure management system, we need to develop a parsimonious representation of the system that captures its principal features and that indicates how these features relate to each other. To do this,

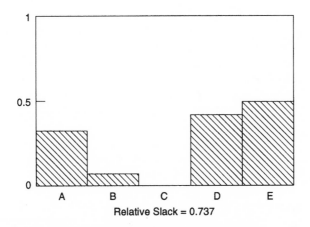

Fig. 10.1   New Zealand—prereform aggregate fiscal discipline

we construct an index for each of the institutional arrangements and, where applicable, for corresponding transparency and accountability mechanisms. The arrangements, mechanisms, and associated indices are presented in detail in Campos and Pradhan 1996.

For a country-specific public expenditure management system, we assign index values to each of the institutional arrangements and transparency/accountability mechanisms in the table. The values are based on responses of an expert on the country's budgeting process to a diagnostic questionnaire that we have prepared as well as an in-depth analysis provided by the expert. For two mechanisms, the openness of financial markets and the freedom of the press, we used objective indices developed elsewhere. Because it is accountability and transparency that bind the governments to institutional arrangements, we give a weight of ⅙ to the arrangement, ⅓ to the transparency mechanism, and ½ to the accountability mechanisms and derive a weighted index for the arrangement cum mechanisms. Where there are no transparency and/or accountability mechanisms, we normalize weights so that the sum of the weights for all applicable factors is 1. For example, if there are no mechanisms associated with an arrangement, then the arrangement gets a full weight of 1, and its weighted index will be equal to its index value. Based on this, we are able to construct a parsimonious representation of each of the three categories of the system in the form of a chart and a corresponding slack coefficient roughly analogous to the Gini coefficient measure of income inequality. For example, figure 10.1 illustrates the relative slack of New Zealand's prereform (circa 1983) system with respect to aggregate fiscal discipline. There are five institutional arrangements under this expenditure category (see table 10.1), represented as A, B, C, D, and E in the horizontal axis. We give equal weights to each of these arrangements and assign a maximum height of 1 to each. The actual country-specific height corresponding to each arrangement is given by the weighted index associated with it, for instance, for A this is 0.325. The unshaded portion represents the slack of the system with respect to aggregate fiscal discipline. Its area (4.18) as a proportion of the total area of the chart (5) gives the corresponding slack coefficient −0.837.

Some arrangements are themselves characterized by subarrangements nested in them. In such cases, we take the average of the actual index values assigned to each of the subarrangements and use that as the index value for the arrangement.

There are also accountability and transparency mechanisms that apply to a whole category. These are the openness of financial markets, which is an accountability mechanism, and the relative freedom of the press, which is a transparency mechanism. Both mechanisms are essentially exogenous to the public expenditure system. For the case of openness of financial markets, we adjust each accountability mechanism under aggregate fiscal discipline by taking the average of the mechanism's index value and the index value for openness. For the case of freedom of the press, we multiply each relevant transparency mechanism by the index value for freedom of the press.

In the case of the prioritization and technical efficiency categories, we assign different weights to each of the arrangements cum accountability/transparency mechanisms based on implications of the preceding analysis. For instance, under technical efficiency, we give line agency accountability twice the weight of competency and autonomy. Without accountability, competency and autonomy can translate into abuse and misuse of resources. With accountability, the government and in particular the line agencies will have strong incentives to improve the overall level of competency and to try to use their autonomy to meet their objectives at least cost. Specifically, under technical efficiency, we assign weights of .5, .5, and 1 respectively to arrangements A, B, and C and, under prioritization, weights of 1, .8, .6, .4, .2 respectively to arrangements A through E (see table 10.1), given their decreasing order of importance as suggested by our analytical framework. In the country-specific analyses, we undertake some sensitivity analysis by comparing our results with the weights with results based on equal weights for each arrangement (Campos and Pradhan 1996).

10.3   New Zealand and Australia

10.3.1   New Zealand

Faced with a severe economic crisis and a heavily interventionist state not dissimilar from former Eastern European centrally planned economies, the government of New Zealand undertook a sequence of radical institutional reforms that sought to completely redefine the role and revamp the functioning of government. The reforms proceeded in four general stages as embodied in the State-Owned Enterprise Act (1986), the State Sector Act (1988), the Public

Finance Act (1989), and the Fiscal Responsibility Act (1993). The State-Owned Enterprise Act took the state out of production activities that the private sector could just as well provide competitively. The act formed the basis of the strategic focus of the reforms that followed. The State Sector Act abolished the permanent tenure of civil servants by putting agency heads on five-year (renewable) performance contracts and granting them the authority to hire and fire employees within their jurisdiction. It also introduced the notion of splitting an agency into two or more focused business units, for example, one as the funder/purchaser and another as the provider. The Public Finance Act introduced two innovations: first, it enhanced the transparency of public financial statements by requiring that all such statements be put on an accrual accounting basis and be published and made available to the general public; and second, it improved accountability by mandating that any given appropriation must be linked to one of seven categories, the main one being outputs. The first innovation made individual agency statements comprehensible to other agencies as well as to the business community. The second created incentives for each agency to clearly specify the outputs that it planned to provide during the fiscal year, for which it could then be held accountable. The Fiscal Responsibility Act enhanced the transparency and accountability of the government for aggregate fiscal discipline through full and frequent disclosure of aggregate fiscal information and benchmarking actual performance vis-à-vis published aggregate fiscal objectives.

In terms of the summary features in table 10.1, the big changes occurred in the second and third columns. Prior to the reforms, most public financial statements and budgetary documents were not available to the general public for scrutiny, and, even if they were made available, they could not be easily understood even by accountants and financial experts in the private sector. Consequently, government performance was largely nontransparent. The Public Finance Act changed this dramatically.

Accountability of line ministries was very weak as well. There were little or no reconciliations of ex ante provisions with ex post outcomes. Line ministries did not face a hard budget constraint. Control of their spending was done mostly through control of their inputs by the central ministries. And because of these, it was not possible to impose sanctions against line ministries. In other words, line ministries had very little autonomy. Consequently, it was difficult to hold them accountable for their performance. The State Sector Act granted considerable autonomy to line ministries but made them accountable for outputs. It introduced sanctions against nonperformance: the chief executive of a line ministry could be dismissed after his or her five-year contract expired and the executive's compensation was based on the delivery of key outputs; employees of the line ministry could be fired by the chief executive. And, in conjunction with the Public Finance Act, it made reconciliations de facto mandatory.

Discussions of accountability and transparency rarely focus on the central ministries. This was certainly the case in New Zealand up to the mid-1980s. In fact, there was a period in which the prime minister held the finance portfolio as well, a situation that could have easily led to fiscal mismanagement (which it did). But accountability and transparency of the central ministries have become a crowning point of the reforms. The Fiscal Responsibility Act has bound the minister of finance to meeting clear-cut fiscal objectives, for example, cutting the deficit to 1 percent. These objectives constitute the outputs that (s)he is responsible for and provide the basis upon which her or his performance is judged and thus upon which her or his compensation and tenure depend.[11]

Accompanying the public-sector reforms were measures that liberalized financial markets. As mentioned earlier, New Zealand was very much like a centrally planned economy prior to the reforms. Concomitantly, the financial sector was highly controlled. Beginning in the mid-1980s, various measures were introduced to ease up the controls. By the early 1990s, financial markets were very much open to international flows. This is indicated by one measure of financial openness that shows the extent to which domestic real interest rates exceed world real interest rates. The index ranges from 0 to 1 in steps of tenths, for example, .1, .2, and so on, with higher numbers reflecting relatively greater openness of financial markets. For New Zealand, the average of the index from 1980 to 1984 was around .3; the average from 1990 to 1994 was .7.

With regard to the institutional arrangements (the first column of table 10.1), the major changes occurred in the third (technical efficiency) and first (aggregate fiscal discipline) categories. As already mentioned, the permanent tenure of agency heads was abolished, and, in its place, a five-year performance contract based on clearly defined key outputs for agency heads (now referred to as chief executives) was introduced. In turn, agency heads were given the authority to hire and fire employees: the typical civil service personnel arrangement was turned on its head. With this also came a great deal of autonomy over agency matters. Under the first category (aggregate fiscal discipline), the reforms introduced formal constraints on aggregate spending and the deficit via the Fiscal Responsibility Act. Comprehensiveness also improved since the output-based system forced line agencies to include all possible expenditures in their proposed budgets: budgets are structured in terms of seven classes of outputs; every expenditure had to fall into one of these classes.

The New Zealand reforms have not been focused on the second category— strategic prioritization *within* the residual, core public sector. Up till recently, there has been no conscious effort to link agency outputs and thus expenditure allocations to strategic outcomes. Only beginning in 1994 was there some attempt to identify broad strategic priorities and to link annual budgetary considerations to these (medium- to long-term) priorities.

In table 10.2, we summarize the changes that the reforms introduced in

---

11. We note also that the contract of the head of the central bank is tied to the inflation rate.

Table 10.2   The New Zealand Reforms

Institutional Arrangements	Accountability	Transparency
1. Aggregate fiscal discipline		
A. Macro framework and coordination mechanisms	Ex post reconciliation	Published
B. Dominance of central ministries	Sanctions	Made public
C. Formal constraints	Openness of financial markets	Freedom of the press
D. Hard budget constraints		
E. Comprehensiveness of the budget		
2. Prioritization		
A. Forward estimates	Reporting on outcomes	Published
B. Comprehensiveness of the budget	Ex post evaluations	Freedom of the press
C. Flexibility to line agencies	Hard budget constraint	Made public
D. Breadth of consultations	Technical capacity of parliament	Comprehensible
E. Use of objective criteria		
3. Technical efficiency		
A. Civil service pay and merit-based recruitment/promotion	Clarity of purpose/ task	Published
B. Relative autonomy of line agencies	Chief executive tenure	Made public
C. Predictability of resource flow	Financial accounts, audits	Freedom of the press
	Client surveys	
	Contestability in service delivery	

terms of the categories and subcategories listed in table 10.1. Items that are shaded indicate the areas where the reforms introduced significant changes. Those that are not shaded represent arrangements or mechanisms that have not been the focus of the New Zealand reforms.

Characterizing Pre- and Postreform Systems

Using the methodology discussed earlier, we are able to capture the essential institutional changes that the above reforms introduced. We derive slack coefficients to both the prereform (circa 1983) and the postreform (circa 1994) systems of New Zealand. The left side of figure 10.2 indicates the weighted indices for each arrangement (i.e., the height) and illustrates the relative slack of the prereform system with respect to the three categories. The corresponding slack coefficients are indicated in the upper right corner. The right side of the figure does the same for the postreform system.

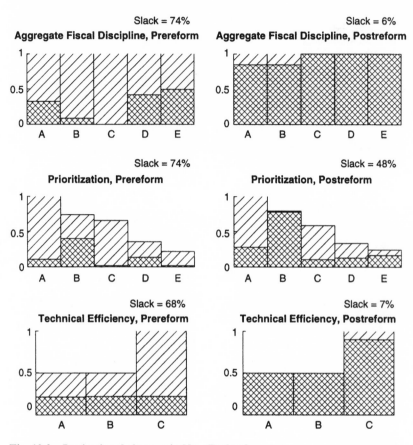

Fig. 10.2   Institutional changes in New Zealand

Correlating Systems with Outcomes

From figure 10.2, we discern that the relative slack of the New Zealand system with respect to aggregate fiscal discipline is substantially smaller today than it was in the prereform era—a slack coefficient of .06 versus .74. Corresponding to this has been a significant fall in the deficit-to-GDP ratio over the period 1984 to 1994, as indicated in figure 10.3. The ratio was about −9 percent in 1983 but gradually fell over the decade so that by 1994 it turned into a small surplus.

Interestingly, the expenditure-to-GDP ratio fell less drastically from about 38 percent in 1983 to around 35 percent in 1994. This is depicted in figure 10.4. However as figure 10.5 illustrates, the composition of spending changed markedly, with the share going to the development of industry falling from about 13 percent in 1983 to approximately 3 percent in 1994 and the share of social services rising roughly from 30 percent to 37 percent and the share of

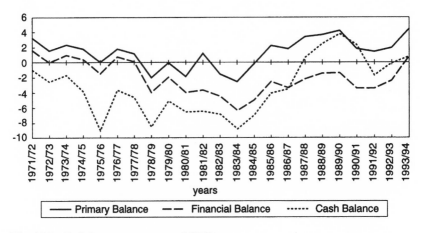

Fig. 10.3   Deficits as percentage of GDP

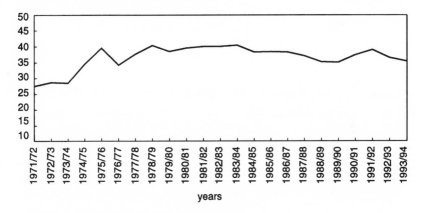

Fig. 10.4   Expenditure as percentage of GDP

health from 7 percent to around 12 percent. Other expenditure ratios remained relatively constant. The slack coefficient of the system (and thus the relative slack) with respect to prioritization is correlated with this change. Circa 1983, the slack was .74; in 1995 it was .48. A look at the left side of figure 10.2 indicates the possible weak points of the prereform system with respect to prioritization. The system scores low on arrangements A, C, and E, which are arrangements that respectively deal with the articulation of strategic priorities, deal with the flexibility of line agencies, and pertain to the use of economic analysis in evaluating expenditures. The right side of figure 10.2 shows that substantial changes were introduced to address C and E. Changes were also introduced to improve on B (the relative integration of the budget). The change in A, which refers to the articulation of strategic outcomes, is consistent with

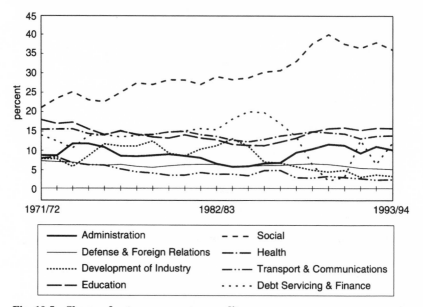

Fig. 10.5   **Shares of net government expenditure**

observed changes in the role of the state, which essentially involved a radical redirection of the role of government from one that supported state-owned enterprises and intervened heavily in industry through massive regulation to one that aggressively encouraged the provision of contestable goods and services by private industry. The articulation of strategic outcomes within the core public sector, however, remains weak.

In terms of the capacity to achieve technical efficiency, the postreform system improved significantly on the prereform system; the former has a slack coefficient of .07 and the latter .67. Unit cost data is not generally available except for a very limited sample of activities and only for a limited time period. The New Zealand Treasury has conducted a pilot study of productivity improvements in a small, select set of activities. The study estimates average unit costs for select activities within four ministries. But as Scott and Ball (1996) comment, there were no adjustments made to inflation and there were a lot of qualifications. That is, the data must be interpreted with caution.

Due to the request of the Treasury that the results be kept confidential (for the moment), we will label the concerned activities anonymously and indicate the changes in unit costs over time estimated for each of them.[12] We emphasize that these results are very preliminary and may change as the Treasury com-

---

12. The Treasury released the study in late 1995; we will identify the activities and present data on changes in unit costs in subsequent research.

Table 10.3 **Percentage Change in Unit Costs in New Zealand, Selected Activities**

Activities	Period of Study	Percentage Change in Average Unit Costs
A	1989–94	Fall of 10 to 20%
B	1989–92	Rise of 25%
	1992–95	Fall of 25 to 30%
C	1990–94	Fall of 10 to 40%
D	1987–94	0%[a]

[a]Unit cost levels dropped down to approximately 1989 levels.

pletes its study. The results, which are indicated in table 10.3, suggest that unit costs are likely to have fallen between 1984 and 1994. This is consistent with the change in the slack.[13]

10.3.2 Australia

Australia has instituted a medium-term expenditure framework, which focuses the budget process on changes in strategic priorities within aggregate fiscal parameters. It has introduced measures that grant considerable flexibility to line agencies and provide them with incentives to identify savings options themselves. At the same time, the reforms have sought to focus attention on outcomes and introduce some form of accountability, although these are not formalized.

These reforms consist of six main, interrelated elements. First, a cornerstone of the Australian reforms has been a system of forward estimates, or three-year forecasts of the minimum cost of existing policies and programs, which are automatically rolled into budgetary allocations if there is no change in policy. This has removed from ministerial consideration the bulk of outlays in any budget that do not involve any changes in policies. Ministers now allocate the limited time for budget consideration to policy development rather than zero-basing an entire set of appropriations; indeed, this has freed up cabinet time as evidenced by the decline in cabinet meetings from 370 in 1981 to 180 in 1988–89 to 121 in 1989–90. The lock-in feature has also provided line agencies with more certainty about present and future resources, thereby potentially enhancing technical efficiency. Finally, the requirement to publish a reconciliation table that shows and explains the deviation between the forward estimates for the year and actual allocations in the annual budget, including their outyear implications, has served as a transparent and accountable mechanism for show-

13. We have also attempted a characterization of the pre- and postreform systems with equal weights on all arrangements (cum accountability/transparency mechanisms) in each of the three expenditure categories. The results indicate that, within reasonable weighting parameters, our characterization has relatively robust ordinal properties, i.e., big changes remain big and small changes remain small (Campos and Pradhan 1996).

ing areas of policy change as well as the future demands on resources of these policies.

Second, mechanisms for macroeconomic planning reconcile the forward estimates with the target deficit to identify the scope for new spending and savings. Aggregate fiscal discipline in the determination of target deficits has in turn been induced by public commitments to aggregate targets (e.g., the Hawke government's trilogy of commitments not to increase spending and taxes, and to reduce the deficit) and implicitly enforced through open financial markets and media. Third, decision-making mechanisms were instituted at a political level through the "Trilaterals" and the Expenditure Review Committee (ERC) of the cabinet to decide upon competing priorities for spending and savings to achieve the net fiscal targets. Individual portfolios are required to submit spending and savings proposals to stay within their targets, but it is up to the ERC to decide whether to choose only the savings or spending options, or both. Fourth, a system of portfolio budgeting was introduced. This devolves priority setting to individual portfolios by encouraging and requiring line agencies to themselves identify savings and spending options within their portfolio to meet their net savings targets. This capitalizes on the superior information of line agencies by inducing them to identify their least cost-effective program in order to fund new programs. Fifth, the development of the running-costs system further devolved authority within departments or portfolios. All administrative and salary expenses, which previously consisted of 20 or more items, were consolidated into a single running-cost item, and department managers were given the authority to allocate this expenditure item to various inputs— including staff numbers and salaries—as they saw fit. Additional flexibility was provided by allowing agencies to bring forward or carry over running costs between years, up to a limit of 10 percent. A partial quid pro quo for this freedom is the annual efficiency dividend of 1 percent that agencies are expected to achieve in their running costs every year.

Finally, while portfolio budgeting and the running-cost system devolved authority to line agencies, program management and budgeting was introduced to focus attention on outcomes. This entailed classification of portfolio activities into programs, and introduction of accountability mechanisms by requiring departments to report on the performance of programs within their portfolios. At the same time, ex post evaluation was introduced to assess whether programs were achieving their intended results. Various reviews, however, have concluded that program budgeting and evaluation has had limited impact on budgetary allocations, but has helped create a performance-oriented culture.

Using the methodology above, we are able to characterize the principal features of these reforms, and assign slack coefficients to both prereform and postreform systems. As shown in figure 10.6, the coefficients corroborate our qualitative findings that the greatest emphasis in the Australian reforms has been on improving strategic prioritization (i.e., slack coefficient declined from 80 percent to 12 percent) and aggregate fiscal discipline (i.e., reduction in coef-

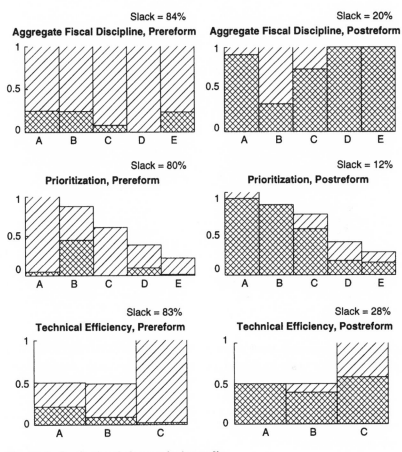

Fig. 10.6 Institutional changes in Australia

ficient from 84 percent to 20 percent). At the same time, there has been less emphasis on introducing measures for accountability to enhance technical efficiency.

The reforms have had a dramatic impact on the level and composition of spending. Aggregate budgetary outlays declined from 29.8 percent of GDP in 1984–85 to 23.7 percent in 1989–90. This involved three consecutive years of negative real growth in outlays (1987–88 to 1989–90) and four years of resulting budget surplus (1986–87 to 1990–91). The budget deficit moved from 4.1 percent of GDP in 1983–84 to a surplus of 2 percent of GDP in 1989–90! The reduction in forward estimates of outlays from 1987 was even more dramatic than the reduction in actual expenditures. Figure 10.7 shows that there was a strong tendency in the early 1980s for forward estimates of outlays on existing outlays to rise steeply. This meant that the reduction in annual growth of spending involved a double task: reversal of growth in forward esti-

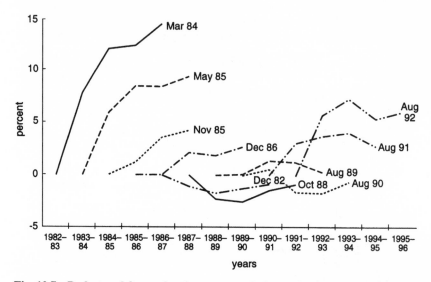

Fig. 10.7   Budget and forward estimates, cumulative real growth, Australia
Source: Dixon 1996, 229.
Note: Excludes asset sales.

mates to bring spending down to the preceding year, and further reductions in spending to achieve net declines. From 1987, however, the forward estimates of outlays begin to show declines in the outyears, under the influence of budget decisions that reduced outlays over a period of time.

What is striking about the Australian experience is that these dramatic cuts were achieved by significant changes in the composition of intrasectoral expenditures on account of savings identified by line agencies themselves (fig. 10.8). The distribution of real savings measures undertaken by line agencies shows that the spending cuts involved some major policy shifts, particularly in the social security function, where a much higher degree of outlays targeting was achieved. However, the bulk of the changes in expenditure composition came from measures of a highly activity-specific nature, involving program redesign and elimination of particular, less cost-effective aspects of program spending. These achievements contrast sharply with an attempt to reduce spending by an earlier administration in the early 1980s, which unsuccessfully tried to eliminate redundant functions in a centralized manner and merely ended up making modest reductions through across-the-board cuts.

10.3.3   New Zealand versus Australia: A Comparison

New Zealand and Australia are often mentioned together as being at the cutting edge of institutional reform. Our analysis above reveals that while they share some important principles in their reform efforts, they have by and large taken dramatically different paths, which provide quite separate paradigms for other countries.

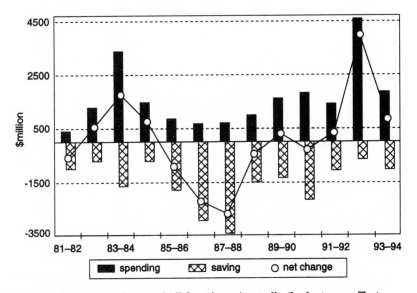

Fig. 10.8   Real new policy, total all functions, Australia (budget year effect, 1981–82 to 1993–94)

Perhaps the most important shared characteristic of the two reforms is that they each have sought to alter underlying *incentives* that govern the allocation and use of resources. Within this, a common feature is *transparency*, which binds key players to particular fiscal outcomes and makes it costly for them to misbehave. Transparency pervades all key aspects of the New Zealand reforms—for example, explicit delineation of outputs, the contracts of chief executives, budgetary appropriations explicitly based upon outputs purchased, publication of balance sheets showing net worth of government, and legislatively mandated full and frequent disclosure. In Australia, transparency is best exemplified in the requirement to publish a reconciliation table for the forward estimates, explicitly indicating how much particular outlays were changed in the annual budget vis-à-vis the forward estimates, the reasons behind these changes, and their outyear implications.

Another shared feature is *considerable devolution to line agencies* to perform their tasks. In both countries, this has created incentives that make it worthwhile for line agencies to identify savings, and move them toward a greater interest in both allocative and technical efficiency. In New Zealand, chief executives have complete autonomy over the allocation of inputs to produce the outputs, including the right to hire and fire. In Australia, all administrative expenses of line agencies have been consolidated into a single running-cost item, and managers have complete flexibility in the allocation of these costs across inputs, including staff numbers and salaries. Further, portfolio budgeting in Australia devolves priority setting to individual departments, encouraging them to identify the specific spending and savings measures to meet

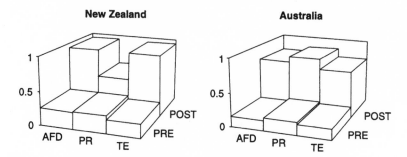

Fig. 10.9   Emphasis of reforms in New Zealand and Australia
Note: AFD = aggregate fiscal discipline. PR = priority setting. TE = technical efficiency.

their net fiscal targets. Another shared feature is *contestability* in service delivery. In both countries, there is a strong emphasis on unbundling the provision of public services, and introducing competition in service delivery—including from the private sector—in order to achieve technically efficient outcomes. While New Zealand has gone much farther down this route, Australia too has instituted explicit measures for contestability—even for policy advice.

A final common characteristic has been a *binding commitment to aggregate fiscal discipline.* Each country has publicly committed itself to targets for fiscal prudence and has instituted mechanisms that facilitate the achievement of fiscal targets. At the same time, the openness of financial markets and the media have provided an external disciplining mechanism to ensure adherence to prudent fiscal targets.

Past this, however, Australia and New Zealand have adopted dramatically different reforms to achieve aggregate fiscal discipline. A principal distinguishing feature has been the relative emphasis placed on *technical efficiency* in New Zealand as opposed to *strategic priority setting* in Australia. This is clearly revealed in their relative slack measures corresponding to the two outcomes as shown in figure 10.9. This in turn reflects relative emphasis on technical efficiency in the delivery of *outputs* (i.e., goods and services produced) in New Zealand, as opposed to the cost-effective achievement of *outcomes* (i.e., the impact of outputs on beneficiaries) in Australia. The different reforms in the two countries have been path-dependent, reflecting the particular background and historical conditions driving each reform.

On the eve of reforms, New Zealand inherited an overexpanded public sector not dissimilar to the command economies of the former socialist countries. Consequently, a principal emphasis was on restructuring the role of the state by privatizing large chunks of the public sector. This extended itself into the paradigm of instituting private-sector incentive mechanisms within the remaining core public sector in order to achieve technical efficiency in the delivery of outputs. There is a strong emphasis on formal contracts for accountability in the efficient delivery of outputs. Management contracts between ministers and chief executives, as well as budgetary appropriations, have been based upon outputs.

By contrast, the Australian reforms were launched when a preceding administration had been unsuccessful in reducing public spending by identifying redundant functions. A centralized, top-down Commonwealth Review of Functions failed to identify egregious anomalies in the role of the state in Australia. Consequently, the Australian reforms sought to rely on a more nuanced and finely surgical process of identifying savings. They did so by focusing the budget process on changes in strategic priorities, and relying heavily on line agencies to themselves identify savings options. The system seeks to achieve results by creating an environment in which strategic priorities are articulated at the political level, and managers are given considerable flexibility—through portfolio budgeting and the running-cost system—to achieve the intended outcomes. The system seeks to achieve accountability through reporting on performance and ex post evaluations, but there are no formal outcome- or output-based contracts.

Consequently, in Australia, tightly specified accountability mechanisms based on outputs, as in New Zealand, have been sacrificed in favor of a greater collective as well as individual focus on outcomes. This reflects a fundamentally different philosophical emphasis driving the two reform efforts, with Australia placing a greater faith on trust and consensual relationships and New Zealand instituting formal accountability mechanisms to resolve incentive incompatibility stemming from a principal-agent paradigm.

The weakness of the New Zealand system is that with everyone focused on outputs and technical efficiency, the link with outcomes has been overlooked until recently. The broad priorities (so-called SRAs and KRAs—see sec. 10.4) have only recently been implemented to forge a closer link with outcomes. The weakness of the Australian system rests in much looser systems of accountability. However, this is necessitated to some extent by a federal structure wherein a large percentage of services are delivered by state governments.

It is worth asking whether a country could not merely adopt the best of the two countries' systems—that is, a focus on strategic priorities as well as technical efficiency. In a world without transactions costs, one could well envisage a system where there is a focus on outcomes, which is then translated into corresponding outputs through formalized contracts. However, our comparative analysis of the Australian and New Zealand reforms indicates that this is easier said than done. Australia adopted a strategy that began with an emphasis primarily on improving strategic prioritization. Given the much greater importance of policymaking at the central government level induced by its federal structure, the benefits relative to the transactions costs of improving strategic prioritization were likely to be higher than the net benefits from improving technical efficiency. In New Zealand, initial reforms were indeed geared toward strategic prioritization, given the vastly overextended public sector: wholescale privatization of state enterprises and departments producing commercial outputs generated substantial early dividends. Having done this to the extent politically feasible, reforms then turned to improving the technical efficiency of remaining public agencies.

10.4 Recent Developments

Recent developments in both New Zealand and Australia suggest that the two reforms are converging toward some common paradigm. In particular, each is placing greater emphasis on the level of expenditure outcome that has hitherto not been sufficiently addressed.

Recently in New Zealand, there have been concerns that formal contracting has led to a massive volume of specification and reporting requirements and thus detracted from attention to strategic policymaking (Schick 1996). In response to this, New Zealand has initiated reforms to improve strategic planning and budgeting (Boston and Pallot 1997). In particular, a focused set of broad strategic outcomes—so-called strategic result areas (SRAs) and key result areas (KRAs)—were identified. Budgetary priorities as well as contracts of chief executives now more explicitly focus on SRAs and KRAs. As noted by Schick (1996, 86), "through the SRAs and KRAs, the medium (and longer) term perspective mandated by the Fiscal Responsibility Act, and increased planning, the strategic capacity of Government departments has been upgraded. What is most pleasing about this development is that it has been accomplished in ways that comport with the logic and practice of the New Zealand model. The SRAs and KRAs emphasize the ex ante specification of objectives, as do other elements of the New Zealand system, and the Fiscal Responsibility Act upholds the value of transparency in public policy." Inevitably, further work will need to be undertaken in refining outcome measures and instituting ex post evaluation systems.

In Australia, the thrust of the reform process was changed significantly in 1996 with the election of a Liberal government that believed in a more minimalist public sector than its predecessor. The new government required agencies to step up the search for activities that might be effectively performed within a purchaser-provider framework, while also according greater freedom to set their own terms and conditions of employment.

This more rapid transition to provision of public services by arm's-length contractors has created a difficult hurdle for a public sector hitherto driven by outcome (rather than output) reporting by its agencies. While the emphasis on program objectives and outcomes over the previous decade had focused agencies on how far their programs were furthering the government's objectives, it did little to assist the preparation of contracts with arm's-length service providers that clearly defined the "deliverables" expected by the government (such as cost, quantity, quality, and timeliness) in return for the funding provided to the contractor. The increased pace of contracting out has therefore triggered a new focus within the Department of Finance on supplementing outcome information with clearly defined measures of program outputs for which service providers can be held contractually responsible. This new focus on outputs is intended to augment rather than displace the long-standing focus on outcomes, and may be incorporated in the accrual budgeting framework (ensuring the proper costing of outputs) by 1999–2000. It remains to be seen whether the rediscovery of an output focus in a public sector that had long focused on outcome measures for its programs will result in a distinctively Australian style of purchaser-provider relationship that blends strengths from both perspectives.

10.5 Concluding Remarks

In this paper, we have developed a methodology for evaluating the quality of a public expenditure management system. Using theories developed within the field of the new institutional economics and the reform experiences of Australia and New Zealand with public expenditure management, we have been able to identify key institutional arrangements that affect aggregate fiscal discipline, strategic prioritization, and technical efficiency in the use of budgeted resources. We have argued that these arrangements can be effective only if there are mechanisms that bind public officials to these arrangements. By this we mean that public officials will incur a sufficiently high cost if they violate the arrangements. Within the limitations of our data, we have been able to show that certain mechanisms that enhance transparency and accountability can indeed introduce such costs and thus lead to better expenditure outcomes.

Our comparative analysis of the Australian and New Zealand reforms highlighted the importance of interactions and potential trade-offs among the three levels of expenditure outcomes. Our findings and framework have enabled us to analyze the impact of donor assistance on the three interrelated levels in aid-dependent countries.

While we have managed to capture the essence of the Australian and New Zealand reforms with our approach, we have still not reached the point at which we can recommend with confidence which elements of the reforms will work and which will not in a different context, for example, developing-country institutional environments. Indeed there have been some attempts in a developing-country context to push a New Zealand type of reform program without adequate attention to the replicability or adaptability of these reforms. As Levy and Spiller (1996) have shown within the context of the design of regulatory systems, the replicability problem is very complex and requires in-depth comparative analysis across countries of more fundamental underpinnings, and their mapping onto specific institutional arrangements. In the context of budgetary systems, the more fundamental underpinnings that will influence replicability include, for instance, administrative capacity, enforceability of the rule of law, and the relationship between the executive and the legislature.

Though this chapter attempts to develop a coherent framework for understanding a public expenditure management system, the set of issues involved are admittedly very complex. Our proposed methodology offers a first cut. Further research can fine-tune this methodology and in particular attempt to explore in further detail the transactions costs inherent in the trade-offs among the three levels of expenditure outcomes.

References

Alesina, Alberto, Ricardo Hausmann, Rudolf Hommes, and Ernesto Stein. 1996. Budget institutions and fiscal performance in Latin America. NBER Working Paper no. 5586. Cambridge, Mass.: National Bureau of Economic Research.

Boston, Jonathan, and June Pallot. 1997. Linking strategy and performance: Developments in the New Zealand public sector. *Journal of Policy Analysis and Management* 16:382–404.

Campos, Jose Edgardo, Hamid Davoodi, and Sanjay Pradhan. 1995. Aggregate fiscal discipline and the role of financial markets: Some preliminary evidence from developing countries. World Bank. Photocopy.

Campos, Jose Edgardo, and Hadi Esfahani. 1996. To initiate public enterprise reform or not: What drives the decision? *World Bank Economic Review,* September, 451–85.

Campos, Jose Edgardo, and Sanjay Pradhan. 1996. Budgetary institutions and public expenditure outcomes. Working Paper no. 1646. Policy Research Department, World Bank.

Campos, Jose Edgardo, and Hilton L. Root. 1996. *The key to the East Asian miracle: Making shared growth credible.* Washington, D.C.: Brookings Institution.

Dixon, Geoffrey. 1996. Budgetary institutions and expenditure outcomes in Australia. Background paper, Policy Research Department, World Bank.

Haggard, Stephan, and Robert Kaufman, eds. 1992. *The politics of economic adjustment.* Princeton: Princeton University Press.

Krehbiel, Keith. 1991. *Information and legislative organization.* Ann Arbor: University of Michigan Press.

Levy, Brian, and Pablo Spiller. 1996. Regulation, institutions, and commitment in telecommunications: A comparative analysis of five country studies. In *Regulations, institutions, and commitment: Comparative studies of telecommunications,* ed. Brian Levy and Pablo Spiller. Cambridge: Cambridge University Press.

McKelvey, Richard. 1976. Intransitivities in multidimensional voting models and some implications for agenda control. *Journal of Economic Theory* 12:472–82.

Schick, Allen. 1996. *The spirit of reform: Managing the New Zealand state sector in a time of change.* Report for the State Services Commission and the Treasury, New Zealand.

Scott, Graham, and Ian Ball. 1996. The influence of fiscal institutions on aggregate fiscal outcomes: Expenditure composition and the effectiveness of resource use in New Zealand. Background paper, Policy Research Department, World Bank.

Shepsle, Kenneth. 1979. Institutional arrangement and equilibrium in multidimensional voting models. *American Journal of Political Science* 23:27–60.

Shepsle, Kenneth, and Barry Weingast. 1994. Positive theories of congressional institutions. *Legislative Studies Quarterly* 19(2): 149–79.

Staniland, Martin. 1985. *What is political economy?* New Haven: Yale University Press.

United Nations. 1992. The control and management of government expenditure. Development Papers no. 13. Bangkok: U.N. Publications.

von Hagen, Jürgen. 1992. Budgeting procedures and fiscal performance in the European Communities. Economic Paper no. 96. Commission of the European Communities.

Weingast, Barry. 1979. A rational choice theory of congressional norms. *American Journal of Political Science* 23: 245–62.

Weingast, Barry, Kenneth Shepsle, and Christopher Johnsen. 1981. The political economy of benefits and costs: A rational choice approach to distributive politics. *Journal of Political Economy* 89:642–64.

World Bank. 1993. *The East Asian miracle: Economic growth and public policy.* New York: Oxford University Press.

11   Budgetary Procedures—Aspects and Changes: New Evidence for Some European Countries

Jakob de Haan, Wim Moessen, and Bjørn Volkerink

11.1   Introduction

Most industrialized countries entered the 1980s with their public finances in disarray. At the time, persistent deficits pushed up public-debt-to-GDP ratios. Still, some countries proved more successful than others in keeping their public finances under control. In recent literature it has been argued that this variation in cross-country fiscal experiences cannot be explained on purely economic grounds, or as a result of the timing of recessions, as implied by Barro's (1979) tax-smoothing theory. Variations in political and institutional arrangements that affect national policy formation might help explain cross-country differences in fiscal policies pursued. This line of research has emphasized political instability, government structure, and electoral systems as potential determinants of budget deficits (see Alesina and Perotti 1995b for a review). For instance, Roubini and Sachs (1989a,b) have argued that the type of government in power is very important in explaining debt policies in OECD countries. These authors found that large coalition governments had higher deficits, other things being equal, than one-party, majoritarian governments. However, subsequent research found less support for this so-called weak-government hypothesis. Edin and Ohlsson (1991) argue, for instance, that the political cohesion variable used by Roubini and Sachs captures the effects of minority governments rather than majority coalition governments. De Haan and Sturm (1994,

Jakob de Haan is the Jean Monnet Professor of Economics at the University of Groningen, The Netherlands. Wim Moessen is professor of economics at the Center for Economic Studies, Catholic University of Leuven, Belgium. Bjørn Volkerink is a Ph.D. candidate in the Department of Economics at the University of Groningen, The Netherlands.

The authors thank the following persons for their assistance: Brian Finn, Francesco Lippi, Per Molander, Roberto Perotti, Giancarlo Salvemini. Thanks are also due Kim Rueben, Jürgen von Hagen, James Poterba, and other conference participants for their comments on a previous version of the paper.

1997) found support for neither the Roubini-Sachs hypothesis nor the position expressed by Edin-Ohlsson. Borrelli and Royed (1995) also dismiss the weak-government hypothesis. However, Alesina and Perotti (1995a) conclude that coalition governments are less successful in adjusting public finances than one-party governments.

Another institutional factor that has been pointed out as a potential determinant of cross-country variation in fiscal policy is budget institutions, that is, the procedures that lead to the formulation, approval, and implementation of the budget (Alesina et al. 1996). Various authors have analyzed the importance of budget rules and institutions on the basis of U.S. state experience with balanced-budget rules and on the U.S. federal experience with antideficit rules (see Poterba 1996 for a review). There are also various studies that compare budget outcomes in nations with different fiscal institutions. It is quite remarkable that the international studies conclude that budget institutions are important. The two aspects that have received most attention in this line of research are the degree of centralization or authority in the budget process, and the degree of budget transparency (Poterba 1996).

On the basis of a survey under the member states of the European Union, von Hagen (1992) has developed two sets of indicators for the strength of budgetary procedures in these countries. The so-called structural indices pertain to testing the hypothesis that fiscal discipline is enhanced by budget procedures in which the prime minister or the minister of finance has a strong position; in which universalism, reciprocity, and parliamentary amendments are limited; and that facilitate strict execution of the budget law. The so-called long-term planning constraint indices pertain to testing the hypothesis that the more budgetary decisions are tied to a multiperiod fiscal program, the greater will be the degree of fiscal stability achieved. On the basis of simple bivariate regressions von Hagen reports strong support for the structural hypothesis, but the role of long-term constraints is not found to be significant. Von Hagen and Harden (1994) also use these indices to evaluate the link between budget processes and sustainability of fiscal policy. They report a significant correlation between their sustainability measures and the structural index. Similarly, the long-term constraint index is positively correlated with the sustainability measure with a six-year time horizon; for the eight-year horizon this is true only if Luxembourg is left out.

As pointed out by Poterba (1996), international research is more likely to be affected by omitted variables that are correlated with both budget institutions and fiscal priorities than cross-state analysis. There is, however, also evidence that even if other variables are included, budgetary institutions still exert a significant influence on fiscal policy outcomes. De Haan and Sturm (1994) have used an index based on all the information that von Hagen provided in a similar model as employed by Roubini and Sachs (1989b) and find that it still has a significant effect on fiscal outcomes in the (at the time 12) EU member countries. However, the importance of budgetary institutions is much less than suggested by simple bivariate regressions.

In a similar vein, Alesina et al. (1996) conclude that centralized and transparent procedures have been associated with more fiscal discipline in Latin America in the eighties and early nineties. Centralized procedures are those that, for example, limit the role of the legislature and attribute a strong role to the Treasury minister in the budget process.

There is one potential problem with this literature (Poterba 1996). Budget institutions may be endogenous, that is, to use them as an explanatory variable it is necessary that the institutions cannot be changed easily as a result of current or past fiscal outcomes. Riker (1980) argues that political institutions reflect the "congealed preferences" of the electorate. In other words, institutions that do not suit a majority of the electorate will be overturned. Still, one could argue that changing budget institutions is not that easy and there are costs involved with revising fiscal rules (Alesina and Perotti, chap. 1 in this volume). There are various ways to deal with the endogeneity problem (Poterba 1996). The first one is to control for some measure of voter preferences. De Haan and Sturm (1994) include a proxy for the political color of the government in their regressions and find that budgetary procedures are still relevant in explaining fiscal policy. A second approach involves analyzing the evolution of budget rules and examining the causes and impact of procedural changes. This is the approach pursued in the present paper.

Another unresolved issue is the question of which features of budget institutions are the most important in influencing fiscal policy (Poterba 1996). The indicators of von Hagen (1992) and of Alesina et al. (1996) broadly focus on similar aspects. Alesina et al. (1996) conclude for their sample of Latin American countries that the two components not significantly related to fiscal performance are those referring to transparency and, in particular, the role of the minister of finance. In the present paper we follow a similar approach, using the information provided by von Hagen–Harden for the EU member states.[1]

The remainder of the paper is organized as follows. The next section outlines our methodology. The third section presents an analysis of aspects of budgetary procedures in EU member states. In the fourth section the experience of some countries (Belgium, Ireland, Italy, and Sweden) is analyzed in detail. These countries show very diverging developments in their public-debt-to-GDP ratio.

---

1. Von Hagen (1992) distinguishes between two groups of (overlapping) indices, namely the so-called structural indices (focusing on the position of the minister of finance, the presence of constraints, the role of parliament in the budget process, the transparency of the budget, and the flexibility in the execution phase) and the so-called long-term constraint indices (focusing on multiannual fiscal programs, the informativeness of the budget, the amendment powers of parliament, and the flexibility in the execution phase). Von Hagen and Harden (1996) present both additive and multiplicative versions of their index of "centralization" of the budget process. The two methods of aggregation lead to very similar results, suggesting that lack of similar degrees of centralization holds at different stages of the same process.

On the basis of a case study approach, we examine whether (and why) budgetary institutions have changed and whether this has affected fiscal policy outcomes. The final section offers some concluding comments.

11.2 Methodology

The focus of this paper is on changes in and aspects of budgetary procedures. To analyze which aspects of budgetary procedures are the most important ones, we follow an approach similar to Alesina et al. (1996), using information provided by von Hagen (1992) and von Hagen and Harden (1996) and distinguishing between the following aspects of the budgetary process (in parentheses the corresponding items of von Hagen are shown):

*A*1. Position of minister of finance (items 1b, 1d, 4a, 4c)[2]
*A*2. Position of legislature (items 2a–e)[3]
*A*3. Presence of some kind of constraints (items 1a, 5d)[4]
*A*4. Transparency of the budget (items 3a–e)[5]
*A*5. Flexibility during execution of the budget (items 4b, d, e, f)[6]
*A*6. Relationship with other parts of government

It has been argued by various authors that a minister of finance (MF)—in contrast to spending ministers—does not strive for a large budget but is more constrained by considerations of general welfare. Consequently, a strong position of the MF—both in the preparatory and execution phase of the budget— may enhance budget discipline.[7] The position of the legislature may also be important. It is generally assumed that if parliament has much power to change the proposed budget, it is likely that budget deficits will be higher than proposed by the government. The presence of various kinds of binding constraints (varying from constraints in the constitution or the law to political agreements) may foster budget discipline. The transparency of the budget may also be im-

2. These items refer to the position of the minister of finance (MF) in agenda setting, the structure of the negotiations, whether MF can block expenditures during execution phase, and whether disbursements require approval of MF.
3. These items refer to room for amendments, whether they have to be offsetting, whether they can cause the fall of government, whether all expenditures are passed in one vote, and whether there is a global vote on total budget size.
4. These items refer to presence of general constraints and the degree of political commitment to a long-term planning constraint.
5. These items refer to whether special funds are included, whether budget is submitted in one document, assessment of transparency by respondents, link to national accounts, and whether loans to nongovernment entities are included.
6. These items refer to presence of cash limits, transfers between chapters, changes in budget law during execution, carryover of unused funds to the next year. We have corrected the codings of item 4f of von Hagen 1992 in our research, as they do not correspond to the possible scorings in the explanation of the contents of the table on p. 72 of von Hagen 1992. A score on item 4f of 1 should be 1.33, 2 should be 2.66 and 3 should be 4.
7. Von Hagen distinguishes between both phases of the budgetary process, but here we follow Alesina et al. (1996), who also focus on the position on the MF in the entire budget process.

portant: the more transparent the budget, the more difficult it will be to use budgetary tricks to increase expenditures. As Alesina and Perotti (chap. 1 in this volume) put it: "at least up to a point, the less the electorate knows and understands about the budget process, the more the politicians can act strategically and use fiscal deficits and overspending to achieve opportunistic goals." A fifth item is the execution of the budget. How binding the budget law is for government depends, inter alia, on the possibility of proposing supplementary budgets and the relative importance of open-ended appropriations in the budget. The final issue that we distinguish is the relationship between central government and other levels of government. Although von Hagen (1992) provides some information on this issue, he does not take it into account in constructing his budget indicators. Still, this issue may be important since the degree of fiscal decentralization is often found to influence fiscal policy outcomes. One reason may be that local governments generally face a harder budget constraint than the federal or national government (Moessen and Van Cauwenberge 1997). Our sixth variable is the score on two items: whether other levels of government face some kind of balanced-budget requirement, and the degree of planning autonomy of regional authorities.[8] All variables that we use are normalized on a scale ranging between 0 and 4.[9] The variable A_{tot} is the sum of variables $A1$ to $A6$.

To analyze whether an aspect of budgetary procedures has changed since the beginning of the 1990s in the four countries that we focus on, we have sent out a survey with questions on the aspects outlined above. The survey is added as appendix A. The survey was sent to the ministry of finance or, in case we did not get a response, to experts at the national central bank. The answers were subsequently checked by experts from outside government. In case of diverging answers we went back to the original respondents to clear these issues. By following this procedure, we are quite certain that our surveys give an adequate representation of the current budgetary process in Belgium, Ireland, Italy, and Sweden.

This approach may yield insights with respect to changes in the budgetary process. Indeed, in the case of Sweden we can clearly identify which aspects of the budgetary process have changed recently. Although it may be necessary to discover what—if anything—has changed in the budgetary process, simply conducting another survey is not without problems. First, the questions that we have asked were not exactly the same questions as von Hagen posed. From a much wider set of questions he included those items where the answers varied

---

8. The information is taken from table A1 in von Hagen 1992. If local governments have no planning autonomy, the second variable is 4; if they have limited autonomy, it is 2.66; if they may be placed under surveillance, it is 1.33, and in case of autonomy it is 0. The first variable measures whether a binding balanced-budget constraint exists: 4 for a binding requirement; 2.66 for the golden rule; 1.33 for not binding; and 0 if there is no requirement.

9. The total score is divided by the number of issues taken into account to construct the variable concerned.

the most across countries. Still, the purpose of our survey is to analyze whether changes in the selected items have occurred, and for that purpose our approach is valid.

Second, the person who answered our questions is in most cases not the same as von Hagen's respondent, and this may yield different answers due to the subjective nature of at least some of the questions. The only exception here is Sweden, where the budget process was evaluated in 1992 on the basis of items as published in von Hagen 1992; after a number of reforms the process was evaluated again (Swedish Ministry of Finance 1995). As the issues raised were exactly the same in both evaluations, the first potential problem also is unlikely to have affected the outcomes for Sweden.

Third, the overall attitude with respect to the importance of sound budgetary procedures—and, more generally, sound fiscal policies—may have changed since von Hagen conducted his survey, and this may affect our survey. Although the purpose of our survey is to find out whether any changes have occurred in those aspects of the budgetary process that we have distinguished in the four countries that we focus on, we have sent out the questionnaire to all EU countries,[10] as this allows us to discover whether any systematic pattern is present. If, for example, the overall score in all countries were higher, this could indicate that increased awareness may have affected our results. Table 11.1 shows the total scores (the sum of A1 to A6) based on the results as reported by von Hagen (1992) and the results of our survey. It follows that indeed in all countries included in von Hagen's (1992) study and in our survey the scores in our survey are higher. Still, the most remarkable increases occur in the budgetary procedures of the countries that we analyze in more detail in section 11.4.

Apart from the factors pointed out above, there are two other possible explanations for any differences between the results of our survey and that of von Hagen. First, interpretations of existing rules in the budget process may have become stricter. We would definitely consider this a change in budgetary institutions, similar to a change in the formal rules. Second, the coding as reported in von Hagen 1992 may have suffered from incomplete information. It is simply impossible for any researcher in comparative analysis to check for all countries whether the answers given are accurate. For those countries that an author is most familiar with, this an easier task. Indeed, for the case of the Netherlands, for example, we have some doubts about certain codings given by von Hagen. For instance, for item 1b (presence of some general constraint) the score of von Hagen indicates that the level of government debt acted as some kind of constraint in Dutch budgetary procedures. However, at the beginning of the 1990s the norms of fiscal policy in the Netherlands related to the budget deficit and the level of taxes and social security payments as share of national

10. Including the new EU member states (Austria, Finland, and Sweden), as this may provide useful new information.

Table 11.1   **Indicators of Budgetary Institutions Based on von Hagen and New Survey**

	Original	Survey
Austria		12.56
Belgium	7.18	15.23
Denmark	15.08	16.61
Finland		13.18
France	20.23	
Germany	15.26	16.41
Greece	9.88	
Ireland	8.35	16.78
Italy	7.03	11.09
Luxembourg	13.06	
Netherlands	14.38	15.11
Portugal	8.38	12.26
Spain	6.33	13.55
Sweden		5.78[a]
United Kingdom	17.24	15.88

Note: The table presents the scores of A_{tot} as constructed on the basis of information provided in von Hagen 1992 and von Hagen and Harden 1996 and on the basis of a new survey.
[a]As of 1999, score is 15.50.

income (see de Haan, Sterks, and de Kam 1992), which is not one of the options given by von Hagen. This brings us to another issue. Sometimes our respondents indicated that the possible answers—which were all taken from von Hagen (1992) for comparison purposes—were not sufficient.[11] For instance, in Ireland parliament has no ability to amend government "estimates"—only to accept or reject them (see appendix B for details). In those cases we took the score for the answer that was closest to the answer actually given.

After this discussion of our methodology we now turn to our results concerning the importance of the distinguished aspects of budgetary institutions.

11.3   Aspects of Budgetary Institutions

Table 11.2 presents a summary of the variables we distinguished in the previous section. The variables are based only on the information provided by von Hagen (1992) (and von Hagen and Harden 1996 for Luxembourg). The data relate to the situation at the beginning of the 1990s. The variable A_{tot} is the sum of all variables ($A1$–$A6$). It is quite remarkable that the scores for the various aspects of the budgetary process show considerable variation across countries.

Table 11.3 shows a simple correlation matrix of the data presented in table 11.2. The variable d(debt) is the change in the debt-to-GDP ratio over the pe-

---

11. We included a question concerning the adequacy of the options given for all clusters of questions (see appendix A).

Table 11.2   Aspects of Budgetary Institutions at the Beginning of the 1990s

	Variable						
	$A1$	$A2$	$A3$	$A4$	$A5$	$A6$	A_{tot}
Belgium	1.25	0.80	0.00	2.00	1.80	1.33	7.18
Denmark	1.75	2.40	3.00	2.67	2.60	2.67	15.08
France	4.00	3.60	2.50	3.66	3.13	3.33	20.23
Germany	3.25	0.80	3.00	3.40	2.82	2.00	15.26
Greece	1.25	0.00	1.00	2.07	2.90	2.67	9.88
Ireland	0.25	1.60	2.50	1.00	3.00	0.00	8.35
Italy	0.75	1.20	2.50	1.00	0.25	1.33	7.03
Luxembourg	2.50	2.00	1.50	3.73	2.67	0.67	13.06
Netherlands	2.75	3.20	2.50	3.60	0.33	2.00	14.38
Portugal	2.50	0.25	1.50	1.47	2.67	0.00	8.38
Spain	0.50	0.80	0.50	3.00	1.53	0.00	6.33
United Kingdom	1.75	3.20	3.50	3.20	2.93	2.66	17.24

Source: own calculations based on information provided by von Hagen (1992) and von Hagen and Harden (1996).
Note: The possible score of all aspects as distinguished in section 11.2 ($A1$–$A6$) ranges between 0 and 4. A_{tot} is the sum of $A1$–$A6$. Differences are possible due to rounding.

Table 11.3   Correlation Matrix

	$A1$	$A2$	$A3$	$A4$	$A5$	$A6$	A_{tot}
$A2$	0.43						
$A3$	0.33	0.61					
$A4$	0.67	0.56	0.19				
$A5$	0.25	−0.00	0.14	0.13			
$A6$	0.49	0.51	0.45	0.44	0.18		
A_{tot}	0.77	0.77	0.67	0.73	0.39	0.76	
d(debt)	−0.50	−0.54	−0.45	−0.58	−0.36	0.05	−0.57

riod 1980–92. It follows that the correlation between the various aspects of the budgetary process that we have distinguished is sometimes quite low. It is, for instance, quite remarkable that the presence of some binding constraint ($A3$) is hardly related to the flexibility in the execution process ($A5$). The correlation between the position of the legislature ($A2$) and $A5$ is even less. It also follows that the total index and the transparency of the budget ($A4$) show the highest correlation with the change in the general government debt-to-GDP ratio over the period under consideration.

The remainder of this section reports the outcomes of a model similar to the one used by Roubini and Sachs (1989b) to analyze which aspects of budgetary institutions affect fiscal policy outcomes most strongly. As Roubini and Sachs have pointed out, the specification of this model is consistent both with elements of optimizing approaches to budget deficits (such as the tax-smoothing model of Barro 1979) and with traditional Keynesian models of fiscal deficits.

Indeed, both theories imply that budget deficits are countercyclical. Variants of this model have also been used in subsequent research (de Haan and Sturm 1994; Hallerberg and von Hagen, chap. 9 in this volume). The model is estimated using panel data for 12 EU member countries over the period 1980–92. Suppressing time indices, the estimated equation is

(1) $DBY = a_0 + a_1 DBYL + a_2 DU + a_3 GR + a_4 DRB + a_5 A + v$,

where the dependent variable (DBY) denotes the change in the public-debt-to-GDP ratio. The explanatory variables are the lagged change in the debt ratio (DBYL), the change in the unemployment rate (DU), the GDP growth rate (GR), the change in debt-servicing costs (DRB),[12] and some indicator for the budgetary process (A); v denotes the error term.

The results using A_{tot} as an indicator for the strength of budgetary procedures are for the coefficients of a_0 to a_5, respectively (t-statistics are shown in parentheses): .03 (3.47), .32 (4.89), .43 (1.51), −.46 (−2.89), 2.65 (6.46), and −.001 (−1.82). The indicator is significant at the 10 percent level, but the coefficient is not very large. All other variables (except the coefficient on the change in unemployment rate) are significant at the 5 percent level. These findings are in line with the results reported in de Haan and Sturm (1994). Budgetary institutions matter, but the effect on fiscal outcomes is quite small.

Next, we have examined whether all aspects of the budgetary process as we have distinguished them in section 11.2 are equally important. The first step is to calculate the F-statistic for the test that all coefficients are the same if all indicators are included in the regression for gross government debt growth. This statistic is .57, which implies that the hypothesis cannot be rejected. Next, we have repeated the regression, each time subtracting one of the aspects that we have distinguished from A_{tot}.[13] If the results are different in comparison with the regression reported above, this would be an indication of the importance of the excluded aspect of the budgetary process. The results are shown in the upper part of table 11.4. As the coefficients of the other included variables are similar to those reported above, we only report the coefficients for the budgetary variables. It follows that the coefficients and their significance levels are very similar, suggesting that all aspects of the budgetary process that we have distinguished are more or less equally important. Similar results are found if we use the various budgetary indicators (A1–A6) as explanatory variables in equation (1) instead of A_{tot} (not shown). However, it is possible that differences

12. We have used two variants for this variable. First, actual interest payments as share of GDP. Second, a similar variable as used by Roubini and Sachs, namely: $d(i - p - n)BY_{t-1}$, where i denotes interest payments on government debt divided by government debt, p is the rate of inflation, and n is the GDP growth rate. Whenever the real interest rate exceeds the rate of real output growth—as was the case in many countries during the 1980s—the outstanding debt imposes a burden on the public finances. If this rising debt burden is transitory, it should be accommodated by a temporary rise in the budget deficit, as argued by Roubini and Sachs. Both variables yielded similar results. The results shown are those using actual interest payments. All data are from the OECD and the European Commission.

13. Von Hagen (1992) followed a similar approach.

Table 11.4   **Estimates of Equation (1) (budgetary variables only), 12 EU Member Countries, 1980–92**

	Variable					
	$A_{tot}-A1$	$A_{tot}-A2$	$A_{tot}-A3$	$A_{tot}-A4$	$A_{tot}-A5$	$A_{tot}-A6$
Coefficient	−0.001	−0.001	−0.001	−0.001	−0.001	−0.002
(*t*-statistic)	(−1.72)*	(−1.81)*	(−1.72)*	(−1.76)*	(−1.59)	(−2.10)**
	Variable					
	A1	A2	A3	A4	A5	A6
Budgetary	−0.003	0.002	0.001	−0.001	0.000	0.003
variable	(−0.99)	(0.58)	(0.27)	(−0.42)	(0.02)	(1.14)
Interaction	−0.001	−0.187	−0.174	−0.081	−0.163	−0.136
variable	(−0.01)	(−2.38)**	(−2.57)**	(−1.37)	(−2.78)**	(−1.48)

Note: The upper part of the table presents estimates of a_5 in equation (1) with various budgetary indicators. These consist of the scores of A_{tot} minus the scores of the various aspects of budgetary procedures as distinguished in section 11.2 (A1 to A6). The lower part of the table presents estimates of equation (1) in which A1 to A6 are used as budgetary indicators. The interaction variable consists of the interaction of GDP growth and the budgetary indicators. *T*-statistics are shown in parentheses.
*Significant at the 10 percent level.
**Significant at the 5 percent level.

in budgetary institutions are more strongly felt during economic downturns. We have therefore reestimated the model, adding each time an interaction variable that consists of the product of the GDP growth rate and the budgetary institution variable. Multicollinearity problems forced us not to include the GDP growth rate as a separate variable. The coefficients of the interaction variables are shown in lower part of table 11.4. The results suggest that the position of the legislature, the presence of binding constraints, and flexibility during the execution of the budget matter most. Our findings are not entirely in line with those of Alesina et al. (1996), who found that the position of the minister of finance and the transparency of the budget showed the lowest correlation with budgetary outcomes in their sample of Latin American countries. They argue, however, that this is probably due to the difficulty of measuring these aspects in their sample.

11.4   Evolution of Budgetary Institutions: Evidence for Some European Countries

11.4.1   Introduction

Figure 11.1 shows the public-gross-debt-to-GDP ratio in Belgium, Ireland, Italy, and Sweden over the period 1979–95. It follows that the debt ratio in these countries has developed quite differently over the period under consideration. In Ireland the upward trend has been reversed. In contrast, in Italy the debt ratio was on the rise until 1994; since then some stabilization has set in. In Belgium the debt ratio has been more or less stabilized since 1987, although

Fig. 11.1   Gross government debt (% GDP), 1979–95
Source: OECD.

Table 11.5   Changes in Codings of Aspects of Budgetary Procedures

Aspect	Belgium		Ireland		Italy		Sweden	
	Old	New	Old	New	Old	New	Old	New
Position of minister of finance (A1)	1.25	3.25	0.25	3.25	0.75	0.75	1.00	1.75
Position of legislature (A2)	0.80	1.60	1.60	3.00	1.20	2.80	1.60	3.20
Constraints (A3)	0.00	3.00	2.50	3.00	2.50	2.50	0.50	4.00
Transparency (A4)	2.00	3.13	1.00	1.53	1.00	0.80	1.00	3.20
Flexibility during execution (A5)	1.80	2.92	3.00	2.67	0.25	1.58	1.68	2.02
Relationship with other parts of government (A6)	1.33	1.33	0.00	3.33	1.33	2.66	0.00	1.33[a]
Total	7.18	15.23	8.35	16.78	7.03	11.09	5.78	15.50[a]

[a]From 1999 onward.

the debt ratio is still very high. In Sweden the debt ratio increased until 1994, but has been stabilized since.

In this section we analyze whether budgetary procedures in the four countries under consideration have changed recently, and if so, why these changes occurred and what their consequences were in terms of policy outcomes. An important input in this process are the results of our survey. Appendix B contains the detailed results of our survey. Table 11.5 summarizes our main findings as reported in appendix B. The table presents the situation at the beginning of the 1990s, mostly based on von Hagen 1992 and the outcomes of our survey. There are notable differences. As described in section 11.2, however, the simple fact that we find other scores for our budgetary variables may not necessarily be caused by actual changes in budgetary institutions (except probably for Sweden). Therefore, the information from our survey is supplemented by information from various other sources to enable us to evaluate developments in the budgetary process in the countries under consideration. We start all country studies with an outline of the budget cycle.

11.4.2 Belgium

In 1989 a major institutional change occurred in Belgium as a new budgetary law (June 28, 1989) was enacted, modifying substantially the previous budgetary law of 1963. Two concerns were explicitly articulated: (i) the presentation of the budget in terms of programs, and (ii) a stricter timing for the parliamentary approval of the submitted budget. In addition some minor modifications were implemented.

Before 1989 the principle of "speciality" was interpreted rather rigorously in the sense that the Belgian budget easily encompassed some 2,400 line items. As usual, these line items were input oriented (e.g., wages, operating costs), and quite often they represented minuscule amounts of money. This required a drastic reduction in the number of budget items. At present the budget covers some 500 items that focus on programs. For each program the total cost is stated together with a program description and a tentatively quantified program output. The further breakdown of the program appropriation into the detailed cost elements is also communicated to the parliament, but no longer requires a formal vote. Moreover, within the same program (and below some precise legal ceilings) the spending minister is entitled to reshuffle the cost items during the execution of the budget. This modification significantly increases the managerial autonomy of the spending minister within the approved budget program and the prespecified rules.

The tardy vote of the budget constituted another major drawback of the previous budgetary procedure. Although the budgetary documents were to be submitted before the end of September, the parliament rarely succeeded in approving the budget before the end of December. Quite often one had to have recourse to the escape route of "provisional twelfths." This means that each month a routine paragraph is approved that allows each spending minister to operate as a going concern, limiting the outlays to one-twelfth of the last budget law. No new activities may be undertaken. This procedure was repeated for several months in a row, quite often until March. The new law drives the formal vote forward to the end of November instead of December (see table 11.6).

When interpreting the codings in appendix B one should also keep in mind that two other events have shaped the budgetary behavior in Belgium. First,

Table 11.6   Budgetary Cycle in Belgium

	Main Events and Activities
FY $t - 1$	
February–March	Minister of the budget and minister of finance send their colleagues a circular setting out guidelines for drawing up budget proposals for the following fiscal year. The instructions have already been approved by the Council of Ministers.
March	On the basis of the guidelines in the budget circular, all the ministers draw up, with the help of their officials, a budget estimate for their department, based on unchanged policies. The appropriations required for any new initiatives must figure separately in the budget estimate. The proposals are sent for his or her advice to the inspector of finance accredited to the department.
April	The budget estimates are then reviewed in bilateral meetings (between each spending department and the Budget Department).
June	When all departmental budget estimates have been bilaterally reviewed, the minister of the budget presents a report on the outcome to the Council of Ministers at the end of June. The minister of finance does the same for the Ways and Means budget estimate.
June–July	Early July marks the beginning of a series of meetings held by the ministerial Select Committee headed by the prime minister.
Early August	Once the budget proposals have been reviewed by the Select Committee, they are submitted to the Council of Ministers for decision in late July–early August.
Late September	Submission to parliament.
Late November	Formal vote in parliament.
FY t	
January 1	Start of fiscal year t.

Source: OECD (1995).

there was a constitutional reform in 1988–89 that transformed Belgium from a unitary to a federal state. In one stroke about one-third of the central government spending was transferred to the regional level. This expenditure shift is highly concentrated on the areas of education, cultural and recreational affairs, public health and welfare services to individuals, transportation, environment, and economic matters. Shared taxes constitute the major financing source for the regional level. More than 90 percent of the tax proceeds originate from a joint personal income tax and VAT. Exclusive taxes are deliberately downsized to a limited scope (such as the inheritance tax, the tax on games and bets) in order to minimize local distortions or an overexploitation of the tax bases. At the same time, it is believed that fiscal federalism can exert some disciplinary force. The golden rule applies de facto for the regional level, which has limited access to public borrowing and no opportunity for seignorage collection. As opposed to the central government, the regional level is confronted with a harder budget constraint. In a federalist setting more government decisions are taken under a hard budget constraint than in a unitary state.

Second, the prescriptions of the Maastricht Treaty (1992) have also reshaped budgetary attitudes. Belgium has committed itself to a first entrance into the EMU. The ambition to reduce the general government budget deficit from 7.2 percent of GDP to 3 percent in five years requires a sustained austerity, which in turn places fiscal discipline high on the political agenda and also emphasizes the relative weight of the minister of finance.

Comparing the old and the new scores of the various indicators that we have distinguished (table 11.5), it follows that the most notable differences for Belgium occur with respect to the position of the MF ($A1$) and the presence of constraints ($A3$). As the Maastricht fiscal targets became more important, the position of the minister of the budget together with the MF became stronger. For instance, in 1992 the minister of the budget got the title of vice prime minister. Still, part of the differences in comparison with the codings of von Hagen may be due to different evaluations of budgetary practices. For instance, according to von Hagen the MF cannot block expenditures. Strictly speaking this is correct. However, the minister of the budget can block expenditures upon instigation of the accredited inspector of finance. As the MF teams with the minister of the budget, we agree with our respondent that the maximum score is therefore more appropriate (see appendix B for further details).

As explained above, from 1992 on the guidelines of Maastricht have oriented, some would say dictated, fiscal policy in Belgium, which is devoted to a first entrance into EMU. Each year, a numerical time-path is specified for the next year and the following years until the start-up of the EMU. This results in a strong political commitment to the deficit and debt targets, in contrast to the past.

The score on $A4$ (transparency) is also higher in our survey. Here at least part of the differences with respect to the results of von Hagen is due to subjective interpretations. For instance, although the budget consists of one document (unity of budget presentation), it materializes in three "books" to make the volumes manageable. This has been the practice for some time now. Our respondent therefore answered that the document consists of one document, while the score of von Hagen implied that this was only the case recently. Another major difference under this heading is the link to the National Accounts, which—in contrast to von Hagen's information—is provided, albeit in a different document; this practice has not changed recently.

11.4.3   Ireland

As follows from the outline of the budgetary cycle shown in table 11.7 the MF takes the lead in the budgetary process in Ireland. In recent years, the practice has been to specify medium-term fiscal objectives. Since 1980 there has been broad political consensus that restoration of fiscal balance is essential for promoting economic growth. To this end, various specific quantitative targets have been used. Recent practice has been to specify specific medium-term fiscal objectives, particularly in relation to the deficit and public debt ratios, as

Table 11.7   Budgetary Cycle in Ireland

	Main Events and Activities
Year t − 1	
February	MF issues circular requesting departments to submit expenditure projections on no-policy-change (NPC) scenario.
March–April	After departments have submitted their three-year NPC projections, negotiations take place between DF and departments.
May–June	Taking NPC projections into account, government decides on targets for budgetary aggregates like general government deficit.
June	MF issues circular to spending departments, which inter alia explain the parameters with which the budget will operate and which seek appropriate adjustments to existing spending plans.
July–September	Departments submit draft expenditure estimates to DF for examination. Subsequently, MF briefs government on remaining areas of dispute. Government decides on detailed expenditure allocations.
October–November	Abridged version of "Estimates for Public Services" is published.
December–January	MF formulates proposals for annual budget statement that is presented to Dáil toward end of January. White Paper on Receipts and Expenditures is published.
Year t	
March	Revised estimates are published, together with public capital program.
April–May	Enactment of Finance Bill. This gives legislative effect to the tax changes proposed in the budget statement.
June–July	Dáil votes on individual spending estimates by way of financial resolutions.
June–December	If necessary, supplementary estimates are submitted for approval by the Dáil.
December	Appropriation Bill is passed.

Source: Public Financial Procedures, June 1996.
Note: With effect from budget year 1998, the budget date will be brought forward from January to October, which will mean presenting the 1998 budget in late October 1997.

Ireland is clearly committed to becoming a member of EMU. Indeed in the policy agreement *A Government of Renewal* between Fine Gael, the Labor Party, and Democratic Left of December 1994, it was stated, "This Government is committed to a firm management of the public finances throughout its period in office. In particular, we accept the public debt philosophy and targets set out in the Maastricht Treaty . . . to adhere strictly to an annual General Government Deficit of no more than 3% of GDP . . . and to reduce the Debt/ GDP ratio towards 60%."

The annual Estimates Circular seeks expenditure demands that comply with these medium-term objectives. Spending departments, in submitting their annual demands for resources, must now provide details of forecast resource requirements for three years ahead. Their demands are then assessed for consistency with the Estimates Circular specifications in a consultative process that clarifies the basis for the bids and focuses on the elimination of excess demand. Despite that process, the aggregate demand typically exceeds the allocation for departmental spending that would be consistent with the target for the overall deficit. The next stage is, therefore, for the MF to undertake a series of *bilateral* meetings with each of his or her colleagues to establish priorities for the allocation of the available resources. The Department of Finance (DF) again aggregates the outcome of these negotiations into a total provision for all departmental spending and presents it to government in an overall budget context. If the outlook remains unsatisfactory, the government will instigate a further round of bilateral meetings to secure further reductions. Finalization of the budget also requires cabinet decisions on specific taxation changes and final adjustments to spending plans.

Recently, the budgetary process was strengthened, as in the 1996 budget a full system of multiannual budgeting was announced. This approach involves three-year benchmark projections for the budgetary aggregates. In setting the budget targets and making budget decisions in year n, the impact of those decisions on the budget positions for years $n + 1$ and $n + 2$ is considered. In year n the budget projections for years $n + 1$ and $n + 2$ on the basis of continuation of policies as pursued in year n are published. So, the 1997 budget contained projections for the main economic and budgetary aggregates for 1998 and 1999, as well 1997. In making these projections, it was also considered prudent to include a contingency provision for unforeseen factors that could have an impact on the budgetary aggregates in the medium term.

In 1996 cash-limited spending programs were introduced after a joint report by the Department of Finance/Comptroller and auditor general. "Cash-limited" means that entitlement to payment in a specific year will be contingent on the availability of funds.

Comparing the old and the new scores of the various indicators that we have distinguished (table 11.5) it follows that the most notable differences for Ireland occur with respect to the position of the MF (*A*1) and the relationship with local governments (*A*6). Our respondent did not indicate that the formal rules concerning the position of the MF have changed. The most notable differences with respect to the codings of von Hagen relate to the position of the MF in the execution phase, as our respondent indicated that the MF can block expenditures and that his or her approval is required for disbursement. Indeed, the expenses of government departments are paid out of moneys provided by the Oireachtas (Irish parliament) to such an amount as sanctioned by the MF under section 2(4) of the Minister and Secretaries Act, 1924, and confirmed by section 3(3) of the Controller and Auditor General Act, 1993. The difference with respect to the codings of von Hagen may therefore reflect the formal rule versus actual practice.

A new system of financing local government has been introduced with effect from budget year 1997. The new system involves the abolition of charges of domestic consumers for water and sewerage services. The revenue loss will be replaced by the assignment of motor tax revenue currently paid directly to central government. In general, local governments have limited autonomy and face, according to our information, a balanced-budget requirement.

11.4.4   Italy

The main features of the budgetary process in Italy are shown in table 11.8. The process is extremely complicated. At the budget formulation stage, three ministries—the Treasury, budget, and finance—are involved. The central role in budgetary matters is played by a department within the Treasury, Ragioneria Generale dello Stato (RGS). The responsibility for economic and fiscal policymaking is shared between the Ministry of Finance and the Economic Planning Ministry: the first has the lead in fiscal revenue policies (taxes and other revenues), the second in macroeconomic forecasting (OECD 1995). The process generates several budget documents, which differ in terms of accounting basis, sectoral coverage, and date of issuance. In May the Documento di Programmazione Economica e Finanziaria (DPEF) is presented, which contains two sets of projections for the next three years: trend projections based on existing legislation and a program projection. The DPEF has a heavy emphasis on planning, and often fails to keep a clear distinction between trends and plans (Alesina et al. 1995). The DPEF quantifies deficit targets, but does not specify measures to reach them (OECD 1997). In July budgetary projections under current legislation *(bilancio a legislazione vigente),* which refer to the state only, are presented to parliament.

At the beginning of 1997 a budget reform was approved that has led to some changes. The main change is that the parliament is no longer going to approve a budget in which expenditure is organized in about six thousand items, and will deal with a simplified structure. The budget is going to be organized according to "functional targets" (that indicate the main political decisions), and according to "base units" (that indicate resources for the responsibility centers of the state administration). This reform may increase transparency and accountability both at the political and at the administrative level.

Comparing the old and the new scores of the various indicators that we have distinguished (table 11.5), it follows that the most notable differences for Italy occur with respect to the position of the legislature (*A2*) and the flexibility during execution of the budget (*A5*). At this stage it should be pointed out, however, that in the case of Italy the answers of our respondent and of our outside expert sometimes differed considerably. On the basis of available evidence and subsequent answers to detailed further questions we have come up with the scores as shown in appendix B. In case of doubt from our side, we indicate so.

11.4.5   Sweden

Budgetary procedures have improved considerably in Sweden (see below for further discussion; see also table 11.9). The acute financial crisis that hit

Table 11.8 Budgetary Cycle in Italy

	February	March	April	May	June	July	September
Preparation of next year's budget		Budget guidelines prepared by RGS	Current and capital account of each ministry submitted to RGS	Document of Economic and Financial Planning (DPEF)	Parliament resolution on DPEF	Annual and three-year budget on current legislation submitted to parliament by July 31	Forecasting and planning report. Draft budget documents submitted to parliament by September 30 (and to be approved by December 31)
Activity during the year				Quarterly Treasury report estimating borrowing requirements for the public sector and the statement of cash accounts[a]			
Conclusion of previous year's budget	Treasury report on cash outcomes for previous year (state sector and other levels of government) submitted to parliament by February 28	General report on the economic situation of the country			Budget adjustment bill for the current year and financial statement for the previous year submitted to parliament by June 30		

Source: OECD 1997.

[a]In May, August, November.

Table 11.9   **Budgetary Process in Sweden**

Date	Main Events and Activities
November–December	Directives from the Budget Department of the Ministry of Finance to spending ministries for five-year expenditure forecast
December–January	Government discusses priorities
February–March	Preparation of background material for government negotiations
April 15	Spring Budget published, which contains three-year expenditure ceilings proposal, outline of the budget of next year, in-year followup report, and the outcome of the previous year
June	Parliamentary decision on Spring Budget
August	Budget amendments presented to parliament (generally minor)
September 20	Budget proposal presented to parliament
November	First budget decision in parliament about the frames for expenditures areas
December	Second budget decision in parliament about appropriation
Late December	Issue letters to the agencies providing authorization for spending

Source: Swedish Ministry of Finance.

Sweden in the beginning of the 1990s was the main motivation of the reform of the budgetary process. In fact, reform of the budget process formed an integral part of the policy of fiscal consolidation (OECD 1996). However, our survey also revealed that recent academic work on budget institutions, notably the work of von Hagen as well as the personal commitment of high-ranking civil servants and the minister of finance—Goran Persson, who became prime minister in March 1996—also played a major role in the reform.

In 1992 a parliamentary commission was installed to analyze possibilities for improving the budgetary process. In a report to the Ministry of Finance (Molander 1992) it was concluded that the Swedish budget process performed relatively poorly in comparison with other European countries with respect to expenditure control. This lack of control reflected a weak role of the minister of finance, a fragmented budget process within parliament, absence of transparency and inadequate information content of the budget, and too much flexibility in the implementation of the budget (see also table 11.5). The result was heavy spending overruns, primarily on transfer programs (OECD 1996).

The aforementioned report of Molander proposed to change the existing procedure, introducing the two-step procedure outlined in table 11.9. The final report of the parliamentary commission contained a further elaborated version of this two-step procedure. Implementation required a change of the constitution. Both the old and the new parliament approved this change in 1994.

A second major change was the introduction of expenditure ceilings in 1996, following a proposal from the government in 1995 (Molander 1997). The lack of control of government expenditure in the past was due to the fact that 70 percent of spending was governed by statutory rules, with no obligation to find matching cuts if estimates were exceeded, or to implement legislative changes in order to bring expenditures in such programs back to a baseline (OECD 1996). Political opposition to expenditure ceilings motivated by fears that they would undermine security as provided by the welfare state has been voiced from the Left Party (formerly the Communist Party). The strong involvement of the new prime minister no doubt has helped to introduce the system of expenditure ceilings. Nowadays three-year ceilings are imposed for the 27 major expenditure areas (including social security transfers, but excluding interest payments). These ceilings are the cornerstone of the new budget process. The total expenditure ceiling is derived ex ante from overall budgetary objectives and not from component commitments embodied in the program setups (OECD 1996). The ceilings for the period 1997–99 were decided upon by parliament in the spring of 1996. The total expenditure ceiling was scheduled to fall from 40.7 percent of GDP in 1997 to 37.5 percent in 1999 (OECD 1996). The following budget rounds consist of decisions as to the expenditure ceiling for the new year, added to the three-year horizon.

Comparing the old and the new scores of the various indicators that we have distinguished (table 11.5), it follows that the indicators $A4$ (transparency of the budget) and $A3$ (constraints) show the highest increase. The budget is now, for example, submitted in one document (see appendix B for further details). The increase of $A3$ is due to the introduction of the expenditure ceilings outlined above and the strong political commitment attached to them. The most important change in the flexibility of the execution of the budget ($A5$) is also due to the system of expenditure ceilings. The increase in $A2$ (position of legislature) is due to the fact that the powers of parliament have been reduced somewhat. Amendments, for example, were not required to be offsetting previously, but they are now. In the past there was only a final global vote, while the new procedure requires approval in the initial stage of the budgetary process (Swedish Ministry of Finance 1995). The position of the minister of finance ($A1$) has also improved slightly, as he or she now proposes budget norms on which the government will decide, whereas in the past a standard bottom-up procedure was applied (Swedish Ministry of Finance 1995). Finally, the position of local governments ($A6$) will change, as a binding requirement on their accounts to balance, combined with requirements to fund their commitments in the area of occupational pensions, will apply from the year 2000 (OECD 1996).

11.5   Concluding Comments

In this chapter we have analyzed which features of budget institutions are the most important in influencing fiscal policy outcomes using data for member countries of the European Union. It is concluded that budget institutions affect fiscal policy outcomes, but that the effect is quite small. There are some indications that the position of the legislature, the presence of binding constraints, and flexibility during the execution of the budget matter most. We have also analyzed the evolution of budgetary institutions in some countries to examine the causes and impact of procedural changes. The countries included in the analysis have divergent public-debt-to-GDP ratios. A survey under experts from these countries was used, together with other information available, to analyze possible changes in budgetary institutions. The most notable changes occurred in Sweden. All aspects of the budgetary process that we have distinguished improved, but the most notable changes relate to the transparency of the budget and the presence of binding constraints. The latter is due to the introduction of expenditure ceilings and the strong political commitment attached to them. The most important change in the flexibility of the execution of the budget is also due to this new system. The acute financial crisis that hit Sweden in the beginning of the 1990s was the main motivation of the reform of the budgetary process. However, our survey also revealed that recent academic work on budget institutions as well as the personal commitment of high-ranking civil servants and the minister of finance also played a major role in the reform. Despite these improvements, the public debt ratio in Sweden has risen considerably since the beginning of the 1990s. It is our contention, however, that without the improvement in the budgetary procedures the rise would probably have been even more pronounced.

In Ireland the debt-to-GDP ratio rose in the 1980s, leading at that time to a broad political consensus that restoration of fiscal balance was essential for promoting economic growth. To this end, various specific quantitative targets have been used. Recent practice has been to specify medium-term fiscal objectives, particularly in relation to the deficit and public debt ratios, as Ireland is clearly committed to becoming a member of EMU. The most notable differences for Ireland in comparison with the survey of von Hagen (1992) occur with respect to the position of the minister of finance, which are not due to changes in the formal procedures, but may reflect the formal rule versus actual practice.

In Belgium the Maastricht criteria have also strengthened the budgetary process since its latest reform in 1989. Belgium has committed itself to a first entrance into the EMU. The goal of reducing the general government budget deficit to 3 percent requires a sustained austerity, which in turn places fiscal discipline high on the political agenda and also emphasizes the relative weight of the minister of finance. It is our contention that the constitutional reform of 1988–89, which transformed Belgium from a unitary to a federal state, may exert some disciplinary force as well, since the golden rule applies de facto for regional governments, which have limited access to public borrowing and no opportunity of seignorage collection.

Finally, in Italy the Maastricht criteria also have some impact. Although there are no differences with respect to the von Hagen survey, our respondent has the impression that the policy constraints have become more rigid as a consequence of the EMU criteria. The most notable changes, in comparison to the results from von Hagen, regard the position of the legislature and flexibility during the execution phase of the budgetary cycle.

Appendix A
Survey

I. Questions relating to the position of the Minister of Finance (MF)

1. Could you please indicate which one of the following is the best characterization of the agenda setting for the budget negotiating process in your country (choose only one):
   □ MF or cabinet collects bids from spending ministers;
   □ MF or cabinet collects bids subject to preagreed guidelines;
   □ cabinet decides on budget norms first;
   □ MF proposes budget norms to be voted on by cabinet:
   □ MF (or prime minister) determines budget parameters to be observed by spending ministers.

2. Could you please indicate which one of the following is the best characterization of the budget negotiating process in your country (choose only one):
   □ all cabinet members involved together
   □ multilateral
   □ bilateral between spending ministers and MF.

3. Can the MF block expenditures: yes/no

4. Is disbursement approval required from MF (or controller): yes/no

It may be that the budgetary process in your country is not characterized adequately by the options outlined above; if so, please indicate in what respect the options are not adequate.

Could you please indicate whether with respect to the questions 1–4 anything has changed since 1991, and if so, why these changes occurred?

II. Questions relating to the position of the legislature

5. Could you please indicate which one of the following is the best characterization of the position of the parliament:
   a. Possibility to propose amendments: unlimited/limited
   b. Are these amendments required to be offsetting: yes/no.
   c. Can (accepted) amendments cause fall of government: yes/no.
   d. Are all expenditures passed in one vote: yes/mixed/votes are chapter by chapter.
   e. Is there a global vote on total budget size: final only/initial.

It may be that the budgetary process in your country is not characterized adequately by the options outlined above; if so, please indicate in what respect the options are not adequate.

Could you please indicate whether with respect to question 5 anything has changed since 1991, and if so, why these changes occurred?

III. Questions relating to the presence of some kind of constraint

6. Could you please indicate whether the government is bound by some general constraint:
   - [ ] none
   - [ ] public-debt-to-GDP ratio
   - [ ] public-debt-to-GDP ratio and deficit-to-GDP ratio
   - [ ] government-spending-to-GDP ratio or Golden Rule
   - [ ] government-spending-to-GDP ratio and deficit-to-GDP ratio.
7. Could you please indicate which characterization is most adequate with respect to the degree of commitment of some long-term planning constraint:
   - [ ] no long-term planning constraint
   - [ ] for internal orientation only
   - [ ] indicative
   - [ ] weak political commitment
   - [ ] strong political commitment.

It may be that the budgetary process in your country is not characterized adequately by the options outlined above; if so, please indicate in what respect the options are not adequate.

Could you please indicate whether with respect to questions 6–7 anything has changed since 1991, and if so, why these changes occurred?

IV. Questions relating to the transparency of the budget

8. Could you please indicate which characterization is most adequate with respect to the transparency of the budget.
   a. Are special funds included: no/some/most/yes, but annexed to budget draft/yes.
   b. Is the budget submitted in one document: no/recently yes/yes.
   c. Is the budget according to your personal view: hardly transparent/ not fully transparent/fully transparent.
   d. A link of the budget to the national accounts is: not provided/possible/provided in separate documents/direct link provided.
   e. Government loans to non-government entities are included in budget draft: no/reported in separate document/yes.

It may be that the budgetary process in your country is not characterized adequately by the options outlined above; if so, please indicate in what respect the options are not adequate.

Could you please indicate whether with respect to question 8 anything has changed since 1991, and if so, why these changes occurred?

V. Questions relating to the flexibility during the execution of the budget

9. Could you please indicate which characterization is most adequate with respect to the flexibility during the execution of the budget.
   a. Are spending ministries subject to cash limits: no/yes.
   b. Transfers of expenditure between chapters are: unrestricted/limited/ require consent of MF/require consent of parliament/only within departments possible/only within departments and with consent of MF.
   c. Changes in budget law during execution are: at the discretion of government/by new law which is regularly submitted during fiscal year/at the discretion of MF/require consent of MF and parliament/ only by new budgetary law to be passed under the same regulations as the ordinary budget.
   d. Carry-over of unused funds to next year are: unrestricted/limited/ limited and requires authorization by MF or parliament/not possible.

It may be that the budgetary process in your country is not characterized adequately by the options outlined above; if so, please indicate in what respect the options are not adequate.

Could you please indicate whether with respect to question 9 anything has changed since 1991, and if so, why these changes occurred?

VI. Questions relating to the relationship between central government and other parts of government

10. Could you please indicate which characterization is most adequate with respect to the budgetary status of regional authorities:
    a. balanced budget required: no/yes, but not considered to be binding/ Golden Rule requirement/yes.
    b. Planning autonomy: lower-level governments are autonomous/ they may be placed under surveillance of higher-level government/ they have limited autonomy/they have no autonomy.

It may be that the budgetary process in your country is not characterized adequately by the options outlined above; if so, please indicate in what respect the options are not adequate.

Could you please indicate whether with respect to question 10 anything has changed since 1991, and if so, why these changes occurred?

Appendix B
Detailed Country Studies

This appendix discusses our detailed results concerning the various aspects of budget institutions as distinguished in section 11.2. Any differences in coding between von Hagen 1992—or in the case of Sweden, with respect to the situation at the beginning of the 1990s—and our survey are indicated in bold.

Belgium

Position of the Minister of Finance (von Hagen Score A1: 1.25; Our Survey: 3.25). The MF teams with the minister of the budget, who usually holds the title of vice prime minister. Even before the Maastricht fiscal targets came to play a major role in Belgian fiscal policy, one witnessed an increased "weight" of the minister of the budget together with the MF. In close cooperation with the prime minister they draft the "budget circular," inviting the spending ministers to submit their budget proposals within specified parameters (item 1b: 1). These instructions are to be approved by the Council of Ministers. In the elaboration of their budget the spending ministers are advised by their higher-ranking civil servants and the inspector of finance who is accredited to the department. Starting from baseline projections, new activities and other priorities are incorporated in the budget proposals. These are submitted in a first round of scrutiny to the minister of the budget. Here they are bilaterally reviewed (item 1d: **4** instead of 0). After aggregation they are confronted with the estimates of the MF for the Ways and Means. In fact there is a kind of division of labor in the sense that the MF handles the revenue side of the budget (taxes, public debt), whereas the minister of the budget focuses on the expenditure side. Several rounds of bilateral "negotiations" may occur to target expenditures to revenues. Finally all items, which remain unresolved, are collected for a final decision procedure called the "Budgetary Conclave." Again bilaterally the spending ministers are now confronted with the "core" of the Council of Ministers (i.e., prime minister, the vice prime ministers, and the MF). These decisions may involve changes in tax laws, privatizations, or new debt management techniques.

According to von Hagen the MF cannot block expenditures (item 4a: 0). In fact, it is the minister of the budget who can block expenditures upon instigation of the accredited inspector of finance. A score of **4** may therefore be more appropriate. A preliminary "visum" of the department of the MF is required before cash disbursements are executed (item 4c: 4).

Position of the Legislature (von Hagen Score A2: 0.8; Our Survey 1.60). Policy outcomes are often compromises of the different parties constituting the coalition government. The parliament consists of a House of Representatives and a Senate. The Senate provides "fairness" appraisals on new laws but is not active in the budgetary procedure, which is the prerogative of the House of Representatives. In principle the possibility of proposing amendments is unlimited. In fact amendments are only marginal and, ironically enough, often address budget lines that are directed toward the operational costs of the House itself. This huge distance between principle and practice explains the difference with the score in the von Hagen paper (item 2a: **4** instead of 0). The amendments are not required to be offsetting (item 2b: 0) and do not cause the fall of a government (item 2c: **0** instead of 4). Usually it is the absence of consensus on fundamental policy issues that causes the collapse of a coalition. Linguistic and ideological differences between Flanders and Wallonia have often reduced the length of tenure of a government in the past.

The proposed budget covers three documents: the expenditure budget, the budget of ways and means, and the budget message (Algemene Toelichting). This latter document is more policy oriented and "readable" for the general public. It is not subject to a formal vote in the House of Representatives. The expenditure budget and the budget of ways and means have the format of a budgetary law that is to be voted upon.

As a rule the three documents are available before the end of September, and votes take place before the end of November. The House has two months to assess and discuss the new budget. The more technical debates are conducted in the specialized committees of the House, regrouping those representatives with a special interest in, for example, foreign policy, social security, finance. The plenary debate, which requires several days in a row, is finalized by a vote chapter by chapter (item 2d: **4** instead of 0; item 2e: 0).

Constraints (von Hagen Score A3: 0.00; Our Survey 3.00). From 1992 on the guidelines of Maastricht have oriented, some would say "dictated," the budgetary behavior of Belgium, which is devoted to a first entrance into the EMU. When elaborating the budget each year, a numerical time path is specified for the next year and the following years until the start-up of the EMU. Remarkably, a consensus is reached between all the parties and interest groups involved. The scientific input for this deliberation is delivered by the High Council for Finance (which includes academia), the Economic Planning Agency, the National Bank, and the Department of Studies of the Ministry of Finance. This results in a strong political commitment to the 3 percent deficit-to-GNP ratio and to a "significant" reduction in the public-debt-to-GDP ratio (item 1a: 0; now **2**; item 5d: 0; now **4**).

Transparency of the Budget (von Hagen Score A4: 2.00; Our Survey: 3.13). As already mentioned, the budget consists of one document (unity of budget presentation) that materializes in three "books" to make the volumes manageable (item 3b: **4** instead of 2). Special funds are annexed to the budget draft (item 3a: **3** instead of 2). The budget presentation is not fully transparent, as it takes some routine and expertise to run through the chapters (item 3c: 2). The link to the national accounts is provided in a separate document called the "economic regrouping," which is published some time later (item 3d: 0; now **2.66**). The "totality" requirement of the budget stipulates that loans to nongovernment entities should be included (item 3e: 4)

Flexibility during Execution of the Budget (von Hagen Score A5: 1.80; Our Survey: 2.92). The von Hagen study reports that the spending ministers are not subject to cash limits. From our information it appears that the Treasury (Ministry of Finance) severely surveys the cash flows (item 4b: **4** instead of 0). In fact, the austerity prescriptions of Maastricht have changed several aspects of the actual budgetary behavior. Nowadays a transfer of expenditures is restricted to line items within the same department and with the consent of the MF (item 4d: 3.2; now **4**).

In the early spring the government organizes a formal assessment of the execution of the budget. The macroeconomic environment may have changed since the drafting of the budget in the summer of the preceding year. There may be new information on real growth, inflation, interest rate levels, tax revenues, and unemployment. If required, the expenditure and/or the revenue side of the budget will be adjusted by a formal law to be voted by the House of Representatives as an annex to the official budget law (item 4c: 4; now **1**). The carryover of unused funds to the next year is limited and requires the authorization of the MF and parliament. The rules are rather detailed and may differ for a recurrent expenditure versus an investment outlay (item 4f: 0; now **2.66**).

Relationship with Other Parts of Government (von Hagen Score A6: 1.33; Our Survey: 1.33). Since the constitutional reform of 1989–90 Belgium has become a federal state. Between the central and the local level (municipalities), the regions (Flanders, Wallonia, Brussels) have now required substantial competence in areas such as economic development, environment, infrastructure, education, and cultural affairs. Tax autonomy is restricted, but the regions benefit from a complex system of shared and assigned taxes *(juste retour).* The lower levels of government are primarily involved in allocation rather than redistribution or stabilization. On average they face a harder budget constraint than the central government. The golden rule applies for the regions and the municipalities. However, within this constraint the own preferences are respected.

Ireland

Position of Minister of Finance (von Hagen Score A1: 0.25; Our Survey: 3.25). As follows from the outline of the budgetary cycle, the MF takes the lead in the budgetary process. In recent years, the practice has been to specify medium-term fiscal objectives. In setting its targets for the 1997 budget, the government set specific targets for the deficit (and debt) and for overall tax/expenditure aggregates for 1997–99, taking account of the foregoing projections. The annual Estimates Circular seeks expenditure demands that comply with these medium-term objectives (item 1b: 1). Spending departments, in submitting their annual demands for resources, must provide details of forecast resource requirements for three years ahead. Their demands are then assessed for consistency with the Estimates Circular specifications in a consultative process that clarifies the basis for the bids and focuses on the elimination of excess demand. Despite that process, the aggregate demand typically exceeds the allocation for departmental spending that would be consistent with the target for the overall deficit. The next stage is, therefore, for the MF to undertake a series of bilateral meetings with each of his or her colleagues to establish priorities for the allocation of the available resources. The Department of Finance again aggregates the outcome of these negotiations into a total provision for all departmental spending and presents it to government in an overall budget context. If the outlook remains unsatisfactory, the government will instigate a further round of bilateral meetings to secure further reductions (item 1d: **4** instead of 0). Finalization of the budget also requires cabinet decisions on specific taxation changes and final adjustments to spending plans. The MF can block expenditures during the execution phase of the budget (item 4a: **4** instead of 0). The Public Financial Procedures (section A4) makes clear that expenditure must have authority of the Department of Finance. Disbursements also require approval (item 4c: **4** instead of 0).

Position of Legislature (von Hagen Score A2: 1.60; Our Survey: 3.00). The legislature (Oireachtas) consists of the president, who is head of state under the constitution, the lower house (Dáil Eireann) and the upper house (Seanad Eireann). Ministers must be members of a house of the Oireachtas. The prime minister, deputy prime minister, and MF must all be members of the Dáil. Only the Dáil has the power to amend legislation involving public monies; however, it is not empowered to amend estimates—only to adopt or to reject them (item 2a: 4). Standing orders (procedural rules) of the lower house preclude any addition or reduction in the annual estimates. According to von Hagen, amendments do not have to be offsetting (item 2b: 0), but one may question this score as parliament cannot amend estimates. (We have dropped this question in the calculation of our new score for A3.) However, the legislature can propose amendments to the taxation side of the budgetary equation, and in the past one government fell after one particular taxation proposal had been voted down by the Dáil (item 2c: 4). The upper house does not debate the budget per se; it does, however, consider the annual Finance Bill (taxation) and Appropriation Bill (expenditure), on which it may make recommendations that the Dáil may either accept or reject.

As follows from the outline of the budgetary process, the parliamentary stage in Ireland is prolonged into the financial year. Budget provisions are enacted into law only after the budget has already come into operation. This requires preliminary spending authorizations. This is provided for by resolutions on individual estimates. The White Paper on Receipts and Expenditure shows the outturn for the previous financial year, estimated receipts and expenditures (both voted and nonvoted, see below), and the estimated borrowing requirement. The estimates are in highly aggregated form in this stage. The white paper is not the subject of a Dáil motion. Individual estimates are updated, and each one is presented and debated on separately only in June/July. When an estimate is passed by the Dáil, it is technically known as a Vote. (The score for item 2d is zero according to von Hagen (1992), but given the procedures as outlined a score of **4** is more appropriate). Only in December is the Appropriation Bill passed, which gives statutory effect to the estimates approved by the Dáil (item 2e: 0).

Government expenditure in Ireland falls into two broad categories: nonvoted expenditure, which the Dáil does not have to vote on (like the service of the national debt), and voted expenditures, which refers to the ordinary services of departments (both capital and noncapital spending). Expenditure is provided for under Votes, one or more covering the functions of each department or office (Public Financial Procedures, 1996).

Constraints (von Hagen Score A3: 2.50; Our Survey: 3.00). Since 1980 there has been broad political consensus that restoration of fiscal balance is essential for promoting economic growth. To this end, various specific quantitative targets have been used. As pointed out above, recent practice has been to specify medium-term fiscal objectives, particularly in relation to the deficit and public debt ratios (item 1a: 2). Ireland's current fiscal policy is based on the maintenance of low budgetary deficits and is formally set out in the policy agreement, *A Government of Renewal* (December 1994) between Fine Gael, the Labor Party and Democratic Left, and *Partnership 2000 for Inclusion, Employment and Competitiveness,* agreed with the social partners in December 1996. Nowadays, there is strong political commitment to the targets formulated (item 5d: **4** instead of 3).

Transparency of the Budget (von Hagen Score A4: 1.00; Our Survey: 1.53). As follows from the outline of the budgetary process, the budget does not consist of one document (item 3b: 0). Some special funds are included (item 3a: 1), while our respondent to the survey regarded the budget as almost fully transparent (item 3c: 2). A link to the national accounts is provided in the budget booklet (item 3d: **2.66** instead of 0), while government loans are included in the finance accounts (item 3e: 2).

Flexibility during Execution of the Budget (von Hagen Score A5: 3.00; Our Survey: 2.67). To ensure tight control of expenditure and adequate notice of potential deviations from target, departments are required to submit a profile of expenditure by month to the Department of Finance for approval at the beginning of the year, and monthly returns of actual and forecast expenditure including explanations of variations from profile. If actual expenditure in any given month is less than the amount specified in the approved profile for that month, this will normally be regarded as a saving for the year; that is, it is not available for spending later in the year (item 4f: **2.66** instead of 4). Approval for expenditure in a particular month in excess of the approved profile is only given where there is a clear-cut understanding that it will be offset by specific compensating measures later in the year. Only a small number of programs are cash limited (item 4b: 0). Transfers are normally only allowed within departments and with consent of the MF (item 4d: 4). As follows from our description of the budgetary process, changes in the budget law during execution require parliamentary approval (item 4e: 4).

Relationship with Other Parts of Government (von Hagen Score A6: 0.00; Our Survey: 3.33). Ireland is a unitary state. There are two layers of government: central government, including the state-sponsored body sector, and regional government, which includes regional health boards and local authorities. There are also extrabudgetary funds (including social insurance funds). Local authorities are responsible for such local services as provision of public housing, construction and maintenance of roads, water supplies and sanitary services, refuse collection, environmental protection, and fire services. Approximately half of their spending is funded by Exchequer grants, most of which are specific grants, and the rest of their funding is raised at the local level. According to von Hagen local governments do not face certain constraints and are autonomous with respect to budget planning. Our respondent answered, however, that they have limited autonomy.

Italy

Position of Minister of Finance (von Hagen Score A1: 0.75; Our Survey: 0.75). At the budget formulation stage, three ministries—the Treasury, budget, and finance—are involved. The central role in budgetary matters is played by a department within the Treasury, Ragioneria Generale dello Stato (RGS). The responsibility for economic and fiscal policymaking is shared between the Ministry of Finance and the Economic Planning Ministry: the first has the lead in fiscal revenue policies (taxes and other revenues), the second in macroeconomic forecasting (OECD 1995). The process generates several budget documents, which differ in terms of accounting basis, sectoral coverage, and date of issuance. Fiscal targets are set by parliament on the basis of a proposal by the three ministries (score 1b: 1.00). This score is based on Alesina, Mare, and Perotti 1995. After that, negotiations take place between the spending departments and notably the Treasury, which are, according to Alesina, Mare, and Perotti (1995), somewhat unregulated (item 1d: 2). (However, according to our respondent a score of 4 [bilateral negotiations] would be more appropriate.)

At the budget implementation stage, the Treasury has responsibility for the management of the state cash resources. The minister cannot block expenditures if authorized by the budget (item 4a: 0). Whether disbursement is required is not entirely clear. According to our respondent it is required, but according to von Hagen and Harden (1994) and our outside expert it is not (item 4c: 0).

Position of Legislature (von Hagen Score A2: 1.20; Our Survey: 2.80). Parliament has two chambers: The Camera dei deputati (lower house) and the Senato della Republica (senate). In general, ministers are members of parliament. The budget documents are submitted by the Government, either first to the lower house and subsequently to the senate, or vice versa. The two chambers have an equally important position regarding all sorts of laws, including budgetary laws. When chambers disagree with each other, the law is examined again (and modified) following the same procedure. Since 1988, the Leggi di Bilancio (finance act) cannot be used to change substantive legislation as it can only reflect existing legislation (art. 81 of the constitution). All interventions must be carried out in the Legge Finanziaria (LF) and Provvedimenti Collegati (PC). Once passed, these become existing legislation and are incorporated in the LB by amending the LB with the Nota di Variazioni (Alesina, Mare, and Perotti 1995; OECD 1995).

The financial law, the connected laws, and the budget are examined by the two houses in the same form. In each house these texts are examined beforehand by parliamentary commissions, but at this stage the real voting process takes place only in the Budget Commission. This will pass the approved text to the full session. Here, the approbation of the financial law starts from article 1, in which the maximum permitted for total budget size is set (item 2e: **4** instead of 0). (Both our respondent and expert gave this score.) Still, as the DPEF sets only the aggregate objectives of the fiscal maneuver, and at an early stage of the budget process, it only provides a very vague description of the government's plan, without any realistic quantification of its expected savings. Thus, at the time parliament votes on the target figure for the SNF, which becomes binding for the subsequent budget process, there is practically no notion of the means to attain it, and therefore, of whether it is realistic (Alesina, Mare, and Perotti 1995).

Both chambers have a limited right to add to or modify proposed revenue and expenditure (item 2a: 4). Parliament can increase expenditures as long as they are covered by additional revenues (Alesina, Mare, and Perotti 1995). According to our respondent a score of 4 on item 2b would be appropriate, as parliament nowadays sets itself lines of conduct that must be followed during the budget sessions. Our outside expert was less optimistic here. While parliamentary amendments must leave the state deficit unchanged, any additional spending being covered by offsetting expenditure cuts or additional revenues *(copertura),* this safeguard can be circumvented by way of parliament proposing higher spending to be implemented by local government and other external agencies (e.g., social security funds). Thus, extra general government spending can arise even when the *copertura* requirement is formally met (OECD 1997) (item 2b: 0). Both our respondent and expert agreed that accepted amendments can lead to the fall of a government (item 2c: **4** instead of 0). Voting is mixed (item 2d: 2).

Constraints (von Hagen Score A3: 2.50; Our Survey: 2.50). Multiyear budgets are based on commitments. They reflect proposed government policy with respect to the new budget and its multiyear consequences (OECD 1995). Targets are formulated in terms of the debt ratio and the deficit (item 1a: 2; item 5d: 3). Although there are no differences with respect to the von Hagen survey, our respondent has the impression that the constraints have become more rigid as a consequence of the EMU criteria.

Transparency of the Budget (von Hagen Score A4: 1.00; Our Survey: 0.80). As follows from the description of the budgetary process, there are various documents at various stages (item 3b: 0). The budget is hardly transparent (item 3c: 0), and there is no link provided with the national accounts (item 3d: 0). Government loans to nongovernment entities are not included (item 3e: **0** instead of 4), but special funds are, according to our respondent and expert (item 3a: **4** instead of 1).

Flexibility during Execution of the Budget (von Hagen Score A5: 0.25; Our Survey: 1.58). Ministries are not subject to a cash limit (OECD 1997) (item 4b: 0). Transfers are only possible within departments according to both respondent and expert (item 4d: **4** instead of 0). There are only limited ways to carry over unused funds to the next year (item 4f: **1.33** instead of 0). Unspent appropriations are "carried over" (up to two years for current expenditure, three years for public works, and five years for capital spending). As a result, annual cash budgets for the state are based on preliminary evaluations of carryovers that tend to be underestimated. Reliable estimates of carryovers are not available before March (OECD 1997). Changes in the budget require a new law (item 4e: 1).

Relationship with Other Parts of Government (von Hagen Score A6: 1.33; Our Survey: 2.66). Italy is a unitary state. There are three layers of government: state or central level, regional and provincial level, and municipalities. The provincial level is by far the smallest in financial terms. Although there has been a slight increase in fiscal autonomy during the last years, the respondent to our survey found that lower-level governments have limited autonomy.

Sweden

The budgetary process of Sweden went through a reform. Any differences in coding in comparison to the situation at the beginning of the 1990s are shown in bold. The sources are an internal memorandum of the Swedish Ministry of Finance (Swedish Ministry of Finance 1995) and information provided by Per Molander.

Position of Minister of Finance (Former Score A1: 1.00; New Score 1.75). The cabinet is involved at all stages of the budget process, although the negotiations on expenditure as a rule are held between the MF and the responsible ministry (item 1d: 4). Late in April, the government presents a revised Budget Bill, summing up the various bills presented after the Budget Bill and containing a revised economic policy and budget statement, a revised revenue estimate, a revision of the economic survey presented in the Budget Bill, the multiyear budget projections, and the three-year economic policy assessment. With respect to item 1b, it was stated that previously a standard bottom-up procedure was applied (0), but that after the reform the cabinet will decide on budget norms to be proposed by the minister of finance (3 instead of 0). The MF cannot block expenditures during the budget year (item 4a: 0), nor does he or she have to approve disbursement (item 4c: 0).

Position of Legislature (Former Score A2: 1.60; New Score: 3.20). Parliament has one chamber (Riksdag). By constitutional law, parliament has to approve the budget before the start of the fiscal year. Parliament has unlimited rights to propose amendments both before and after the reform (item 2a: 0), and these were not required to be offsetting previously (item 2b: 0), but they are since 1996 (4). Budget decisions can cause the fall of the government both in the old and the new procedure (item 2c: 4). Voting is chapter by chapter (item 2d: 4). There is a global vote on total budget size, which used to be final only (item 2e: 0), but is since 1996 initial (4).

Constraints (Former Score A3: 0.50; New Score: 4.00). A frame budget process has been adopted in parliament, which is in effect from 1996 onward. In the spring of 1995, a nominal, multiannual expenditure ceiling for the public sector was proposed in the economic spring bill, a proposal endorsed by parliament. With the expenditure ceiling in place, constraints are even more binding than the most restrictive alternatives (item 1a was 0, now 4). Before the reforms, the degree of commitment to planning constraints was limited to internal orientation (item 5d: 1); after the reform there is strong political commitment (4).

Transparency of the Budget (Former Score A4: 1.00; New Score: 3.20). With respect to the transparency of the budget, it appears that only some special funds were included (item 3a: 1), but that now all special funds are included (4). Before the reform, the budget was not submitted in one document (item 3b: 0), but now it is (4). According to the respondent, the budget was previously not fully transparent (item 3c: 2), but after the reform it is (4). Links to national accounts are not supplied (item 3d: 0). Government loans to non-government entities used to be recorded by the National Debt Office in a separate document (item 3e: 2), but are now included in the budget (**4**).

Flexibility during Execution of the Budget (Former Score A5: 1.68; New Score: 2.02). There were no cash limits before (item 4b: 0). They will be tested in some areas, although not where third-party obligations are binding. According to our respondent this implies a score of 4, but here we disagree. Transfers between chapters require the consent of parliament and the MF both before and after the reform (item 4d: 2.4) The same applies to changes in the budget decision (item 4e: 3). Carryover possibilities used to be limited (item 4f: 1.33), but now also require the consent of MF (**2.66**).

Relationship with Other Parts of Government (Former Score A6: 0.00; New Score: 1.33). Sweden is a unitary state. There are three layers of government: the state or central government, county councils, and municipals. The latter two supply the bulk of public consumption (regional: health care; municipal: schooling, care for children and elderly), and have a constitutional right to tax the citizens in order to finance this production. Social security expenditures outside the budget consist mainly of supplementary old-age pensions, a pay-as-you-go system that is currently being transformed into a sort of simulated premium-reserve system. A golden rule requirement will be in effect as of 1999 for both the municipal and regional levels. Lower levels of government have relatively large autonomy.

References

Alesina, A., R. Hausmann, R. Hommes, and E. Stein. 1996. Budget institutions and fiscal performance in Latin America. NBER Working Paper no. 5586. Cambridge, Mass.: National Bureau of Economic Research.

Alesina, A., M. Mare, and R. Perotti. 1995. The Italian budget procedures: Analysis and proposals. Columbia University Working Paper no. 755.

Alesina, A., and R. Perotti. 1995a. Fiscal expansions and adjustments in OECD countries. *Economic Policy* 21:207–48.

———. 1995b. The political economy of budget deficits. *IMF Staff Papers* 42:1–31.

Barro, R. J. 1979. On the determination of public debt. *Journal of Political Economy* 87:940–71.

Borrelli, S. A., and T. J. Royed. 1995. Government strength and budget deficits in advanced democracies. *European Journal of Political Research* 28:225–60.

de Haan, J., C. G. M. Sterks, and C. A. de Kam. 1992. Towards budget discipline: An economic assessment of the possibilities for reducing national deficits in the run-up to EMU. Economic Papers no. 99. Commission of the European Communities.

de Haan, J., and J.-E. Sturm. 1994. Political and institutional determinants of fiscal policy in the European Community. *Public Choice* 80:157–72.

————. 1997. Political and economic determinants of OECD budget deficits and government expenditures: A reinvestigation. *European Journal of Political Economy* 13:739–50.

Edin, P., and H. Ohlsson. 1991. Political determinants of budget deficits: Coalition effects versus minority effects. *European Economic Review* 35:1597–1603.

Moessen, W., and P. Van Cauwenberge. 1997. Federalism, the status of the budget constraint, and the relative size of government: A bureaucracy approach. Photocopy.

Molander, P. 1992. Statsskulden och budgetprosessen. ESO report DS 1992:126.

————. 1997. Reforming budgetary institutions: The case of Sweden. Forthcoming.

OECD. 1995. *Budgeting for results*. Perspectives on Public Expenditure Management. Paris: OECD.

————. 1996. *OECD economic surveys: Sweden, 1996/97*. Paris: OECD.

————. 1997. *OECD economic surveys: Italy, 1996/97*. Paris: OECD.

Poterba, J. M. 1996. Do budget rules work? NBER Working Paper no. 5550. Cambridge, Mass.: National Bureau of Economic Research.

Riker, W. 1980. Implications for the disequilibrium of majority rule for the study of institutions. *American Political Science Review* 74:432–46.

Roubini, N., and J. Sachs. 1989a. Government spending and budget deficits in the industrial countries. *Economic Policy* 8:99–132.

————. 1989b. Political and economic determinants of budget deficits in the industrial democracies. *European Economic Review* 33:903–38.

Swedish Ministry of Finance. 1995. Re-evaluating the Swedish budget process. Photocopy.

von Hagen, J. 1992. Budgeting procedures and fiscal performance in the European Community. Economic Paper no. 96. Commission of the European Communities.

von Hagen, J., and I. Harden. 1994. National budget processes and fiscal performance. *European Economy: Reports and Studies* 3:311–418.

————. 1996. Budget processes and commitment to fiscal discipline. IMF Working Paper no. 96/78.

12   Subnational Budgetary and Stabilization Policies in Canada and Australia

Thomas J. Courchene

12.1   Introduction

At first blush, Canada and Australia appear to be very similar nations. Both are former British colonies and are members of the Commonwealth. Both are parliamentary federations and constitutional monarchies, although Australia may be close to becoming a republic. The land masses of the two countries qualify them among the largest nations on earth. They are both small, open economies endowed with ample natural resources. Both nations have significant aboriginal or First Nations populations, both have vast parts of their territory that are sparsely populated, and on and on. And at the broad policy level, Canada's system of equalization payments was patterned, conceptually, after the philosophy underpinning Australia's Commonwealth Grants Commission. And Australia has followed Canada in relying on "executive federalism" as a key policy and coordination institution, even to the point where COAG (the Council of Australian Governments) is currently operating much more effectively than Canada's FMCs (First Ministers' Conferences).

To be sure, there are some important differences. Australia does not have a United States on its border with the resulting dominant impact on trade, cultural identity, and policy independence. Moreover, Australia has no equivalent to Quebec—a province that is linguistically, culturally, and legally (civil law rather than common law) distinct. At the institutional level, Canadian scholars

Thomas J. Courchene is the Jarislowsky-Deutsch Professor of Economic and Financial Policy at the School of Policy Studies and director of the John Deutsch Institute for the Study of Economic Policy at Queen's University.

The author thanks Rob Nicholl of the Tasmanian Treasury, Paul Boothe of the University of Alberta, Colin Telmer of Queen's Department of Economics, and Teresa Courchene of the Research Department of the Toronto Dominion Bank for their assistance in preparing this paper. He also acknowledges the valuable comments of the editors of this volume and the conference participants.

have duly noted the differences in our upper chambers and, on more than one occasion, we have unsuccessfully attempted to convert our appointed Senate into the Australian "triple E" version—elected, equal, and effective. Even recognizing these important differences, Canadians and Australians (let alone others) tend, nonetheless, to assume that the similarities far outweigh the differences, with the result that relevant literature is replete with Canadian-Australian comparisons, the most recent of which is Boothe 1996.

From this vantage point, therefore, one might assume that the rationale for comparing subnational budgetary and stabilization policies in Canada and Australia is to assess important or intriguing differences in what otherwise is an essentially similar approach to the conduct of provincial/state fiscal policies.

Reality, however, is quite another matter: one can make a convincing case that the taxation, spending, and borrowing autonomy of the Canadian provinces and of the Australian states represent the polar extremes in modern, mature federations. The wide-ranging powers and fiscal autonomy of the Canadian provinces place them at least on par with the Swiss cantons. Contrast this with the Australian states, which have no effective access to broad-based taxation (sales and/or income taxes) and, therefore, suffer from an incredible vertical fiscal imbalance—Commonwealth transfers exceed the states' own-source revenues. And, of course, the operations of the Australian Loan Council have traditionally limited the states' borrowing *autonomy,* although it may have increased the states' borrowing *ability* since they did so with the imprimatur of Canberra.[1] Given all of this, it should then come as no surprise that Australia has in place an institutional framework designed to ensure that the states' budgets are harmonized and/or coordinated with the Commonwealth's overall philosophy and objectives. Likewise, it should not come as a surprise that on far too many occasions the fiscal policy initiatives of the Canadian provinces have created significant negative spillovers for the Canadian macro strategy.

Cognizant of these divergent subnational fiscal environments, the analysis begins by detailing the different constitutional/institutional frameworks for Canadian provinces and Australian states (sec. 12.2). Beyond the tabular approach to constitutional differences, attention is directed to the allocation of taxing powers, to the extent of vertical fiscal imbalance, to the degree of conditionality of fiscal transfers, to an assessment of the two countries' equalization programs, and, finally, to regional disparities. With this as backdrop, and in line with the budgetary-institutions theme of the volume, section 12.3 highlights the operations of the extensive degree of Commonwealth-state fiscal coordination, while section 12.4 contrasts this with the lack of federal-provincial fiscal coordination in the Canadian federation.

The analysis then shifts to the 1990s fiscal history at the national level (sec-

---

1. For purposes of this paper, "Canberra" and the "Commonwealth government" are used interchangeably to refer to the central government in Australia while "Ottawa" and the "federal government" will be the Canadian counterparts.

tion 12.5 for Canada and section 12.6 for Australia), replete with the manner in which national fiscal policy interplays with provincial and state fiscal policy. The final substantive section presents and assesses Standard and Poor's credit ratings for Australian states and Canadian provinces. An integrative conclusion completes the paper.

Because of the polar nature of these two fiscal systems, this comparative case study may provide useful insights with respect to some of the analytical issues that feature prominently in other papers in the volume. In particular, the decentralized budgetary and borrowing flexibility of the Canadian provinces probably has some implications for the EU in the era of monetary union. Likewise the impressive recent deficit turnaround in Canada may shed light on issues such as the role of a strong finance minister, the role of deficit targets, and the importance of transparency—issues that occupy center stage in the analyses of other papers in this volume. And with its Charter of Budget Honesty, Australia has carried transparency to new heights. Where relevant, these relationships between budgetary institutions and fiscal performance will be highlighted.

12.2   The Constitutional/Institutional Frameworks Relating to Subnational Budgetary Autonomy

The theme of this section is that a comparative analysis of the subnational fiscal/budgetary policies and processes of the Canadian provinces and Australian states can only be understood in the context of the differing constitutional/institutional frameworks in the two countries. Toward this end, table 12.1 provides selected salient features of the comparative constitutional backdrop. We begin the more detailed analysis by directing attention to the allocation of taxing powers.

12.2.1   The Allocation of Taxing Powers

In the 1930s, both the Australian states and Canadian provinces had, de facto, significant and similar taxing powers. For example, the Canadian provinces (including municipalities) accounted for nearly 70 percent of total own-source revenues in the federation. In Australia, the states accounted for 46 percent of total taxation, including 60 percent of income tax revenues (Walsh 1996, 125). In the 1940s, both countries dramatically centralized their taxation systems as part of the war effort. To this point, therefore, their experiences were roughly similar.

In the postwar period, however, the Canadian provinces regained their former taxation powers, whereas, in Australia, the Commonwealth effectively precluded any resurgence in state taxation. As noted in table 12.1, there were two key events that led to the maintenance of the Commonwealth's monopoly of broad-based taxation. One was the High Court's peculiar decision to interpret a state-levied general retail sales tax as a customs duty, thereby prohibiting

Table 12.1 **Fiscal Federalism in Canada and Australia: The Constitutional/ Institutional Framework**

Area	Australia	Canada
A. General provisions 1. Powers	Formal listing of Commonwealth powers. Most of these are concurrent, but with Commonwealth paramountcy. Residual powers to states.	Federal and provincial governments have own listing of powers, section 91 for Ottawa and section 92 for the provinces. Residual power to federal government.
2. Internal economic union (and judicial interpretation)	Commonwealth trade and commerce power given expansive reading by the High Court (similar to scope of U.S. interstate commerce power). Substantially enhances Commonwealth powers.	Federal trade and commerce power given much less expansive reading by the Supreme Court. Provincial head of power ("property and civil rights") serves as de facto residual clause. Canada is much more decentralized than is Australia.
B. Taxation 1. Direct taxes	Commonwealth and states can both levy direct taxation.	Both federal and provincial governments can levy direct taxation.
Income taxes	However, Commonwealth has effectively monopolized personal and corporate income taxes: States will lose Commonwealth grants if they reenter income taxation. No state has yet done so.	Provinces collect roughly 40 percent of personal income taxation. Nine provinces piggyback off federal income tax, while Quebec has its own separate PIT. Three provinces have separate corporate income tax (Quebec, Ontario, Alberta) while the rest piggyback on Ottawa's corporate tax.
2. Indirect taxation	Except for customs duties, are concurrent powers. But High Court prohibited state sales taxes on grounds that they were the customs duty. Australia has no general sales tax.	Provinces cannot levy indirect taxes. But provincial sales taxes (following British interpretation) were viewed as a direct tax. All provinces except Alberta now levy sales taxes. Federal government levies value-added tax (GST). Hence, joint occupancy with limited harmonization (only Quebec, New Brunswick, Newfoundland, and Nova Scotia have harmonized their PST with federal GST).

Table 12.1   (continued)

Area	Australia	Canada
3. Natural resources	Concurrent, with Commonwealth paramountcy	Provincial jurisdiction, except for resources on Canada (nonprovince) lands. When Saskatchewan and Alberta joined the federation in 1905, Ottawa maintained the subsurface property rights. It transferred these subsurface rights to these provinces around 1930. The result is that these two provinces own the subsurface rights on virtually all the (energy rich) lands within their borders.
C. Intergovernmental grants	Section 96 states that the Commonwealth may grant financial assistance to any state on such terms or conditions as parliament thinks fit. As noted above, the Commonwealth has used this power to prevent states from levying income taxes. This provision provides the authority for the Commonwealth's specific-purpose grants and for the general revenue grants falling under the Commonwealth Grants Commission.	Generalized federal spending power provides mechanism for Ottawa to make grants to the provinces (but probably not in a way that serves to regulate activities in the provincial domain). The principle of equalization (but no precise formula) has been enshrined since 1982. Recently, the federal government has agreed to curtail the exercise of its spending power in areas of exclusive provincial jurisdiction—now requires broad provincial support and opting out with compensation for those provinces not on side.

state action (since customs duties were the prerogative of the Commonwealth). More recently, the High Court has also struck down state excises on gasoline and tobacco. The other, and more important, decision was the Commonwealth's threat under s.96 (panel C, table 12.1) to withdraw financial transfers from any state that reentered the income tax field. Given the critical role that these Commonwealth-state transfers play in state revenues (elaborated in the following section), it is perhaps not surprising that no state has seriously considered reentering the income tax field.

The result of all of this appears in tables 12.2 and 12.3 for Australia and Canada respectively. Focusing initially on the Australian data, a few features merit highlighting. First, very few tax bases are shared. Of the first ten entries

Table 12.2　　　　　**Access to Revenue Sources: Australia, 1992–93**

	Total ($ billions)	Percentage Distribution		
		Commonwealth	States/ Territories	Local
A. Taxes, fees, and fines				
1. Income taxes (personal and corporate)	63.2	100.00	0.00	0.00
2. Property taxes				
Financial transactions	4.9	0.00	100.00	0.00
Other	6.7	0.00	30.9	69.1
3. Sales taxes				
General sales tax	9.3	100.00	0.00	0.00
Excises	10.8	95.5	4.5	0.00
Gambling and insurance	3.5	0.00	100.00	0.00
International trade	3.3	100.00	0.00	0.00
4. Payroll taxes				
General	5.8	0.00	100.00	0.00
Selective	1.4	100.00	0.00	0.00
5. Taxes on use of goods and performance of activities	6.5	3.6	96.4	0.00
6. Fees and fines	2.4	39.0	46.9	14.1
Total taxes, fees, and fines	117.7	75.3	20.5	4.2
B. Operating surplus of public trading enterprises (PTEs)	11.5	34.6	62.9	2.5
Total revenues	129.2	71.7	24.2	4.1

Source: Australian Bureau of Statistics 1995, section 24.

in table 12.2 (up to and including row A5) eight are allocated 100 percent to either the Commonwealth or the state/local level, with the remaining two having at least a 95 percent share allocated to one or the other level of (95.5 percent of excises accrue to the Commonwealth, while 96.4 percent of taxes on goods accrue to the state/local level). Of the 12 Canadian tax categories (table 12.3), only 3 fall in this 95 percent plus range—all property taxes are local, the international component of sales taxes (customs) is federal, and virtually all natural resource revenues are provincial.[2] The second general point is that

2. While this observation obviously depends on the manner in which tax sources are classified, the thrust of the argument would hold under alternative classifications as well. In terms of the classification utilized in tables 12.2 and 12.3, some elaboration is probably in order. In table 12.2, the states' general payroll taxes accrue to the consolidated revenue fund and are part of the states general revenues; i.e., they are not social insurance levies. Indeed, in the OECD definition of social insurance levies, Australia has none. It has no unemployment insurance program. Workers' compensation is compulsory for firms, but this is run largely through third-party (private) insurance. And there is no Australian equivalent to the Canada/Quebec Pension Plan, the compulsory public pension system. Entry B of table 12.2 (public trading enterprises) is probably quite similar to entry 9 in table 12.3—for example, they would both include the provincial/state monopolies for the various utilities. The "financial transactions" entry under the property tax heading in table 12.2 is generally referred to as "stamp duties"—taxes on securities transactions. And so on.

Table 12.3 **Access to Revenue Sources: Canada, 1992**

	Total ($ billions)	Percentage Distribution	
		Federal	Provincial
1. Income taxes			
Personal	103.7	62.8	37.2[a]
Corporate	14.0	65.0	35.0[a]
2. Property taxes	27.8	0.00	100.00[b]
3. Consumption taxes			
General sales	35.6	47.9[c]	52.1[d]
Fuel	8.0	37.0	63.0[a]
Alcohol and tobacco	6.8	57.5	42.5[a]
International (customs)	4.0	100.00	0.00
4. Social insurance levies	24.7	62.6[e]	37.4[e]
5. Sales of goods and services	13.4	23.0	77.0
6. Licences and permits	4.2	6.6	93.4
7. Natural resource revenues	4.6	1.0	99.0[a]
8. Miscellaneous taxes	11.0	56.0	44.0
9. Return on investments and other revenue	23.5	26.6	73.4[a]
Total revenues	277.5	46.7	53.3

Source: Canadian Tax Foundation 1994, table 4.3.

[a]Entirely or largely provincial.

[b]Largely local.

[c]Primarily the GST, a value-added tax.

[d]Primarily general retail sales taxes at the provincial level.

[e]Federal component is largely unemployment insurance premiums, and provincial component is premiums for workers' compensation. The public pension premiums (CPP/QPP) are not included.

not only are the states left with a narrow set of own-source revenues, but even these are under increasing competitive pressure. Payroll taxes (which are probably the closest thing the states have to a broad-based tax) are increasingly viewed as problematic in an era of high unemployment, and they are under further pressure because the Commonwealth has recently begun encroaching on this base with pension contributions. As a result of the recent (1995) Competition Principles Agreement, which opens the state's public-sector business enterprises to interstate competition, it will be more difficult for the states to maintain their large revenues arising from the operating surplus of Public Trading Enterprises (row B of table 12.2). And because of the inherent mobility of financial transactions, the various taxes on financial transactions (stamp duties) are also coming under pressure—in the mid-1990s Queensland cut its stamp duties on marketable securities by 50 percent in order to attract securities business from New South Wales. Given the inherent mobility of this tax base, other states had no choice but to follow Queensland's lead.

Table 12.3 presents comparable tax allocation data for the Canadian federation. Ottawa maintains just under two-thirds of the personal and corporate income taxation and about half of the general sales taxation (the federal share is the GST, a value-added tax, and the provincial share relates to the point-of-sale retail sales taxes). While most of the remaining detail is left to the reader, the natural resource revenues entry (row 7) is critical for the ensuing analysis. It is not just that nearly 100 percent of the revenues from this source accrue to the provinces. It is also that, for two provinces, Saskatchewan and Alberta, the subsurface rights (e.g., for oil and gas) rest with the province, not with the owners of the land (see row B3 of table 12.1).

The final row of each table presents aggregate revenues and their distribution between the national and subnational governments. In Australia, the Commonwealth's share is 71.2 percent, while the federal share in Canada is less than 50 percent (46.7 percent). What is also very evident is that, subject to some adjustment for exchange rates,[3] the level of overall taxation in Australia is much lower than in Canada. In a recent paper comparing taxation in Canada and Australia, Dahlby and Wilson (1996) argue that one of the reasons for this likely has to do with the fact that so many tax sources are shared in Canada. The analogy here is that of a common-property resource. Hence, sharing a common tax base will lead to "overtaxation" in the same way that the "tragedy of the commons" leads to "overgrazing." For example, on at least two occasions over the last decade Ottawa reduced personal income taxes in order to bring Canadian personal income tax rates more in line with those in the United States. On both occasions, some provinces (e.g., Ontario) responded by raising their own tax rates, thereby "taking up" the vacated tax room. This is a fiscal federalism example of the common-pool or $1/N$ problem that plays center stage in many papers in this volume.

For our purposes, however, the key message that emerges from tables 12.2 and 12.3 is that the Canadian provinces have much more in the way of meaningful tax autonomy and flexibility than have the Australian states, including access to broad-based tax sources such as sales and personal/corporate income taxation. As Walsh (1996, 115) has noted, "Australia has by far the highest degree of vertical fiscal imbalance among the major federations in the industrialized world. It is even high by the standards of most unitary countries."

12.2.2 Vertical Fiscal Imbalances

Tables 12.4 and 12.5 present data on vertical fiscal imbalances, inter alia, for the two federations. While the fiscal years differ, the qualitative implications derived from putting the Canadian data on a comparable fiscal year would

---

3. The Canadian dollar depreciated relative to the Australian dollar over the recent period. In terms of the number of Canadian cents per Australian dollar, the average of monthly exchange rates was 91.1 cents in 1990, 89.2 cents in 1991, 88.7 cents in 1992, 87.6 cents in 1993, 100 cents in 1994, 101.7 cents in 1995, and 107 cents in 1996. The PPP values are quite different because the Canadian dollar is considerably undervalued. On a PPP basis for 1996, the Australian rate is 135 Australian cents per U.S. dollar, and the Canadian rate is 122 cents per U.S. dollar, with roughly similar values for 1994 (134 and 125 respectively [OECD data]).

Table 12.4   **Horizontal Equalization in Action: Australia, 1993–94**

	Own Revenues (standardized)		Commonwealth Grants ($ per capita)		Grants Plus Revenues (1+3+4)		Grants as a % of Own Revenues ((3+4)÷1)
	$ per capita (1)	% of National Average[a] (2)	General (3)	Specific Purpose (4)	$ per capita (5)	% of National Average (6)	(7)
New South Wales	1,774	105.0	686	910	3,370	96.9	90.0
Victoria	1,618	95.8	699	914	3,231	92.9	99.7
Queensland	1,658	98.2	902	924	3,484	100.1	110.1
Western Australia	1,907	113.0	945	969	3,821	109.8	100.4
South Australia	1,502	88.9	1,113	1,033	3,648	104.9	142.9
Tasmania	1,269	75.2	1,326	1,033	3,628	104.3	185.9
Northern Territory	1,788	105.8	5,001	1,546	8,335	239.6	366.2
Australian Capital Territory	1,641	97.2	1,154	763	3,558	102.3	116.8
Australian standard	1,689	100.0	847	943	3,479	100.0	106.0

Sources: Commonwealth Grants Commission 1995, table VI-10 (columns 1–2); table 3, Budget Paper no. 3, pursuant to the 1993–94 Australian budget (columns 3–4).

[a]These percentages represent the difference in revenue-raising capacity across the states, since tax effort is held constant.

Table 12.5   **Horizontal Equalization in Action: Canada, 1991–92**

| | Own Revenues (standardized)ᵃ | | Own Revenues Plus Equalizationᵇ | | Own Revenues Plus Equalization, CAP, and EPF | | | Financing Share | Net Transfers | | | | Grants as a % of Own Revenuesᶠ |
| | $ Per Capita | % of National Average | $ Per Capita | % of National Average | $ Per Capita | % of National Average | $ Millionsᶜ | ($ millions)ᵈ | Net ($ millions)ᵈ | Net ($ per capita) | Net (as a % of own revenues)ᵉ | |
	(1)	(2)	(3)	(4)	(5)	(6)	(7)	(8)	(9)	(10)	(11)	(12)
Newfoundland	2,991	67	4,440	93.5	5,077	94	1,196	315	881	1,536	0.51	70
Prince Edward Island	3,019	67	4,440	93.5	5,089	94	271	82	189	1,446	0.48	69
Nova Scotia	3,506	78	4,440	93.5	5,118	95	1,452	754	698	775	0.22	46
New Brunswick	3,171	71	4,440	93.5	5,116	95	1,426	519	907	1,249	0.39	62
Quebec	3,958	88	4,440	93.5	5,186	96	8,377	5,393	2,984	436	0.11	31
Ontario	4,761	106	4,761	100	5,352	99	5,863	10,878	–5,015	–506	–0.11	12
Manitoba	3,681	82	4,440	93.5	5,080	94	1,526	764	762	697	0.19	38
Saskatchewan	3,970	89	4,440	93.5	5,017	94	1,011	653	388	390	0.10	26
Alberta	5,937	133	5,917	125	6,565	122	1,586	2,395	–809	–321	–0.07	11
British Columbia	4,840	108	4,840	102	5,487	102	2,081	3,067	–986	–306	–0.07	13
All provinces	4,478	100	4,751	100	5,397	100	24,819	24,819	–1			21
High/low		1.99		1.34		1.31						

Source: Reproduced from Courchene 1994, table 17; author's calculations.

ᵃRevenues from representative tax bases at national average tax rates—that is, fiscal capacity.

ᵇ$4,440 is the five-province standard.

ᶜEqualization plus CAP plus the cash components of EPF (plus the tax abatements for Quebec).

ᵈThe shares of federal taxes by province appear in Courchene 1994, chapter 2, note 3.

ᵉColumn 10 ÷ column 1.

ᶠ(Column 5 – column 1) ÷ column 1.

not differ. The first point to note is that standardized own revenues (i.e., at comparable tax rates and standardized tax bases) are considerably more variable across the Canadian provinces. From table 12.5, standardized own revenues for Alberta are twice that of Newfoundland and Prince Edward Island (i.e., the high/low ratio is 1.99, from the last row), whereas Western Australia's own revenues are only 1.5 times that of Tasmania. Second, on average, own revenues for the Canadian provinces are well in excess of those for the Australian states ($4,478 from the second to last entry in column 1 of table 12.5 vs. $1,689 from the "Australian Standard" row of column 1 in table 12.4). This follows directly from the earlier data on the allocation of tax sources: there is simply no scope for the Australian states to raise anywhere near the own-source revenues of the Canadian provinces. While Commonwealth-state transfers as a percentage of own-source revenues are, as elaborated below, much higher than federal-provincial transfers, it is still the case that, after transfers, the provinces' revenues significantly exceed those of the Australian states ($5,397 vs. $3,479, from the last entries of column 5 in both tables). Much of this relates to the allocation of expenditure functions—for example, welfare is a provincial matter in Canada but a Commonwealth responsibility in Australia. Some also reflects the fact that, as a percentage of GDP, Australian taxes overall are much lower than Canadian taxes.

One measure of the degree of vertical fiscal imbalance appears in column 6 of table 12.4 for Australia and in the last column of table 12.5 for Canada. At the all-province level, federal-provincial transfers represent 21 percent of standardized own revenues in Canada, while Commonwealth-state grants actually exceed average own revenues—grants are 106 percent of standardized own revenues. The most fiscally autonomous state in Australia (New South Wales, with a grants-to-own-source-revenues percentage of 90 percent) is far more grant-dependent than any Canadian province. The Canadian ratios range from a high of 70 percent for Newfoundland to 11 percent, 12 percent, and 13 percent for Alberta, Ontario, and British Columbia, the three "have" (or non-equalization-receiving) provinces. Indeed, in the fiscal year 1996/97, Alberta's budget *surplus* was well in excess of *all* transfers from Ottawa, so that this province's own revenues *exceeded* its total expenditure. And Alberta has by far the lowest tax effort of all the provinces. Thus, Alberta is fully autonomous fiscally!

12.2.3   Conditional versus Unconditional Grants

Given the centralist and egalitarian features of the Australian federation, it should follow that the Commonwealth grants to the states should be tilted in the direction of conditional or specific-purpose payments (SPPs). From columns 3 and 4 of table 12.4, this is precisely the case—specific-purpose transfers exceed general-purpose transfers ($943 per capita vs. $847 per capita). What is not shown in table 12.4 is that SPPs have been increasing relative to unconditional grants. The situation in Canada is precisely the reverse. With the recent move to "block funding" of federal transfers relating to health, postsecondary education, and welfare in the form of the CHST (Canada Health and Social Transfer), there remain *no* specific-purpose transfers in the Canadian federation. To be sure, *all* provincial monies spent on health must abide by five principles (universality, accessibility, comprehensiveness, portability, and public administration). However, these principles relate more to the requirements of an "internal social union" than to conditions on the transfers themselves.

Australia may well be unique among modern federations in terms of having its intergovernmental grants gradually shift from general purpose to specific purpose or from an unconditional to a conditional basis. Indeed, even the general-purpose grants that fall under the rubric of the Commonwealth Grants Commission (CGC) are not as unconditional as they might appear. This is because one of the determinants of the CGC grants is "expenditure disabilities." If there is a greater expenditure "need" in a given state, it will receive a larger share of the grant for that specific expenditure purpose. What appears to be occurring is that special interests are increasingly aware of this and are pressuring the states to spend these monies more *in accordance with the associated expenditure needs.* And if the special interests fail in this endeavor to bring the states in line, they can then lobby Canberra to remove this category from general-purpose grants and to convert it to a specific-purpose grant. This is part of the dynamic in favor of tied grants in Australia, and without access to broad-based taxation the states are rather helpless to combat this dynamic. In this sense, the core problem relates to the enormous degree of vertical fiscal imbalance. Hence Australian policy analysts desirous of enhancing state autonomy are, not surprisingly, focusing on creative approaches to significantly enhancing the states' taxation powers and, therefore, fiscal autonomy (e.g., Walsh 1996). In line with the earlier analysis, these efforts will probably not succeed unless the Commonwealth alters its centralist/egalitarian philosophy. Now that we have broached the operations of the CGC, it is appropriate to focus on this celebrated institution in more detail and to compare it with Canada's equalization program. To anticipate the analysis, nowhere is Australian egalitarianism more evident than in its approach to these CGC "equalization payments."

12.2.4   Equalization

By way of an introductory set of comments on revenue equalization in Canada and Australia, the first point to note is that the CGC approach (which relates to General Revenue Grants, not specific-purpose payments although, as noted later, some of the SPP's are indirectly taken into account in the CGC calculations) combines both vertical and horizontal balance considerations, whereas the Canadian equalization program is concerned only with horizontal balance (i.e., only seven of the ten provinces qualify for equalization). Second, the CGC model equalizes for both "revenue means" and "expenditure needs," whereas the Canadian model is limited to ensuring that all provinces have access to some "standard level" of per capita revenues (currently a "five-province standard," where the five provinces in the standard are Ontario, British Columbia, Saskatchewan, Manitoba, and Quebec). Third, Canadian provinces with per capita revenues in excess of this five-province standard level of per capita revenues *keep* their excess revenue. In other words, rich provinces are not "leveled down." Because the CGC model integrates both vertical and horizontal transfers, there are no "tall poppies"—Australian states are fully leveled, both up and down. Finally, the CGC model only determines the states' "shares" or the "relativities" with respect to the overall general-revenue grant. The Commonwealth government determines the amount to be distributed. This differs from the Canadian equalization formula, which simultaneously determines the distribution and the magnitude of the payments, except when ceilings and/or floors apply, as they have on occasion over the past decade.

The CGC Model

The Commonwealth Grants Commission model is a computational nightmare in the sense that it equalizes across 19 categories on the revenue side and 40 on the expenditure side. Having spent months wrestling with the mechanics and mathematics of the CGC model, I have come to the conclusion that whatever the merits of the CGC (and there are many—its independence, its accessibility, its competence) one of them is not its expositional ability. Thankfully, there is a much more intuitive approach to the CGC model, one employed in the article *Horizontal Fiscal Equalization,* the Report of the Heads of Treasuries Working Party to the 1994 Premiers' Conference (1994). Essentially the grants to each state can be expressed as

- an equal per capita share of the total revenue grant;
- *plus* revenue needs $[R_S/P_S\,(1 - p_i)]$, where revenue-rich states ($p_i > 1.0$) will be leveled down from the standardized per capita revenue (R_S/P_S), and vice versa;
- *plus* expenditure needs $[E_S/P_S(\gamma_i - 1)]$, where "needy" states ($\gamma_i > 1.0$) will receive a larger share of the standardized expenditures (E_S/P_S), and vice versa;
- *minus* the excess of those Specific Purpose Payments that are included in the analysis (and not all of them are) in relation to the amounts that the CGC model would call for.[4]

This approach is applied in table 12.6 for 1993/94. Column 1 contains the equal per capita value of the grant, which is $980 (i.e., the $17,400 million figure in column 7 divided by total population). Column 2 corrects for revenue

---

4. Some but not all SPPs are integrated into the CGC model. If the amount of these SPPs across states is in excess of what would result if these SPPs were allocated on the basis of the CGC's approach to *expenditure need,* then the excess (deficiency) is subtracted (added) in order to determine the CGC grant for the state in question.

Table 12.6   The Anatomy of CGC Grants, 1993–94

	Equal Per Capita Share of General Revenue ($ per capita) (1)	Revenue Needs[a] ($ per capita) (2)	Expenditure Needs[b] ($ per capita) (3)	Adjustment for Receipt of Other Commonwealth Payments[c] ($ per capita) (4)	General Revenue Grant Requirement (sum of columns 1–4) ($ per capita) (5)	Per capita relativities (column 5 ÷ column 1)[d] (6)	CGC Grants ($ millions) (7)	Source of Funds ($ millions) (8)	Interstate Redistribution Difference (column 7 − column 8) ($ millions) (9)	($ per capita) (10)
New South Wales	980	−91	−66	13	836	0.853	5,046	6,197	−1,151	−191
Victoria	980	23	−203	17	818	0.834	3,658	4,905	−1,247	−279
Queensland	980	35	46	9	1,070	1.092	3,367	2,502	865	274
Western Australia	980	−95	247	−39	1,094	1.116	1,842	1,730	112	66
South Australia	980	203	40	−28	1,196	1.219	1,752	1,229	523	357
Tasmania	980	335	177	−44	1,449	1.478	686	335	351	755
Northern Territory	980	−4	4,064	−356	4,685	4.778	795	165	630	755
Australian Capital Territory	980	141	−296	21	847	0.864	255	337	−82	−273
Average (columns 1–5) or total (columns 7–8)	980	0	0	0	980	1.000	17,400	17,400	0	0

Sources: Report of the Heads of Treasuries 1994, table 2.1 for first six columns. Distribution in column 8 is taken from table 2 of Brosio 1994. Author's calculations for the remainder.

[a]Negative revenue needs mean above-average revenue-raising capacity, and vice versa.

[b]Negative expenditure needs means below average expenditure requirements, and vice versa.

[c]Negative adjustment means above-average receipt of relevant payments.

[d]These relativities differ slightly from the Premiers' Conference relativities due to a minor technical adjustment.

[e]This column allocates the grants according to the distribution by state of the source of Commonwealth revenues.

needs, that is, New South Wales loses $91 per capita because it is revenue rich, and so on. Column 3 corrects for expenditure needs. Victoria and the Australian Capital Territory are the big losers here since, they are in effect, deemed less "needy" than the remaining states. Column 4 adjusts for those SPPs that are included in the CGC model. The per capita entitlements appear in column 5 and the resulting relativities in column 6. Note that the *net* adjustment in each of columns 2, 3, and 4 is zero, so that the overall $980 per capita value of the average grant is maintained.

As noted in the introduction to this section, the Australian approach to general revenue assistance embodies both horizontal and vertical equalization. Column 5 of table 12.6 provides a way of disentangling, conceptually, these two components. The per capita payment for Victoria is the lowest among the states, at $818 per capita. One could call this the *vertical equalization* component of the general revenue grants, that is, the component that all states receive. Any amounts above this $818 represent, in effect, *horizontal equalization,* namely payments necessary to bring every state to the Victorian level, as it were, that is, to enable other states to provide the average standard of state-type services, assuming they do so at the average level of operational efficiency and that they make the average effort to raise revenues from their own sources (CGC 1995, 51).

The Analytics of the Canadian Equalization Formula

The five-province standard (FPS) Canadian equalization formula can be expressed as follows:

(1)
$$\frac{E_{ij}}{P_i} = t_{cj}\left(\frac{B_{Rj}}{P_R} - \frac{B_{ij}}{P_i}\right)$$

for all j (revenue sources) and all i (provinces), where E_{ij} = equalization to province i from revenue source j; P_i = population of province i; E_{ij}/P_i = per capita equalization to province i from revenue source j; t_{cj} = the national average (all-province) tax rate, defined as total revenues from revenue source j (that is, TR_j) divided by the total base for source (that is, B_{cj}), where subscript c refers to Canada or, more correctly, the all-province total; B_{Rj}/P_R = the per capita base for source j in the five-province standard (FPS). The five provinces comprising the standard are Ontario, Quebec, British Columbia, Manitoba, and Saskatchewan. Subscript R refers to the representative five provinces.

For each of the 33 revenue sources that enter the formula, a common base is established and a national average tax rate is calculated. Note that even if a province does not tax a given revenue source, it will still be assigned a tax base. For example, Alberta has no sales tax, but it obviously does have a sales tax *base,* namely the value of retail sales in the province. Thus, the focus of the formula is on equalizing fiscal capacity, not actual revenues.

As equation (1) indicates, if a province has a per capita tax base that is less than the average per capita base of the five provinces that make up the standard, that is, if the term in parentheses in equation (1) is positive, the province in question will have a positive entitlement for this revenue source and vice versa. Entitlements are summed for each province over all revenue sources, and the resulting total, if positive, represents the province's equalization entitlement. If the sum is negative, the entitlement is set to zero. That is, rich provinces' revenues are *not* brought down to the five-province standard (FPS). Indeed, there is no transfer of monies between provinces—equalization payments are made from the federal government's consolidated revenue fund. The seven equalization-receiving provinces are typically referred to as the "have-not provinces," with the remaining three (Alberta, Ontario, and British Columbia) enjoying the title of the "have provinces." Finally, equalization payments are *unconditional*—they can be spent as the receiving provinces wish.

Equalization in Action: A Comparison

Equalizing Impact. From column 2 of table 12.5, per capita differences in the Canadian provinces standardized own-source revenues range from Newfoundland's 67 percent of the all-province average to Alberta's 133 percent. As noted beneath the table, the five-province standard for 1991–92 was $4,440 per capita. The operations of the equalization formula mean that all provinces with less than this per capita revenue level will be brought up to $4,440. The postequalization revenues appear in columns 3 and 4. The high/low ratio falls from 1.99 pre-equalization (column 2) to 1.34 postequalization (column 4) and further to 1.31 once the vertical transfers (for health, postsecondary education, and welfare) are added in. Indeed, were one to remove energy-rich Alberta from the comparison, the "relatives" would range from 94 percent of the all-province average to 102 percent. Intriguingly, the differences in these per capita revenue levels (again excluding Alberta) are not much different from those for Australian states, posttransfer, as recorded in column 6 of table 12.4, especially if one excludes the Northern Territory.[5] However, the differences in per capita revenues for Australian states are *deliberate* and are *designed to create effective equality in providing services*.

One final note in this context. The Canadian data in table 12.5 relate to standardized revenues, not actual revenues. Estimates of *actual* per capita revenues across provinces for fiscal year 1996–97 reveal that six provinces have per capita revenues *in excess* of those of Alberta. In other words, Alberta has taken out its superior fiscal capacity in terms of a low tax effort (i.e., the lowest personal income taxes, no provincial sales tax, etc.).

---

5. Note that the Australian data include the Northern Territories, whereas the Canadian territories (Yukon and the Northwest Territories) are not included in table 12.5, in part because, unlike the Northern Territory, their fiscal transfers do not fall under the rubric of the general equalization formula. Were one to include them in the analysis they, like the Northern Territory, would be "upside" outliers because their transfers also incorporate a "needs" component.

Net Interstate Distribution. The last four columns of table 12.6 focus on the net interstate redistribution as a result of the operations of the CGC. The dollar values of the CGC grants by state appear in column 7. The resulting total ($17.4 billion) is then reallocated across states in accordance with the source of Commonwealth revenues. Thus, Victoria receives $3.658 billion in CGC grants, but its citizens' share of financing the overall grant would be $4.905 billion; that is, it contributes $1.247 billion net (or $279 per capita) to the financing of the general-purpose revenues. This amounts to over one-third of its actual CGC grant.

Columns 7 through 11 of table 12.5 repeat this exercise for Canadian transfers. From column 7, Ontario receives $5.8 billion in transfers, but its citizens' share of Ottawa's consolidated revenue to pay for the transfers is $10.8 billion, for a net contribution of $5.015 billion or nearly 90 percent of its own transfer. But this is not the identical exercise as in table 12.5, because Ontario also gets to keep its tax revenues in excess of the five-province average level. Nonetheless, these data help clarify the actual degree of interprovincial redistribution. For example, overall grants to Quebec equal 31 percent of its own revenues (column 11). But when one takes into account who pays for these transfers, the *net* transfer to Quebec as a percentage of its own revenues is 11 percent (column 10). Even on this net basis, transfers remain high for some provinces— 51 percent of own revenues for Newfoundland and 48 percent for Prince Edward Island.

Stabilizing Features of Equalization: Canada. Under the Canadian equalization system, a have-not province is guaranteed the average per capita revenue of the five provinces that make up the equalization standard. Thus, if the tax bases collapse in a have-not province that is not included in the five-province standard because, say, of an asymmetric negative shock, its revenue level will be *unaffected.* This is 100 percent stabilization, as it were. This result is symmetric, in the sense that equalization will "confiscate" any revenues arising from an increase in these provinces' tax bases. That this is the case is obvious from equation (1) above, because the fall in B_{ij}/P_i does not affect B_{Rj}/P_R for those provinces that are *outside* the five-province standard.[6] For have-not provinces that are part of the standard, the offset is not complete because any fall in that province's tax base will also reduce the five-province standard. Assume that Quebec has a 30 percent weight in the five-province standard. If Quebec's tax bases were to fall by 10 percent, the five-province standard would fall by 3 percent and Quebec's total revenues would accordingly fall by 3 percent (as would the equalization for *all other have-not provinces*).

On the other hand, the three "have" provinces receive no insulation on either

---

6. For a detailed discussion of the analytics of the Canadian equalization formula, readers can consult Boadway and Hobson 1993 or Courchene and Wildasin 1984.

the up or down side. If Alberta suffers a 10 percent fall in its tax bases, then its revenues fall by 10 percent and vice versa. The same applies for Ontario and British Columbia, with one important proviso—their tax bases enter the five-province standard. With its 50 percent weight in the FPS, a 10 percent increase in Ontario's tax bases implies a 5 percent increase in the level of the five-province standard for *all* have-not provinces. In the last half of the 1980s, the Ontario economic boom meant a rapidly rising FPS, so much so that the ceiling provisions of the equalization program came into play. And the dramatic collapse in Ontario's revenues in the 1990s recession served to lower the five-province standard, so that the "floor" provisions of the equalization formula came into play.

Therefore, in terms of stabilization properties, Canada's equalization program has, at one extreme, zero stabilization for the three "rich" provinces, and, at the other, full (100 percent) stabilization for the four have-not provinces outside the FPS, with the remaining three provinces occupying the middle ground.

Two final comments are in order. First, have-not provinces can gain, revenue-wise, from an increase in their tax *rates*. But this is not a realistic alternative in the current environment where all the pressures are in the direction of tax cuts, not tax increases, and this applies with even more force in have-not provinces, which tend to already have higher-than-average tax rates.

The second point is that the equalization schemes are, on balance, probably more *redistributive* than *stabilizing*. Because Ontario has a 50 percent weight in the five-province standard, the equalization payments received by Nova Scotia depend as much, if not more, on what happens in Ontario as in Nova Scotia. For example, Nova Scotia's GDP need not be deviating from a trend line (i.e., no stabilization problem, per se) yet its equalization could still increase if Ontario's tax revenues are revving upward and vice versa. That many of the so-called stabilization programs in federal nations embody substantial redistribution is a key theme in Goodhart and Smith 1993.

Both these final two comments also apply to the CGC model, to which I now turn.

Stabilizing Features of Equalization: Australia. The CGC model has potential stabilizing features since the total amount to be equalized is set annually by the Commonwealth. On a timely basis, this could be increased in a recession and vice versa. But this would apply to *all* states in accordance with the existing "relativities": on an immediate basis, it cannot be targeted to a state with a negative economic shock because the CGC approach employs a five-year average, lagged three years.

More generally, the Australian states are severely revenue constrained: they cannot pocket the proceeds of an economic boom (except for the initial three years before their newfound fortune becomes reflected in the revised relativities). To see this, consider the following example, drawn from the early 1990s.

Western Australia received a $750 million Commonwealth transfer relating to offshore energy initiatives. Apart from the initial three years, this will enter WA's relativities and WA may not even retain its population share of this revenue. This will depend on the relevant revenue and expenditure relativities. And if the Commonwealth holds overall revenue transfers constant, WA will experience a sharp fall in its transfers, offset by increases in all other states. Whether this results in a confiscatory drop in transfers will, as noted, depend on WA's relativities. Were this revenue windfall to occur in Alberta, the province would pocket *all of it.* Since Alberta is not part of the FPS, there would be no impact on equalization in other provinces. Were British Columbia the recipient province, it also would pocket all of this windfall, but since the FPS would rise as a result (since British Columbia is part of the FPS), all other provinces would stand to have their equalization increased somewhat, financed from Ottawa's consolidated revenues.

At this juncture, it is important to raise an important issue. Whatever philosophy is behind these equalization programs, they have a common defect—there is precious little *revenue incentive* for Australian states and Canadian "have-not" provinces to implement policies that ensure state/provincial growth. As already noted, a revenue increase resulting from growing tax bases for poor provinces outside the FPS in Canada is fully confiscated by the Canadian equalization formula. And this confiscation is presumably high as well for *all* Australian states. While there are admittedly other rationales for states and provinces to embark on growth-producing policies, the incentives in the equalization formula are, nonetheless, perverse.

12.2.5 Regional Disparities

Two final issues merit attention in preparing the ground for a focus on subnational budgetary policies and institutions. Since they are drawn from the existing literature, the analysis will be brief.

The first is that per capita regional income (GDP) disparities are much higher across Canadian provinces than across Australian states (Courchene 1993a, 1996a). With Victoria on the high end (for 1991) and Tasmania on the low end, the high/low ratio for the Australian state is 1.30, or 130 percent. For the Canadian provinces, the corresponding 1991 high/low ratio is 1.79, or 179 percent (with Alberta on the high end and Newfoundland and Prince Edward Island essentially tied for the low end). Were one to replace Alberta with Ontario, the high/low ratio would still be above 170 percent. The ratio of employment to the labor force (i.e., unity minus the unemployment rate) reveals an even greater disparity—a high/low ratio for the Australian states of 1.03 compared with 1.13 for the Canadian provinces, or four times as disparate for Canada. These results should come as no surprise. With wage grids roughly identical across states, with automatic stabilizers (e.g., welfare) located at the center, and with full fiscal leveling, there is nowhere near the scope in Australia for an Alberta resource boom or an Ontario manufacturing surge to ratchet up these provinces' revenues and for them to become capitalized in wages and rents.

However, were one to focus on personal income per capita (as distinct from GDP per capita) the variation in the degree of regional disparity is substantially reduced—1.21 for the Australian high/low ratio across states and 1.30 across the Canadian provinces. What this means is that Canada has a (relatively) more generous set of federal transfers to individuals, particularly to individuals in the poorer provinces. Much of this relates to the operations of the Canadian unemployment insurance program—eligibility criteria are tilted toward poorer regions, as are the duration of benefits. (Australia does not even have an unemployment insurance program.) Indeed, Canada's interpersonal transfers are such that, for Newfoundland and Prince Edward Island, personal income actually *exceeds* provincial GDP in 1991. For no Australian state is this even close to being the case.

This leads to an important observation. Just as the Canadian provinces have more effective powers than the Australian states, so too does Ottawa have more maneuverability than Canberra. Except for the Commonwealth's free reign on designing transfers to the states (section 96), the Commonwealth is prohibited from discriminating in favor of particular states in its other policies. There is no similar provision in the Canadian Constitution, and Ottawa is notorious for building regional preferences into programs other than equalization. Indeed, at one point in the recent past, investment incentives in *national* income taxation were tilted in favor of have-not provinces. One result of the proliferation of federal policies (replete with perverse incentives) designed to combat Canadian regional disparities is that these disparities have become long-standing and entrenched. Elsewhere (1993b and 1994) I have referred to this as "transfer dependency" or a "policy-induced equilibrium." At the analytical level, one could probably make the case that these Canadian initiatives at the regional level are rather inevitable. While the Canadian federation is not structured to deliver an Australian type of egalitarianism, the Canadian Constitution does commit governments to "promote equal opportunities for the well-being of all Canadians" (s.36(1)(a) of the Constitution Act, 1982). Since equal opportunity is deemed not to arise out of the interplay of market forces (as evidenced by the degree of provincial per capita disparities in GDP), it falls on the federal government to become an active regional player in programs beyond the formal equalization program. Indeed, Ottawa is finding itself more and more driven to regionally redistributive roles. On the other hand, Canberra is able (and, actually, constitutionally bound) to play a regionally neutral role in delivering national programs. This poses no particular challenge to the Australian egalitarianism, since the concerns relating to individual and state equity/equality are accommodated within the confines of the operations of fiscal federalism and the centralized nature of the federation.

With this admittedly lengthy constitutional/institutional/empirical backdrop, we now direct attention to the frameworks within which the Australia states and Canadian provinces conduct their fiscal/budgetary policies. To anticipate the ensuing analysis, it should come as no surprise that the Australia case is a model of coordination and harmonization, while the Canadian case is neither and, in some aspects, actually borders on the dysfunctional.

12.3   Commonwealth-State Fiscal Coordination in Australia

12.3.1   The Original Commonwealth Loan Council (CLC)

In 1927, the Commonwealth and the governments of the six states entered into a Financial Agreement to coordinate and centralize their borrowings. This agreement took effect in 1929. The thrust of the agreement was as follows (Saunders 1990, 38–39):

> The Commonwealth would finally use its long-neglected power in Section 105 of the Constitution to take over all state debts. The Commonwealth would contribute the amount it had previously paid in per capita grants toward the interest due on the debts for a period of fifty-eight years, which was assumed to be sufficient to amortize them. For the future, a Loan Council, representative of all governments, would be established to make decisions about the terms and levels of borrowings. Most decisions would be by majority, with the Commonwealth having two votes and a casting vote and the states one vote each. With a few exceptions all borrowings would be carried out by the Commonwealth. The states would be liable to the Commonwealth for interest on the loans and the Commonwealth would be liable to the bondholders.

The Loan Council has had a very checkered history, important details of which appear in Saunders 1990. Of interest for present purposes are a few main points. First, the role of the respective governments within the Loan Council was a function of the financial resources available to them. This altered dramatically in 1942 when the Commonwealth assumed sole responsibility for income taxation. As Saunders (1990, 42) notes, "one important result was virtually to eliminate Commonwealth reliance on Loan Council decisions for borrowing for its own purposes." Relatedly, the Commonwealth's power in the Loan Council became preeminent, since the states were wholly dependent on revenue transfers from the Commonwealth.

There was a more serious problem however. There were a set of exemptions in the 1929 legislation that allowed the states to utilize semigovernment or local government "authorities" to effectively borrow for them, with some of the resulting funds appearing in their consolidated revenues. This "end run" on the Loan Council eventually reached dramatic proportions. For example, in 1989–90, "states or their authorities are expected to borrow $3.7 billion on their own behalf, in both domestic and overseas markets. A significant portion of these funds will find their way into state consolidated revenue" (Saunders 1990, 40). Thus, the 1929 version of the Loan Council was essentially in shambles by the 1990s. However, the basic principles underlying the council were still alive and well and were embodied in the reconstituted Loan Council.

12.3.2   The Reconstituted Loan Council

As of 1993, the Loan Council was reconstituted. It now operates largely under voluntarily agreed arrangements rather than the legislated provisions of the earlier Financial Agreement. The council is a Commonwealth-State Ministerial Council comprising the Commonwealth treasurer (as chair) and the premier or treasurer of each state, with the Commonwealth Treasury providing the Loan Council Secretariat. The goals of the new council as reflected in Commonwealth Loan Council 1993 are intended to

- facilitate financial market scrutiny of public-sector finances via better reporting and so make jurisdictions more accountable to the markets
- enhance the role of the Loan Council as a forum for coordinating public-sector borrowings in light of the discussion of fiscal strategies
- promote greater understanding of budgetary processes
- provide the basis for states and territories assuming greater freedom and responsibility in determining their financing requirements consistent with their fiscal and debt position and overall macroeconomic constraints

The macro coordination role is a carryover from the old Loan Council. What is new is that the states will now borrow in their own right rather than via the Commonwealth or through their various borrowing authorities. But this borrowing will be filtered through the Loan Council process in a way that facilitates transparency, public accountability, and enhanced financial market monitoring. What is not as yet clear is whether the financial markets will view the states as "independent" market participants or whether they will assume that the Commonwealth, via the Loan Council process, is implicitly or explicitly guaranteeing the state debt. (More on this in section 12.7 below.)

It is too soon to tell whether this new procedure will work, particularly since the arrangements are voluntary. In the first couple of years or so, all has worked well because the Loan Council has accepted the LCA nominations submitted by the states and because, as will be evident in section 12.6, the Commonwealth's deficit bore the brunt of the 1990s recession.

I now turn to a brief discussion of the context within which the Loan Council and, more generally, Australian fiscal federalism operates.

12.3.3   The Anatomy of Australian Financial Federalism

Figure 12.1 presents my interpretation of the anatomy of Australian financial federalism. The budget cycle begins with the National Fiscal Outlook. This is an overarching document to the entire process of Australian intergovernmental financial relations. It presents projections, on a comparable and consistent basis, for all governments' fiscal outlooks for the medium term (i.e., the current year and the following three years) under both a high- and low-growth scenario. The underlying assumption in these forecasts is that the fiscal parameters

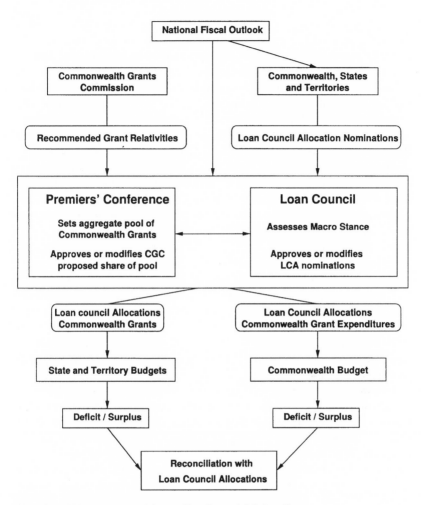

Fig. 12.1   The anatomy of Australian financial federalism

remain unchanged over the projection period, including the *real* value of revenue assistance from the Commonwealth to the states and territories. Initially, these forecasts were provided in advance only to state and territorial governments and were made public only at the time of deliberations of the Loan Council and the Premiers' Conference. In 1995, however, these projections were made public in advance of the Premiers' Conference. As an important aside, this official public document providing an assessment of all governments' fiscal stances on a consistent basis does not exist in Canada, although some private-sector agents (e.g., the economics department of the Toronto Dominion Bank) have partially filled the gap.

The National Fiscal Outlook (NFO) feeds into the Commonwealth, state, and territorial Loan Council Nominations (LCAs in figure 12.1). In tandem, the NFO and the LCAs provide the public and the financial markets with a prebudget overview of the various fiscal positions, which, in turn, enhances the transparency and accountability of the overall budgetary process.

Roughly coincident with the preparation of the National Fiscal Outlook is the publication of the Commonwealth Grants Commission "relativities," that is, the state/territorial shares of Commonwealth grants. These grant relativities and the LCAs then feed into the daylong meeting of the Loan Council and the Premiers' Conference. The role of these meetings is at least threefold: (i) to ratify or otherwise reconsider the LCAs; (ii) likewise to ratify or otherwise adjust the "relativities" recommended by the Commonwealth Grants Commission; and (iii) to decide on the *total* amount of the Commonwealth-state general-revenue grants, which will then be allocated in line with the shares or relativities. These decisions are also released immediately to the public and the financial markets.

Given the grant-dependent nature of the Australian states, as outlined earlier, the effective coincidence (i.e., on the same day) of the decisions relating to loan allocations and Commonwealth transfers means that the Commonwealth government is clearly in the driver's seat. For example, one could conceive of generous Loan Council allocations along with a curtailment of overall Commonwealth transfers; that is, the Commonwealth could force the states to borrow. There is precious little that the Australian states could do, at least in the short term, in response to such a tactic.

This comment aside, the next stage in the process, in terms of figure 12.1, is the preparation of budgets. Because data on deficit projections and Loan Council allocations are already public, the incentives facing the various governments are clearly to do "better" than this in terms of their bottom line.

This focus on transparency, on accountability, and on linking overall government deficits to the underlying macro strategy stands in stark contrast to the laissez-faire approach in Canada. Even though the reconstituted Loan Council arrangements are voluntary, the revenue dependence of the states on the Commonwealth is such that it is highly unlikely that the errant Ontario fiscal scenario (elaborated later) could ever be replicated in Australia. More generally, Australia has in place a fiscal, or at least a borrowing, coordination process that appears to ensure that the aggregate fiscal stances are rendered consistent with the overall macro strategy. None of this should come as a surprise, given the centralist/egalitarian nature of the Australian federation.

12.4   Federal-Provincial Fiscal Coordination in Canada

In a word, there is no coordination! Moreover, any monitoring of provincial finances is done by the capital markets (bond-rating agencies), not by Ottawa. As Kneebone (1994) argues, these capital market constraints were effective (at least in the 1980s) in terms of keeping the lid on provincial borrowing, but they did not really constrain the federal government.

However, one can report some recent progress in related areas. Canada now has a version of a budget cycle. The federal budget comes down in late February or early March of each year. This fixed date does serve as a harmonization element of sorts in the sense that most provinces will know what Ottawa is doing when they present their own budgets. In particular, provinces are obviously interested in any changes in federal-provincial transfers, which, except for equalization, typically appear in federal budgets. In addition, federal and provincial finance ministers and/or deputies do apparently share basic budgeting information in closed-door meetings prior to the beginning of the budget cycle. An important initial step in terms of providing greater transparency, information, and even potential coordination would be to make these projections public à la Australia's National Fiscal Outlook.

Beyond these measures, however, Canada has nothing to compare to the Australian institutional process. Phrased differently, the provinces can tax and spend as they wish and they can borrow as long as they can find markets for their bonds.

However, the real subnational fiscal story in Canada is the potential conflict between provincial and federal policies. I shall focus here only on the province of Ontario and deal with three periods within the last decade or so where its policies ran fully counter to Ottawa's fiscal/macro thrust. Then, I shall focus on errant behavior by the federal government.

12.4.1   Fiscal Conflict: Ontario versus Ottawa

To illustrate the problems that can arise in a highly decentralized federation with effective fiscal autonomy at both levels of government, it is convenient to focus on three recent episodes where the policies of the province of Ontario (which has roughly 40 percent of Canada's GDP) either offset or dramatically complicated Ottawa's macro agenda.

The first occurred in the mid-1980s when the federal government followed the Americans in reducing personal and corporate income tax rates. Ontario responded by "taking up" the vacated federal tax room. That is, it increased its provincial income taxes by the same amount. Overall, taxpayers in Ontario were left in a "neutral" position—total personal income taxes remained constant, but more now went to Ontario and less to Ottawa. I should note in passing that Ontario was not the only province to adopt this strategy. The effect was to negate what the federal government was intent on achieving—a reduction in personal income taxation to bring Canada's tax rates more in line with those in the United States, especially since this was the run-up period to the Canada–United States Free Trade Agreement. Moreover, the tax break was intended primarily for the footloose manufacturing sector (i.e., for Ontario) in order to alleviate the high marginal tax rates on upper-echelon management. But all for naught. Essentially, this is the common-property-resource issue in yet another guise since both Ottawa and the provinces share the income tax bases.

The second episode occurred in the latter half of the 1980s. Ontario was in the throes of a very substantial economic boom. Real GDP growth rates for the province averaged over 5 percent annually for the 1984–89 period. But Ontario was also launched on a veritable spending spree. As a result, inflation pressures were beginning to emerge in the province. Partly to counter this and partly because of a philosophical conversion, the Bank of Canada launched its price stability strategy in early 1988. Yet Ontario's spending increases kept marching along at midteens growth rates. Given that Ontario accounts for roughly 40 percent of Canada's GDP, this severely complicated the price-stability strategy. Interest rates and exchange rates soared—for example, the Canada-U.S. exchange rate appreciated from the low 70 cent range in 1986 to nearly 90 U.S. cents per Canadian dollar in 1991. These rates were much higher than would have been required had Ontario's fiscal policy been coordinated with the overall macro strategy. In the event, rough justice prevailed, as it were, since Ontario was the principal loser in early 1990s recession. Nonetheless, the lack of policy coordination generated substantial economic costs to *all* Canadians.

The third episode follows from the second. Thanks to the spending and taxing spree of the 1980s, Ontario entered 1990 with one of the highest tax rates in the country and with a legitimate claim to be the premier social spender at the provincial level. Both of these features were wholly out of character for the province of Ontario—traditionally a low-tax and moderate-spending province. In any event, the 1990s recession pulled the rug out from under Ontario's revenue base. Ontario's newly elected New Democratic Party (Canada's version of a socialist party) responded by attempting to spend its way out of the recession. The result was a $10 billion budget deficit for Ontario for the fiscal year 1990–91, compared to budget balance in 1988, for example. And not once in the five-year mandate of the New Democrats did Ontario's deficit fall beneath $10 billion. From a net public debt level of just over $40 billion in fiscal 1990–91, Ontario's debt mushroomed to $99 billion in fiscal 1995–96—an increase of nearly 150 percent. During this same period, the federal government was launched on a determined deficit-reduction course, which was obviously and seriously compromised by Ontario's deficit spending. Although Canada's inflation rate was running below that in the United States, our nominal interest rates and, therefore, our real interest rates were well above comparable U.S. rates. We only achieved the interest-rate "crossover" (i.e., Canadian nominal rates for short- and medium-term maturities *below* U.S. nominal rates) once the new Conservative government in Ontario (elected in 1995) committed the province to budget balance by the end of the century.

Several implications arising from Ontario's debt run-up merit highlighting. The first relates to severity of the early 1990s recession for Ontario. The revenue collapse was such that it would have been impossible to keep the province out of the red. The New Democrats may have thrown fiscal caution to the winds, but achieving budget balance, at least in the first year or two of the recession, would have required draconian measures. The second is related. Because Ontario is a "have" province (and remained a have province throughout the recession), it has no equalization "safety net" underpinning its revenue base. Third, Ontario entered this period in rather enviable fiscal shape. Its budget was balanced in 1988–89 (table 12.7), and its debt-to-GDP ratio was less than 15 percent. (Only British Columbia had a lower debt/GDP ratio in this era.) Indeed, as late as 1990 Ontario had a (Standard and Poor's) AAA rating. Therefore, Ontario had ready access to capital markets, at least initially. However, it did not take long for the capital markets to react. Standard and Poor's dropped Ontario's rating to AA+ in 1991, to AA in 1992, and then to AA− in 1993, where it still remains. Nonetheless, the province was able to float roughly $60 billion in new bonds over a five-year period—undoubtedly a record for a subnational government, anywhere, anytime.

The fourth point situates Ontario's behavior in the EU context. As I have argued elsewhere (1993b), the challenge to coordinated macro policy in either Canada or the EU is not likely to come from the smaller provinces or countries. In part, this is precisely because they are small and, hence, likely to have minimum impact on the overall stabilization strategy: errant behavior by Portugal or Newfoundland will have little effect on EU or Canadian inflation targets. In part, also, the capital markets will tend to keep these countries or provinces in check. On both counts, this is less likely to apply to the powerful nations or provinces. For example, in the second of the above two episodes, Ontario was well within any sort of Maastricht-type guidelines. In terms of the 1990s, however, Ontario's deficit-to-GDP ratio did exceed 3 percent from 1991–92 onward (3.9 percent in 1991–92, 4.4 percent in 1992–93, 3.9 percent in 1993–94, 3.3 percent in 1994–95, dropping finally to 2.8 percent in 1995–96), while the debt/GDP ratio increased from 14.2 percent in 1989–90 to 31.3 percent in 1995–96. The point I am making here is that large countries in the EU that are "intramarginal" in terms of the Maastricht guidelines are far more likely to wreak havoc with overall macro and inflation guidelines than are some of the smaller and likely capital-markets-constrained countries who are likely to be bumping against the Maastricht guidelines in any event.

The key message in the Canadian case is that the federation is in dire need of some coordinating, perhaps even harmonizing, mechanisms that would address the deleterious spillovers arising from fiscal and budgetary decentralization. Note that this is not meant to downplay the potential for stabilization policies at the provincial level, especially for the three have provinces. In particular, there is an important provincial role in terms of "tempering" their economic booms.

12.4.2   Fiscal Conflict: Ottawa versus the Provinces

While Canada's taxation system is very decentralized, it is at the same time quite harmonized. The decentralized personal income tax allows the provinces (except for Quebec, which has its own personal income tax) to levy a single tax rate against federal taxes payable. For example, a 50 percent provincial tax rate would imply that the province in question would receive one-third of over-

Table 12.7 Canadian Federal and Provincial Governments: Surpluses and Deficits (as of July 21, 1997)

	1989–90	1990–91	1991–92	1992–93	1993–94	1994–95	1995–96	1996–97	Projections 1997–98	1998–99
					Surpluses/Deficits ($ millions)					
Total federal and provincial	−33,253	−42,060	−57,005	−65,941	−62,205	−53,368	−40,544	−23,116	−18,768	−10,622
Federal	−28,930	−32,000	−34,357	−41,021	−42,012	−37,462	−28,617	−15,000	−10,000	−5,000
Total provincial	−4,323	−10,060	−22,648	−24,920	−20,193	−15,906	−11,927	−8,116	−8,768	−5,622
Newfoundland	−175	−347	−276	−261	−205	−127	9	−29	−20	−10
Prince Edward Island	−8	−20	−50	−82	−71	−2	4	−7	−17	1
Nova Scotia	−266	−257	−406	−617	−547	−235	−201	5	4	4
New Brunswick	−24	−182	−348	−259	−250	−69	51	74	26	23
Quebec	−1,760	−2,967	−4,301	−5,014	−4,921	−5,821	−3,950	−3,245	−2,200	−1,200
Ontario	90	−3,029	−10,930	−12,428	−11,202	−10,129	−8,800	−7,470	−6,580	−4,800
Manitoba	−142	−292	−334	−566	−431	−196	157	56	27	30
Saskatchewan	−378	−360	−842	−592	−272	128	18	369	24	79
Alberta	−2,116	−1,832	−2,629	−3,415	−1,384	958	1,132	2,527	154	252
British Columbia	456	−774	−2,532	−1,686	−910	−414	−347	−395	−185	0

Surplus/Deficit-to-GDP Ratios (% of GDP)

Total federal and provincial	-5.1	-6.3	-8.4	-9.6	-8.7	-7.1	-5.2	-2.9	-2.2	-1.2
Federal	-4.4	-4.8	-5.1	-5.9	-5.9	-5.0	-3.7	-1.9	-1.2	-0.6
Total provincial	-0.7	-1.5	-3.3	-3.6	-2.8	-2.1	-1.5	-1.0	-1.0	-0.6
Newfoundland	-2.1	-3.9	-3.0	-2.8	-2.2	-1.3	0.1	-0.3	-0.2	-0.1
Prince Edward Island	-0.4	-1.0	-2.4	-3.8	-3.1	-0.1	0.2	-0.3	-0.6	0.0
Nova Scotia	-1.7	-1.5	-2.3	-3.5	-3.0	-1.3	-1.1	0.0	0.0	0.0
New Brunswick	-0.2	-1.4	-2.6	-1.9	-1.7	-0.4	0.3	0.5	0.2	0.1
Quebec	-1.2	-1.9	-2.8	-3.2	-3.0	-3.5	-2.3	-1.9	-1.2	-0.6
Ontario	0.0	-1.1	-3.9	-4.4	-3.9	-3.4	-2.8	-2.3	-1.9	-1.3
Manitoba	-0.6	-1.3	-1.5	-2.4	-1.8	-0.8	0.6	0.2	0.1	0.1
Saskatchewan	-1.9	-1.7	-4.1	-2.9	-1.3	0.6	0.1	1.4	0.1	0.3
Alberta	-3.2	-2.6	-3.7	-4.7	-1.8	1.2	1.3	2.8	0.2	0.2
British Columbia	0.6	-1.0	-3.1	-1.9	-1.0	-0.4	-0.3	-0.4	-0.2	0.0

Sources: Federal and provincial budgets and governments, Statistics Canada, and TD Economics, Toronto Dominion Bank.

Note: Federal government deficits for 1996–97 to 1998–99 are estimated by TD Economics. Nominal GDP forecast by TD Economics as of July 1997. Provincial surplus/deficit data are government estimates. Fiscal years begin on April 1 and end on March 31. Data may not be comparable across years. The consolidated surplus/deficit estimates generally include operating and capital items, and equal consolidated revenues less consolidated expenditures. Some provinces include a portion of sinking-fund earnings when reporting their consolidated balances. Ontario's deficit for 1993–94 to 1998–99 is presented on a PSAAB basis, and is not strictly comparable to data for prior years. B.C.'s Consolidated Revenue Fund excludes most capital spending. Manitoba's 1997–98 operating revenue includes $100 million from the Fiscal Stabilization Fund. Saskatchewan's 1996–97 consolidated revenue includes a special CIC dividend of $364.7 million.

all personal income tax revenues. The overall tax is harmonized because the federal government determines all the relevant parameters (definitions of income, definitions of tax credits, overall progressivity, etc.) and because the tax compliance for the provincial portion of the tax is minimal (the provincial tax component occupies only a line or two in the overall tax form). While the harmonization of the personal income tax remains, Ottawa introduced a 7 percent European-style VAT (the goods and services tax, GST) beginning in 1991. This replaced the former manufacturers' sales tax. The rationale for the switch is not in question. The GST, like any VAT, is export-import neutral and, therefore, ideally designed for the enhanced U.S. and North American integration under the FTA and NAFTA. Unfortunately, this tax was introduced in the face of almost universal opposition from the provinces. Initially, only Quebec agreed to harmonize its PST (provincial sales tax) with the GST base (and was rewarded with the power to collect both the GST and its harmonized PST). For the nine other provinces (actually eight, since Alberta does not levy a PST), the tax bases of the GST and the PST are very different. In particular, the PSTs generally exclude services. This has introduced a very substantial compliance cost on businesses and, generally, has led to a sales tax "jungle," as it were. As of April 1, 1997, Ottawa offered a $1 billion dollar bribe to three Atlantic provinces (Nova Scotia, New Brunswick, and Newfoundland) to adopt a "blended" (GST plus PST) sales tax at a combined rate of 15 percent. This billion-dollar subsidy has not been well received by the other provinces (who were not offered the subsidy), and the sales tax disharmony still prevails in these other provinces. Whatever the problems and challenges of Commonwealth-state fiscal relations in Australia, this degree of lack of harmonization could never occur.

The other, and more far-reaching, federal-provincial dysfunction is that the Canadian federal government has achieved its quite remarkable deficit-turnaround by "off-loading" or "deficit shifting" much of its problem to the provinces. This issue will be addressed in the context of Canada's recent fiscal history, to which I now turn.

12.5   Recent Fiscal History: Canada

Canada came out of the severe 1990s recession in absolutely dreadful fiscal shape.[7] In fiscal year 1992–93, the federal deficit was $41.0 billion (5.9 percent of GDP) and the combined (federal and provincial) deficit was $65.9 billion (9.6 percent of GDP), as revealed in table 12.7. Federal net public debt was $466 billion (68 percent of GDP) and the combined federal and provincial debt was $660 billion, or 95.7 percent of GDP. Beyond this, our current account deficit was running at 4 percent of GDP. Spilling this amount of red ink was tantamount to an open invitation to what we Canadians call the "kids in red

7. For a longer sweep of Canada's macro history, see Courchene 1997.

suspenders" (the international capital markets) to exert some external pressure on our fiscal profligacy. And they did, not only by downgrading Canada's foreign currency debt (which as a percentage of GDP was well above any other G7 nation) but also by providing an external discipline that in turn provided the needed catalyst for bringing Canadians to their fiscal senses. The fiscal story from 1993, and especially 1995, to the present is one of a quite remarkable turnaround: in 1998 Ottawa is forecast (by Finance Canada) to be the only G7 nation to run a financial requirements surplus. What follows is a brief survey of the key elements of this turnaround.

12.5.1   Inflation, Interest Rates, and Exchange Rates

In 1988 the Bank of Canada adopted a price stability strategy. The immediate result of this was that interest rates spiraled upward, the Canadian dollar appreciated from the low 70 cent range to nearly 90 U.S. cents in 1991, and Canadian competitiveness vis-à-vis the United States (as measured by comparative unit labor costs expressed in a common currency) deteriorated sharply, all of which exacerbated the early 1990s recession.

Nonetheless, the price stability policy did achieve its intended results by early 1992, when Canadian inflation rates dipped below U.S. inflation rates, where they have stayed ever since. And the exchange rate fell back to the low 70 cent range. The problem, however, was that until early 1996, Canadian short-term nominal rates remained above, often well above, comparable U.S. rates with the result that Canadian *real* interest rates were well in excess (often by 4 percent) of U.S. real rates. It was not until early 1996 that Canadian treasury bill rates dipped below comparable U.S. T-bill rates, and it was not until early 1997 that Canadian interest rates were below comparable U.S. rates up to a maturity of 10 years. This "interest-rate crossover" is a historic development and clearly a feather in the Bank of Canada's cap.[8] While not downplaying the role that the Bank of Canada's credibility played in this interest-rate crossover, it is nonetheless the case that the Bank probably needed the commitment to deficit reduction and the budget credibility of the finance minister. Moreover, it probably also needed the newly elected (1995) Conservative government of Ontario to ride herd on the province's five-year average of $10 billion-plus annual deficits.

At the time of writing, interest rates are at 30- or 40-year lows, inflation remains roughly at the midpoint of the 1–3 percent target range and lower than U.S. inflation, the Canadian economy is probably as competitive vis-à-vis the

8. Elsewhere (1997), I expressed some pessimism in terms of Canada's (and the bank's) ability to generate this interest-rate crossover. Obviously, I was wrong. However, the larger point relates to the wisdom of pursuing a lower inflation rate than the Americans, when 80 percent of exports are destined for U.S. markets. Canada cannot tolerate the massive exchange rate swings of the last decade (70 U.S. cents per Canadian dollar in 1986, roughly 90 cents in 1991, and back to the low 70 cent range recently). What may guarantee more exchange-rate fixity is that the U.S. Federal Reserve is also targeting on a low inflation rate. While others (e.g., Fortin 1996) are also concerned about Bank of Canada policy, we are clearly in the minority of the Canadian economics profession.

Americans as it has ever been, the merchandise trade surplus is running at nearly 5 percent of GDP, and the current account is balanced. Fiscal policy is an integral part of this impressive turnaround.

12.5.2   The Fiscal Story

The Chrétien Liberals were elected in 1993 on a platform that included, à la Maastricht, bringing the federal deficit down to 3 percent of GDP. However, Finance Minister Paul Martin, pressured by domestic and international financial markets and the Canadian economics policy community, buoyed by substantial citizen support, and chastened with the reality that debt-servicing costs were running at 33 percent of revenues (in fiscal year 1993–94), utilized this Maastricht window to pursue a much more thorough exercise in fiscal restraint. The key fiscal blueprint was the 1995 federal budget. This budget trimmed the federal civil service by 45,000 persons (25 percent), generated major cuts to program spending (especially federal-provincial transfers), led to the passing down of many areas to the provinces (mining, forestry, tourism, training, etc.), and extricated the federal government from a wide range of areas (privatization, contracting out, desubsidization, etc.).

Almost as important as the budget content was the budgetary *process* adopted by Finance Minister Paul Martin. Apart from opening up the process, these initiatives included

- Setting rolling targets for only two years in the future, but ensuring that these targets would be met. For example, the deficit target for 1995–96 was set for $32.7 billion and that for 1996–97 for $24.3 billion (3 percent of GDP). Actual deficits came in much under target—under $30 billion for 1995–96 and an estimated $15 billion for 1996–97 (table 12.7). The new targets are $17 billion (2 percent of GDP) for 1997–98 and $9 billion (1 percent of GDP for 1998–99). These targets will be met "come hell or high water," to quote from the 1997 budget, and virtually all analysts would agree. Indeed, the 1996–97 deficit is already under the 1997–98 target.
- To ensure that the targets are met, the finance minister has adopted deliberately "prudent" estimates for forecasts of variables like GDP growth and interest rates. For example, the average of private-sector forecasts of nominal GDP growth for 1998 is 4.7 percent. The budget forecasts assume a 4.1 percent growth rate. And the average private-sector forecast for ten-year government bonds is 6.6 percent, whereas the budget forecast uses 7.1 percent.
- In addition, Finance Minister Martin's deficit targets also include a contingency reserve ($3.0 billion for 1997–98), which cannot be spent elsewhere. For 1997–98, the impact of this contingency reserve is such that the deficit target will be met "even if interest rates were 100 basis points higher, and growth one-half percentage point lower, relative to the *prudent* assumptions" (Finance Canada 1997, 47).

The result of all of this is that the finance minister and his budgets have acquired a degree of credibility hitherto unknown in Canadian fiscal circles.

Prior to focusing on a few performance indicators, it is critical for purposes of the present paper to note that much of the successful federal expenditure restraint came at the expense of the provinces: Ottawa took a page out of the Australian hymn book and engaged in significant "deficit-shifting" or offloading to the provinces. The equalization system was untouched, but the cash transfers for health, postsecondary education, and welfare (now rolled into the block-funded CHST) were reduced from $18 billion in 1995–96 to (a projected) $11 billion at the turn of the century. This represents, roughly, a 40 percent cut in CHST cash transfers to the provinces.

For their part, the provinces found themselves with little room to maneuver. The bond rating agencies were poised to lower credit ratings further if the provinces attempted to accommodate this dramatic cash transfer reduction in terms of deficit increases. Since provincial tax rates were already very high, this avenue was effectively closed off. Moreover, the citizen concern over deficits that led to the general acceptance of federal fiscal constraint also applied at the provincial level. Accordingly, these federal cash transfer cuts to the provinces were transformed into roughly equivalent expenditure reductions at the provincial level.

Ontario is especially interesting in this context. The new market-oriented Progressive Conservative government of Ontario (elected in mid-1995) launched the province on both a tax-cutting and deficit-reducing strategy. Ontario's personal income tax rates have been reduced by 30 percent and the budget is to be balanced by the millennium. Ontario also adopted the federal budgeting strategy—very conservative income/revenue growth estimates for its forecasts and a large contingency reserve. As a result, Ontario's deficit has also come in "under forecast," as it were, so that Ontario's budgetary policy is also acquiring considerable credibility. Intriguingly, this approach carried over to the other fiscally errant province—Quebec. Faced with an Ontario tax cut, the separatist Parti-Québécois government in Quebec also had to begin the process of sharp expenditure reduction rather than tax increases. Moving on the tax side would have led to a (further) exodus of Quebec businesses to Ontario or elsewhere.

The result of all of this was that all Canadian governments are currently moving quickly toward budget balance. As already noted, Ottawa's deficit for 1996–97 will probably come in at less than 2 percent of GDP, down from 6.5 percent earlier in the decade. Table 12.7 presents the evolution of federal and provincial deficits from fiscal year 1989–90 through to (forecasts for) 1998–99. Several features of the table merit highlight:

- Both levels of government recorded very substantial increases in their deficits as a result of the 1990s recession—provincial deficits increased from

$4.3 billion in 1989–90 to $24.9 billion at the peak of the fiscal damage (1992–93), while the federal government's deficit increased from $28.9 billion to $41.0 billion over this same period (and actually increased further in 1993–94).

- Unlike the Australian case (detailed later) where the 1990s recession primarily affected the Commonwealth deficit, the Canadian provinces have shared roughly equally in the Canadian deficit increases. This is because the provinces share the cyclically sensitive revenues with the federal government and also share in the automatic stabilizers on the expenditure side (welfare is provincial, employment insurance is federal, and both mushroomed in the recession).
- The aggregate deficit-to-GDP ratio nearly touched 10 percent in 1992–93—indeed, five *provinces* had deficit/GDP ratios in excess of the Maastricht guideline of 3 percent!
- The real "problem" provinces in 1992–93 were Alberta, Ontario, and Quebec. Alberta has made a remarkable turnaround (thanks to an increase in revenues from oil and gas production); in 1996–97 it ran a surplus of 2.5 percent of GDP.
- More generally, the post-1992–93 fiscal story is one of dramatic improvement. The 1996–97 data, when finalized, are projected to yield an aggregate (federal plus provincial) deficit just under the 3 percent Maastricht guideline, with further improvement in sight.
- In 1996–97, five of the ten provinces are in surplus, and the forecast is for seven to be in surplus in 1998–99. Ontario and Quebec remain the errant fiscal provinces, but both are on track for budget balance by the millennium.
- Although not detailed in table 12.7, the result of this deficit-cutting exercise was very dramatic in government program spending as a percentage of GDP. From the 1992–93 level of roughly 37 percent of GDP (20 percent provincial and 17 percent federal), program expenditures will fall to less than 30 percent in 1997–98 (under 16 percent for the provinces and roughly 13 percent for Ottawa). Reductions of this magnitude in EU nations would qualify virtually all of them for EMU entry!

However, the fiscal news is not all good. Were one to reproduce table 12.7 for debts and debt ratios, the results would reveal a rise in the debt/GDP ratio from 74.7 percent in 1989–90 to 105.9 percent in 1996–97. While this latter percentage is down slightly from the peak of 106.3 percent in 1995–96, the reality is that Canada has not yet come to grips with its massive debt overhang. Not to put too fine a point on all of this, Canadian governments now need to develop debt-reduction targets along the lines of the earlier deficit-reduction targets. More to the point, the Canadian fiscal position is clearly vulnerable to either an economic downturn or a rise in interest rates, or both.

12.5.3 Summary

Since much of this volume focuses on the relationship between fiscal institutions and budgetary performance, it seems appropriate to attempt to recast the Canadian experience in the context of some of the conference themes. The commitment to the 3 percent Maastricht-type deficit target in the 1993 electoral platform of the victorious Liberals was no doubt an important catalyst to deficit reduction. But it was not much more than this because it was cast as a five-year goal and only applied to the federal government: the provinces were also running deficits in the range of 3 percent of GDP in 1993. Moreover, Finance Minister Paul Martin's first budget (1994) was not only very unimpressive on the deficit front but held out the promise for major social policy reform that, arguably, could have led to increased rather than decreased expenditures. Beyond this, it became evident that the Canadian public was well ahead of the finance minister in terms of its willingness to accept deficit reduction.

What this disappointing 1994 federal budget triggered was a dual set of processes—one internal to the government and one that was capital-markets driven—that led to the watershed 1995 budget. The former took the form of an intense struggle within cabinet between the finance minister and the social policy minister. This is superbly documented in *Double Vision* (Greenspon and Wilson-Smith 1996). The result was a near-complete victory by the department of finance—social policy reform became subordinated to fiscal priorities, and, as important, restoring fiscal integrity would be achieved principally by expenditure paring. On the external and capital-markets front, the major think tanks in the country came down forcefully on the side not only of deficit reduction, but deficit elimination over a short time frame. Virtually all mainstream economists and bank/financial economists came down on this side. This domestic pressure was reenforced by capital-market developments. One key aspect here was the peso crisis in the fall of 1994 and the suggestion, in the U.S. financial papers, that Canada could well be next. The other was a most unusual move by Moody's—a month or two before the 1995 budget, Moody's placed Canada under a "credit watch."

In tandem, these developments stiffened the finance minister's resolve and led to the watershed 1995 budget, including the budgetary innovations in the area of targets, prudence, and transparency that eventually led to budget credibility. So confident was the finance minister that the 1995 budget would assuage capital markets that he invited the chief economists of domestic and foreign financial institutions to a special budget "lock-up." One measure of the newfound transparency and credibility of successive Canadian budgets is that this lock-up tends no longer to attract chief economists but, rather, their designates. Indeed, now that these budgetary processes have become standard fare, it will be very difficult for the federal government to pull back from them, so much so that pressures are now mounting to shift the focus from deficit reduction to debt/GDP targeting. This view of the Canadian experience lends support to the thrust of many of the papers in this volume.

There is, however, another way to view the evolution of Canadian fiscal history. In my own work (1997), I have argued that one of the principal reasons for the run-up of deficits and debts over the last two decades had to do with some unpleasant fiscal arithmetic, as it were. Up until the first energy crisis in 1973–74, real growth rates exceeded real interest rates, often by a significant amount. In turn, this meant that, ceteris paribus, the debt/GDP ratio would fall. From the mid-1970s on, real interest rates increased relative to real growth rates and, in Canada's case, eventually exceeded real growth rates by 4 percent. Under the old regime, one could run primary deficits (i.e., excluding debt servicing) and still have a falling debt/GDP ratio. No longer. Running primary *surpluses* may not lead to a falling debt/GDP ratio in an environment when real interest rates exceed the real growth rate. The argument would be that governments and fiscal institutions were very slow to recognize this profound change in underlying parameters and, in the process, saddled themselves with debt levels that began to be self-reinforcing.

In a recent paper, Ronald McKinnon (1997) takes a different slant on this historical evolution. For McKinnon, the major turning point was the end of Bretton Woods and the de facto "softening" of budget constraints under the resulting flexible rate regime. Hence, he views EMU as an attempt by member countries to reimpose "hard" budget constraints on themselves, via "monetary separation" (severing the link between national central banks and national budget authorities) and the no-bail-out clause of the EMU. This approach focuses on an *external* imposition of hard budget constraints that would apply to all varieties of electoral systems and fiscal institutions, whereas most of the papers in this volume focus on *internal* innovations that would serve to "harden" budget constraints. In the Canadian case, one could mount a case that aspects of the McKinnon analysis appear to ring true. The federal government recognized that the Bank of Canada could not be deterred from its price stability strategy. Despite the fact that Canadian inflation rates were lower than U.S. rates, if nominal and, therefore, real interest rates were to fall, this required some determined action on the deficit front. Note that this assertion embodies two assumptions, both of which were widely accepted in Canada at the time: (i) that the existing high nominal rates embodied an inflation premium that related to the possibility that the deficit could eventually be monetized and (ii) that over the short term the Bank of Canada would hold firm to its price-stability stance. In essence, this is the definition of a hard budget constraint since the fiscal authorities became boxed in—lowering interest rates required deficit paring. Likewise, the deficit shifting to the provinces was also passed onward in terms of expenditure cuts at the provincial level since the provinces also faced hard budget constraints, largely enforced by the capital markets.

How much relevance the Canadian and McKinnon perspectives have for other countries, and the EMU in particular, is best left for others to assess.

12.6   Recent Fiscal History: Australia

Like Canada, Australia was savaged by the 1990s recession. From a 1989 manufacturing employment index of 102.7 (1990 = 100), the index was still languishing at 92.9 in 1995. Comparable Canadian data are 107.5 in 1989 and 93.4 in 1995 (International Monetary Fund 1997, line 67ey). In terms of the overall labor market, Fortin (1996, 762) comments as follows: "Relative to the 1989 unemployment level, Canada accumulated 15.7 point-years of excess unemployment over 1990–95. According to OECD standardized unemployment statistics, this is significantly more than Japan (2.3 point-years), the United States (6.3) and the European Union (10.7). Our bad unemployment result has been matched only by Australia (16.3 point-years)." Hence, it should come as no surprise that Australia also registered substantial deficits during this period.

However, where Australia differed markedly from Canada is that it entered the recession with an aggregate net debt/GDP ratio in 1990 that was not much above 10 percent (panel A of figure 12.2), compared with the Canadian counterpart of nearly 80 percent. By 1995, Australia's ratio of aggregate net debt to GDP exceeded 25 percent, with almost all of this increase accounted for by the Commonwealth government. This is clear from panel B of figure 12.3: the Commonwealth budget balance deficit went from a surplus of almost 2 percent of GDP, prerecession, to a deficit of over 4 percent in 1992–93, whereas overall state deficits increased only slightly (lower panel). This was primarily the result of the operations of automatic stabilizers. In particular, in the face of the dramatic and sustained fall in employment (alluded to earlier) the Commonwealth spending category "social security and welfare" soared from $25.5 billion in 1988–89 to nearly $50 billion in 1994–95. This was one half of the problem: the other half was the revenue collapse. The behavior of outlays and revenues appear in figure 12.4. Note that this allocation of the burden for accommodating a recession is quite different from that which applied in Canada. As noted earlier, on the expenditure (outlay) front, automatic stabilizers are shared (unemployment insurance at the federal level and welfare at the provincial level) as are the cyclically sensitive taxes (income taxes and sales taxes). Hence, the 1990s recession in Canada resulted in substantial increases in both federal and provincial deficits. Not so in Australia, since on both the outlay and revenue side, the cyclically sensitive programs rest with the Commonwealth.

However, the seemingly benign behavior of state and territory deficits (fig. 12.3) and outlays and expenditures (fig. 12.4) masks a great deal of variation at the state level. All of the states in panel B of figure 12.2 record substantial debt increases, while low-spending Queensland (panel C) increased its net assets as a percent of GDP from 1 percent in 1988 to roughly 11 percent by 1996.

As is evident from these figures, Australia is now putting its fiscal house in order, at least on the deficit side—the projections for the Commonwealth are

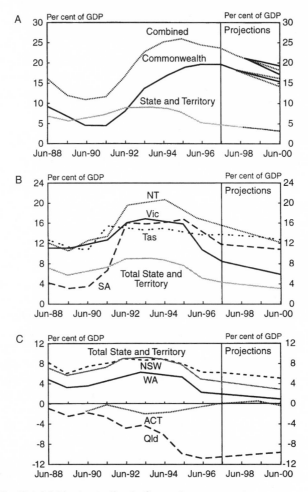

Fig. 12.2   Net debt in Australia: A, General government; B, C, State governments

Source: Working Party of Commonwealth 1997.

Note: In panel A, bands indicate the impact of GDP growth varying by half of one percentage point each side of the central case. "Combined" is the combination of the Commonwealth and the state and territory sector. In panels B and C, the total state and territory sector is expressed as a percentage of GDP.

for a budget surplus before the millennium. This arises largely from an "unwinding" of the operations of the automatic stabilizers in light of the recent strength in Australia's real growth rate.

The projected decline in state revenues from now to the turn of the century (panel C of figure 12.4) has a different explanation. As a result of the 1995 Competition Principles Agreement (elaborated below), CGC grants have been indexed for inflation through to 1998–99. But this means that they will fall as

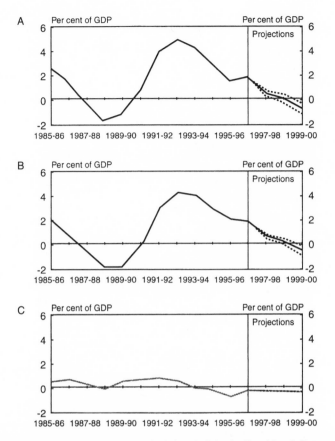

Fig. 12.3   General government underlying deficit: A, Combined Commonwealth and state and territory sector; B, Commonwealth; C, State and territory sector
Source: Working Party of Commonwealth 1997.

a percentage of GDP since the latter is growing in real terms. Beyond this, the Commonwealth will extract a 2 percent "efficiency dividend" from specific-purpose payments made to the states. For both reasons, aggregate state revenues are forecast to fall as a percentage of GDP.

In contrast to the earlier Canadian scenario, the Australian states are relatively sheltered from the impacts of a major recession. This, too, is consistent with the centralization/egalitarian thrust of Australia fiscal federalism.

12.6.1   Budgetary Process Initiatives

The Commonwealth budgetary process incorporates a feature that may well be unique to Australia. In comparing forecasts with actual outcomes the budget classifies (and publishes!) the deviations in terms of two components—parameter changes (e.g., errors in forecasting GNP) and discretionary changes. In

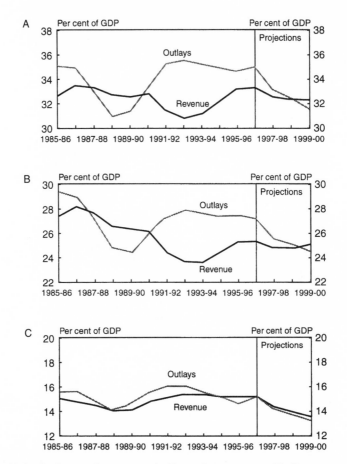

Fig. 12.4   Outlays and revenues: A, General government; B, Commonwealth; C, State and territory sector
Source: Working Party of Commonwealth 1997.

theory, this should make for much better analysis of budgetary policy, since discretionary decisions are now fully transparent. Utilizing this data set, Dixon (1993) conducts an illuminating analysis of discretionary Commonwealth policy over the period 1983–84 to 1992–93. This is a degree of transparency that has no counterpart in Canada.

The major institutional change in the Australian federation over this period occurred in 1995. This was the so-called microeconomic reforms, embodied in the Competition Principles Agreement signed by the heads of government (COAG). This agreement introduces structural reform (enhanced competition, including cross-border competition) for state monopolies and state enterprises (e.g., gas, electricity, water, rail, urban transit [including taxis], ports, self-regulating professional organizations, agricultural marketing boards, and so on). Beyond this, the agreement seeks competitive neutrality between the public and private sector and provides prices oversight of utilities and other corporations with significant monopoly power. This is truly landmark reform/legislation that will serve to dramatically free up the internal common market or the internal economic union. More to the point, such legislation is well beyond the fondest dreams of even the most ardent centralists in Canada!

Intriguingly, the states are the principal losers (financially) from the reform because their erstwhile fees, profits, royalties, and so on from these public trading enterprises will decrease as a result of enhanced (and cross-border) competition. In return, the states were promised an additional $600 million in CGC grants (in three tranches of $200 million each) provided that they implemented the reforms. Moreover, the CGC grants in totality are also indexed for inflation until fiscal year 1998–99. Relatedly, and quite significantly, COAG agreed on a mechanism for voting amendments to the Competition Code. The Commonwealth will have two votes and a casting vote, with each of the other parties having a single vote. As the COAG communiqué notes: "This will provide meaningful State and Territorial participation in changes to the competitive conduct rules while maintaining a consistent national scheme" (COAG 1995, 2).

Not only does this provision further erode the states' revenue-raising powers, it also *increases* the already high degree of vertical fiscal imbalance in the Australian federation. Perhaps Richard Bird (1986, 242) was right when he noted "had Australia not been established initially as a federal country, it seems rather unlikely that it would be one today." And no less an authority on federalism than W. H. Riker (1964, 113) proclaimed that "the divisions in Australian culture seem to be economic and religious with hardly any geographical basis. . . . One wonders why they bother with federalism in Australia." In any event, and as alluded to in the introduction, Australia appears fully embarked on a version of *intrastate* federalism—centralizing powers at the Commonwealth (or national level) but giving the states a greater say in policy promulgation. What is not readily apparent is whether this amounts to a *real* say for the states, given the enormous leverage of the Commonwealth arising from the degree of vertical fiscal imbalance.

The final budgetary process initiative draws upon a similar New Zealand initiative. Frustrated by the fact that during the 1996 election campaign, the then-serving Labor Government declared that the 1996–97 budget deficit would be $590 million with a surplus of $2.7 billion in 1997–98, when the postelection reality revealed deficits of $7.6 billion and $7.3 billion for 1996–97 and 1997–98, respectively, Liberal treasurer Peter Costello introduced a Charter of Budget Honesty. The purpose of the charter is to provide comprehensive fiscal information *prior to elections*. Among the provisions are (Costello 1996, 4)

- An independent preelection report prepared by the secretaries to the Treasury and the Department of Finance that will provide updated fiscal and economic projections;
- Arrangements for more equal access to Treasury and Finance costings of election commitments by the Government and the Opposition to allow the electorate to be better informed of the financial implications of election commitments.

The latter provision is voluntary: the request for costing must come from the leaders of the parties. However, one can be certain that if one party submits to such a costing, the other will certainly be pressured to do so as well. In the above analysis, I noted that the existence of the National Fiscal Outlook substantially enhanced fiscal transparency and accountability. In part, the Charter of Budget Honesty can be viewed as a further step in this direction. If this process meets with any success, it will only be a matter of time, and probably not much time, before it is replicated at the state level.

12.7   States and Provinces: S&P Credit Ratings

To conclude the analysis of subnational budgetary policies in Australia and Canada, table 12.8 presents the analysis by Dafoe, Shepherd, and Thiemann (1996) of comparative state and province credit ratings, fortuitously published in the November 1996 issue of Standard and Poor's *Canadian Focus*. (This is a variant of the analysis of Poterba and Rueben, chap. 8 in this volume.) Prior to focusing on the ratings themselves, it is instructive to focus on the data relating to per capita GDPs for the states and provinces. The Canadian data serve as the numeraire for the comparison. The Australian data in column 3 are presented in Canadian dollars using the then-existing exchange rates— 102.2 Canadian cents per Australian dollar. Column 4 presents the Australian data in terms of purchasing power parity—135 Australian cents per U.S. dollar and 122 Canadian cents per U.S. dollar (OECD data)—and, obviously, reflects the fact that the Canadian dollar rate is dramatically undervalued vis-à-vis the Australian dollar. In terms of the "operating balance" column, the outliers are clearly Queensland on the up side (an operating balance equal to 18 percent of revenues) and Ontario and Quebec on the downside (operating "deficits" of 12.5 percent and 9.4 percent respectively). As documented earlier, both Ontario and Quebec have begun to significantly turn around their deficit burdens. However, the real story in the table has to do with indebtedness, and here the evidence is clear—the provinces are much more indebted than are the Australian states. Setting aside British Columbia (with a debt to total revenues ratio less than that of Tasmania and Victoria), all the other provinces have debt/revenue ratios well in excess of the Australian states. Intriguingly, S&P does not focus on net debt as a percent of *own-source revenues*. Because of the degree of vertical fiscal imbalance, this would essentially double the ratios for

Table 12.8   S&P Subnational Credit Ratings: Canada and Australia

	Senior Rating[a] (1)	Outlook (2)	Nominal GDP Per Capita (C$) 1995–1996[c] (3)	Nominal GDP Per Capita (purchasing power parity)[b] (4)	Real GDP Growth (%)[b] (5)	Operating Balance as a % of Operating Revenues (6)	Total Balance as a % of Total Revenues (7)	Net State/Provincial Debt as a % of Total Budget Revenues, 1996[c] (8)	Public-sector Pension Plan Unfunded Liabilities as a % of Total Revenues, 1996[c] (9)
Australian states									
Australian Capital Territory	AAA	Stable	33,240	29,392	4.0	4.0	1.3	14	43
New South Wales	AAA	Stable	27,029	23,900	9.8	9.8	(0.0)	56	38
Queensland	AAA	Stable	24,500	21,664	18.3	18.3	8.6	22	0
Victoria	AA+	Stable	29,187	25,809	8.4	8.4	12.1	90	41
Western Australia	AA+	Positive	30,504	26,973	8.2	8.2	4.6	55	6.3
South Australia	AA	Stable	24,449	21,619	5.5	5.5	3.5	84	40
Tasmania	AA–	Stable	22,389	19,797	7.3	7.3	0.6	115	44
Canadian provinces									
British Columbia	AA+	Stable	27,057		2.6	2.7	(7.1)	87	17
Alberta	AA	Stable	31,092		3.0	6.4	0.9	125	52
New Brunswick	AA–	Stable	20,833		2.2	6.0	(0.4)	104	35
Ontario	AA–	Stable	28,385		3.1	(12.5)	(20)	207	16
Manitoba	A+	Stable	23,140		2.5	5.6	(0.1)	118	37
Quebec	A+	Stable	23,783		2.1	(9.4)	(16)	165	10
Nova Scotia	A–	Stable	20,000		1.1	2.4	(3.0)	175	17
Saskatchewan	A–	Stable	23,899		2.6	2.6	(0.7)	166	66
Newfoundland	BBB+	Stable	17,318		(0.6)	3.4	(0.5)	137	78

Source: Dafoe, Shepherd, and Thiemann 1996, 19.

Note: GDP = gross domestic product.

[a]Local currency ratings.

[b]Three-year average, 1994–96 (1996 estimated).

[c]Estimated.

the states in the second to last column of the table, with much smaller increases for the Canadian provinces. Hence, it is clear that from S&P's perspective, the national/subnational transfers are essentially viewed as own-source revenues. As noted later, I find this to be a peculiar assumption.

Now to the ratings. For Australia, they vary from AAA for the ACT, Queensland, and New South Wales to a low of AA− for Tasmania. The provincial ratings are much lower—from British Columbia with AA+ to Newfoundland with close to a junk bond rating, BBB+. These ratings may make eminent sense in terms of the debt/revenue ratios in the second to last column of the table. But they make much less sense if the focus were on the ratio of debt to own-source revenue. In my view, therefore, there are important other factors that S&P is (implicitly) factoring in. One is the fact that Ottawa is much more heavily indebted than is Canberra. Indeed, while Canberra has an AAA rating across the board, Ottawa has an AAA rating for its domestic debt, but only an AA+ rating for its foreign debt. All credit-rating agencies impose the notion of a "sovereign ceiling"; that is, Alberta could not acquire an AAA rating across the board if Ottawa only has an AA+ rating on its foreign debt. Beyond this issue, I find these ratings to be very peculiar. As noted in the above analysis, not only has Alberta been running a surplus for several years (and, therefore, paying down its debt) but, in addition, its own-source revenues exceed its expenditures and it has by far the lowest tax effort of all the provinces. Yet its credit rating exceeds only that of Tasmania and is lower than five of the Australian states. Since the publication of these ratings, S&P has upgraded Alberta's "outlook" (column 2) to "positive." But this does not address the core of the issue. Specifically, despite the recent alteration in the Loan Council arrangements (which are intended to have the states borrow on their own hook, as it were), it seems that S&P is *implicitly* assuming that Canberra is ultimately responsible for the states' debts. Given the nature of the Commonwealth-state fiscal interaction (as reflected in figure 12.1 above), this may well be an appropriate assumption, but it is an assumption nonetheless. How else can one explain the fact that S&P rates Ontario AA−, tied with Tasmania and lower than any other Australian state? With Commonwealth grants equal to 185 percent of its own revenues, Tasmania's debt to own-source revenue ratio would be in the order of 330 percent, while that of Ontario would be somewhere in the 230 percent range. Surely the implicit imprimatur of Canberra comes into play here. Thankfully, some Australians also believe that these state credit ratings are inflated. Walsh (1996, 119) remarks that

> notwithstanding the potential for Australia's federal fiscal arrangements to encourage and sustain inefficient state decision making, the size of the Commonwealth's share in funding the states' budgets almost certainly results in the states, collectively and individually, receiving "ratings" from the international agencies consistently higher than their less "dependent" counterparts in other federations. That is, the role of the ratings agencies in disciplining state decision making, increased in significance though it may have become,

is moderated by an "understanding" (or presumption) that the capacity of the Australian states to meet their future obligations is implicitly underwritten by the Commonwealth.

Even with this important caveat, the fact of the matter is that with an overall debt/GDP ratio exceeding 100 percent, all levels of government in Canada are perilously overindebted. This is true in absolute terms, and it is even more evident in relative terms, given that Australia's overall indebtedness is between one-fifth and one-fourth of Canada's indebtedness.

12.8 Conclusion

The preceding analysis of subnational fiscal/budgetary policies and institutions in Canada and Australia has been a comparison of polar extremes. What is very apparent is that the fiscal institutions buttress the salient features of the respective national polities. In Australia, the Commonwealth-state fiscal relationships are fully consistent with the centralist/egalitarian nature of the federation, while the decentralized nature of the Canadian federation is surely enhanced by features such as the degree of subnational tax autonomy and the move toward unconditionality for all federal-provincial transfers. What is not so apparent is whether these fiscal institutions play a determining role in terms of defining their respective polities or whether they are largely a reflection of (i.e., endogenous to) deep-seated societal values. One could probably mount a case to the effect that Canada's decentralization has, historically, been associated with the demands of the province of Quebec, although in more recent years decentralization has probably been fiscally triggered. This issue is more complicated in Australia: for example, was the key High Court decision to label a state sales tax as equivalent to an excise tax and, therefore, preclude the states from entering this field, a reflection of juridical principles or was it more a reflection of the justices' view of what was appropriate for Australian society? Note that this is not intended to be a slight against the judiciary. Now that Canada–United States free trade is a reality, the Canadian Supreme Court will presumably give a more expansive reading to the internal free trade provisions of the Canadian constitution. Beyond these few observations, however, the role of this conclusion is to look to the future.

For the next few years, at least, Canada is locked into more decentralization. Some of this is being driven by the very real threat of a successful independence referendum in Quebec (likely to be held in 1999). However, globalization is also taking its toll on the federation. Only tiny Prince Edward Island now exports more to the rest of Canada than to the rest of the world. Ontario's exports to the United States are running at 2.5 times the value of its exports to its sister provinces and are growing nearly a magnitude faster. Hence, Canada is no longer an east-west economy but more and more a series of cross-border (north-south) economies. This increases the pressures for devolution and asymmetry. Hence, the challenge to the Canadian federation is how to accommodate the increasing policy interdependencies among and between Ottawa and the provinces. One recent intriguing initiative is that the provinces have become more active in generating "pan-Canadian" public goods (Courchene 1996a).

Highly centralized Australia is also being whiplashed by the forces of globalization. At one level, the polarization of market incomes following in the wake of global integration will wreak havoc with Australian egalitarianism, if it has not already done so. At another level, Australia is experiencing challenges similar to those in Canada. Western Australia is progressively integrating internationally rather than nationally. WA's net imports from the rest of Australia have remained fairly constant at $4 billion over the 1985–86 to 1992–93 period, whereas its net export surplus internationally has increased to $11 billion in 1992–93 from $4 billion in 1987–87 (Courchene 1996b). Queensland also has a substantial export surplus with the rest of the world offset by a similar import surplus with the rest of Australia. For the largest states—Victoria and New South Wales—the situation is reversed: they have large external import surpluses and large export surpluses with the rest of Australia. Hence the pressures for increased decentralization, at least on the part of several states, are potentially very strong and very pervasive.

Earlier I indirectly suggested (drawing from Richard Bird) that had Australia not been constituted as a federation it would not now be one. And there is some sympathy in influential Australian circles to do away with the states (Macphee 1994). However, the thrust of the previous paragraph is that there are also powerful countervailing forces pointing in a decentralizing direction. When in opposition, the now-ruling Liberal Party adopted a strong (for Australia!) states' rights perspective. And in the run-up to the Australian Constitutional Centenary, which is replicating the various constitutional conferences one hundred years ago, one of the propositions that was passed was what might be termed the principle of "fiscal coincidence," namely that the jurisdiction responsible for spending should also be responsible for raising the equivalent revenues. Later constitutional conferences will address the issue of vertical fiscal imbalance in more detail. In any event, the real challenge facing Canberra as Australia approaches the millennium is whether or not it can maintain its centralist-egalitarian thrust. Intriguingly, Canberra's current approach appears to be that of bringing the states more fully and more formally into national decision-making processes rather than decentralizing powers, per se.

In summary, my personal view is that *internal pressures* (i.e., policy interdependencies and externalities) will drive the Canadian federation toward more harmonization and coordination of national/subnational policies, even if this coordination is "national" rather than "federal" (Ottawa imposed), while *external pressures* will eventually drive Australia toward a greater decentralization of powers and taxation authority to the states.

References

Australian Bureau of Statistics. 1995. *Year book Australia, 1995.* Canberra: Australian Bureau of Statistics.

Bird, Richard. 1986. *Federal finance in comparative perspective.* Toronto: Canadian Tax Foundation.

Boadway, Robin, and Paul Hobson. 1993. Intergovernmental fiscal relations in Canada. Canadian Tax Paper no. 96. Toronto: Canadian Tax Foundation.

Boothe, Paul, ed. 1996. *Reforming fiscal federalism for global competition: A Canada-Australia comparison.* Edmonton: University of Alberta Press.

Brosio, Giorgio. 1994. The balance sheet of the Australian federation: Some tentative estimates. Discussion Paper no. 37. Federalism Research Center, Australian National University. August.

Canadian Tax Foundation. 1994. *National finance.* Toronto: Canadian Tax Foundation.

Commonwealth Grants Commission. 1995. *Report on general revenue grant relativities: 1995 update.* Canberra: Australian Government Publishing Services.

Commonwealth Loan Council. 1993. *Future arrangements for loan council monitoring and reporting.* Canberra: Commonwealth Loan Council, July 5.

Costello, the Honorable Peter, Treasurer of the Commonwealth of Australia. 1996. *Charter of budget honesty.* Canberra: Commonwealth of Australia, August 20.

Council of Australian Governments (COAG). 1995. Communique April 11.

Courchene, Thomas J. 1993a. Globalisation, institutional evolution, and the Australian federation. In *Federalism and the economy: International, national, and state issues,* ed. Brian Galligan, 64–117. Canberra: Federalism Research Centre, Australian National University.

———. 1993b. Reflections on Canadian federalism: Are there implications for European economic and monetary union. In The economics of community public finance, special issue of *European Economy* 5:123–66.

———. 1994. *Social Canada in the millennium.* Toronto: C. D. Howe Research Institute.

———. 1996a. The comparative nature of Australian and Canadian economic space. In *Reforming fiscal federalism for global competition: A Canada-Australia comparison,* ed. Paul Booth, 7–22. Edmonton: University of Alberta Press.

———. 1996b. Preserving and promoting the internal economic union: Australia and Canada. In *Reforming fiscal federalism for global competition: A Canada-Australia comparison,* ed. Paul Boothe, 185–222. Edmonton: University of Alberta Press.

———. 1997. International dimensions of macroeconomic policies: Canada. In *A handbook on macroeconomic policies in open economies,* ed. Michele Fratianni, Dominick Salvatore, and Jürgen von Hagen. Forthcoming.

Courchene, Thomas J., and David E. Wildasin. 1984. A note on the analytics of the RFPS equalization formula. Appendix to Thomas J. Courchene, *Equalization payments: Past, present, and future,* 409–26. Toronto: Ontario Economic Council.

Dafoe, Stephan, Rick Shepherd, and Jeff Thiemann. 1996. Canadian provinces and Australian states: Contrast and counterpoint. In *Standard & Poor's Canadian Focus,* 18–20. Toronto: Standard & Poor's, November.

Dahlby, Bev, and Sam Wilson. 1996. Tax assignment and fiscal externalities in a federal state. In *Reforming fiscal federalism for global competition: A Canada-Australia comparison,* ed. Paul Boothe, 87–108. Edmonton: University of Alberta Press.

Dixon, Geoff. 1993. Managing budget outlays, 1983–84 to 1992–93. In *Federalism and the economy: International, national, and state issues,* ed. Brian Galligan, 29–55. Canberra: Federalism Research Centre, Australian National University.

Finance Canada. 1997. *Budget chart book: February 1997.* A background document to the 1997 federal budget. Ottawa: Department of Finance.

Fortin, Pierre. 1996. The great Canadian slump. *Canadian Journal of Economics* 29, no. 4:762–87.

Goodhart, C. A. E., and S. Smith. 1993. Stabilization. In The economics of community public finance, special issue of *European Economy* 5:417–56.

Greenspon, Edward, and Anthony Wilson-Smith. 1996. *Double vision: The inside story of the Liberals in power.* Toronto: Doubleday Canada.

International Monetary Fund. 1997. *International financial statistics yearbook, 1996.* Washington, D.C.: International Monetary Fund.

Kneebone, Ronald D. 1994. Deficits and debt in Canada: Some lessons from recent history. *Canadian Public Policy/Analyse de Politiques* 20, no. 2:152–64.

Macphee, Ian. 1994. Towards a model for two-tier government. Paper presented at the conference Australian Federalism: Future Directions, Structural Change, University of Melbourne, Centre for Comparative Constitutional Studies.

McKinnon, Ronald I. 1997. Monetary regimes, government borrowing constraints, and market-preserving federalism: Implications for the EU. In *The Nation state in a global/information era: Policy challenges,* ed. Thomas J. Courchene, 101–42. John Deutsch Institute for the Study of Economic Policy, Queen's University.

Report of the Heads of Treasuries Working Party to the 1994 Premiers' Conference. 1994. Horizontal fiscal equalisation. *Economic Round-Up,* spring, 61–69.

Riker, W. H. 1964. *Federalism.* Boston: Little, Brown.

Saunders, Cheryl. 1990. Government borrowing in Australia. *Publius* 20, no. 4:35–52.

Standard and Poor's. 1996. Canadian provinces and Australian states: Contrast and counterpoint. In *Canadian Focus: Provincial Edition,* 18–20. Toronto: Standard and Poor's.

Walsh, Cliff. 1996. Making a mess of tax allocation: Australia as a case study. In *Reforming fiscal federalism for global competition: A Canada-Australia comparison,* ed. Paul Boothe, 109–40. Edmonton: University of Alberta Press.

Working Party of Commonwealth, State, and Territory Treasury Officials. 1997. *National fiscal outlook: A report to the 1997 premiers' conference.* Canberra: Australian Government Publishing Service.

13   Coping with Fiscal Stress: Illusion and Reality in Central Government Budgeting in Japan, 1975–1997

Maurice Wright

Most of the empirical studies in this volume present comparisons of budget rules and budget outcomes in different jurisdictions. Yet there are important insights to be gained by analyzing the detailed process of budgeting in a given nation in more detail than any cross-national or cross-jurisdictional study can allow. Detailed analysis of the factors that determine budget deficits can provide an empirical basis for evaluating models of deficit determination, such as the "common pool" model of Velasco (chap. 2 in this volume). This chapter focuses on the fiscal experience of the Japanese economy during the last two decades.

Japan's fiscal situation in 1997 was the worst of any G7 country, having deteriorated rapidly with the collapse of the "bubble economy" in 1991 and the deep and prolonged period of economic recession that ensued, and from which recovery has been slow and modest. The deficit on the General Government financial balance in FY 1996 was 7.4 percent of GDP, with a gross debt of over 90 percent. The inclusion of the surplus on social security reduces that deficit to 4.8 percent, but even that figure is exceeded only by Italy among G7. More significantly, as figure 13.1 shows, all but Japan of the G7 countries have a trend from the early 1990s of improving financial balances. While gross debt continued to increase in all G7 countries, the rate slowed, leveling out in the early 1990s, but with the striking exception of Japan, as figure 13.2 shows.

Throughout most of the 1980s and 1990s, the governments of G7 countries experienced conditions of fiscal stress—budget deficits, accumulating debt,

Maurice Wright is professor of government at the University of Manchester, England. He was visiting professor at the Ministry of Finance in Japan in 1992–93, and at the Bank of Japan in 1993–94.

The research and data presented in the paper are part of a study of Comparative Budgetary Systems in G7, supported by the ESRC (R000234125), the Leverhulme Trust, and the European Commission's Programme for Scientific and Technological Development.

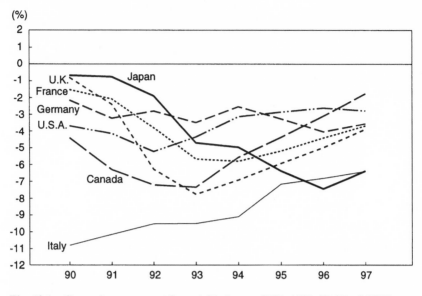

Fig. 13.1   General government financial balance of G7, 1990–97 (% of GDP)
Source: OECD, *Economic Outlook,* June 1996.
Note: Japan and U.S.A.: excludes social security.

and increasing costs of debt-servicing preempting increasing proportions of the total budget. Responding to those pressures, they attempted to reduce the level of deficit and debt and aspired to restore a balanced central/federal budget in the medium term. Many of the budget rules that are analyzed in other parts of this volume (see the summary in Alesina and Perotti, chap. 1 in this volume) have attracted attention precisely because they may affect deficit levels. This chapter explains how the Japanese central government coped with the conditions of continuing fiscal stress in the period 1975–97.

Analysts within Japan (e.g., Asako, Ito, and Sakamoto 1991; Shibata 1993; Kawai and Onitsuka 1996; Ihori 1996) and outside (OECD, *Japan Annual Survey*) attribute the improvement in Japan's financial balance on General Government expenditure that took place in the 1980s to the implementation of tough policies of fiscal reconstruction by Japan's Ministry of Finance (MOF). In doing so they fail to distinguish the appearance of discipline and control from the underlying reality. I shall argue that MOF was largely unsuccessful in reconstructing the fiscal system, and unable to control the growth of central government's spending, the primary cause of fiscal stress. After a brief introduction to the complexities of the Japanese budgetary system, and the various measures used to assess fiscal performance, the chapter traces the origins of the fiscal crisis of 1975. There follows an account of the aims and objectives of policies to "reconstruct" and "consolidate" the central government finances and an assessment of the effectiveness of their implementation. The concluding sections

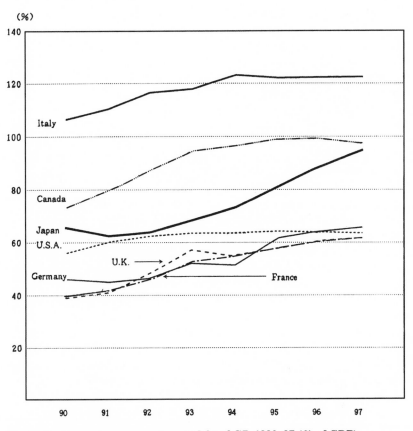

Fig. 13.2   **General government gross debt of G7, 1990–97 (% of GDP)**
Source: OECD, *Economic Outlook,* June 1996.

explain why MOF failed to achieve its fiscal objectives, and compares it with the response of the U.K. and Canadian central/federal governments to similar conditions of fiscal stress.

13.1 Fiscal "Smoke and Mirrors"

Central government budgeting in Japan is complex, and the processes of making budgets opaque. Besides the main (General Account) budget, there is the Fiscal Investment Loan Program (FILP), the so-called second budget, and the budgets of 38 special accounts with hypothecated revenues and specific expenditures. Each year there is at least one, sometimes several supplementary budgets. In addition, there are 91 public corporations, part of whose capital expenditures and trading losses are defrayed from the main budget and FILP. Social security contributions are not counted as general revenues, but paid into separate special accounts, which are, however, partly subsidized by transfers from the main budget. There are, annually, numerous complex cash-flow transfers of revenues and expenditures between the main budget, supplementary budgets, and FILP and between them and the 38 special accounts and the public corporations. There is a considerable potential for the manipulation of those transfers to relieve spending pressures on the main budget.

MOF and Japanese academic analysts tend to measure fiscal performance in terms of the central government's main budget, reflecting MOF's primary focus on fiscal objectives and targets set for it, rather than for General Government as a whole. In fact for a variety of fiscal and political reasons MOF emphasizes the limitations of analysis based on the concept of General Government as applied to Japan. System of National Accounts (SNA) calculations conventionally include the financial balances of social security funds. Japan's pension system is a partially funded system, accumulating funds in advance of payment of future benefits. MOF insists therefore that the accumulated surplus should be regarded as a debt owed to future beneficiaries and not as a source of revenue to offset expenditures elsewhere in the budget; and that with a rapidly aging population, the accumulated surplus will run down. MOF also argues that the conventional exclusion from calculations of General Government of the financial balances of public corporations gives a misleading picture because many of those corporations (especially the nine public finance corporations and two banks, like the Japan Development Bank) implement capital investment programs under the direct control of the central government, amounting to one-fifth of the total public fixed capital formation in Japan. They have been in deficit for most of the period 1979–97. The exclusion of the substantial surpluses on the social security fund, and the inclusion of public corporations' deficits therefore has a marked effect on the financial balance of General Government so defined. The resulting fiscal deficit is therefore much larger and more persistent than that of General Government measured according to the conventions of SNA. At various times in the 1980s and 1990s it was used by the Japanese Government as an important fiscal weapon with which to resist international pressures to stimulate the economy through additional public spending, allowing MOF to claim that apparent surpluses on General Government from 1987 to 1991 were in reality substantial deficits.

Leaving aside the argument about the inclusion of the deficits of public corporations, the exclusion of social security fund surpluses (which OECD concedes) qualifies the picture of progression from deficit to surplus on the overall General Government financial balance in the period of fiscal reconstruction in the 1980s. Thus defined, General Government remains in deficit throughout, although the size of that deficit was reduced.

A second qualification to the perception of successful fiscal reconstruction in the 1980s is that the reduction in the deficit on General Government calculated as a proportion of GDP is partly attributable to the growth of the latter, especially in the period of the "economic bubble" from 1987 to 1991, when the greatest improvement in the deficit occurred.

To what extent was the (qualified) improvement in the overall financial balance of General Government directly attributable to the implementation of policies of fiscal reconstruction in central government's budgeting? If we compare the contribution of the financial balances of central and local governments to the reduction of the deficit in General Government (excluding social security), the latter's fiscal performance is superior. This was partly the result of the central government's shifting the responsibility for the costs of fiscal reconstruction to subordinate levels of government. From 1977 local government's deficit decreased annually from 1.8 percent of GDP, to achieve a surplus in 1988. Central government's deficit on its financial balance increased until 1979, when it stood three times higher than that of local government. Thereafter it too decreased annually, but less rapidly; it never achieved surplus. More revealingly, central government borrowing increased faster than that of local government throughout the whole of the period of fiscal reconstruction, contributing more than three times as much to the overall gross debt of General Government. In 1974 central government's gross debt was 16.9 trillion and local governments' 9.9 trillion. By 1987, *before* the occurrence of the bubble economy, the figures were 211.5 trillion and 59 trillion respectively. As a proportion of GDP, central government's gross debt increased from 12.2 percent in 1974 to 59.5 percent in 1987; local governments', from 7.12 percent to 16.6 percent.

In the light of such evidence, how can we account for the persistence of the myth that MOF's policies of reconstruction were succeeding in restoring fiscal discipline and control before the occurrence of the "bubble economy" in 1987 and the onset of the deep economic recession of 1991–95? The short answer is that through its rhetoric and the presentation of its fiscal performance, MOF *appeared* to have controlled central government spending, an image consistent with its reputation as a strong central organization, coordinating multiple political, economic, and bureaucratic interests in the budget process, able to impose firm discipline and control on the spending ministries and agencies. The reality was otherwise. The reduction that occurred in the overall deficit on General Government that is attributable directly to the improvement in the financial balance of the main budget controlled by MOF was more apparent than real. We shall now show that in the period of fiscal reconstruction during the 1980s (and beyond) it was unable to contain the pressures for more public spending or to reform the inadequate tax base. The underlying cause of fiscal stress— the continuous growth of public spending—remained throughout the 1980s and 1990s. The symptoms of that stress—deficits and debt—were exacerbated by the fiscal consequences of the "economic bubble" of the late 1980s and the collapse into recession that followed; but they were only the proximate cause of the sharp deterioration that occurred in the 1990s. The roots of that fiscal crisis lie much deeper, and it is to those that we turn first.

13.2   The Origins of the Fiscal Crisis of 1975

The fiscal crisis that emerged full-blown in FY 1975 had both long- and short-term causes. With transition to slower economic expansion, it had been apparent for some time that large annual increases in public expenditures could no longer be financed wholly from the revenues generated by economic expansion, as they had been in the era of high growth in the 1950s and 1960s. Secondly, the structure of the taxation system inherited from the U.S. Shoup Mission after the Second World War relied excessively on revenues from direct rather than indirect taxation, which were more affected by cyclical changes than the latter. Two shorter-term factors contributed to the emergence of the crisis in the middle of the 1970s. First, the ratcheting up of public spending at the beginning of the decade, as Japan entered upon its welfare era, encouraged the expectations of Liberal Democratic Party (LDP) politicians, special interest groups, and the electorate about its continued growth in the future. The other immediate and proximate cause of the crisis in 1975 was the fiscal consequences of the first oil crisis in 1973, which led to a sharp contraction of economic activity in Japan and a decline in GNP.

The significance of the growth of public spending in the 1970s was much less the growth of government and its absorption of GNP, which was still growing, albeit more slowly than in previous decades: rather it was the financing of that growth of public spending that caused MOF anxiety and was to create difficulties for the next 20 years. In 1975 the rapid increase in *current* spending could no longer be financed solely out of taxation and other revenues, and it became necessary to issue "special deficit bonds" in addition to the ordinary, so-called construction bonds to finance capital spending. The latter had been issued for the first time since the end of the American occupation when the budget became unbalanced in 1965. Thereafter deficit financing became the norm.

The growing imbalance and widening fiscal deficit that occurred between 1970 and the beginning of fiscal reconstruction in 1979 are shown in table 13.1. As deficits widened, the government borrowed larger amounts; the annual costs of servicing new government borrowing and the cost of accumulated debt rose steeply in the middle of the 1970s (table 13.1). By 1975 the symptoms of a major crisis in the national finances were fully exposed: fast-rising expenditure, inadequate revenue growth, burgeoning fiscal deficits, accumulating debt, and increasing budget rigidity. The latter was especially worrying for MOF. The anxiety expressed in the 1960s about the prospect of "fiscal rigidification" was now being realized as the fixed costs of servicing the debt began to squeeze the amount available in the budget to finance discretionary program expenditures, themselves subjected to the pressures of the new "welfare politics" inaugurated in 1970. To those difficulties was added the looming prospect of an increase in the number of elderly people in Japan in the early decades of the next century, threatening an additional burden on discretionary budgetary expenditures.

Table 13.1   Japan's Central Government Budget: Deficit, Debt, and Debt-Service, 1970–96

	Deficit		Debt Outstanding as % GDP (Nominal)	Debt-Service Costs as % Budget (Initial)
	% Budget (Settled)	% GDP (Nominal)		
1970	4.2	0.4	3.7	3.7
1971	12.4	1.4	4.8	3.4
1972	16.8	2.0	6.0	4.0
1973	12.0	1.5	6.5	4.9
1974	11.3	1.5	7.0	5.0
1975	25.3	3.5	9.8	4.9
1976	29.4	4.2	12.9	6.9
1977	32.9	5.0	16.8	8.2
1978	31.3	5.1	20.4	9.4
1979	34.7	6.0	25.0	10.6
1980	32.6	5.7	28.7	12.5
1981	27.5	4.9	31.6	14.2
1982	29.7	5.1	35.3	15.8
1983	26.6	4.7	38.4	16.3
1984	24.8	4.2	39.9	18.1
1985	23.2	3.8	41.5	19.5
1986	21.0	3.3	42.8	20.9
1987	16.3	2.6	42.7	20.9
1988	11.6	1.9	41.3	20.3
1989	10.1	1.6	39.6	19.3
1990	10.6	1.6	37.9	21.6
1991	9.5	1.4	37.0	22.8
1992	13.5	2.0	37.7	22.8
1993	21.5	3.4	40.4	21.3
1994	22.4	3.4	43.2	19.2
1995	28.0	4.4	46.0	18.6
1996	27.6	4.2	49.0	21.8

Source: Budget Bureau, MOF, Japan, 1997.

This in outline was the *problematique* with which MOF was confronted throughout the next 20 years. In the next section we examine the aims and objectives of policies to "reconstruct" and "consolidate" the central government finances.

13.3   Fiscal Reconstruction, 1979–87: Principles, Objectives, and Policies

MOF could not embark upon policies to reconstruct the national finances without first obtaining political recognition that there was a fiscal crisis and that it was not a temporary phenomenon. Second, MOF had to convince the LDP leadership that fiscal reconstruction was a necessary and appropriate response to the underlying causes of the crisis; and to prescribe a set of guidelines broadly acceptable to it, but which crucially could be invoked subsequently to validate its policies and commit ministers to them. This was achieved by the public articulation of the underlying principles of "sound management" of the national finances.

The basic principle was a balanced budget, which the government pledged to restore at "the earliest possible opportunity." The other principles were all contingent on the symptoms of annual budget deficits. Two related specifically to the management of the economy: first, the risk of "fiscally induced" inflation, and of "crowding out" private-sector investment through the increase and sale of government bonds; and, second, the costs of current expenditures as a burden on future generations of taxpayers, for example by the issue of government bonds to finance a deficit that arose from a shortfall of revenue. "Sound management" also required that the fiscal system should be operated flexibly.

None of these principles was wholly novel. Hitherto largely unstated or unemphasized, their public articulation, affirmation, and reiteration now served three purposes essential to MOF's evolving strategy for dealing with the causes and consequences of the fiscal crisis. First, cabinet ministers and senior LDP politicians could not repudiate the implications for fiscal policy that followed logically from their acceptance of those principles, namely, the reconstruction of the expenditure and tax system that MOF advocated. Second, in order to attempt fiscal reconstruction MOF had to try to change political perceptions and expectations of the role of public spending in the economy. Here the principles provided a set of guidelines to which MOF officials and ministers could refer in the preparation, discussion, and presentation of the annual budgets. Repetition and reiteration helped in the process of "educating" politicians, bureaucrats in the spending ministries, interest groups, the media, and the public to acknowledge and accept the fiscal consequences of changed and changing economic circumstances. Third, the principles of sound management provided a set of broad contextual constraints within which annual bids for more spending, and demands for less taxation, from ministers, bureaucrats, local politicians, and special interest groups could be negotiated. There was of course no guarantee that in practice participants in the budgetary processes would exercise self-restraint when their own interests or those of their clients or supporters were threatened by MOF policies to cut spending or raise taxes. What is important to emphasize here is that by signing up publicly to the principles of "sound management" the LDP legitimized MOF's reformulation of the fiscal agenda.

MOF repeatedly drew attention to the accumulating size of the national debt and its absorption of increasing amounts of GDP, and to the annual costs of servicing the total of the debt outstanding. The latter costs, it argued, led to fiscal rigidification; discretion to vary expenditures on programs to reflect political priorities was being progressively eroded. The implication was clear. If LDP ministers and their back-bench supporters could deliver less to their constituents and clients because of the fixed costs of servicing the debt, they were more vulnerable politically. The LDP's electoral success, and its domination of the Diet had been built and then rebuilt on the politics of distribution to supporters and compensation for aggrieved or disaffected groups (Calder 1988). Fears and anxieties about future prosperity were also exploited skillfully by MOF as it warned repeatedly of the fiscal consequences of an aging population.

These longer-term implications of continuing fiscal deficits and consequential government borrowing were less persuasive arguments for LDP politicians than those where MOF was able to demonstrate that short- and medium-term effects of "fiscal rigidification" limited their discretion to adjust the amount and distribution of expenditure on favored programs, for example public works and agricultural subsidies and support. Nevertheless, both arguments were deployed with increasing sophistication and emphasis through the 1980s to justify MOF's policies of fiscal reconstruction.

13.3.1   Policy Objectives

The main objectives of fiscal reconstruction were unchanged throughout the period 1975–97: first to eliminate the issue of special deficit bonds. The second related objective, of reducing the overall bond-dependency ratio (the proportion of the total budget financed by the issue of government bonds), was broader in its intent, including not only the elimination of those bonds but a reduction in the issue of "ordinary" (construction) bonds as well. The restoration of the conditions of a balanced budget that prevailed until 1965 remained an aspiration, an unstated premise of its policies for fiscal reconstruction. Realistically, MOF accepted the argument for financing a proportion of capital investment by issuing ordinary (construction) government bonds. But nevertheless reduction in the issue of those bonds too was implicit in its third objective: to reduce the size and accumulating service costs of the total of outstanding government debt.

13.3.2   Policies for Reconstruction

These three objectives drove fiscal policy for the next 15 years. Alarmed by the huge revenue shortfall that occurred after the preparation of the initial budget for FY 1975, MOF began simultaneously to search for ways to raise additional revenue, and to cut expenditures to plug the gap. For the moment, these were mainly ad hoc, short-term measures, marginal adjustments to existing patterns of expenditure growth and sources of revenue.

The target date for the elimination of the issue of special deficit financing bonds was FY 1980, but continuing increases in expenditures and depressed revenues combined to produce a sharp increase in the number of bonds issued to raise more revenue to cover the deficit, and the bond-dependency ratio rose from 29.7 percent in FY 1977 to 32 percent in 1978 and to a peak of 39.6 percent the year after. In January 1979, MOF was forced to concede that the aim of eliminating special bonds by the following year would not be achieved, and set a new target date of 1984. It also acknowledged publicly that the causes of the deficit were structural and could not be remedied by "natural increases" to revenue that would occur when (lower) economic growth was resumed. Short-term, ad hoc marginal adjustments to expenditures and to tax brackets had proved inadequate to deal with the rapid growth of the deficit, and failed completely to address its root cause. The structure of the tax system needed to be changed to increase the proportion and yield of indirect taxes compared with direct taxes, and MOF confidently committed itself to "introduce a new general consumption tax in FY 1980." This provided the context and the rationale for the launch of the second of three such attempts to introduce such a tax in the period 1975–97. The first attempt in 1978 failed partly because of opposition within the LDP, but mainly because the proposed tax was universally unpopular. The poor showing of the LDP in the 1979 election for the House of Representatives was widely attributed to it.

Explicit confirmation that MOF was now thinking about reconstruction more strategically was apparent in the reorientation of its main policy objectives to a longer time horizon. This appeared in the new five-year national economic plan *Outlook and Guidelines for the Economic Society for the 1980s* prepared by the Economic Planning Agency under MOF's guidance, and approved by the cabinet in August 1983. The hope that one of the main objectives of fiscal reconstruction could be achieved by 1984 with the elimination of special deficit bonds was dashed by the sharp downturn in economic activity the previous year that necessitated an increase in public spending financed by the issue of additional government bonds in a package of emergency economic measures. The target date was now revised a second time to 1990, and the budget for FY 1984 reflected this new concern for the longer term. Expenditure policy was aimed at securing more radical reforms of some expenditure programs to deliver cuts over several years ahead, for example medical insurance, pensions, and employment insurance. In the short term, the guidelines for budget requests for the coming fiscal year, FY 1984, were drawn more tightly still. Cuts in some categories of current expenditures were raised from 5 percent to 10 percent. Investment expenditures were cut for the first time by 5 percent. As a result, budget policy was now tighter than at any time since the emergence of the fiscal crisis in the mid-1970s. Fiscal austerity was (ostensibly) maintained for three successive years.

13.4   Policies for Fiscal Consolidation, 1987–91

The transition from the policy of fiscal reconstruction to the resumption of a more expansionary, looser fiscal policy that MOF euphemistically dubbed "fiscal consolidation" occurred in the course of FY 1987, marked precisely by the stimulus to domestic demand provided by the emergency economic measures introduced in May 1987, which added 5.0 trillion to public spending, and cut taxes by 1.0 trillion. Fiscal reconstruction evolved pragmatically and (at first) cautiously into fiscal expansion. Following the Plaza Accord of 1985 and the appreciation of the value of the yen that followed, Japan had come under increasing pressure from the international economic community to expand domestic demand to help generate more global economic activity. Domestically, after three years of tight budgets, the LDP was looking for more spending in the run-up to the general election of 1989. These measures effectively marked the end of the period of fiscal reconstruction.

The fiscal austerity associated with the objectives and policies of the ten years of reconstruction was over. However, despite *apparent* progress toward the main objectives of eliminating the issue of special deficit bonds and reducing the bond-dependency ratio, the broader objectives of restructuring the tax system and introducing more flexibility into the composition of the budget remained unfulfilled. MOF's second attempt to introduce a sales tax in 1987 was no more successful than the first, but for different reasons. However, the attempt served to politicize the wider issue of the reform of the tax structure, and to move it up the political agenda, paving the way for the third (successful) attempt in 1988. (On the politics of tax reform see Kato 1994.) The costs of servicing the national debt continued on a rising trend to absorb a fifth of the General Account budget, more than double the figure at the beginning of reconstruction a decade earlier. The total of debt outstanding continued to grow annually, and by 1987 was preempting nearly 43 percent of GNP, its highest ever level (table 13.1).

The cautious, modest fiscal expansion was soon overwhelmed by a tide of public spending as, first, the economy entered the frenetic period of the "bubble" and then collapsed into a deep and persistent recession. Revenues grew strongly throughout the period 1986–90, the direct consequence of the speculative appreciation of land and asset prices in the bubble economy. The short-lived period of unstable, higher economic growth provided the means and the political rationale for a rapid increase of public spending. In such circumstance, and with a general election for the lower house imminent, growth of the General Budget was irresistible. Nevertheless the fiscal deficit narrowed sufficiently (or more accurately, was narrowed by MOF's exploitation of off-budget resources, see below) for MOF to achieve its long-held objective of eliminating the issue of special deficit-financing bonds in 1990. It was also able to make steady progress in the reduction of the number of construction bonds issued. As a result, the bond-dependency ratio fell to 7.6 percent in the planned budget for FY 1991, the lowest level achieved by MOF for 20 years.

With the apparently successful elimination of the special deficit-financing bonds, MOF turned its attention to the "second stage" of reconstructing the national finances, a restatement of the existing objectives to constrain the growth of the massive national debt, and to restore flexibility in the allocation of discretionary expenditures within the General Account budget. In the light of recent experience it was felt necessary to emphasize the need to make the budget more flexible so that it could be used to implement countercyclical economic policy without the need to resort to the issue of special deficit bonds. The bond-dependency ratio was to be progressively reduced below 5 percent, the first occasion that a target figure had been set by MOF since the emergence of the crisis in 1975. With the ratio set at 7.6 percent in the budget about to be proposed for FY 1991, this seemed a realistic target. FY 1995 was set as the date for its achievement.

13.5   The Reemergence of Fiscal Crisis, 1991–96

MOF's public confidence that it would be able successfully to reconcile the competing demands of an expansionary economic policy to stimulate domestic demand with tight fiscal policy to consolidate the gains made in the period of reconstruction evaporated with the pricking of the "bubble economy." The imperatives of countercyclical economic policy quickly overrode the residual concern with the tight control of public spending, as the economy plunged into deep and prolonged recession. More severe than that which had prompted the policy of fiscal reconstruction in the late 1970s, it proved more enduring and intractable than those that had occurred briefly twice before in the 1980s when MOF was faced with a similar dilemma of reconciling contradictory policy aims.

The reemergence of the symptoms of acute fiscal crisis was the result simultaneously of a large and sustained shortfall in revenue and a rapid buildup of public spending. The sharp decline in revenues resulting from the slowdown in domestic economic activity yet again exposed the underlying, structural weakness of the tax system, to which MOF had repeatedly drawn attention during the past decade. While it had achieved some rebalancing of direct and indirect taxes, most notably the introduction of a general consumption tax in 1988, the shock to the tax system of the collapse of the economic bubble was severe. Revenues declined for six successive years, from FY 1991 to FY 1996. As they did so, the need to stimulate demand in the economy led to political and business pressures for tax reductions, and threatened still further loss of revenues.

As the means to finance additional public spending contracted, so the political-economic pressures for larger expenditure budgets and countercyclical packages of fiscal measures intensified. Responding to them, MOF was powerless to prevent a sudden and dramatic widening of the fiscal deficit. Despite this, for the moment the budgetary policies were aimed to slow down the growth of the General Account budget from 6.2 percent in FY 1991 to 2.7 percent, rather than to impose widespread real cuts. By the following year, the full impact of the fiscal crisis was felt. There was a shortfall of more than 5 trillion in the revised estimate for tax revenues for FY 1992. The eventual yield proved even more disastrous: 8.1 trillion less than that planned. MOF had no alternative but to resume heavy borrowing through the issue of ordinary government bonds to finance the deficit. Within the space of two years, MOF had been obliged to resume borrowing at levels comparable to the worst years of fiscal crisis a decade earlier. The planned bond-dependency rate rose from a low point of 7.6 percent in FY 1991 (initial) to 18.7 percent in FY 1994 (initial). The reality was still worse. The implementation of countercyclical fiscal policy through supplementary budgets in-year led to further borrowing still, and the actual bond-dependency rate was more than 22 percent.

With the resumption of the issue of special deficit-financing bonds in 1994, the fiscal wheel had turned full circle. While MOF had treated some of the earlier symptoms successfully, the underlying causes of too little revenue and too much public spending remained. But this time around, the symptoms were more acute, the crisis deeper, and MOF's authority to deal with it weakened by its failure to constrain the growth of the General Account budget; by the paralysis of the governmental process that followed the breakup of the old political order in 1993; and by the progressive erosion of its own authority as the banking crisis (and other events) unfolded in the wake of the collapse of the bubble economy. The fiscal consequences of that collapse destroyed the credibility of MOF's medium-term strategy for achieving those fiscal objectives set out in the 1990 Medium-Term Fiscal Policy to rebalance revenue and expenditures, reduce the size and burden of the accumulated national debt, and restore flexibility in the allocation of budgetary expenditures. The budget was now less, not more, flexible as the growth of the cost of borrowing and accumulated debt exerted a tighter squeeze on discretionary general expenditure programs (table 13.2); it had proved impossible to implement countercyclical economic policy without resorting to the issue of special deficit-financing bonds; progress toward reducing the bond-dependency ratio to less than 5 percent had been reversed; and the redemption of special bonds had been deferred, as MOF sought to constrain the pressures on the General Account budget.

Yet again, the vicissitudes of economic activity had exposed the underlying structural weakness of the tax system. In times of recession revenue yields were unreliable and inadequate to cover the increasing costs of the major spending programs. The general consumption tax was too little and too late to address the fundamental cause of that weakness. Moreover, it soon became apparent that the recession that began officially in 1991 was different in kind and in duration from those that had preceded it in 1985–86, 1980–82, and 1974–75, which were largely consequential or contingent on global economic conditions.

This time round the Japanese economy proved stubbornly resistant to the improvement in international trade that helped deliver the U.S. and European economies from conditions of recession; moreover the appreciation of the yen—the "yen bubble"—and the large surplus on the current balance of trade made it more difficult than in earlier periods to stimulate the economy through

Table 13.2   Servicing the Debt of Japan's Central Government, 1975–96 (initial budget)

	Debt Service (trillion yen)	Debt Service/Budget (%)
FY 1975	1.03	4.9
FY 1976	1.66	6.9
FY 1977	2.34	8.2
FY 1978	3.22	9.4
FY 1979	4.07	10.6
FY 1980	5.31	12.5
FY 1981	6.65	14.2
FY 1982	7.82	15.8
FY 1983	8.19	16.3
FY 1984	9.15	18.1
FY 1985	10.22	19.5
FY 1986	11.31	20.9
FY 1987	11.33	20.9
FY 1988	11.51	20.3
FY 1989	11.66	19.3
FY 1990	14.28	21.6
FY 1991	16.03	22.8
FY 1992	16.44	22.8
FY 1993	15.44	21.3
FY 1994	14.36	19.6
FY 1995	13.32	18.6
FY 1996	16.37	21.8

Source: Budget Bureau, MOF, Japan, 1997.

the promotion of exports. Ever-larger packages of countercyclical economic and fiscal policies, in all totaling 63 trillion between 1992 and 1995, had little immediate effect on stimulating domestic demand.

The state of the national finances deteriorated rapidly throughout FY 1995 and FY 1996. MOF was forced to borrow 22.0 trillion to finance a deficit swollen by the large fiscal stimulus in September 1995, resulting in a bond-dependency ratio of 28.2 percent, its highest level since 1980. In FY 1996 the planned issue of 10.1 trillion of special deficit bonds exceeded all previous experience. By the end of FY 1997 the accumulated debt was expected to total 254 trillion, equal to 48 percent of GDP. The servicing of that debt absorbed more than a fifth of the total General Account budget. The principles of "sound management" were necessarily sacrificed to political-economic expediency. The achievement of the three policy objectives—the elimination of special deficit bonds, the reduction of the bond-dependency ratio to reduce fiscal deficits on the path to a balanced budget, and the reduction of the size and service costs of the accumulated debt—was more distant in 1997 than when they were formulated 20 years earlier. MOF had, however, succeeded at the third attempt in implementing its long-term aim of changing the tax structure; more accurately, it had begun on the process of implementation. Once it had secured the principle of a consumption tax, it was able to exploit the circumstances of a continuing shortfall of revenue during the economic recession to persuade the coalition governments of 1994–96 led first by Murayama and then Hashimoto to agree to increase the rates levied. However, the benefits in the yield of gross revenues were offset in the short term by the costs of financing tax reductions in the recession; the longer-term significance would emerge only with the resumption of sustained economic growth.

Despite the gravity of the fiscal situation the planned budgets for FY 1996 and 1997 nevertheless provided for further increases of expenditure, of 5.8 percent and 3.0 percent. Not only were fixed costs rising, those for discretionary expenditures continued to rise as well. Limiting the latter to 1.5 percent in FY 1997 was claimed by the Government and MOF as a sign of new fiscal austerity. Whether the budget for FY 1998 will mark the beginning of a new realism in the control of public spending promised in PM Hashimoto's vision of fiscal reform will not be apparent for some time to come. There is a strong sense of déjà vu in his earlier declaration of FY 1997 as the first year of fiscal reconstruction.

13.6   Fiscal Reconstruction: Illusion and Reality

How successful was MOF in its attempts to reconstruct the fiscal system after 1975? We look first at its claim to have made substantial progress toward the achievement of its policy aims by the end of the 1980s using its own preferred performance indicators, and then contrast that apparent progress with the underlying reality.

13.6.1   Raising Revenue

MOF's success in narrowing the fiscal gap in the period of fiscal reconstruction was partly the result of the buoyancy of revenues in conditions of sustained, albeit modest, economic growth, but also partly due to marginal changes in the tax structure and in tax rates and thresholds. Its longer-term aim to change the balance of direct to indirect taxation was almost wholly unsuccessful. Even the substantial increase in indirect taxes resulting from the introduction of a national consumption tax in 1988 did little more in the early 1990s than reverse the trend of increasing dependence on direct tax revenues, and to restore the 2.5:1 ratio that obtained in the late 1970s. In reality, the ratio was closer to 4:1, if we take the net tax revenues available (after the hypothecation of revenues to local governments) to finance the General Account budget. Finally, while the burden of national taxes as a proportion of both national income and GDP increased marginally year by year, the Japanese electorate remained lightly taxed compared with other G7 countries in the mid-1980s. Only the United States had a lower ratio than Japan.

As the economy moved into deep recession, total revenues fell for the first

Table 13.3   Japan's Central Government Debt Outstanding, 1975–95
                  (settled budget)

	Government Bonds Outstanding (trillion yen)	GDP %
FY 1975	14.9	9.8
FY 1976	22.0	12.9
FY 1977	31.9	16.8
FY 1978	42.6	20.4
FY 1979	56.2	25.0
FY 1980	70.5	28.7
FY 1981	82.2	31.6
FY 1982	96.4	35.3
FY 1983	109.6	38.4
FY 1984	121.6	39.9
FY 1985	134.4	41.5
FY 1986	145.1	42.8
FY 1987	151.8	42.7
FY 1988	156.7	41.3
FY 1989	160.9	39.6
FY 1990	166.3	37.9
FY 1991	171.6	37.0
FY 1992	178.3	37.7
FY 1993	192.5	40.4
FY 1994	206.6	43.2
FY 1995	225.2	46.0
FY 1996	244.7	49.0

Source: Budget Bureau, MOF, Japan, 1997.

time for over 25 years in FY 1992; tax revenues declined for six successive years. Without the revenues from the new consumption tax, the disastrous shortfall would have been still worse.

13.6.2   The Fiscal Deficit and Government Borrowing

MOF twice failed to achieve its main aim of eliminating special deficit bonds, succeeding on the third attempt in 1990. Their reissue in 1994 and their continuation thereafter represented a humiliating failure of MOF's reconstruction policies. It achieved steady progress in reducing the bond-dependency ratio, partly the result of improving control of total expenditure in the General Account budget and some modest success in revenue raising, but did not succeed in reducing it to less than 5 percent by the prescribed target date of 1995. Although it had come close to doing so in 1991, thereafter the ratio moved sharply upward. Both the size of the accumulated debt and the annual cost of servicing it grew inexorably through almost the whole of the period (tables 13.2 and 13.3). Debt outstanding during the period 1975–96 rose from a total of 14.9 trillion to 240.5 trillion (planned), an increase in the proportion of GDP

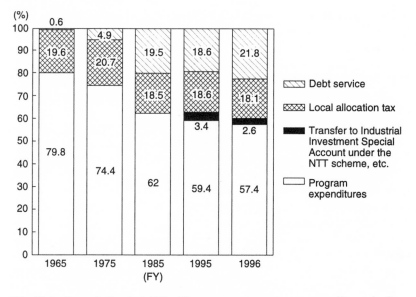

Fig. 13.3   Japan's fiscal rigidity: The squeeze on program expenditures in the central government budget, 1965–96 (initial budget)

from below 10 percent to nearly 50 percent. In the period of fiscal reconstruction, the volume of debt doubled, rising as a proportion of GDP from 31.5 percent to 42.7 percent. Throughout more than a decade of "fiscal reconstruction" and "consolidation," debt-service costs continued to absorb a fifth or more of the total General Account budget, exerting a considerable and continuous squeeze on discretionary expenditures. "Fiscal rigidification" increased throughout the whole of the period 1975–96 (fig. 13.3).

13.6.3   Restraining the Growth of Public Expenditure

MOF's objective for public spending was set and constantly reaffirmed only in the broadest terms: to restrain the growth of public expenditures as much as possible. No numerical targets were prescribed, nor dates for the achievement of some desirable state of restraint. Assessment of performance is therefore more difficult to make, and is to a large extent inferred from the various time-series data that accompanied the presentation of the budget, and in MOF's selection of preferred performance indicators.

MOF claimed to have controlled the growth of expenditure in the General Account budget for much of the period of fiscal reconstruction and consolidation. While planned (initial) expenditure increased in every year from 1975 to 1995, the annual rate of increase slowed, especially in the period of fiscal reconstruction, declining steadily from a peak of 24.5 percent in 1975 to reach standstill in 1987. Thereafter, the economic growth of the bubble allowed, and the conditions of recession which followed obliged, MOF to increase public spending substantially, and the annual percentage changes moved upward once again.

While after 1981 MOF managed to reduce only marginally the proportion of GDP absorbed by the General Account budget as a whole, its focus on the narrower definition of General Expenditure (excluding debt and other fixed costs) showed a much larger reduction in the GDP ratio from 12.6 percent in 1980 to 8.6 percent in 1995. The latter, it emphasized, represented "less than 67% of the FY 1980 peak," approximately the same proportion as that of FY 1970. The inference that MOF wished to be drawn was clear: it had returned the public finances to the status quo ante that prevailed before the era of welfare spending began. That congratulatory self-assessment of its achievement in restraining the growth of public spending in the period of fiscal reconstruction is subject to qualification. First, it was able to make only small cuts in planned General Expenditure for a brief period; no such cuts were made in the totals for the General Account budget as a whole. Even that apparent restraint of the growth of General Expenditure is less impressive when the outcome ("settled") rather than planned ("initial") expenditure is measured (fig. 13.4). This shows that MOF was much less successful in controlling expenditure demands and pressures *in-year* than in the budget-making processes preceding the planned initial budget. This is partly because it was more willing to acquiesce in some of the demands for additional spending financed in supplementary budgets that were not subject to the strict controls of budget ceilings and guidelines and partly because the pressures to stimulate the economy in-year often proved irresistible. Thus the real cuts in the total of General Expenditure claimed for five successive years in the mid-1980s were cuts in *planned* expenditure that MOF was unable to deliver, in all but one of those years. Second, reductions in the General Expenditure/GDP ratio were achieved more as a result of the growth of GDP than a reduction of the level of General Expenditure. In such circumstances public spending can continue to rise (as it did), while simultaneously absorbing a smaller proportion of GDP. That combination was significant in the politics of the budgetary process in the period of fiscal reconstruction, allowing MOF to accommodate political-bureaucratic pressures for more spending without apparently sacrificing its fiscal objectives, measured by the General Expenditure/GDP ratio.

13.6.4   Manipulating Budgets and Special Accounts and Managing the Presentation

MOF's claimed success in restraining the growth of public spending was only partly the result of the implementation of policies of tighter control, most notably in more tightly drawn guidelines for budget requests. It was mainly the result of the effective manipulation of revenues and expenditures between the General Account budget, FILP ("the second budget"), and the 38 special accounts, and by its management of the presentation of its fiscal performance.

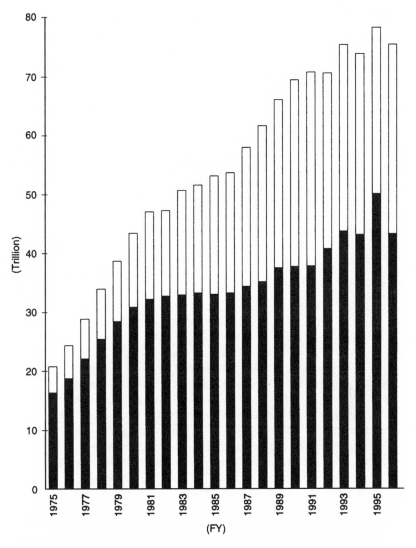

Fig. 13.4   The growth of Japan's central government budget, 1975–96 (settled budget)
Note: 1995, revised budget; 1996, initial budget. GDP: 1995, estimate; 1996, forecast. *Solid bars* are program expenditures; *open bars* are budget including program expenditures.

There were three main budgetary stratagems designed to relieve pressure on the General Account budget. First, MOF exploited the statutory provision for the "carry-forward" of surplus revenues at the end of the financial year to defer redemption of the national debt. In 1982 and for eight consecutive years it suspended the statutory requirement of the fixed-rate appropriation from the General Account budget to the National Debt Consolidation Fund. Payments

Table 13.4   MOF's Deferred Liquidation of Japan's National Debt, 1982–96
                    (settlement—trillion yen)

	Deferred Payments
FY 1982	1.37
FY 1983	1.60
FY 1984	1.82
FY 1985	2.02
FY 1986	2.24
FY 1987	2.41
FY 1988	2.53
FY 1989	2.61
FY 1990	Payments resumed (2.49)
FY 1991	Payments resumed (2.56)
FY 1992	Payments resumed (2.63)
FY 1993	3.04
FY 1994	3.08
FY 1995	3.2
FY 1996	Payments resumed (4.54)

Sources: 1982–89: calculated from bonds outstanding at end of previous financial year, Budget Bureau, MOF, Japan, 1996; 1994–96: *The Japanese Budget in Brief,* Budget Bureau, MOF, 1994, 1995, 1996.

were resumed in FY 1990, but suspended again from 1993 to 1995. From time to time MOF also suspended the transfer to the fund of that surplus on the settlement of the General Account budget, the legislation permitting the priority of the allocation of that surplus to general-purpose funds over that of debt redemption. By these means throughout almost the whole of the period of fiscal reconstruction and consolidation MOF was able to relieve some of the pressures on the General Account budget by suspending the statutory arrangements for the liquidation of a part of the national debt by fixed-rate appropriations from the budget. The resulting "savings" from the suspension of the fixed-rate transfer alone were considerable, averaging annually between 1.5 and 2.5 trillion yen throughout the period of fiscal reconstruction (table 13.4). Added to other fixed costs in the budget, they would have had the effect of further squeezing the amount available for discretionary expenditures and hence exacerbating "fiscal rigidification"; or, if not offset, would have resulted in larger budget totals. Faced with the prospect of massive and recurring annual redemption costs as the (mainly ten-year) special deficit bonds issued in the crisis of 1975 matured, MOF began "refinancing" in FY 1984. From time to time MOF also reduced the proportion of nationally collected taxes statutorily assigned as hypothecated revenues to local governments, achieving a temporary reduction in the total of fixed costs in the budget.

Reducing the scale of the fixed costs, either that of the local assigned taxes or the debt redemption, or both was thus a very effective means of "cutting" public expenditure. It was also a useful means of partly financing the additional

expenditures in supplementary budgets. Suspending the arrangements for re-
deeming the national debt had the further short-term advantage for MOF, that
(unlike the manipulation of local assigned taxes and some other "temporary
special measures" for postponing payments) it was not required to make up
repayments in subsequent years. But such suspension contributed to longer-
term difficulties. MOF's dilemma was that short-term budget reductions to
achieve fiscal reconstruction were purchased at the expense of longer-term
costs: unredeemed debt imposed a burden on future generations, a further example of the triumph of expediency over the principle of "sound management"
of the national finances.

The second budget stratagem derived from the privatization of NTT in 1985,
which provided MOF with another potential source of funds to relieve pressure
on the General Account budget. Funds derived from the sale of shares were
used in part to provide interest-free loans totaling 1.3 trillion per annum for
specified projects of capital investment for the three years 1986–88. Those
resources helped to relieve fiscal pressure on the General Account budget by
enabling MOF to reduce expenditure on the public works programs financed
through it: at the same time it provided a short-term "cost-free" means of sus-
taining support for the public works program as a whole, as the LDP wanted.
For example, in FY 1988, a preelection year, general public works expenditure
was increased by over 20 percent compared with the previous year.

Loans to finance the special capital investment projects through the "NTT
scheme" had ultimately to be repaid from the General Account budget to the
Special Account for National Debt Consolidation. MOF began to do so, just
as the revenues on the General Account began to deteriorate as a result of the
recession, thus exacerbating the emerging fiscal crisis.

13.6.5   The Manipulation of Special Accounts and FILP

The third budgetary stratagem involved the manipulation of cash flows between the General Account budget and other "off-budget" sources. From time
to time during the period of fiscal reconstruction, MOF suspended some statutory annual payments from the General Account budgets into various special
accounts, most notably those for welfare insurance and for national pensions.
At the end of FY 1996 MOF estimated the size of these and other "hidden
debts" that had accumulated from previous manipulations at 16 trillion yen,
excluding the long-term debt of the privatized Japanese National Railways,
27 trillion.

More significant even than those "special temporary measures," MOF used
FILP, supplementary budgets, and some of the 38 special accounts as permanent alternative sources of "off-budget" funding for some public expenditure
programs. The financing of public works programs is a classic example of illusion and reality in Japanese budgeting. The "headline" totals for public works
in the planned General Account budget show a decline from annual increases
of over 20 percent before 1979 to a position of standstill and then reduction of

about 2.5 percent per annum in the period of fiscal reconstruction. In reality the programs enjoyed continuous and substantial growth of between 50 and 100 percent between 1980 and 1996, financed through supplementary budgets, FILP, and ad hoc temporary schemes of investment. A similar phenomenon is observable in the budget allocations for small businesses.

FILP provided the main financial support for housing construction and loans for house purchase, and for agricultural infrastructure. By FY 1994 the government's housing program was financed mainly "off-budget" through FILP; at 13.205 trillion it was more than 12 times the share borne by the General Account budget. The total value of those and other less obvious substituted funds is impossible to calculate; but had the General Account budget been obliged to fund a greater share of the housing program and other public works projects and capital development schemes financed by FILP and designed to improve "social overhead capital," several trillion yen would have been added annually to the General Account budget through the period of fiscal reconstruction, and beyond. Besides the "second budget," MOF also used some special accounts as a substitute for the General Account budget to fund some kinds of capital development, for example the special accounts for road construction, hospitals, and schools. The validity of this growing practice was even more questionable and questioned than its exploitation of the potential of FILP. In short, as a result of these and other "temporary special measures," and the budget stratagems mentioned earlier, MOF was able to set each year a much smaller aggregate for the General Account budget, borrow less to cover a smaller deficit, and record and present apparent progress toward its policy objectives. One effect of the substitution of FILP for the General Account budget was that FILP grew faster and absorbed a rising share of GDP. By 1996 it was two-thirds the size of the General Account budget.

13.7   Explaining MOF's Failure

For most of the period 1975–97, Japan had a stable, one-party, right-wing majority government, and a centralized budgetary system. Crucially, it had a "strong" Ministry of Finance with a formidable combination of formal constitutional and legal powers to raise taxes, control budget and off-budget expenditures, and regulate financial and monetary policies. It possessed hierarchical, organizational, and informational resources unmatched by any other ministry or agency; it was committed to the principle of a balanced budget and "sound financial management"; it prescribed and progressively tightened guidelines for determining the size of the budget and the relative priority of spending programs and set budget ceilings for each ministry and agency. Such a combination of institutional variables would appear to be favorable to the avoidance of fiscal stress, or to the relief of its symptoms. Yet as we have shown, MOF was largely unsuccessful in reconstructing the fiscal system and achieving its policy aims of reducing the deficit and level of accumulated debt. Why was an apparently "strong" Ministry of Finance unable, unwilling, or frustrated in its attempts to implement agreed policies to constrain the growth of public spending, the main cause of fiscal stress?

The aging of the population, the "yoke of prior commitments," and unsustainable rates of growth in debt, factors that help to explain the failure of industrialized countries to control long-term fiscal policy (Steuerle and Kawai 1996), all contributed to the increasing pressures in the budgetary system for more public spending. While they made it more difficult to restrain the growth of demand-led programs such as pensions, social security, and health and welfare programs for the elderly, and to cut back existing spending commitments in other programs, none was a major cause of MOF's failure to control the growth of public spending. There were five main factors. First, MOF's failure to win LDP politicians and business groups to its cause of radical tax reform until the late 1980s left it with an inadequate revenue base in an era in which a "decelerated economy" generated insufficient "natural increases" of revenues to accommodate the double burden of inescapable fixed costs and irresistible discretionary expenditures without recourse to regular heavy borrowing. The consequential costs of servicing the accumulating debt exacerbated that difficulty. Second, throughout the whole of the period 1975–97 MOF was faced with the dilemma of trying to reconcile the contradictory aims of economic policy, which frequently dictated the need for increased public spending and tax cuts (often in response to international pressures) to stimulate the economy with the narrower fiscal aims of reconstruction. The need to do so on several occasions in the period 1975–97 meant that that spending imperative dominated much of the period. It helps to explain and justify why faced with the conflicting policy aims, MOF resorted to temporary expedients, and the budget stratagems and manipulations mentioned earlier. While MOF was able to emerge from short bouts of countercyclical spending with its objectives for fiscal reconstruction still realistically attainable, even if progress toward them was deferred or delayed, as happened on three occasions for example with the target date set for the elimination of special deficit bonds, it could not reconcile them with the rapid, huge expansion of the General Account budget and FILP that the prolonged recession made inevitable.

The third factor inhibiting the effectiveness of its policies for fiscal reconstruction was the need to try to reconcile their implementation with the often conflicting political-electoral strategic aims of the LDP designed to sustain itself in power. Through government and party organizations, the LDP had begun to play a more active and interventionist role in policymaking generally from the early 1970s. The party was incorporated into the budgetary processes, both formally through such structures as the functional committees of its Policy Affairs Research Council, and informally through the intervention of senior party officials and members of special policy tribes (*zoku*). By such means the interests of the party and their clients were accommodated directly or by bureaucratic "anticipated reactions." Spending programs for public works, small businesses, and agriculture financed both through the General Account budget and FILP, implemented locally by local governments, and both locally and regionally through the aegis of Public Finance Corporations, provided a source of patronage and clientelistic distributive politics for the LDP, helping to nourish and sustain Dietmen's personal electoral-constituency networks. While the LDP acquiesced in the introduction of tougher budget guidelines in the mid-1980s, their effectiveness was tempered in practice by the exploitation of spending loopholes provided by the exemption of priority programs, and ad hoc dispensations for public investment and public works, and agricultural infrastructure and subsidies. These provided it with the means to continue to distribute substantial political favors and benefits in the outputs of expenditure programs, and to frustrate MOF's policies for fiscal reconstruction.

A transparent budget process is an oxymoronic concept. But even by conventional standards, Japan's is remarkably complex, opaque, and labyrinthine. However, the lack of transparency was not a major factor in the explanation of the continuance of deficits and debt. The underlying reality of Japan's fiscal situation was no secret. MOF did not conceal the details of its annual budget stratagems and manipulation; the size and composition of the "hidden debt" was public knowledge. More significantly, neither the LDP's own back-bench supporters nor the main opposition parties in the Diet were disposed to argue for less spending or more taxation to reduce the level of deficit and debt. Indeed, the wilder demands of the former were kept in check by the LDP leadership; the (then) Japan Socialist Party used its position as the official opposition in the lower house from time to time to obstruct the passage of budget bills as a means of extracting spending concessions from the government. While there was some support among Diet parties for clean government, there was none of any significance for smaller government. It is unlikely therefore that more transparency in the budget processes, for example by involving legislators in the determination of the size of the budget(s) and its distribution, or in the prescription of budget guidelines and targets, would have checked the growth of public spending.

The fourth factor was the nature of the budgetary process, through which the aggregate budget total was determined, and its distribution negotiated between the spending ministries and MOF's Budget Bureau. The aggregate or "ceiling" for the General Account budget and for FILP was set by MOF after discussion with senior LDP politicians and ministers; throughout the whole of the period 1975–97, even at times of crisis, the planned aggregate was always greater than that of the preceding fiscal year. The only attempt at a planned cut, in FY 1995, was made possible only by suspending the statutory payment of national debt redemption. Even so, the outcome total was several trillion greater than that planned. Top-down limits are a necessary condition of effective control of spending, but as Japan's experience shows, they are not sufficient. The "ceiling" for each ministry's budget was negotiated with the Budget Bureau, together with the distribution of new money allocated to priority programs. Although the prescription of budget guidelines nominally limited the amount of spending on each program, in practice categories of exception and exemption provided both the opportunity and incentive for ministers and their officials to argue for more spending in their annual negotiations with the Budget Bureau. Crucially, the budget guidelines did not apply to supplementary budgets, which provided a further annual opportunity for spending ministries to argue for more public spending.

Fifth, MOF is very much less powerful in the budget processes than is commonly supposed, or appears from an inspection of *formal* budget institutions and arrangements. The latter provide the basis of the framework within which budget decisions are made, but a more complete and informed guide to how and why particular budget outcomes occur requires an analysis of the *informal* politics of the budgetary process, the interaction among the participants in those processes—the roles and strategies of ministers, party officials, bureaucrats, and special interest groups, and the unwritten rules of the game that regulate their behavior in informal structures such as policy networks (Wright 1991; Thain and Wright 1995). As in the United Kingdom and Canada, MOF's exercise of the formal discretionary authority vested in it by the constitution and by statute is constrained in practice by the exercise of countervailing discretionary power by other participants. Like the Treasury and the Department of Finance/Treasury Board, MOF is locked into a system of mutually constrained power relationships, mainly with the LDP and the spending ministries, and rarely able to impose its constitutional and hierarchical authority on them and other participants, or to implement a directive strategy for determining the budget aggregate and its distribution. The paradigm of the politics of public spending is "negotiated discretion" (Thain and Wright 1995).

Finally, compared with other G7 countries, "how to pay for it" questions have not thus far been a central concern of the budgetary processes. Maturity in the public sector has developed more slowly, partly because experience of "welfare spending" came much later, and partly because of the tradition of high economic growth generating substantial revenue surpluses (Steuerle and Kawai 1996).

13.8 Coping with Fiscal Stress

MOF's pragmatic and expedient response to continuous fiscal stress throughout the period of fiscal reconstruction and beyond was understandable and from its perspective politically rational. By exploiting the potential of FILP as a "second budget"; by using it and several special accounts as alternative sources of finance to the General Account budget; by suspending statutory payments, by temporary "borrowings" and the manipulation of cash flows— by all these short-term expedients MOF was able to keep the fiscal ship afloat through the troubled waters of the early 1980s, and allowed it to present an illusion of public spending control consistent with apparent steady progress toward the achievement of its main policy objectives. It not only avoided (or at least postponed) the breakdown of the fiscal system: it reasserted and reiterated the principles of "sound management." Without the annual ceiling on the General Account budget and the imposition of ceilings on ministerial budgets, public spending would have grown at a still faster rate. Guidelines for determining the relative priority of competing spending programs at least obliged ministers and LDP back-benchers to talk the language of priority and the allocation of scarce(r) resources, even if in practice the application of those guidelines was less rigorous than MOF intended. In a period in which the internal spending pressures that resulted from the expansion of welfare spending in the 1970s was fueled by the expectations of LDP politicians, their clients, and aggrieved groups of still more public spending and lower taxes, this was no small achievement.

That said, any hopes that it had of making the surface appearance consistent with the underlying reality—in short to make a reality of reconstructing the fiscal system according to the principles of "sound management"—were destroyed by the fiscal effects of the bubble economy that ratcheted up levels of public spending insupportable by the recent historic trends of GDP growth and contingent revenue yields; and by the plunge into deep and prolonged economic recession in the years that followed. Whatever progress had been made was slowed, then halted, and ultimately reversed as the fiscal imperative of the recession dictated massive amounts of borrowing to finance countercyclical spending, and tax cuts and concessions. Any gains that accrued from implementation of the policies of reconstruction and consolidation evaporated. The status quo ante of 1975 was quickly restored. But this time around the fiscal crisis was much deeper and enveloped FILP, now swollen to two-thirds the size of the General Account budget and experiencing its own crisis of identity in the era of deregulated interest rates and liberalized capital markets. Fiscal reconstruction in the second half of the 1990s now had a much broader connotation than the earlier concern with the tax structure, the budget system, and the growth of the General Account budget: it touched all parts of the fiscal system. The crisis of the national finances was itself both a contributory cause and a symptom of a much broader crisis of the state, in which its role and that of the political, bureaucratic, and economic institutions that sustained it were the subject of sustained critical debate.

Were other G7 governments more successful than those of Japan in the period 1975–97 in achieving their objectives to relieve stress and bouts of acute crisis? To stem the tide of rising expenditure through the 1980s and 1990s, both U.K. and Canadian governments responded annually with budget policies designed to exert continuous downward pressure on the size and cost of departmental expenditures programs. In practice, in both countries until the early 1990s, bottom-up pressures for more spending regularly overwhelmed the top-down planned totals, as they did in Japan. In the United Kingdom, central government's own spending, excluding local authorities and nationalized industries, grew in real terms by about a third between 1979 and 1992 (Thain and Wright 1995). The trend of General Government expenditure, apart from a dip in spending in the mid-1970s and the late 1980s, shows a steady and continuous rise in real spending. Conservative governments from 1979 failed to slow the trend rate of growth, roughly 2 percent per annum in real terms. As in Japan, they were able to achieve neither the heroic objectives set in 1980, nor the less ambitious revised ones set in the mid-1980s. What was stress in the second half of the 1980s collapsed into crisis after the general election of 1992, requiring urgent action to cap the budget aggregate and to change the budget machinery and processes for determining and delivering it. Despite that, public spending continued to grow annually in real terms at a faster rate than in any five-year period since 1979.

Unlike the United Kingdom or Japan, Canadian objectives for controlling public spending were in the early 1980s expressed more vaguely, normally without precise targets and dates for achievement. The Trudeau Government had pledged to hold the growth of spending of the federal budget to that of GNP and to reduce the deficit, and this had been achieved by 1978. However, after reelection, the recession of 1981–82 led to a rapid deterioration in federal finances, and from 1980–84, federal spending was rising above the trend line of GDP. From 1975–76 to 1982–83 federal spending as a proportion of GDP increased by 3.2 percent, and for the whole of the period to 1989–90, by an average of 10.4 percent per annum. Spending increased from 1987, deficits increased for five consecutive years from 1989 to 1993, and with higher interest rates, the costs of servicing the growing debt grew rapidly. Numerical targets for the progressive reduction of the deficit were prescribed annually in the federal budget, and revised as they were missed. But from 1994, federal spending and the deficit appeared to be set on a downward trend, and the medium-term objective of achieving a balanced budget a practical proposition. Canada's achievement of its fiscal objectives, both short-term control of the capped budget aggregate and the progressive reduction of the budget deficit and debt over the medium-term period were unmatched by either the United Kingdom or Japan or by other G7 countries. It is perhaps too early to say whether the apparent success of the last three years will endure and be sustained through the business and electoral cycles. But thus far, the federal government has treated not only the symptoms of fiscal stress, persistent deficit and rising debt, but through real cuts in programs and operating budgets begun to remedy the main cause of that stress, the growth of federal spending.

References

Asako, K., T. Ito, and K. Sakamoto. 1991. The rise and fall of the deficit in Japan. *Journal of Japanese and International Economies* 5:451–72.

Calder, K. 1988. *Crisis and compensation: Public policy and political stability in Japan, 1949–1986.* Princeton: Princeton University Press.

Ihori, T. 1996. Prior commitments, sustainability, and intergenerational redistribution in Japan. In *The new world fiscal order,* ed. C. E. Steuerle and Kawai Masahiro. Washington, D.C.: Urban Institute Press.

Kato, Junko. 1994. *The problem of bureaucratic rationality: Tax politics in Japan.* Princeton: Princeton University Press.

Kawai, M., and Y. Onitsuka. 1996. Fiscal policy, global saving and investment, and economic growth. In *The new world fiscal order,* ed. C. E. Steuerle and Kawai Masahiro. Washington, D.C.: Urban Institute Press.

Shibata, Tokue, ed. 1993. *Japan's public sector.* Tokyo: Tokyo University Press.

Steuerle, C. E., and Kawai Masahiro, eds. 1996. *The new world fiscal order.* Washington, D.C.: Urban Institute Press.

Thain, C., and Maurice Wright. 1995. *The Treasury and Whitehall: The planning and control of public expenditure, 1976–1993.* Oxford: Oxford University Press.

Wright, Maurice. 1991. The comparative analysis of industrial policies: Policy networks and sectoral governance structures in Britain and France. *Staatswissenschaften und Staatspraxis* 4:503–33.

Contributors

Alberto Alesina
Department of Economics
Harvard University
Cambridge, MA 02138

Adriana Arreaza
Department of Economics
Box B
Brown University
Providence, RI 02912

J. Edgardo Campos
The World Bank
Room G2-101
1818 H Street, NW
Washington, DC 20433

Thomas Courchene
Policy Studies Building
Queens University
Kingston, Ontario K7L 3N6
Canada

Lars P. Feld
SIASR, Institutsgebäude
University of St. Gallen
Dufourstr. 48
CH-9000 St. Gallen
Switzerland

Alejandro Grisanti
Inter-American Development Bank
1300 New York Avenue, NW
Washington, DC 20577

Jakob de Haan
Faculty of Economics
University of Groningen
PO Box 800
9700 AV Groningen
The Netherlands

Mark Hallerberg
Sam Nunn School of International
    Affairs
Georgia Institute of Technology
Atlanta, GA 30332

Jürgen von Hagen
Zentrum für Europäische
    Integrationsforschung
University of Bonn
Walter-Flex-Strasse 3
53113 Bonn
Germany

Mark P. Jones
Department of Political Science
Michigan State University
East Lansing, Michigan 48824

Gebhard Kirchgässner
SIASR, Institutsgebäude
University of St. Gallen
Dufourstr. 48
CH-9000 St. Gallen
Switzerland

Yianos Kontopoulos
301 West 53rd Street, Apt. 11K
New York, NY 10019

Wim Moessen
Center for Economic Studies
Catholic University of Leuven
Naamsestraat 69
B-3000 Leuven
Belgium

Roberto Perotti
Department of Economics
Columbia University
420 West 118ᵗʰ Street, 10ᵗʰ Floor
New York, NY 10027

James M. Poterba
Department of Economics, E52-350
Massachusetts Institute of Technology
Cambridge, MA 02142

Sanjay Pradhan
The World Bank
1800 H Street, NW
Washington, DC 20433

Kim Rueben
Public Policy Institute of California
Suite 800
500 Washington Street
San Francisco, CA 94111

Pablo Sanguinetti
Departamento de Economia
Universidad Torcuato Di Tella
Minones 2159/77
1428 Buenos Aires
Argentina

Bent Sørensen
Department of Economics
Box B
Brown University
Providence, RI 02912

Ernesto Stein
Inter-American Development Bank
1300 New York Avenue, NW
Washington, DC 20577

Ernesto Talvi
CERES
Circumvalacion Durango 383
Esc. 301
Montevideo
Uruguay

Mariano Tommasi
Universidad de San Andrés
Vito Dumas 284
1644 Victoria
Buenos Aires
Argentina

Andrés Velasco
Department of Economics
New York University
269 Mercer Street
New York, NY 10003

Bjørn Volkerink
Department of General Economics
Faculty of Economics
University of Groningen
PO Box 800
9700 AV Groningen
The Netherlands

Oved Yosha
Eitan Berglas School of Economics
Tel Aviv University
Ramat Aviv, Tel Aviv 69978
Israel

Maurice Wright
Department of Government
The University of Manchester
Oxford Road
Manchester M13 9PL
United Kingdom

Author Index

Subject Index

Accountability: Australian priority setting, 239–40; Australian public spending management reform, 254–55; costs imposed on politicians by, 235, 242; for efficient delivery of public services, 237t, 244; of government for allocating resources, 241; to mitigate tragedy of the commons, 236–38, 243; New Zealand prereform and reform measures, 1, 237t, 246–53

Advisory Council on Intergovernmental Relations (ACIR): data on state-level balanced-budget rules, 191; state antideficit provisions index, 185–86, 190–91t

Antideficit rules: argument for, 182; effect of weak, 32; effect on borrowing costs of state-level, 204; effect on measured deficits, 182; of EMU countries, 2

Argentina: decentralized fiscal structure in, 136–37; fiscal reform, 121–23; Law of Financial Administration (1992), 121; politics, 139–46; public spending, 139–46. *See also* Provinces, Argentina

Australia: Competition Principles Agreement (1995), 307, 338, 340; equalization of tax revenues, 312–19; federal and state coordination of fiscal policy, 321–24; federal government neutrality toward subnational entities, 320; fiscal federalism, 304–5t; limited autonomy of states in, 302; prioritization of resource allocation, 9, 239–40; recent fiscal policy (1990s), 337–42; Standard & Poor's credit ratings

of states, 342–45; transparency of budget, 303. *See also* States, Australia

Belgium: budgetary cycle, 277t; fiscal institution changes in, 275t, 276–78; from unitary to federal state, 277, 291

Bond market, U.S. tax-exempt: comparison of state-level differences in yields, 188–204; model of determinants of bond yield, 183–85; yield determination studies, 185–87

Borrowing, government: with antideficit rules, 204; Australian states' arrangements for, 321–22; effect of Canadian subnational, 9–10; in model of budget process in cabinet government, 214. *See also* Bond market, U.S. tax-exempt; Debt, government

Budget, government: as common resource pool, 235; cycle in Canada, 324–25; growth of Japan's (1975–96), 365–69; Japan's General Account, FILP, and supplementary budgets, 351–52, 361–69; lack of transparency in Japanese, 351–53; model of process in cabinet government, 212–14; tax-smoothing theory of, 151

Budget Act (1974), United States, 18–19

Budgetary institutions. *See* Fiscal institutions

Budget deficit: arising from common-pool problem, 3; Canada (1990s), 330–31; effect of antideficit rules on, 182; Japan (1970s, 1990–97), 349–50, 354; levels effect smoothing function of government, 61; relation of referenda in Switzerland

Fiscal policy (*cont.*)
Argentina, Peru, Costa Rica, and Colombia, 121–23; Swiss voter participation in decision making for, 154–65; testing for party differences in Argentina, 142–46; U.S. interstate differences in, 181–82. *See also* Common-pool problem; Consumption smoothing; Fiscal target commitment; Income smoothing; Tax-smoothing theory

Fiscal Responsibility Act (1993), New Zealand, 247–48, 260

Fiscal rules: financial market response to, 182; subnational level, 7. *See also* Antideficit rules

Fiscal system, Japan: centralized (1975–97), 370; fiscal crisis (1991–96), 360–63; origins of crisis (1975), 354–55; policies for consolidation (1987–91), 358–60; reconstruction (1979–87), 355–58

Fiscal target commitment: budget process in single-party or coalition cabinet government, 216–19; impact on budget deficit, 230

Fragmentation: of budget process, 3; effect on fiscal policy outcomes, 6; in fiscal decision making, 81; government executive and legislative, 33, 83–85; model of decision making with, 41–44; procedural, 84; specification of model to estimate, 87–89

Free riding: within idea of common pool, 138; incentives for, 7

Governments: coalition or commitment approach in EU countries, 222–25; delegation or commitment approach to fiscal process, 214–17; relation of size to electoral systems in Latin America, 124–29; size in Latin American countries, 105–6; size in OECD countries, 105–6. *See also* Budget process; Cabinet government; Debt, government; *specific countries*

Gross domestic product (GDP) smoothing, 60–61

Impossibility theorem (Arrow), 17–18

Income smoothing: channels in EU and OECD countries for, 62–67; cross-country, 63–64; international, 78–79; mechanisms for regional and country-level, 63–64; related to risk sharing among countries, 64–67

Information: for consensus building and resource allocation, 239

Institutions: collegial, 16–17; hierarchical, 16–17; to mitigate tragedy of the commons, 236–38; for prioritization of common-pool resource allocation, 242. *See also* Fiscal institutions; Voting procedures

Interest groups: endogenous budget deficit derived from dynamic game, 44–47; in fragmented fiscal decision making, 38, 81; influence on fiscal institution design, 123; model of fragmented fiscal policy decision making, 41–44; in model of fragmented policy strategies, 40–50; switching strategies and equilibria related to debt, 50–52

Interest rates: Canada (1990s), 331; link to deficits and debt levels, 209; state-specific, 182. *See also* Bond market, U.S. tax-exempt

Ireland: budgetary cycle, 279–80; current fiscal policy, 293; financing local government, 280–81, 294; fiscal institution changes in, 1, 275t; role of minister of finance, 291–92

Italy: budgetary process in, 281–82; budget reform (1997), 281; legislature, 295–96; limited autonomy of subnational governments, 296; role of minister of finance, 294–95

Japan: "bubble economy" effects, 353, 359; causes of fiscal crisis (1991–96), 360–63; central government budget (1970–96), 354–55; collapse of "bubble economy" (1991), 349; fiscal policy (1980s), 350; General Account, FILP, and supplementary budgets, 351–52, 361–69; opaque budget process, 351–53

Laws: arguments against balanced-budget, 15–16; related to limits on state-level tax or spending, 190–91t, 192–93. *See also* Rules

Legislatures: Belgium, 289–90; choices of pork barrel projects, 19–22; Ireland, 292–93; procedures for voting on budget, 18–19, 22–23

Maastricht Treaty: antideficit measures for EMU, 1–2; effect of fiscal targets on EU member countries, 278; influence on Bel-